After Appropriation

University of Calgary Press
2500 University Drive NW
Calgary, Alberta
Canada T2N 1N4
www.uofcpress.com

LIBRARY AND ARCHIVES CANADA CATALOGUING IN PUBLICATION

After appropriation : explorations in intercultural philosophy and religion / edited by Morny Joy.

Based on papers presented at the workshop: Comparative Philosophy and Religion, held at the University of Calgary, Calgary, Alta., in 2006.
Includes bibliographical references and index.
Also issued in electronic format.
ISBN 978-1-55238-502-9

1. Religions. 2. Philosophy, Comparative. 3. Philosophy and religion. I. Joy, Morny

BL51.A48 2011 201'.61 C2011-906852-4

The University of Calgary Press acknowledges the support of the Government of Alberta through the Alberta Multimedia Development Fund for our publications. We acknowledge the financial support of the Government of Canada through the Canada Book Fund for our publishing activities. We acknowledge the financial support of the Canada Council for the Arts for our publishing program.

This book has been published with the aid of a grant from the Social Science and Humanities Research Council of Canada.

Government of Alberta
Canada
Canada Council for the Arts
Conseil des Arts du Canada
Social Sciences and Humanities Research Council of Canada
Conseil de recherches en sciences humaines du Canada
Canada

Cover photo courtesy of Morny Joy
Cover design, page design, and typesetting by Melina Cusano

edited by

Morny Joy

After Appropriation

Explorations in Intercultural Philosophy and Religion

University of Calgary Press

TABLE OF CONTENTS

Introduction vii
MORNY JOY

Comparative Studies in Philosophy/Religion and Dialogue as Mutual "Strangification" (*Waitui* 外推) 1
VINCENT SHEN

The Philosopher as Stranger: The Idea of Comparative Philosophy 25
MICHAEL MCGHEE

Locating Intercultural Philosophy in Relation to Religion 41
TINU RUPARELL

The Connecting *Manas*: Inner Sense, Common Sense, or the Organ of Imagination 57
ARINDAM CHAKRABARTI

Studying the "Other": Challenges and Prospects of Muslim Scholarship on World Religions 77
AHMAD F. YOUSIF

The Vices of Ethics: The Critique of Morality in Nietzsche, Kierkegaard, and Daoism 95
KATRIN FROESE

Comparative Philosophy of Religion and Modern Jewish Philosophy: A Conversation 119
MICHAEL OPPENHEIM

Philosophy, Medicine, Science, and Boundaries 139
DAN LUSTHAUS

Religious Intellectual Texts as a Site for Intercultural Philosophical and Theological Reflection: The Case of the *Śrīmad Rahasyatrayasāra* and the *Traité de l'Amour de Dieu* 173
Francis X. Clooney, S.J.

Phenomenology of Awakening in Zhiyi's Tiantai Philosophy 203
Chen-kuo Lin

Ibn Rushd or Averroës? Of Double Names and Double Truths: A Different Approach to Islamic Philosophy 221
Tamara Albertini

The Use of *Lakṣaṇā* in Indian Exegesis 239
Christopher G. Framarin

Women's Rights as Human Rights: Explorations in Intercultural Philosophy and Religion 257
Morny Joy

Notes on Contributors 281

Index 287

Introduction

MORNY JOY
University of Calgary

This edited volume is the result of a special workshop funded by the Social Science and Humanities Research Council of Canada and held at the University of Calgary in 2006. The purpose of the workshop was to bring together a group of leading scholars in the two fields of what has been called "comparative religion" and "comparative philosophy." The mandate was to explore the current state of affairs in these fields and to explore whether there can be a rapprochement between them. To further this task, it set out to investigate certain problems and/or to suggest alternative approaches. While there may already be numerous specialized books in the fields of comparative philosophy and comparative religion, there are a limited number of scholars who can address both disciplines. Such scholars attended this workshop. It thus marked the beginning of an interdisciplinary and intercultural project to bring these scholars together to initiate discussion that would continue to take place on a regular basis.[1] The unique aspect of the workshop was that this was the first time to my knowledge that a group of scholars had been intentionally assembled where there were scholars with expertise in both areas of comparative philosophy and comparative religion. As such, it is a ground-breaking volume.

While the division between the two disciplines of Religious Studies and Philosophy is commonplace in Western academia, this bifurcation does not necessarily apply in non-Western settings, where religion and philosophy tend to be integrated. As a result, when the disciplines are virtually mutually exclusive, as in the West, a full appreciation of non-Western approaches to either religion or philosophy is not easily attained, and distortions, such as appropriation, often occur. Within the last ten years, there has been a concerted effort on the part of a number of scholars to try to address these deficiencies, but it is necessary to distinguish this project from others that are occurring. It is not a project in inter-religious dialogue, which occurs only among believers and practitioners. Nor is it an exercise in apologetics where one religion would maintain dominance. Instead, it is an academic activity, undertaken with the goal of re-examining many ideas that have been misappropriated or otherwise excluded in comparative studies. These errors have resulted from a traditional approach where the religions and philosophies of non-Western peoples have been interpreted by reducing or manipulating their ideas and values to fit solely with Western concepts and categories. As such, this project is conducted with full awareness of the post-colonial critique of such enterprises. As a result, the overall aim of the project is not to reach a final solution or to recommend a definitive procedure – the intricate and often impenetrable jargon employed in many undertakings of comparative philosophy has been noted by many scholars. It is easy to get lost. This book seeks to avoid such interferences with a more modest endeavour of initiating constructive discussion.

In undertaking to organize this conference, there was also the intention, in accordance with SSHRCC regulations, to have a significant number of Canadian scholars represented, and to have a balance of gender as well as of scholars at different stages of their career. The actual impetus for this conference resulted from two new joint appointments to the departments of Philosophy and Religious Studies at the University of Calgary in 2006. These two appointees are: Chris Framarin (Hinduism and Analytic Philosophy) and Katrin Froese (Chinese Philosophy/Religions and Continental Philosophy). This brought about a critical mass of scholars in these departments working in the area of comparative religion and philosophy – adding to the work of Morny Joy (Comparative Method and Theory in History of Religions/Continental Philosophy) and

Tinu Ruparell (Hinduism and Christianity). The four of us comprised the organizing committee of this workshop. I take this opportunity to thank my Calgary associates for all their dedicated work, which helped to realize the conference. At this stage I would also like to acknowledge and thank the generous support of the Social Sciences and Humanities Research Council of Canada, without whose grant to Scholarly Conferences and Workshops this venture – including publication of this volume – would not have been realized. The University of Calgary was also generous in granting both a Conference Grant and a Grant for a Visiting Speaker.

One of the central questions that interested us was how comparative philosophy and religion would change if the concepts and categories of non-Western philosophies and religions were taken as primary in their terms of reference. This is the principal reason that we determined to frame this project as an exercise in intercultural philosophy and religion in a way that attempted to bridge the two various areas of study. While some scholars preferred to retain the term "comparative" – their approach was not uncritical and their usage was basically compatible with what we understand by the term "intercultural." This workshop is timely and constitutes a major contribution to the burgeoning field of intercultural study in philosophy and religion.

We each nominated a number of thinkers that we considered to be doing groundbreaking work in this area. Seven scholars accepted our invitations. Of those who accepted, only five could come. Those who could not come submitted papers that were discussed at the conference. All papers were then revised as a result of the discussions. As a result, the volume comprises an excellent selection of essays that touch on vital issues in all the major religions and their relation to philosophy, from both substantive and methodological perspectives.

All participants were asked to reflect on the problems and difficulties that they had encountered in their attempts to undertake work of such an interdisciplinary, intertextual, and intercultural nature. The essays that were presented at the workshop reflected the diverse nature of the dilemmas and insights that had been perceived already, or arose in the course of writing the workshop paper. The workshop examined the overlapping terrain between the fields of philosophy and religion. On the one hand, one workshop was particularly pertinent because it allowed not only for the examination of the religious undercurrents that have informed philosophy, but also for the exploration of whether the division in the West has served to narrow the horizons of much contemporary Western philosophy in a way that excludes modes of thinking that are not amenable to its procedures of classification. On the other hand, the academic study of religions has often tended to focus on one aspect in an in-depth study of one particular religion, and it has made grandiose claims of similarity with non-Western religions, based on broadly organized typologies of a phenomenological nature.[2] This often led to vague generalizations or inaccurate accommodation in accordance with Western constructs.

In contrast, this workshop on intercultural philosophy and religion fostered a philosophical dialogue between diverse traditions that allowed for a re-examination within Philosophy and Religious Studies of ideas that have often previously been taken for granted. Such an approach also threw into question the predominant trend towards specialization in academia. In this spirit, the conference also encouraged interdisciplinary discussion between scholars working in a wide variety of cultural, religious, and philosophical fields. The book that has resulted from this workshop consists of thirteen essays, all of which address an issue or illustrate a problem in the interdisciplinary field of intercultural religion and philosophy as it is presently conceived.

At this stage it would seem appropriate to delineate the understanding of the notions of "intercultural philosophy and religion" that are being used here, as the concept "culture" is itself a loaded, if not overdetermined, word. In this context, we have adopted the term "intercutural" to acknowledge its recent usage in a number of conferences and publications. It has come to be employed instead of the term "comparative" so as to distinguish its approach as one that neither privileges nor takes as normative Western concepts, categories, or methods. Such a usage of "intercultural" is to be applauded as it attempts to remedy what are viewed as past distortions and impositions.[3] Yet any unqualified use of the term "intercultural" is unacceptable without further investigation of its implied meaning(s). This is because the term "culture" is by no means objective or innocent in the way that it is being applied today.[4] In an article on human rights, Martin Chanock supplies a reason why the contemporary Western usage(s) of the word "culture," are in need of interrogation because of its past compromised employment as an agent of imperial enculturation: "All we can say about 'culture' comes from a history of imperialism, and from the current dual framework of 'orientalising' and 'occidentalising' in a world of globalised symbolic exchange. If we are to treat 'culture' as a fundamental factor in our analyses of rights, and of government and institutions we need a very high degree of self-awareness of the history and current circumstances of the deployment of the concept."[5]

It is somewhat ironic, in contrast to the above colonialist deployment of "culture" by western nations, that in non-Western and formerly colonized countries a contemporary use of the word "culture" promotes it as a conservative defence against any change – especially those that are associated with "Western values." In some instances, it is connected with appeals to either an idealized or pristine society that predated colonization, or to rejection of the impact of selective Western influences. Uma Narayan eloquently discusses fascinating variants of this phenomenon in her book *Dislocating Cultures*.[6] Contemporary anthropology also has had something of importance to add, particularly given the lively discussions that have taken place since James Clifford's book, *The Predicament of Culture*.[7] As I have said elsewhere: "Clifford acknowledges the seemingly paradoxical engagement in ethnography as it both negotiates and evaluates the very procedures it both introduces and participates in."[8] The resultant self-reflective stance, which incorporates an examination of one's own presuppositions, would seem to recommend a stance whereby anthropology no longer regards culture as a consistent or timeless and stable entity. As Sherry Ortner observes in relating the development of her own understanding of the construction of culture: "[There] are larger shifts in the conceptualization of 'culture' in the field of anthropology as a whole, [that go] in the direction of seeing 'cultures' as more disjunctive, contradictory, and inconsistent than I had been trained to think."[9] "Culture" then, while it still needs to be understood as the amalgamation of influences such as ideals, forces, institutions, and traditions, including those of religion and philosophy, should never be reified as a static entity. It would seem that all of the above observations need to be kept in mind when the term "intercultural" is invoked. They function as a healthy precaution against the attempted enforcing of any one particular viewpoint as holding any special prerogative to authority or precedence. A healthy hermeneutics of suspicion would seem necessary.[10]

Questions of method and theory are obviously essential to such an undertaking, and another task envisioned by this workshop was to provide as clear an exposition as possible of the respective contributions of both Philosophy and Religious Studies to this interdisciplinary venture. The late Raimundo Panikkar suggested that the basic business of comparative philosophy and religion was what he called "diatopical hermeneutics." This is the practice of bringing one culture, language, or philosophy into another culture, language and religion/philosophy for the purposes of a clearer exposition of the relevant questions, contexts, and topoi. It also undertakes a constructive search for new and more useful responses to these questions and topoi. In such a context, comparative philosophy and comparative religion engage in an encounter between fundamentally different traditions and address issues of how to deal with the "foreign." Not only does this necessitate working between languages that may not readily lend themselves to translation, but it also demands an exposure to ways of thinking that may be either unknown or marginalized within one's accustomed canon. In one respect, however, this project seeks to enlarge on this accustomed understanding of the "foreign." Not only must one avoid the pitfalls of simply superimposing familiar categories onto another tradition in order to achieve a comfortable synthesis but, by venturing into such unfamiliar terrain, one needs also to examine familiar traditions from the "outside" and thereby reveal presuppositions that are often taken for granted. This may well foster an awareness of incongruities within "known" paradigms that might otherwise go unnoticed. Almost all the papers contain reflections on the nature of such foreigness or otherness, or, as Vincent Shen termed it, adapting a Chinese word *waitui* (外推), "strangification." At the same time, there is one position that is evident in all the papers. This is that each tradition involved in a comparison is accorded equal weight. No tradition is regarded as having a superior stance or a more privileged access to truth, however that may be understood.

Over the past fifty years, the journal, *Philosophy East and West,* has published numerous insightful articles of a comparative nature, where both philosophy and religion have been featured. But there has not been a specific issue where the methodological problems of such interactions have been addressed in a systemic or thematized way. There have also been, of course, a large number of single-author volumes written from either a philosophic or religious studies perspective of a comparative nature that reflect the accepted methods of their respective disciplines. One example is Lee Yearley's highly nuanced comparative study of Aquinas and Mencius on both virtue and courage. His astute readings broach both philosophic and religious topics. Distinguishing carefully between areas of theory and practice, or reason and ethics, Yearley is particularly sensitive to differences as well as to commonalities in both traditions in the way they foster human flourishing.[11] Another example of comparative work that illustrates how attitudes can be changed is that of Roger Ames. He demonstrates that an encounter with Chinese thought sensitizes the reader to the truly original nature of a thinker such as Nietzsche who is a maverick within his own tradition.[12] Other scholars have highlighted certain issues of a methodological nature pertaining to comparative philosophy. The work of Gerald J. Larson and Eliot Deutsch[13] and that of Fred Dallmayr[14] have been particularly helpful. Katrin Froese, who is a contributor to this volume, has also written an excellent comparative philosophical study.[15]

It needs to be observed that this type of investigation has not been the prerogative of Western scholars alone, as recent books by Chinese scholars illustrate. For example, Cheng Zhongying (1991)[16] has drawn parallels between Confucianism and western hermeneutics, and Li Chenyang in *The Tao Encounters the West*,[17] describes how democracy and eastern values can fruitfully be combined. Another recent edited volume in the same vein is that of Shun Kwong-loi and David B. Wong.[18]

It is also noteworthy, that there have not been many edited collections comparing and contrasting eastern and western philosophy and religion. There has been, however, one such volume already published. This was entitled, *East-West Encounters in Philosophy and Religion,* edited by Professor B. Srinavasa Murthy and Ninian Smart, published in 1996.[19] It was Professor B. Srinavasa Murthy who first organized a conference of this nature in Mysore in 1991, with a second one taking place in Long Beach, California, in 1993. The book comprises selected papers from both conferences. Examples of papers or sections in the book have titles such as: "Person: East and West," or "Asian and Western Thought." It is obviously wide in scope but contains very little reflection on issues of methodology. Nevertheless, it marked a rich and eclectic attempt to take the measure of the immense interest stimulated by the two conferences.

I believe that our workshop and the resultant papers can make an extremely important contribution to the continuance of such undertakings, both nationally and internationally, to the rapidly expanding field of intercultural studies in both philosophy and religious studies. Thus far, there has been no book published that attends to a multi-faceted discussion of method and theory from an intercultural philosophical and religious perspective. I also believe that it is both a substantial and an original undertaking. One of our principal intentions in inviting scholars in philosophy from both analytic and Continental backgrounds as well as scholars in religion, all of whom are well versed in method and theory, was to raise the discussion on these issues to a more sophisticated level, particularly in light of contemporary debates on the role of pluralism and globalization. The aim was not to find solutions, but the hope was to arrive at some clearer insights into the various obstacles that can hinder such exchanges.

* * *

Vincent Shen proposes the term "strangification" – a translation of the Chinese term *Waitui* – as a constructive way of appreciating the task that is involved in undertaking intercultural study in philosophy and religion. His intention in using this term is to describe a process of "going outside oneself in order to go to many others"; that is, to strangers and to strange worlds that engage with different forms of philosophy and religion. His paper contributes to this volume by laying out certain methodological foundations for his philosophy of contrast as a strategy of strangification. As part of this strategy, dialogue is understood as a process of mutual strangification. In his study, Shen illustrates his discussion by contrasting Chinese philosophy with Western philosophy. He does this by first clarifying his concept of "many others," as well as those of contrast and strangification, with reference to their origin in Chinese philosophical traditions such as Confucianism and Daoism. He then places these terms in dialogue with a number of Western Continental philosophers. Shen's own discussion is set against the contemporary context of globalization and with particular reference to his own traditions of Chinese philosophy and religions.

After defining globalization as a historical process of deterritorialization or border-crossing, Shen places intercultural studies within a framework of cross-cultural philosophy and religion. From his perspective, intercultural study can be appreciated as leading to potential communication with a view to mutual enrichment, instead of simply doing comparison simply for comparison's sake. By replacing certain post-modern French thinkers' concept of "the other" with a concept of "many others," Shen also elaborates on the concept of "contrast." For Shen, comparison, communication, and dialogue always start with a mutual act of going outside of one's self-enclosure to many others, an act initiated by an original act of generosity that makes reciprocity possible. In the resulting process of mutual strangification, all parties involved endeavour to make their own scientific/cultural/religious/life world understandable to each other. From a methodological position, Shen's paper focuses on the strategy of strangification and the idea of dialogue as mutual strangification as ideas and processes that can take place on a number of levels – linguistic, pragmatic, and ontological.

Michael McGhee wonders about a different sort of strangeness – that of the philosopher who, in ancient times, as described in the work of Pierre Hadot, was a seeker of wisdom and thus not necessarily motivated by the same goals as ordinary citizens of the world. McGhee reflects on his own feelings of estrangement from contemporary philosophy – specifically that of analytic philosophy – and suggests ways that could revitalize contemporary philosophy from its basically secular preoccupations. He considers comparative philosophy as one possibility – but not simply as an exercise that would enlarge the canon. McGhee considers the impetus that prompted Henri Corbin to undertake his explorations in comparative philosophy, but McGhee seeks to move beyond its idealistic Platonic orientation. Nevertheless, he recognizes the need for a skilled application of the Platonic tools of dialogue, both *agon* and *elenchus*, in any comparative exercise where searching questions need to be asked, though probably to different ends than Plato and Corbin had in mind. This is because McGhee is only too well aware that the present situation, with its globalized networking and commodification, needs to be taken into consideration. In such a complex world, a solution can no longer be sought in easy appeals to former times, such as Corbin's approach. McGhee is seeking a way that would mediate between the all-too-familiar contemporary extremes of nihilism and idealism, or other simplistic dualisms that tend to occur in contemporary debates of inclusion/exclusion. From a comparative perspective, McGhee finds guidance for a responsive and tolerant approach in his own Buddhist practice. He finds it particularly helpful in the way it provides insight into how states of consciousness influence either the expansiveness or constraint of human experiences and action. Such knowledge is a form of wisdom and would be helpful in intercultural philosophy as a way of encountering strangeness or otherness. It could help foster the innovative connections that can take place when a philosopher, as a stranger, enters into previously alien or unknown ways of philosophizing that challenge ideals regarded as normative in his or her own time, culture, and philosophical tradition.

Tinu Ruparell is also interested in the question of strangeness and the stranger as a component of intercultural philosophy and religion – but this time the stranger is cast as the Other. As Ruparell attests, the authentic voice of the Other is a subject that has exercised many scholars. This includes those who, from a postcolonial perspective, view colonialism, with its mandate of "civilizing" the religious other as involving the imposition of foreign values and beliefs. At the same time, there are philosophers, like Emmanuel Levinas, who seek to rectify the failures of the Western ethical code that did not prevent the Holocaust from occurring. As Ruparell observes, Levinas's prescription for a new understanding of an ethical orientation is to place one's responsibility for the other person before one's self-related inclinations, be they charitable or egocentric. In his own search to find a process that would be suitable for intercultural philosophy and religion – one that allows an alienated person or subaltern figure to find his or her voice – Ruparell proposes that Levinas's approach might be of help. In this approach, the philosopher goes towards the other, in a manner similar to Shen's "strangification." In fact, again one becomes a stranger to oneself on order to be open to the other. Ruparell, however, would see a further qualification to Shen's proposal to initiate a dialogue by means of a *kenosis*, or emptying of self. This is because for Ruparell, in attempting to constitute him- or herself in a different mode of receptivity, a person must not just become receptive but place oneself entirely at the disposal of the other. Only by taking such a radical step, Ruparell proposes, can a genuine self-transformation take place.

All the above three variations on the theme of strangeness and the stranger by Shen, McGhee, and Ruparell find echoes in other essays in this volume, though different terms are employed to describe such a moment or movement. They are all symptomatic of the difficult situation involved when a Western academic tries to come to terms with a legacy that has prevented him or her from full appreciating the dimensions of religions and philosophical systems that are substantially at variance with their own particular notions of belief or ethical ideals.

The contribution of **Arindam Chakrabarti** is a study of the Sanskrit philosophical concept of "*manas*", controversially translatable as "inner sense." Among the many functions assigned to this internal instrument by the *Bṛhadāraṇyaka Upaniṣad* (1.5.3), such as desire, resolution, doubt, memory, and introspection, one crucial function is that of cross-modal comparison and connecting the data from different external senses. The paper discusses seven distinct arguments for postulating such an inner sense. In the Sāṃkhya, Vedānta, and Nyāya schools of philosophy, it becomes a distinct sense organ, responsible for attention, comparison, imagination, and reflective awareness of cognitive and hedonic states. Since it is an organ of comparison, *manas* deserves special attention of comparative philosophy. Chakrabarti illustrates this point by actually comparing the Indian concept of inner sense with a corresponding conception in Aristotle's *De Anima* (425a–426b), where such a sixth inner sense is proposed and rejected. But the comparable idea of a *sensus communis* is taken seriously by Aristotle. In Kant's philosophy, inner sense also has a very crucial role to play, but it is distinguished from the common sense, which is central to aesthetic reflective judgment. Chakrabarti suggests a richer theory of a sixth common sense-organ for imaginatively perceiving possibilities. The essay concludes by discussing Ibn Rushd's (Averroës') original metaphysics of the inner common sense, in his commentary on *De Anima*, and indicating the possibility of connecting the concept of sense-organs with the Vedic Hindu concept of multiple divinities.

Ahmad Yousif's paper is a constructive proposal that would help situate the notion of comparative religion as an acceptable approach in Islam. In this way it features more as a preamble to the further development of intercultural philosophy and religion. Yousif understands his contribution to constitute the beginnings of a move towards a possible dialogue of Islam with Western and Eastern religions. He states that, in most institutions of higher learning in the Muslim world today, scant attention is given to the field of comparative religion. This is in distinct contrast to similar institutions in Western countries. Yet, to bring the situation into perspective, Yousif states that this was not always the case. Between the ninth and twelfth centuries, Islamic civilization witnessed the rise – and also eclipse – of the discipline of *'ilm al milal wa n-nihal* (literally, "knowledge of religious groups and sects"). Classical Muslim scholars, such as al-Shahrastani, al-Biruni, al-Kalbi, al-Baghdadi, Ibn Ḥazm, and others, made numerous investigations and contributions to the field. The modern period has also witnessed the emergence of a number of Muslim intellectuals, such as al-Faruqi, Shalaby, al-Hashimi, Daraz, and others, who have made serious endeavours to investigate the field. Frequently, the methodology utilized by Muslim scholars towards the study of major world religions, however, differs from their Western counterparts. Yousif's paper first explores the historical developments of the discipline of comparative religion from Islamic and Western perspectives. Second, it compares and contrasts methodological approaches among Muslim and non-Muslim scholars in the field of comparative religion. Then, it examines some of the challenges encountered by scholars studying "other" religions. In conclusion, it discusses the importance and significance of studying major world religions at the tertiary educational level, in the West and in the Muslim world, to help in the mutual understanding and appreciation of both philosophy and religion.

Katrin Froese's exercise in intercultural philosophy and religion is achieved by putting seemingly disparate philosophers in dialogue on a particular subject. In her paper, she examines the criticisms of ethics undertaken by Nietzsche and Kierkegaard as well as in the Daoist philosophies of the *Daodejing* and Zhuangzi. All of these thinkers expose an unethical underbelly to ethics. They reveal an intractable paradox at the heart of ethics, which is that the same processes that enable human beings to become moral also produce immorality. Such a formulation suggests that morality and immorality may share a common core. By way of comparison, Froese first portrays Nietzsche as seeking redemption from selfish Christian morality by attempting to infuse life into what he views as its moribund precepts. He does this by adopting a universal ethic of embracing life that is based on affirmation of this world rather than self-contempt and a longing for eternity. Then, by describing Kierkegaard's critical philosophy, Froese demonstrates the trouble that western ethics has in accommodating the radical other. This is due to the spectre of egoism that undermines all such human endeavours. As a remedy, Kierkegaard states that faith demands a readiness to relinquish all attachments of the ego so as to be able to enter into a direct relationship with God.

Froese also portrays the way that Daoist thinkers view morality as worrisome because it is directly linked to the use of language. For Daoists, language, by definition, must parcel the world into fragments. Thus language constrains, and, because of this, it is often linked to the desire for closure or possession. The resultant addiction to language suggests that moral imperatives are very closely wedded to the desire for knowledge, which is understood as a way of rendering the world amenable to human comprehension. Words thus divide, and so exclude, as well as include. As a result, morality, by positing the good, must inevitably depend on the notion of evil against which it defines itself. This means that moral systems all too often rest on the ostracism of the stranger who symbolizes the unknown and cannot so easily be embraced within the linguistic paradigm. In order to counteract this, Daoist philosophy, both in the *Daodejing* and the *Zhuangzi*, underlines the importance of an attunement to nothingness. This is because nothingness represents a kind of radical openness that has banished desire. Thus, despite their seemingly obvious differences, Nietzsche, Kierkegaard, and Daoist thinkers would concur that conventional morality is predicated on a kind of resistance that can stamp out the particularity of others, rather than celebrating it. As such, Froese's exercise in comparative philosophy and religion helps to demonstrate commonalities of viewpoint regarding ethical ways of living in traditions that are often regarded as completely distinct.

In his paper, **Michael Oppenheim** begins with a guiding question to help him in his explorations: "What might a conversation between comparative philosophy of religion and modern Jewish philosophy contribute to each participant?" While he appreciates that such a conversation is only just beginning to take place, he believes that there are important insights that each side can contribute to the other. He begins by reflecting on the nature of contemporary philosophy and Jewish philosophy from a comparative perspective. This is followed by an examination of some basic problems in these two areas. In terms of comparative philosophy, he first examines the failure of philosophy generally to respond to contemporary feminist philosophy. He then laments its failure to include Jewish philosophy (as well as Islamic philosophy) and to recognize them as having historic roles in its own narrative history. Oppenheim then highlights what he considers to be the two problem areas in contemporary Jewish philosophy: 1. the way the relationship between (Western) "philosophy" and Jewish philosophy is usually depicted, and 2. its own reticence to recognize and enter into dialogue with feminist Jewish philosophy. In the concluding section, Oppenheim explores the potentialities for each side to address these problem areas in the mode of the other as proposed by Levinas.

Dan Lusthaus's essay is a wide-ranging rumination on what it has meant to do comparative philosophy of religion. In his approach, since all thinking is comparative – where, hopefully, comparative philosophy stimulates insightful thinking – comparative philosophy and religion needs to draw its strength from expanding the range of philosophies and religions it compares. In Lusthus's view, for a Western philosopher to think about Indian or Chinese or Arabic or Jewish philosophies is basically no different from a North American philosopher thinking about Plato, Spinoza, Hegel, or Wittgenstein. Each task requires looking at the other through similarities and differences of language, culture, context, foundational categories, historical developments, and a host of other factors. Lusthaus posits that the basic differences are not between East and West, as is often assumed, but between styles of philosophizing and root metaphors from which different traditions take their orientation. In this vein, Lusthaus explores the similarities and differences between religion, philosophy, and science, especially medicine. Taking the fact that *pramāṇa* theory (the means of acquiring knowledge) first appeared in India in a medical text, the *Caraka-saṃhitā*, as a jumping-off point, he illustrates that philosophy, religion, and medicine have always been intertwined, especially in ancient and medieval philosophy. He concludes with a concise examination of the *Caraka-saṃhitā*'s *pramāṇa-theory*, with special attention to a unique *pramāṇa* found only in one text, *yukta-pramāṇa*. This is an inductive synthetic type of reasoning that seeks to analyze transformation in terms of coordination of multiple factors converging into a transformative trajectory. Lusthaus's analysis thus proposes a fascinating mode of pursuing comparative studies in philosophy and religion. In a sense, such an exercise is also in the spirit of intercultural philosophy and religion in that it does not privilege a specific religion but attempts to discern their similar roots.

In his essay, **Francis X. Clooney** proposes that religious texts – considered seriously, and in depth – constitute a most appropriate and fruitful place for reflection on philosophical and theological issues in a comparative context. Such texts provide access to worlds of thought that are invariably complex and inhabit diverse terrains – partly accessible and partly particular – or present insider discourse that can all branch off in various diverse and elusive ways. For Clooney such texts are also often especially rich in style as they are in readers' expectations. Two such texts from two traditions, in this instance, Hinduism and Catholicism, if they are read together, create an array of comparative possibilities that, in turn, can then generate a considerable range of philosophical and theological reflection. Clooney regards this kind of reflection on complex texts that are both philosophical and theological, both highly rational and richly imaginative, as being superior to thematic comparisons. This is because the texts resist conclusive generalizations and keep introducing cultural and religious specificity back into such generalizing discourses.

Because the emphasis is on thinking-through-reading, half of Clooney's essay is dedicated to giving a passage from each of the two classic texts that are to be read together – that *need* to be read together, if their religious and philosophical significance is to be made accessible in a comparative context. Each of the texts that are excerpted – the *Treatise on the Love of God* (*Traité de l'Amour de Dieu*) of Francis de Sales, a major seventeenth-century Catholic theologian, and the *Essence of the Three Mysteries* (*Śrīmad Rahasyatrayasāra*) of Vedānta Deśika, a major medieval Hindu theologian – "works" on multiple levels and makes connections among linguistic, philosophical, theological, mystical, and other tradition-based resources. When the texts are read together, their possibilities are maximized and intensified, and the new text thus generated, comprised of traditional, religious, and rational insights, facilitates further conversation.

Such a shared reading provides a complex starting point – reference, foundation, directions – for intercultural reflection, philosophical or religious. This is because each text is itself a synthesis compounded by its author. Together, the paired texts constitute a still more complex conversation in which the reader who is philosophically or religiously inclined reads his or her way back and forth across the spectrum of matters both philosophical and religious, or rational and affective.

Chen-kuo Lin explores the Buddhist phenomenology of awakening as exemplified in the philosophical writings of Zhiyi (538–597 C.E.), the founder of the Tiantai School of Buddhism, and then investigates in what way the Western notion of phenomenology, especially as pursued by Edmund Husserl, could be enriched by comparison with this Chinese philosopher's work. The phrase "phenomenology of awakening" is deliberately used in contrast to "phenomenology of mundane experience." In the Buddhist context, the former may be referred to as "phenomenology of insight," whereas the latter is classifiable as "phenomenology of consciousness." In both forms of phenomenology, a distinct method is required for the disclosure of truth. Lin's article is mainly concerned with how the truth of awakened experience is disclosed through the meditative method in the Buddhist phenomenology of Zhiyi. As an illustration of one of the impetuses of this volume, which is an attempt to investigate the ways in which Western philosophy and religion can be rethought through non-Western categories, two questions are raised by Lin. The first asks: in what sense can Zhiyi's Tiantai philosophy be characterized as a form of phenomenology? The second asks: in what way can Husserlian phenomenology be further developed into a phenomenology of awakening as envisioned in the Buddhist tradition? In reply to these questions, Lin divides his study into two sections. The first section lays out the Buddhist distinction between mundane knowledge and trans-mundane insight. In the second part, Lin focuses on Zhiyi's soteriological phenomenology with special attention to the problems of truth, meditation, and insight. In conclusion, he sums up the religious spirit in Zhiyi's phenomenology, where the experience of awakening should never be regarded as exclusionary. In this way, it differs from Husserl's more explicitly personal approach. For Zhiyi, true awakening, which manifests the enlightened world, must be experienced *along with* all other worlds that have yet to be enlightened. That is, true liberation must be experienced *along with* all other worlds that are still in suffering. In his study, Lin describes how Husserl's understanding of phenomenology can be enriched by an intercultural study with Chinese philosophy, which is indeed a reversal of many earlier ones where the terms of reference were usually provided by the Western scholar and traditional categories of analysis.

Tamara Albertini's paper is an appeal to study, discuss, and assess philosophy in non-Western traditions by returning to criteria afforded by these same traditions. It is an appeal that Islamic philosophy should be read and appreciated on its own terms, rather than assessed according to Western standards. Rather than being preoccupied with what "counts" as philosophy, or with what constitutes a "good thought" or a "good methodology" according to standards developed to measure the philosophical merits of Western texts, the focus of inquiry ought to be placed on the devices, concepts, and strategies that are of concern to the tradition to be studied. Ideally, for Albertini, the inter-cultural investigation begins once the intellectual intricacies of the two (or more) traditions involved in an in-depth study or discussion have been appreciated – each one in its own right.

Albertini then graphically illustrates what happens when centuries of misunderstandings and missed opportunities stand in the way of Western scholars' "appreciation" of another tradition of thought, such as, for example, Islamic philosophy. Ironically, the difficulty in this comparative setting lies not in Muslim thought being perceived as being too *different* but rather as too *similar*. This over-emphasizing of the commonalities has its roots in an approach that has long looked upon Islamic philosophy and sciences as a gold mine for Western intellectual needs. For Albertini there is, nevertheless, something to be gained from recognizing this ill-balanced perception: Islamic philosophy has been no stranger to the European historical landscape in the past. Yet while the scientific, philosophical, and, to a lesser degree, cultural debt toward Islamic civilization has long been acknowledged, contemporary research on Muslim thought requires a new direction. In Albertini's view, what needs to be created is an understanding of why it should matter to study Islamic philosophy for its own sake, independently of how or whether it *speaks* at all to the Western world. To achieve this, a non-utilitarian approach should be adopted, or, at the very least, one in which the primary *use* of studying Muslim thought is to know it on its own terms.

Chris Framarin examines an approach that is utilized in Indian philosophy and explores how *lakṣaṇā* and its application could be of benefit to Western scholars in their own work of interpretation and translation of Indian texts. *Lakṣaṇā* is an Indian exegetical principle that permits an interpreter to revert to a less literal reading of a claim when the literal reading is sufficiently implausible. If the literal reading implies a contradiction or absurdity, for example, an interpreter is often permitted – and sometimes required – to understand the claim figuratively. Contemporary interpreters of Indian philosophy employ this strategy extensively, but often without acknowledging its limitations. In this paper, Framarin argues that contemporary interpreters of Indian philosophy should adopt and utilize the principle of *lakṣaṇā*, but only in accord with the criteria set forth by classical Indian philosophers.

Morny Joy's paper introduces the topic of women's rights as human rights as a subject that could benefit from intercultural discussion by both philosophy and religion. It may not seem immediately to be a relevant topic for such an undertaking, but it is an emerging area of interest and concern that needs to be addressed by women. At stake is the shifting boundary between public/private as this affects the secular/religious divide. In many recent instances, fundamentalism has attempted to interfere in the public and political sphere, while keeping women under tight private control. At the same time, many feminists have proclaimed "the personal is the political." Such diverse impulses would only seem to confuse the situation. Yet what is being contested in both cases concerns the rights of women, particularly with reference to the control of their bodies. Joy discusses how in the wider parameters of the globalized women's movement, reactionary activities by fundamentalists from a number of religions and countries at the United Nations have tried to prevent any further advances by women in the area of rights, citing reservations on matters of culture and tradition. These are basically shorthand terms for religion. Such cases involve extraordinarily complex and sensitive issues that need extremely careful discernment of the religious sensibilities involved. They are not easily solved. Yet they are in need of input from scholars in religion because of their specific skills in both religious/ethical traditions and fine-tuned exegesis or textual interpretation. As yet there has not been much work done on a comparative basis that would bring scholars of religion and philosophy into dialogue with activists from all regions and religions of the world to address this most important issue. This paper is an attempt to bring it to notice and further discussion from a comparative perspective.

Notes

1 As a follow-up to this conference, the group decided that it would like to continue the conversation that it started and applied for Seminar status at the American Academy of Religion. It has met at its annual conference for the past four years and has one more year of its five-year mandate.

2 Perhaps one of the more popular examples of this genre is Mircea Eliade's work, *Patterns in Comparative Religion*, trans. Rosemary Sheed. (New York: World Publishing, 1972, c1958).

3 There is always the fear that the introduction of such a new term could be just the latest fad in academic circles. As with all such terms, it is necessary to keep a careful watch on the development of its continuing usage.

4 See Morny Joy, "Method and Theory in Religious Studies: Retrospect and Prognostications," *Temenos* 43, no. 2 (2008): 199–222.

5 Martin Chanock, "Culture and Human Rights: Orientalising, Occidentalising and Authenticity," in *Beyond Rights Talk and Culture Talk*, ed. Mahmood Mamdani (New York: St. Martin's Press, 2000), 15–36.

6 Narayan describes the manner in which such claims function in contemporary forms where there is movement to unite nationalism with religion, as in India. She is as concerned about the "demonic other" produced by colonialism, as she is about the ensuing manufactured nostalgic essentialism of an idealized, ancient India. See Uma Narayan, *Dislocating Cultures, Identities, Traditions, and Third World Feminisms* (New York: Routledge, 1997), 33.

7 Clifford, James. *The Predicament of Culture: Twentieth-Century Ethnography, Literature and Art* (Cambridge, MA: Harvard University Press, 1988).

8 Morny Joy, "Beyond a God's-Eye View: Alternative Perspectives in the Study of Religion," in Armin W. Geertz and Russell T. McCutcheon (eds.), *Perspectives on Method and Theory in the Study of Religion, Adjunct Proceedings of the 17th Congress of the International Association for the History of Religions*. (Leiden: Brill, 2000), 132.

9 Sherry B. Ortner, *Making Gender: The Politics and Erotics of Culture* (Boston: Beacon Press, 1996), 175.

10 Paul Ricoeur introduced this term in his book, *Freud and Philosophy: An Essay on Interpretation*. New Haven, CT: Yale University Press. He there referred to Nietzsche, Marx, and Freud as the "masters of suspicion." By this term, he wished to alert people that they may not always be totally in control of what they presume to be their free and transparent thoughts. But there is also another element to the definition of this term. He has also stated that: "The hermeneutics of suspicion functions against systems of power which seek to prevent confrontation between competing arguments at the level of genuine discourse." This is found in an essay, "Imagination,

Testament and Trust," in *Questioning Ethics: Contemporary Debates in Philosophy*, ed. Richard Kearney and Mark Dooley (London: Routledge, 1999), 17.

11 Lee Yearley, *Mencius and Aquinas: Theories of Virtue and Conceptions of Courage* (Albany, NY: SUNY Press, 1990).

12 Roger Ames, "Nietzsche's Will to Power and Chinese Virtuality," in *Nietzsche and Asian Thought*, ed. Graham Parkes (Chicago: University of Chicago Press, 1991).

13 Gerald Larson and Eliot Deutsch, eds., *Interpreting Across Boundaries: New Essays in Comparative Philosophy* (Princeton: Princeton University Press, 1988).

14 Fred Dallmayr, *Beyond Orientalism: Essays on Cross-Cultural Encounter* (Albany, NY: SUNY Press, 1996).

15 See Katrin Froese, *Nietzsche, Heidegger and Daoist Thought: Crossing Paths In-Between* (Lanham, MD: Lexington, 2006).

16 Zhongying Cheng, *New Dimensions of Confucian and Neo-Confucian Philosophy* (Albany, NY: SUNY Press, 1991).

17 Chengyang Li, *The Tao Encounters the West: Explorations in Comparative Pluralism* (Albany, NY: SUNY Press, 1999).

18 Shun, Kwong-loi, and David B. Wong, *Confucian Ethics: A Comparative Study of Self, Autonomy, and Community.* (New York: Cambridge University Press, 2004).

19 Ninian Smart and B. Srinivasa Murthy, eds., *East-West Encounters in Philosophy and Religion* (Long Beach, CA: Long Beach Publications, 1996).

comparative studies in philosophy/religion and dialogue as mutual "strangification" (*Waitui* 外推)

VINCENT SHEN
University of Toronto

FROM COMPARATIVE PHILOSOPHY/RELIGION TO INTERCULTURAL PHILOSOPHY/RELIGION

For me, comparative studies in philosophy and religion today should be put in the context of reaching out to meet many others in all cultural traditions and political communities, a phenomenon of border-crossing or deterritorialization characteristic of today's world process of globalization. Elsewhere I have defined 'globalization' as "a historical process of deterritorialization or border-crossing, in which human desire, human interconnectedness and universalizability are to be realized on the planet as a whole, and to be concretized in the present as global free market, trans-national political order and cultural glocalism."[1] All people of the world are involved in the process of going beyond themselves to many others, to meet them and understand them, either ideally for dialogue in view of mutual enrichment or unfortunately for dealing with conflict in the case of oppositional confrontation.

It is in this context that comparative studies become pragmatically meaningful. I don't think, at least for myself, that there is any positive interest for doing comparison for comparison's sake. Comparative studies in philosophy, religion, social sciences and culture, etc., always presuppose and indeed involve, on the one hand, the existence of many others and the act of going outside of oneself to many others, and, on the other hand, a deeper understanding of one's true self and potentiality, and the precious values accumulated in one's own tradition.

Now, when the world is entering an era of globalization, two interrelated questions concerning the future of philosophy/religion emerge for our attention: First, how could each philosophical/religious tradition draw the best of its cultural resources for the benefit of other philosophical/religious traditions in the world? Second, how could each philosophical/religious tradition achieve self-understanding by regarding impartially other philosophical/religious traditions and, furthermore, by allowing philosophizing and religiosity to become indispensable for the mutual understanding of all cultural traditions in the world? Facing the challenge of these two questions, we are led to put more and more emphasis on intercultural philosophy/religion.

It is an undeniable fact that philosophy/religion was, and still is, culturally bound. Western philosophy was very much related to the long cultural heritage from ancient Greek, through Roman, to medieval and modern Europe. In the non-Western world, for example, in China, we find other traditions such as Confucianism, Daoism, and Buddhism. As Martin Heidegger has well pointed out, Western philosophy has developed from a decisive choice made by the Western culture in the time of Parmenides and Plato. Even now, many works in the history of Western philosophy are still unjustifiably called "The History of Philosophy"; regrettably, this exclusiveness and arrogance arbitrarily sets aside many other possibilities.

In this context, to study intercultural philosophy/religion means not to enclose one's own vision of philosophy/religion within the limit of one's own tradition, especially that of Western philosophy/religion. This is particularly necessary today when the type of rationality and religiosity so basic to Western civilizations is now much challenged and even collapsing. Now the world is open to other types of rationality and religiosity, or it would be better to say a more comprehensive function of human reason and human feeling.

It is well recognized that we live now in an age of multiculturalism. As I see it, the concept of "multiculturalism" should mean, of course, but not only, a request for cultural identity and a respect for cultural difference, as Charles Taylor has well argued. In the meanwhile, it has been limited to a kind of "politics of recognition."[2] For me, "multiculturalism" means, at the start, that each and every culture has its own cultural identity and that each should respect each other's cultural differences; besides, it should mean, above all, mutual enrichment by cultural differences and an unceasing search for universalizable elements embodied in various cultural traditions.[3] I understand that we can obtain this *upgraded* meaning of multiculturalism only by conducting dialogues among different cultural worlds. In this context, different ways of doing philosophy and religion in different cultural traditions could enrich our vision of the multi-layered and multi-faceted reality. Especially in this time of radical change, any philosophy/religion capable of facing this challenge has to include in itself an intercultural dimension.

PHILOSOPHY OF CONTRAST AND INTERCULTURAL PHILOSOPHY/RELIGION

What is intercultural philosophy/religion? This should not be limited only to doing comparative philosophy/religion, as in the cases of comparative linguistics, which is quite often limited to the studies of resemblance and difference between two different languages. Although doing comparative philosophy/religion in this manner could lead to a kind of relativism in philosophy/religion, it could not really help the self/mutual understanding and the practice of philosophy/religion itself. A maximal vision of comparative study should lead to interaction and dialogue among different cultural, philosophical, and religious traditions.

For me, the real target of doing intercultural philosophy/religion is to put different philosophical/religious traditions into contrast, rather than engaging in a sheer comparison. I understand "contrast" as the rhythmic and dialectical interplay between difference and complementarity, continuity and discontinuity, which leads eventually to the real mutual enrichment of different agents, individual or collective, such as different traditions of religion or philosophy.[4]

I have proposed a philosophy of contrast as an alternative to both structuralism and Hegelian dialectics. Structuralism sees only elements in opposition but not in complementarity. It also over-emphasizes synchronicity to the negligence of diachronicity, and therefore human historicity is reduced to mere structural determinism. It could be said that historical movement is essential to Hegelian dialectics, which sees dialectics as both methodology and ontology, i.e., as the historical movement of Spirit seen as the True Reality. In Hegel, however, Spirit moves by means of *Aufhebung*, which is understood in a negative way that tends finally towards the triumph of negativity and thus overlooks the positivity in dialectical movement. However, my concept of contrast rediscovers the dynamic tension of both difference and complementarity, structurality and historicity, and it integrates both negative and positive forces in the movement of history as the process of Reality's unfolding and manifestation.

The wisdom of contrast has its origin in Chinese philosophy, such as the *Book of Changes*, the *Laozi* and other Chinese philosophical texts. It suffices to mention that the diagram of the Great Ultimate seems to give us a concrete image of a philosophy of contrast, though apparently it represents only what I call "structural contrast." Still, we can put it into movement on the axis of time and thereby obtain an image of "dynamic contrast."

By "structural contrast" I mean that in any moment of analysis, the multiple objects appearing in our experience are constituted of interacting elements, different yet related, opposing yet complementary to each other. It is synchronic in the sense that these elements appear simultaneously so as to form a well-structured whole. Being different, however, each element enjoys a certain degree of autonomy; while being related, they are mutually interdependent.

On the other hand, by "dynamic contrast" I mean that, on the axis of time, all beings, all individual life-stories, collective histories, and cosmic processes are in a process of becoming through the continuous and discontinuous interplay of the precedent and the consequent moments. It is diachronic in the sense that one moment follows another moment on the axis of time, to form a history, not in a discontinuous or atomic succession, but in a contrasting way of development moving continuously and discontinuously. As discontinuous, the novel moment has its proper originality, never to be reduced to any preceding moment. As continuous, it always keeps something from the preceding moment as residue or sedimentation of experience in time. This concept of dynamic contrast could explain all the processes of becoming, such as the relationship between tradition and modernity.[5]

In this sense we are different from structuralism for which the structure is anonymous, as it determines the constitution of meaning without being known consciously by the agent.[6] For us, on the contrary, a system or a structure is always the outcome of the act of structuration by a certain agent or group of actors in the process of time.

On the other hand, the process of time can also be analyzed through our vision or intellectual gaze in order to uncover its structural intelligibility. An historical action can be analyzed in terms of systematic properties and be integrated into a structural totality. This is true, for example, in communication where the system and the agent are mutually dependent and promoting one another. The contrasting interaction between structure and dynamism leads finally to the evolution process of complexification. Structural contrast puts interacting elements into a kind of organized totality, but it is only through dynamic contrast that continuity and the emergence of new possibilities can be properly understood.

The wisdom of contrast reminds us always to see the other side of the story and the tension between complementary elements essential to creativity in time. The wisdom of contrast reminds us of the contrasting situation between concepts such as agent and system, difference and complementarity, continuity and discontinuity, reason and rationality, theory and praxis, understanding and translatability, process and reality, etc.

Let us consider now the epistemological strategies we can adopt in view of a good comparative or intercultural philosophy/religion. Two consecutive strategies could be proposed here: First, the strategy of appropriation of language, which means, more concretely, speaking and learning the language that makes other cultural/philosophical/religious traditions understandable. Ever since our childhood, learning a language takes place by interacting with the generous act of those who take the initiative to speak to us and thereby open to us a world of meaningfulness. Later, when we are grown up, we learn the languages of different disciplines, cultural practices, and linguistic communities, which open us to ever-enlarging worlds. As Wittgenstein says, different language games correspond to different life-forms; therefore, appropriation of another's language would give us access to the life-form implied in that specific language. By appropriating different languages of different cultural/philosophical/religious traditions, we could enter into different worlds and thereby enrich the construction of our own world.

Second, there is the strategy of *strangification* (or *waitui* 外推, in Chinese). By this I mean the act of going outside of oneself to go to many others, from one's familiars to one's strangers, from one's cultural/religious world to many others' cultural/religious worlds. Later, I'll discuss in more detail three types of strangification, that is, linguistic, pragmatic, and ontological strangification, and my notion of "dialogue" as mutual strangification.

CONTRAST INVITES STRANGIFICATION

Philosophies/religions from different cultural traditions may be seen as in a situation of contrast, that is, different yet complementary, which allows them to go beyond one's own side to multiple others, from one's own familiarity to strangers. We may, for example, put Chinese philosophy and Western philosophy into contrast, by saying that, first, Western philosophy uses languages based on alphabetical systems and are therefore more abstract, while Chinese philosophy uses pictograms and ideograms, which express ideas through images such as 人 (*ren*, human beings), 天 (*tian*, Heaven), 仁 (*ren*, humanness), 道 (*dao*, the Way), and 心 (*xin*, mind/heart). Second, Chinese philosophy expresses itself by *image-idea*, different from Western philosophy, which aims at *pure ideas*; Chinese philosophy prefers metaphors and narratives, and thus is different from concepts and argumentations used by Western philosophy. We may also put them into contrast by saying that Western philosophy can be traced back to its origin in the Greek notion of *theoria*, the disinterested pursuit of truth and sheer intellectual curiosity,[7] while Chinese philosophy seems to be without such a purely theoretical interest and is more pragmatically motivated. Generally speaking, the *episteme* in Western philosophy began as a result of the attitude of *wonder*, which led to the theoretical construction of scientific and philosophical knowledge, whereas Chinese philosophy began with the attitude of concern, which led finally to a practical wisdom for guiding human destiny.

In the case of Western philosophy, Aristotle pointed out in the *Metaphysics* that the way of life in which knowledge began was constituted of leisure (*rastone*) and recreation (*diagoge*), as in the case of the Egyptian priests who invented geometry in such a way of life. Aristotle believed that, in leisure and recreation, human beings need not care about the daily necessities of life and could thereby wonder about the causes of things and go in search of knowledge for knowledge's sake. The result of wonder was theories. Aristotle wrote in the *Metaphysics*:

> For it is owing to their wonder that men both now begin and at first began to philosophize; they wondered originally at the obvious difficulties, then advanced little by little and stated difficulties about the greater matters ... therefore since they philosophized in order to escape from ignorance, evidently they were pursuing science in order to know, and not for any utilitarian end.[8]

According to Aristotle, the philosophical meaning of "*theoria*" was determined, on the one hand, with respect to praxis, or, as Aristotle put it, "not in virtue of being able to act but of having the theory for themselves and knowing the cause."[9] On the other hand, it was determined with respect to a universal object, which was seen by Aristotle as the first characteristic of *episteme*, thus leading itself to philosophy and ending up with ontology.[10]

We now know well that the emergence of *theoria* in Greece also had its religious origin. In the beginning, *theoroi* were the representatives from other Greek cities to Athens's religious ceremonies. It was through looking at and not acting in the ceremony that they participated in religious ritual. Analogically, philosophers, emerging from *theoria*, began to look at the universe in a disinterested way instead of looking only at the altar or the stage. Western philosophy was historically grounded in this Greek heritage of *theoria*, which no longer regarded human life as determined by diverse practical interests but rather submitted itself henceforth to a universalizing and objective norm of truth. *Theoria* and philosophy, in

Aristotle's *Metaphysics*, culminated ultimately in the science of ontology, which, according to Aristotle, investigated being as being as the most general and comprehensible aspect of all beings.

By contrast, Chinese philosophy in general originated with the attitude of *concern*, which led not to universalizable theories but to *universalizable praxis*. It was because of his concern with the destiny of individual and community that a Chinese mind started to philosophize. The *Great Appendix* to the *Book of Changes*, arguably attributable to Confucius, started to give an explanation of the beginning of the *Book of Changes* and saw its author to be in a situation of anxiety and calamity with compassionate concern. There we read:

> Was it not in the last age of *Yin* 殷 ... that the study of the Changes began to flourish? On this account the explanations in the book express a feeling of anxious apprehension, and teach how peril may be turned into security, and easy carelessness is sure to meet with overthrow. The way in which these things come about is very comprehensive, and must be acknowledged in every sphere of things. If in the beginning there be a cautious apprehension as to the end, there will probably be no error or cause for blame. This is what is called the Way of Changes.[11]

This text shows that, in the eyes of its author, Philosophy of Changes, as a serious intellectual activity, began with the attitude of concern in the situation of anxiety and calamity, not at all in the situation of leisure and recreation, as Aristotle would suggest. It emerged with the concern for both personal and collective destiny. The proposition that "the way in which these things come about is very comprehensive, and must be acknowledged in every sphere of things" suggests that Chinese philosophy intends to be a practical wisdom capable of guiding a universalizable *praxis*.

Since whether or not there is universality pure and simple is still a question open to debate, we prefer to use the term "universalizability," – a common concern of which may show us a convergence between Western philosophy and Chinese philosophy. Even if Western philosophy concerns itself more with the universalizability of theories, whereas Chinese philosophy concerns itself more with practical universalizability, nevertheless, both of them try to go beyond particular interest and to transcend the limit of particularity in view of a universalizable value. In a certain sense, both of them target the ideal of universality in which *theoria* and *praxis* might be seen as complementary. In a certain sense, *theoria* and *praxis*, though different, are complementary and constitute thereby a structural contrast between Chinese philosophy and Western philosophy.

THOUGHT, EXPERIENCE, AND THEIR UNITY

Another contrast, this time on the level of epistemic principle, puts Chinese philosophy and Western philosophy in another situation of difference and complementarity. The close relation of Western philosophy to mathematics is itself a fascinating philosophical problem. Not to mention the philosophy of ancient Greece, it suffices to say that geometry, algebra, and, more generally, to use Heidegger's term, '*mathesis universalis*' have founded the rationality of European modern science. This, in its rational aspect, is a process of theory-construction using logical-mathematically structured language to formulate human knowledge. In modern Western philosophy, rationalism since Descartes, Spinoza, and Leibniz has laid the rational foundation of modern European science. Their philosophy and many of their works, written according to the order of geometry, offer us the most articulated examples of *mathesis universalis* in modern Western philosophy.

Compared with this, Chinese philosophy did not use logico-mathematic structures for its theory formation. It did not ponder its own linguistic structure to the point of having elaborated a logic system for the formulation and control of scientific discourse. Mathematics, though highly developed in ancient China, was used only for describing or organizing empirical data, not for formulating theories. Lacking in logical mathematical structures, Chinese philosophy and its proto-scientific theories were mainly presented through intuition and speculative imagination. These theories might have the advantage of being able to penetrate into the totality of life, nature, and society as a whole, to give them a reasonable interpretation, but they lacked somehow the rigour of structural organization and logical formulation.[12] Even today, Chinese philosophy may still learn from Western philosophy in the more rigorously logical formulation of its theoretical propositions, but, with its essential concern with life-meaningfulness, it would never go so far as to indulge itself in mathematic/logical formulations.

On the other hand, empirical data are also very much emphasized in both Chinese philosophy and Western philosophy. For the latter, such as in the case of classical empiricism, philosophers like Locke, Berkeley, and Hume have well justified the empirical side of Western modern science, characterized by its unrelenting quest of empirical data and well-controlled systematic experimentation. We should, however, notice that modern science works on information, not *passively given* as understood by classical empiricism, but rather *actively constructed* by theoretical and technical devices. Modern science, by elaborating on the sensible data and our perception of them, assures itself of keeping in touch with the environment, the supposed "real world," but in a very artificially and technically controlled way.

As to Chinese philosophers, they made empirical observations too, looking up to the heavenly movement and down to various things on earth. These could be very detailed but passive observations, with or without the aid of instruments, with the intent to penetrate into the true nature of all things. But it had seldom tried any systematically organized experimentation to the extent of effecting any active artificial control over the human perception of natural objects.

In fact we should say that, if there is need of empirical data, it is because there is need to go outside of our thought to reach the Reality over there so as to form a reliable knowledge. The search for empirical data could therefore be seen as a particular form of strangification, but, if control of our perception is indispensable, the technical manipulation of the object might not be necessary. Chinese philosophers preferred, as *Zhong Yong* (中庸, the *Doctrine of the Means*) said, to allow all things, including oneself and many others, to unfold their own nature.

Furthermore, in Western philosophy of science, there is always a conscious checking of the correspondence between theories and empirical data so as to combine them into a coherent whole and to serve human beings' purpose of explanation and prediction for the control of world events. This idea of correspondence could be found either in the tradition from classical empiricism to logical positivism, which assumes that there is truth where there is correspondence of theory to empirical data, or in

Kant's critical philosophy, for which the world of experience must enter into the a priori framework of our subjectivity in order to become known by us. The idea of correspondence is always there behind all tentative forms of verification (R. Carnap), falsification (K. Popper), or other forms of confirmation.

As to Chinese philosophy, we should say that the unity between empirical knowledge and human thinking was also much emphasized.[13] This is what Confucius affirmed when he told his disciple *Zi Gong* (子貢) that he was not merely aiming at learning many things and retaining them in memory but rather that there was a unity that bound them all together.[14] Confucius seemed to affirm, as Kant did, the complementary interaction between empirical data and thinking when he said, "To learn without thought leads to confusion. To think without learning leads to danger."[15] These words of Confucius remind us of Kant's saying that sensibility without concept is blind, whereas concept without sensibility is void. However, it is different in the sense that the mode of unity in Confucianism is achieved by ethical praxis, and, in the case of Daoism, by life praxis, both in reference to the Dao or Heaven as the Ultimate Reality. Here "*praxis*" or "practical action" was not interpreted as a kind of technical application of theories to the control of concrete natural or social phenomena. On the contrary, it was understood as an active involvement in the process of realizing what is properly human in the life of the individual and of society. As to science and technology, they are not to be ignored but must be reconsidered, transformed, and upgraded in the context of ethical praxis and life praxis.

REASONABLENESS ENCOURAGES STRANGIFICATION

The function of reason in Chinese philosophy is better characterized as *reasonableness* rather than by *rationality*. "Reason" in the Chinese sense refers always to the totality of existence and to its meaningful interpretation by human life as a whole, which in principle would encourage the act of going to the other side of reality to see holistically and therefore encourage strangification.

On its cognitive side, reasonableness concerns the dimension of meaning: meaning of literary or artistic work, life, society, culture, existence itself, etc. The model of this cognitive activity could be found in the understanding and interpretation of a text or a work of art. This activity of understanding and interpretation could be extended to any form of relationship that human beings entertain with the dimension of the totality of existence. In the understanding of meaning, we have to refer, not only to its linguistic meanings, but also to the totality of my self and the totality of relationships that I entertain with the world. In some sense, it has to start from my self as the subject of my experience and my understanding in order to reconstruct the meaning of a text, but it refers inevitably to the level of ontology where human life is integrated into a profound relationship with the Ultimate Reality.

On its practical side, when we ask the question, what are those actions that are subject to the function of reasonableness, the answer is that all actions are concerned with personal as well as collective involvement in meaning constitution. For example, we could think of those actions concerned with the creation and appreciation of works of art, with the realization and evaluation of moral intention, and even those political actions concerned with the decision of historical orientation of a certain social group. Finally, we could consider the meaning of life and existence as an unceasing process of meaning realization in the universe.

We have to notice that the function of reasonableness that refers itself to the totality of one's self and one's relationship with the world, as exemplified by Confucianism, is still quite limited to human-centred orientation. There is still another function of reasonableness, of a more speculative character, which is concerned more with the totality of Being and Reality Itself and is not limited to human subjectivity and human meaningfulness. This is more exemplified by Daoism.

In Chinese philosophy, it is necessary to ask the question about the relation we have with Reality Itself, or the Ultimate Reality. I would say that Chinese culture is characterized by its intimacy with Reality Itself. It cherishes always some sort of communicative union with the Reality Itself or Ultimate Reality, understood as Heaven, Sincerity, Dao, Nature, Emptiness, Mind, or Life.

Confucianism's function of reason, though focusing on human beings as the centre of the cosmos, is nevertheless still open to the dynamism of nature in supposing that human beings are interconnected with and responsive to many others, such as nature and Heaven. The concept of "Heaven," which had represented a personal God in ancient China and thereby represented an implicit Ultimate Reality, changed its meaning after the arrival of Confucianism, so as to represent now the philosophical ground of human existence and moral praxis. The focus therefore was shifted to the concern with human self-awareness and responsiveness to many others, nature and Heaven. This self-awareness and responsiveness, this interconnectedness, which Confucius expresses by the term *ren*, serves as the ontological foundation of the manifestation of Reality Itself and humans' original communicative competence. By way of sincere response, human beings can even attain the Ultimate Reality. That is why the *Doctrine of the Means* posits "sincerity" (誠, *cheng*) as its core concept, which means both metaphysically the true Reality itself and psychologically the true self. On the transcendental level, it is in union with the true Reality before its expressions evolve into empirical psychic states such as being happy, angry, sad, or joyful.

Confucianism tends to see human language and knowledge as human ways of manifesting Reality Itself. This could be achieved through the rectification of names and a sincerity of purpose. In today's situation, Confucianism would look upon science and technology as capable of being integrated into the process of constructing a meaningful world. In general, the process of human intervention into the process of nature is seen by Confucianism as humankind's participation in and assistance in the creative transformation of Heaven and Earth. It concerns a kind of participative construction instead of dominative construction.

For Daoism, the Dao, as the Ultimate Reality, manifests itself in Nature, and Nature is seen as a spontaneous process not to be dominated and determined by human beings' technical intervention. Human beings themselves are considered by Daoism as part of nature, and their ontological status is much like that of plants, animals and other beings in nature, all taken to be sons of the same Mother, the Dao. Daoism teaches us how to respect the spontaneous process of nature and that human beings' knowledge should be constructed in such a way that it unfolds the spontaneous dynamism of nature.[16] According to Daoism, human beings should be aware of the limit of all kinds of human construction and, by way of deconstructing the already constructed, keep their minds always open to the spontaneous dynamism of nature. Knowledge and Life-world, necessary for human existence, should not be constructed according to the structural constraint of human language and thought but according to the rhythmic manifestation of nature.

In general, Chinese culture cherishes the Life-world, which is partly constructed by human beings and partly unfolds itself spontaneously in the rhythm of nature. Confucianism puts its emphasis more on the human construction of a meaningful existence, while, in contrast to it, Daoism would emphasize the spontaneous unfolding of natural rhythm.

STRANGIFICATION AS WORKABLE STRATEGY OF INTERCULTURAL PHILOSOPHY

We are now facing a multicultural situation, together with more and more conflicting differences in interests, ideologies, and worldviews. In this pluralistic world, the search for self-identity, for respect of difference, and for mutual enrichment becomes more urgent than ever. The exception is found in the domain of artistic creation, where there will be no space for compromise and consensus, and there we can accept Jean-François Lyotard's idea of a radical preference for difference in language games in view of originality and creativity. But in the public sphere, in any case, we always need more communications and more effort for consensus. In the public sphere, life could not go without communication, and policy-making could not be done well without consensus.

I accept Lyotard's view that we should respect each language game and its differences. But this does not mean that we should not try to understand each other's language and to appropriate it or to translate ours into language of or understandable to others. Otherwise, we will not really be able to appreciate the difference of the other, and our respect for this difference is deprived of a real appreciation of it. In fact, if person *P* can really say that language game *A* is in such and such aspects different from language *B*, even to the degree of being incommensurable, it means that both language games are intelligible and understandable to *P* and *P* understands them. This fact presupposes *P*'s appropriation of both languages and his act, at least implicitly, of strangification between them.

That is why Lyotard's respect for different language games remains abstract and unrealizable. In order to understand the difference of other philosophical/religious/cultural traditions, we need language appropriation and strangification, and these do not necessarily presuppose any tentative of integration, not to say unification. Strangification presupposes language appropriation, but it does not presuppose the target of a final unification. Unwillingness to appropriate another's language and an unwillingness to strangify, however, would mean self-contentment with, or self-enclosure in one's own micro-world, cultural world, or religious world.

The concept of "strangification" could be seen as a workable strategy of communication between different agents. I have modified and extended Fritz Wallner's idea of "strangification" (*Verfremdung*, in German; first proposed to serve as an epistemological strategy for interdisciplinary research on the level of science) to levels of intercultural exchange and interreligious dialogue. "Strangification," an act of going outside oneself to multiple others, from one's familiarity to strangeness, is properly human and universal to all human activities and can therefore be applied to all kinds of communication, including cultural interaction and religious dialogue. For me, the process of dialogue should be a process of mutual strangification.

Presupposing an act of previous appropriation of language, intercultural philosophy can proceed first of all to conduct *linguistic strangification*, by which we translate the language of one's own philosophical/religious or cultural tradition into the language of (or understandable to) another tradition, to see whether it thereby becomes understandable or absurd. In the latter case, reflection and self-critique should be made of one's own tradition instead of self-defence or other more radical form of apologetics. Although there is always some untranslatable residue or hard core of meaningfulness, its commonly shareable intelligibility would be enough to prove its own universalizability. If one can only boast of the meaningfulness of one's philosophy/religion within one's own cultural tradition, as some nationalist philosophers and scholars of religion would maintain or pretend, this is only a proof of its own limit rather than of its merit.

Then comes the *pragmatic strangification*, by which we draw out one philosophical idea or cultural value/expression from its own cultural context to put it into another cultural context to see whether it is still understandable/workable there or whether it loses its ability to adapt itself in the new context and become ineffective. If it still works, this means it has more pragmatic possibilities and is pragmatically more universalizable. Otherwise, it should check its own limit by self-reflection and self-critique.

Finally, there is *ontological strangification*, by which we attempt to travel from one micro/cultural/religious world to other micro/cultural/religious worlds in order to understand them through the detour of a direct contact with or the manifestation of Reality Itself.[17] This level of strangification is especially important when there is a religious dimension in the philosophical traditions or in religious dialogue. Without a certain engagement to an experience of Ultimate Reality, it would be superficial in conducting religious dialogue. Our experience of the Ultimate Reality, if indeed ultimate, should be universalizable and shareable, otherwise it could be only a pretext of religious exclusivism.

In fact there are many cases of successful intercultural or interreligious strangification. One of them is Buddhism's success in China. We know that Buddhism came from India to China and became one of the three basic constituents of Chinese philosophy and religion. Buddhism accomplished this by taking all the measures of linguistic, pragmatic, and ontological strangifications. As to linguistic strangification, Buddhism first of all appropriated Daoist and Confucian languages to make itself understandable to Chinese intellectuals and then proceeded to the systematic translation of its scriptures into Chinese. As to pragmatic strangification, Buddhism made an effort to re-contextualize itself in Chinese ethics (such as filial piety), politics (such as relation with political leadership), and economics (such as monastery economics). On the ontological level, with its experience of Emptiness or One Mind as Ultimate Reality, Buddhism made itself understandable to other endogenous traditions such as Confucianism and Daoism. The Buddhist experience of Emptiness and Mind, the Daoist experience of *Dao* and *wu*, and the Confucian experience of *ren* (humanness, humanity, and cosmic innerconnectedness) and *cheng* (sincerity and true reality), though quite different in themselves, still enjoy some similarity and complementarity in their experiences of the Ultimate Reality.[18]

Unfortunately, not all Buddhist strangification into China communicated the right message to Chinese people, and this was deeply related to the linguistic strangification. This is to say that linguistic strangification can affect pragmatic strangification and *vice versa*. This can be found in some Chinese translations that missed or even distorted the original message that was potentially good for Chinese culture in the long run. For example, the translation of terms expressing ethical relationship such as "mother and father" and "wife and husband" in Indian Buddhist scriptures became "father and mother" (sometimes even modified as "paying filial piety to father and mother"), and "husband and wife." The phrase "marry one's wife" was quite often translated as "marry one's wife and concubines." As to political relations, "republican relation" was translated as "imperial relation." In the volume 2 of the *Dīrghāgama*, Sākyamuni praised the country of Vraja people, who often held meetings to discuss righteous affairs in a republican way. However, when translated into Chinese, it reads "the Emperor and his subjects are in harmony and the superior and inferior respect each other" (君臣和順, 上下相敬).[19] The consequence of this was that the messages of more egalitarian ethics and republican politics contained in the Indian Buddhist scriptures were turned into hierarchical and totalitarian terms in order to adapt to Chinese culture and thereby the Chinese people were unable to learn for their own long-term benefit.

The most basic of all these three is linguistic strangification, by which one translates an idea/value/expression from one cultural/religious world into language of (or understandable to) other cultural/religious world. Even if in the process of translation, we lose by necessity some meaningful content, especially in the case of poetic, aesthetic, and religious expressions, this should not be an excuse for not making any effort of strangification. We should not argue from the fact of losing meaning in translation for a radical intranslatability of different language games. We could say that there must be a minimum of translatability among different language games, so as to allow the act of strangification. The act of strangification presupposes also the will to strangify and the effort of strangification. Strangification is thus the minimum requirement in intercultural interaction.

I would say that strangification is a very useful strategy, not only for different scientific disciplines, but also for different cultures and religions. It is even more fundamental than Habermas's concept of "communicative action." In fact, Habermas's communicative action is a process of argumentation in which the proposition-for and the proposition-against, by way of *Begründung*, search for consensus in a higher proposition acceptable to both parties. Although Habermas has proposed four claims for an ideal situation of communication, including understandability, truth, sincerity, and legitimacy, unfortunately, in the actual world of communication, it happens very often that there is either total conflict or compromise, without any real consensus. The Habermasian argumentation tends to fail if in the process of *Begründung* and in the act of searching for consensus there is not first of all any effort for strangification. In this case, there will be no real mutual understanding and no self-reflection during the process of argumentation. Therefore, the strategy of strangification could be seen as a prerequisite for any successful communication.

Religious and/or philosophical dialogue should be conceived as based on a mutual act of strangification or mutual *waitui*. In the dialogue between *A* and *B*, on the level of linguistic strangification, *A* should translate his propositions or ideas/values/belief system into the language of *B* or a language understandable to *B*. In the meanwhile, *B* should translate his propositions or ideas/values/belief system in the language of *A* or understandable to *A*. On the level of pragmatic strangification, *A* should draw his proposition(s), supposed truth(s)/cultural expression/value/religious belief out from his own social, organizational contexts and put it into the social, organizational context of *B*. In the meanwhile, *B* should draw his proposition(s), supposed truth(s)/cultural expression/value/religious belief out from his own social, organizational context and put it into the social, organizational context of *A*. On the level of ontological strangification, *A* should make an effort to enter into *B*'s micro-world, cultural world, or religious world through the detour of his experience with Reality Itself, such as a person, a social group, Nature, or the Ultimate Reality. Meanwhile, *B* should also make an effort to enter into *A*'s micro-world, cultural world, or religious world through the detour of his experience with Reality Itself.

This is to say that comparison, communication, and dialogue will never be conducted within one's self-enclosure. On the contrary, it starts with a mutual act of going outside of one's self-enclosure to the other, what I call "a process of mutual *waitui*." I go outside of myself to you and you go outside of yourself to me, so as to form a dialogue leading to mutual enrichment. When we conduct mutual *waitui*, we make our own scientific/cultural/religious/life-world understandable to each other by translating our languages into the language of each other or understandable to each other, by putting it into another's pragmatic context or by going through the detour of Reality Itself or the other's life-world. This process of mutual *waitui* is to be conducted not only in everyday life, in scientific research, and in cultural and religious life, but also in economic and political life, where different political parties, interest groups, governments, and people should always commit themselves to a process of communication leading to mutual enrichment rather than to conflict or war.

Strangification and dialogue in the form of mutual *waitui* are more fundamental than the communicative action understood by Habermas as argumentation. For me, Habermasian argumentation presupposes a previous effort of strangification in expressing one's proposal(s) in another's language or in a language understandable to others, without which there will be no real mutual understanding and no self-reflection in the process of argumentation. Habermas's four ideal claims for understandability, truth, sincerity, and legitimacy just cannot work in the real world without previous mutual *waitui*. I would think I am sincere, but you would think I am a hypocrite; I would think that I am telling the truth, but you may consider that just absurd; and, since a commonly acceptable norm does not yet exist, or that the law necessary for legitimacy is still an issue under debate, there is no accepted legitimacy, so to speak.

THE FOUNDATION OF STRANGIFICATION IN CHINESE PHILOSOPHY

Philosophically speaking, the strategy of strangification has its condition of possibility in human communicative competence. In Chinese philosophy, Confucianism would propose *ren* (仁) as the original communicative competence, the ontological condition of possibility that renders feasible and legitimate the act of strangification as well as communication and self-reflection. From this original communicative competence, Confucianism proposes the concept of *shu* (恕), which could be seen as an act of empathy and strangification, a better strategy for fruitful communication than Habermas's argumentation. Confucianism, in positing the existence of a *sensitive responsiveness* as a condition of the possibility of strangification, has elevated strangification to the ontological level.

Based on the sensitive responsiveness of *ren*, Confucianism affirms the existence of an innate knowledge (良知, *liangzhi*) and the dimension of tacit consensus, which could serve as the pre-linguistic foundation for further argumentative consensus. If deprived of all these, during the process of argumentation, Habermas's suggestion of four ideal claims would not be able to work in actual political debates, even to the point of leading towards total conflict, because of the difference in political languages and in interpreting concepts such as truth, sincerity, and legitimacy. There will be no real mutual understanding and no self-reflection during the process of argumentation, if we do not communicate our position in considering the others and in speaking the other's language or in a language understandable to the other.

In Confucianism, the concept of *shu* represents this ability to go to multiple others and to communicate with others through language understandable to him/her/them. Especially under the post-modern condition, when any difference in race, gender, age, class, or belief system could create total conflict, any part in confrontation, difference, or opposition with another part should communicate with the other part in a spirit of *shu*.

On the other hand, from the Daoist point of view, strangification does not only presuppose the appropriation of and translation into the language of other traditions. It is also necessary to render oneself present to the Reality Itself. In Laozi's word, "Having grasped the Mother (Reality Itself), you can thereby know the sons (micro-worlds). Having known the sons, you should return again to the Mother."[20] Daoism posits an ontological detour through Reality Itself as the condition *sine qua non* for the act of strangification into other worlds (micro/cultural/religious worlds).

In terms of Laozi, we grasp the Reality Itself by the process of "retracing regard" (觀, *guan*), an act of intuition into the essence of things by letting things be as they are. A holistic knowledge is seen therefore by Daoism as a back and forth process between the act of interacting with manifested worlds (sons) and the act of returning to Reality Itself (the Mother). The act of returning to Reality Itself and communicating with it is therefore considered by Daoism as nourishing our strangification with other worlds. This act of ontological detour through Reality Itself bestows an ontological dimension to strangification. Ontological strangification in this sense is especially important for religious dialogue, when the relation with the Ultimate Reality is most essential to religious experiences.

For Chinese philosophy, it is always preferable to encourage the act of strangification and dialogue to maximize harmony in one's relation with many others. I use the term "many others" (or multiple others) to replace the post-modern concept of the "Other" proposed by Lacan, Levinas,

Derrida, and Deleuze. For me the "Other" is a mere abstraction. In no moment of our life are we facing purely and simplythe "Other." We are all born into the many others and we grow up among many others. The Confucian concept of *wulun* (五倫, five relationships), the Daoist concept of *wanwu* (萬物, myriad things), and the Chinese Buddhist concept of *zhongsheng* (眾生, all sentient beings) all imply an undeniable idea of many others. It is better for our life of sanity that we keep in our mind the existence of many others and our relation with multiple others.

CONCLUSION

As I see it, now that we are in the beginning years of the twenty-first century, philosophy is also facing the challenge of globalization. We should not limit ourselves to a single type of national philosophy or to a philosophical tradition. Although philosophizing is a common interest of many cultural traditions in the world, it is still too early to boast of a world philosophy, and philosophy still exists in plural forms. In today's situation, philosophers are commonly facing three major interrelated issues:

First, the swift and enormous development of science and technology will soon become the leading factors of human historicity and cultural development. In fact, this is the real power leading to a world of globalization. How to deepen the development of science and technology through philosophical reflection and how to elaborate ethical reflection to make science and technology more human will be very important issues in the future of human civilization. This will not be achieved by any single philosophical tradition whatsoever and, by virtue of the complex nature of the problem, invites the effort of intercultural philosophy.

Second, the more and more frequent and intimate interactions between different cultural traditions is putting us inevitably in a world of multiculturalism. How are we to enrich ourselves and promote others by means of cultural interactions in which we share the best part of our own, while being aware of our own limitations in contrast to others? This task will become even more urgent in the future. In this sense I think that intercultural philosophy is a key to the future of philosophy.

Third, as we have seen, the philosophy of the twentieth century was too much human-centred. Just think of phenomenology, existentialism, structuralism, critical theory, neo-Marxism, hermeneutics, post-modernism, and modern Neo-Confucianism; all of these philosophical tendencies were all human-centred. However, as we observe, the difficulties of humankind became unsolvable in the bottleneck jammed with all these human-centred ways of thinking. Fortunately, the ecological movement and new discoveries in astronomical physics leads us to a greater concern with Nature, and the religious renaissance in the end of the last century leads us also to a concern with the transcendent or the absolute other and also with inter-religious dialogue. In this new era, we will have to redefine human experience in the context of nature and inter-religious dialogue.

We hope, and we should say, that the domination of the philosophical forum by Western philosophical/religious discourses should from now on cede its way, with self-critique and self-understanding, to the wisdom of concordant contrast, paying more respect to both difference and complementarity and leading to the optimal harmony among many philosophical/religious traditions. In this context, traditional comparative philosophy/religion should move on to intercultural philosophy/religion. In the multicultural context, now and in the future, the search for self-identity, reciprocal respect, and mutual enrichment could be reached through a new vision and practice of intercultural philosophy/religion. For this, Chinese philosophy/religion will have a lot to say. I am not saying that Chinese philosophy/religion will be another dominant trend in the future but rather that Chinese philosophy/religion could contribute to a more balanced intercultural philosophy/religion better for all philosophical/religious traditions and cultural interactions. With the vision and method of contrast, mutual strangification, and dialogue, we will be able to deal with the problems of the impact of science and technology on all cultures, the situation of multiculturalism, and the redefinition of human experience in both the cosmic and inter-religious context, which are the major challenges of twenty-first century intercultural philosophy/religion.

Notes

1 Vincent Shen, "A Book Review of Michael Hardt and Antonio Negri's *Empire* (Cambridge, MA: Harvard University Press, 2000), 478 pages + xvii," *Universitas: Monthly Review of Philosophy and Culture* 361, Taipei (June 2004): 109–12.

2 Charles Taylor, "Politics of Recognition," in *Multiculturalism*, edited by A. Gutmann (Princeton: Princeton University Press, 1994), 25–36.

3 Vincent Shen, "From Politics of Recognition to Politics of Mutual Enrichment," *The Ricci Bulletin*(Taipei Ricci Institute for Chinese Studies) 5 (February 2002): 113–25.

4 I have worked out a philosophy of contrast in my works, especially in my *Essays in Contemporary Philosophy East and West* (Taipei: Liming Publishing, 1985).

5 Vincent Shen, *Essays in Contemporary Philosophy East and West*, 7–8, 24–27.

6 For my critique of structuralism, see ibid., 257–90.

7 Vincent Shen, *Disenchantment of the World* (Taipei: China Times, 1984), 31–37.

8 Aristotle, *Metaphysics*, 982b 12–22, trans. W.D. Ross, in Introduction to Aristotle, edited by Richard McKeon (New York: Modern Library, 1992), 261–62.

9 Aristotle, *Metaphysics*, 981b 6–7, ibid., 258.

10 Aristotle, *Metaphysics*, 982a 20–982b 10, ibid., 260–61.

11 *The Text of Yi Ching*. Chinese original with English translation by Z.D. Sung, (Taipei: Wenhua Books, 1973), 334. The English translation of this book is actually that of James Legge with some modifications and additions.

12 As Joseph Needham has suggested, "Mathematics was essential, up to a certain point, for the planning and control of the hydraulic engineering works, but those professing it were likely to remain inferior officials." Joseph Needham, *Science and Civilization in China*, vol. II (Cambridge: Cambridge University Press, 1959), 30. For me, this social and political reason given by Needham partly explains the unimportance of mathematics in Confucianism. A more internal rationale of it might be that mathematics was considered to be a technique of calculation and an instrument of organizing empirical data, not as an objective structure of reality and discourse.

13 Concerning Confucianism, B. Schwartz is right when he says, "To Confucius knowledge does begin with the empirical cumulative knowledge of masses of particulars, ... then includes the ability to link these particulars first to one's own experiences and ultimately with the underlying unity that binds this thought together." Benjamin Schwartz, *The World of Thought in Ancient China* (Cambridge, MA: Belknap Press, 1985), 89.

14 Confucius, *Analects* (*Lun Yu*, 論語), XV-3.

15 Confucius, *Analects* (*Lun Yu*), II-15, my translation.

16 Vincent Shen, "Annäerung an das taoistiche Verständnis von Wissenschaft. Die Epistemologie des Lao Tses und Tschuang Tses," in F. Wallner and J. Schimmer, ed., *Grenzziehungen zum Konstruktiven Realismus* (Vienna: WUV-Univ. Verl.,1993), S188ff.

17 Fritz Wallner understands "ontological strangification" on the level of interdisciplinary research and takes it to mean the movement by which we transfer from one micro-world in one discipline to another micro-world. For me, the fact that we can move from the micro-world of one discipline or research program to another is still limited to the ontic level. It is only when this transfer happens through the detour by Reality Itself that there is ontological strangification.

18 Cf. Vincent Shen, "Appropriating the Other and Transforming Consciousness into Wisdom: Some Philosophical Reflections on Chinese Buddhism," *Dao: A Journal of Comparative Philosophy* (December 2003): 43–62.

19 *Taishō Shinshū Daizōkyō*, ed. J. Takakusu and K. Watanabe (Tokyo: Taisho Issaikyo Kankokai, 1924–32): I:12.

20 Laozi, *Daodejing*, chap. 52. in *Laozi Sizhong* [Four Versions of Laozi] (Taipei: Da An Publishing, 1999), 45.

The philosopher as stranger: The idea of comparative philosophy

MICHAEL MCGHEE
University of Liverpool

The title and sub-title of this essay seem to name incongruous themes arbitrarily bolted together – but their unexpected congruence is the theme of the reflections that follow. The idea of the philosopher as "stranger" comes from a comment in Pierre Hadot's book, *Philosophy as a Way of Life*,[1] a book now associated with a philosophical movement that seeks to re-engage with the ancient, practical conception of the philosopher as a seeker after wisdom. This re-engagement, however, is also an expression of dissatisfaction with the contemporary condition of philosophy. The claim I wish to make in this paper is that what we now call "comparative philosophy" is not only an expression of this same dissatisfaction but is also one of the main strands of its development. Comparative philosophy, particularly as it is associated with the work of Henry Corbin, is another *form* of philosophy as a way of life, a particular way of seeking to revitalize the ancient conception of philosophy as a search for wisdom.

PHILOSOPHERS AND THE "WORLD"

> Thus philosophers are strangers, a race apart.... By the time of the Platonic dialogues Socrates was called *atopos*, that is, "unclassifiable." What makes him *atopos* is precisely the fact that he is a "philo-sopher" in the etymological sense of the word; that is, he is in love with wisdom. For wisdom, says Diotima in Plato's *Symposium*, is not a human state, it is a state of perfection of being and knowledge that can only be divine. It is the love of this wisdom, which is foreign to the world, that makes the philosopher a stranger in it.[2]

It is useful and sobering to be thus reminded by Hadot of this ancient image of the philosophers, whose love of wisdom makes them strangers in the world. It reminds us, in the first place, of the subtle resonances of the expression – "the world" – that Hadot here introduces, which is at once a formation of desire and a perspective on reality embodied in a population. It reminds us that "the world" in this sense has *always* moved, as Eliot once wrote, "in appetency, on its metalled ways/ Of time before and time after," and it also reminds us that this spirit of appetency is what *defines* "the world." The origins of philosophical estrangement from the world must lie in the exposure to its cynical view of knowledge and opinion as instruments of policy and power. Speaking *truth* to power, *parrhesia*, is one of the virtues of the philosopher, not just because it is dangerous but also because it can hardly be heard.

Hadot's words are sobering because they imply a high vocation for philosophy that seems now either dauntingly unattainable or foolishly irrelevant, especially in those whose avocation is to teach philosophy in institutions of higher education. Is it possible for an academic philosopher of the early twenty-first century really to be a philosopher under the ancient conception, a member of a race apart, one who has become a stranger because of their love of a "wisdom" defined "as a state of perfection of being and knowledge that can only be 'divine'"?

The crucial contrast here is with a "human" *imperfection* of being and knowledge. The concept of "the world" might be taken as referring to one form of this imperfection, a condition in which a prior state of being determines what might be appropriated as knowledge, rather than one in which being progressively alters with the knowledge that is appropriated. But all this language is embedded in the Platonic spiritual tradition whose downfall Nietzsche had announced along with the death of God. Such a sense of "being philosophical," which we retain in common speech as a way of representing a distinctive and admirable demeanour, particularly of fortitude in the face of adversity, seems otherwise remote from dominant contemporary conceptions of the vocation of philosopher and seems, indeed, closest to religious notions of sainthood.

There are few enough voices now in philosophy that even hint at such a vocation for philosophers as "strangers in the world." Surprisingly, though, there *is* a hint of a leaner but only an apparently more secular version of this conception found in a short remark in Wittgenstein's *Zettel*.[3] He observes there that "the philosopher is not a citizen of any community of ideas. That's what makes him a philosopher."[4] This is at least a conception in which the philosopher is in some way set apart – from those who *are* the citizens of a "community of ideas." But now, this comment is juxtaposed in *Zettel* to an intriguingly long and quite unexpected quotation from Plato's early dialogue, *Charmides*, whose topic is how to understand the idea of temperance or temperateness, the Greek virtue of *sophrosune*. What is under discussion in the passage copied out by Wittgenstein is the proposal that *sophrosune* should be defined as "knowledge of knowledge and ignorance." This is obscured for Anglophone readers by the translation of *sophrosune* as "wisdom," though the German text has the more accurate *Besonnenheit*, with its sense of the self-possession that belongs to temperateness or temperance. The implication of making this connection between what appears on the surface to be a "purely" practical virtue and that of "knowledge of knowledge and ignorance" is that our states of mind in some fundamental way govern our access to and experience of reality, and do so in a way that is not reducible to the sort of propositional or conceptual knowledge that is independent of the states of mind of the knower. The idea is not that the relevant state of mind can be identified separately from the knowledge to which it gives access. We are speaking, rather, of a *single state* of being and knowledge, in which conduct and demeanour are natural expressions of the state of the knower. This is almost the defining Platonic thought that sets the philosopher apart as a stranger. Their distinctive knowledge is attained through transformations of their inner experience, in the sense that what they come to know and their interior disposition form a unity, a transformation of their whole being. This makes them *a-topos* and takes them precisely out of "the world," which is thus defined as the expression of a contrasting mental condition that stands in need of transformation. This is perhaps the point of the contrast between "human" and "divine" in Hadot's reference to the speech of Diotima in the *Symposium*. But now, why is *sophrosune* or temperance defined as knowledge of knowledge and ignorance? It is time to consider Plato's greatest metaphor.

One of the most striking aspects of Plato's image of the cave is that the prisoners are not in a position to see that they are prisoners. We could put it more strongly and say that, were they to be told that they were prisoners, *they would have no reason to believe what is nevertheless true*. The Platonic irony is that we know that the real claim is that our own position is that of the prisoners and that *we have no reason to believe it either*. The truth or reality of our situation is beyond the grasp of our concepts; there is something that transcends or surpasses them. This does not imply that we know nothing – we know a lot about shadows for instance – but only that we are ignorant of the real nature of our situation, or, somewhat differently, are *deluded* in our estimate of it. If we have an estimate of it, as many people do, it features as a kind of baseless assumption that what lies within our fixed horizon exhausts reality. What is striking about the way the metaphor unfolds is that at a certain point the liberated prisoner is brought to a position where he can now *see the mechanisms* that determined the scope of the limited knowledge previously available to him, which he can now see was, by contrast, a restricted knowledge only of shadows. It is just these mechanisms that prevent the prisoners from seeing any reason to believe that they are prisoners, and the ironic implication is that there are analogous mechanisms – of human bondage – that obscure the alleged fact that we are in the same position as the prisoners. The liberated prisoner sees the flames of the bonfire and the traffic on the road whose shadows are cast onto the walls that confront the chained prisoners. One way of understanding this significant moment in the cave, with the liberated prisoner looking back at the scene and at the workings of the mechanisms that limited perception, is that it is an image precisely of the enlargement and liberation that depend upon *sophrosune*. It is also, therefore, a picture of the idea of "knowledge of knowledge and ignorance" since the liberated prisoner at least knows *this*: – he knows both what the chained prisoners know and what they are ignorant of. In other words, it is the moment when the prisoner has become a stranger to the world of which he was once an inhabitant: he now speaks a foreign language.

These Platonic reflections imply claims about what it is to be a human being at all and about what it is to be a philosopher. The underlying thought is that within us there is a divided and conflicted self, something all too human contending against and resisting something "divine," a self that at once belongs to and clings to "the world" and at the same time has the possibility of transcending and becoming a stranger in it. The question that remains is whether the ancient conception can be disentangled from what is crudely known as the "two worlds" doctrine of Platonism.

COMPARATIVE PHILOSOPHY, COLONIALISM, MULTICULTURALISM

Now so far I have said nothing to indicate that my topic will impinge on the theme of comparative philosophy. However, I said at the beginning that recent interest in the ancient conception grew out of dissatisfaction with a state of the discipline that seemed by contrast sterile and disengaged. I also remarked that the turn to comparative philosophy expressed a similar dissatisfaction. But it also has other grounds, which brings us at once to our contemporary situation, in which the turbulence of geopolitics is complicated by tensions between tradition and modernity, religion and secularism, tensions rendered global by the historical processes of colonization, "westernization," and migration. In our multicultural societies in the West, we find that the spiritual and intellectual division that began to emerge in the eighteenth century exists now as a division within and between both relatively indigenous and relatively recent immigrant communities.

Non-Western countries were exposed not only to the foreign culture of the colonists but also to its tensions and conflicts, and the dismay that many felt in the West as secularization took its course was transferred to the countries that were being "westernized." It would be naïve to see this dismay as simply moral, since the undermining soft power that accompanies hard economic and military power – a natural expression of "the world" as it moves in appetency – is also a major political reality. Many outside the West must find it ironic that the expression "the clash of civilizations" was coined in the West. Thus, for example, Roy Mottahedeh[5] discusses the Iranian writer Al-e Ahmad's sense of the cultural illness that he felt had stricken the towns and cities of Iran. Mottahedeh comments:

> For this illness Al-e Ahmad seized on a newly coined word, and he made this word a rallying cry for Iranians from the sixties to the present. The word translated literally, piece by piece, is "West-strickenness," but even this clumsy translation fails to convey the sense of the Persian original, *gharbzadegi*. "I say that *gharbzadegi* … is like cholera (or) frost-bite. But no. it's at least as bad as saw-flies in the wheat fields. Have you ever seen how they infest wheat? From within. There's a healthy skin in places, but it's only a skin, just like the shell of a cicada on a tree."[6]

The Indian philosopher J. L. Mehta, who was a well-known commentator on the work of Heidegger, once referred to the disruptive forces unleashed by the Western "marriage of science and technology."[7] But it's not so much the marriage that is the problem as the perspectives and energies that have driven its direction. Mehta asked whether it might not be true that "Western thought … enters … like a Trojan horse … into the thinking of the non-Western world" or "like a virus … invisibly altering our perception of reality."[8] And the point here, surely, is the "invisibly." It *may* be that one's perception of reality *ought* to be altered, but only, surely, on the basis of what you judge to be compelling reasons. If there is an abrupt caesura, then the old way of thinking remains unresolved, becomes unconscious and works itself out underground. In 1929 Krishna Chandra Bhattacharya[9] had written that cultural subjection occurs "when one's traditional cast of ideas and sentiments is superseded *without comparison or competition* by a new cast representing an alien culture which possesses one like a ghost" (emphasis added).[10] The consequence, as he says, addressing his Indian audience, is that "we either accept or repeat the judgments passed on us by Western culture, or we impotently resent them but have hardly any estimates of our own, wrung from an inward perception of the realities of our own position."[11]

The states of mind that find expression in the dispositions of "the world" are hardly absent in non-Western countries. As we know, present victimhood is hardly a guarantee of present or future virtue. Even the distinctively *moral* anxiety about western sexual excess can also veil a harsh patriarchal impulse to control women. It would be difficult to show that the alleged moral decline of the West extends to the disappearance of exemplars of courage, justice, and compassion. However, the alleged moral decline of the West and the perceived degeneracy of the culture it has exported are quite closely connected to one of the most influential essays into comparative philosophy.

PLATONISTS OF THE WORLD

Perhaps it would be prudent if I confessed the misgivings I had when I was invited to contribute to this project on the state of "comparative philosophy" – misgivings, I should say, in the first instance, about my own competence as a contributor to what appeared to be a serious and well-developed specialist field of philosophical *scholarship*, but also the sceptical misgivings of an outsider looking in, about the nature and value of the enterprise, its interest for *philosophers*. My misgivings took the form at once of a suspicion that what is called "comparative philosophy" might represent a *dilution of philosophy* and, admittedly somewhat in tension with that, an anxiety that crucial philosophical work might be ignored because its name allows "mainstream" philosophers to shunt it into a specialist siding of marginal interest.

However, and especially when one takes into account historical periods of intense intellectual contact between cultures, whether Greeks and Romans, Europeans and Arabs, Moguls, Hindus and Buddhists, it seems to me that in fact "comparative philosophy" is just *philosophy*, that philosophy is *intrinsically* "comparative" if we mean by that term that it critically compares and examines the merits of ideas whatever their provenance. In other words, philosophy has frequently in its history been refreshed by "cross-cultural comparison." Indeed the *failure* to engage with other traditions probably stands more in need of explanation than the readiness to do so.

One fairly obvious explanation extends at least to the mainstream of analytic philosophy – it is both deeply implicated in and partly the product of the Western process of secularization. Philosophers of this tendency are the least likely to feel any need to look abroad, as it were, apart from for the sake of recruitment to its own ranks. And there is no doubt that many have been very happy to be recruited, as Bhattacharya and others have lamented. Those who are most likely to look abroad for sustenance, both to other traditions and to poetry and literature, are those who feel most strongly that something profound is missing, that the focus is too narrow, and that subjectivity, interiority, spirituality, have all gone from it and need to be restored. But this returns us to the *agon* of philosophy in the modern age and the problem of how, if at all, philosophers can resolve the tensions between religion and secularism. Are not these latter notions also the most contestable, the most implicated in the traditional worldview from which western philosophy has rescued us? And if we claim that we are in a period in which an arid, over-technicalized and self-referential philosophy needs to be refreshed, we should state our grounds, refer to some failure in its *adequacy to human reality* and show that it is of the kind imaginatively represented by the case of the released prisoner. This challenge is not easy to meet, since it invites a conversation between different formations of subjectivity. Not to put too fine a point on it, it is invidious to make this claim, as there is a problem in principle about communication between the chained and the released prisoner, and this problem must lie at the heart of our present philosophical difficulties. And claiming to be a released prisoner is not a comfortable public position. Alternatively, and to introduce a Freudian thought, just as we can judge that an individual is showing resistance in the vicinity of repressed material, we must be able to say that there is material, including significant aspects of human experience, that is not yet incorporated into the world of the philosophers. Their account of experience and reality is unsatisfactory because the way they represent how things are is distorting and deluded.

That its practitioners in the West who have felt compelled to coin a special term for an ancient and intrinsic practice implies, then, a *philosophical critique* of "straight" or mainstream philosophy. "Comparative philosophy" is a coinage that belongs nevertheless to the *politics* of philosophy, and we take it seriously, as more than merely wounded and resentful *amour propre*, only when it can show that there is inadequacy or lack in the tradition. This is that it is blind to significant insights into human nature that are available elsewhere, or that its general conception of the possibilities of human action and experience, and the forms of our general understanding of the nature of reality, stand in need of significant correction.

But the crucial thing that it also seeks to acknowledge is the political reality that we do philosophy now in a global rather than a merely regional context, and in multicultural not monocultural societies, and that a monocultural philosophy is itself as it were a pale reflection of the tendency towards *assimilation* rather than *integration*. Although politicians regularly distinguish between these two terms, they also regularly conflate them. When we hear it declared that Muslims in the UK, for example, must learn to integrate themselves into some host community, it is hard to see how this is not simply a demand for assimilation. Assimilation is a one-way process, whereas integration is a reciprocal process. Nor is integration achieved simply by the presence of different communities living side by side in mutual indifference. It only takes place when the whole is altered by the participation of the parts in dialogue with one another, generating a new *intercultural* reality. The image of this in a philosophy that recognized and benefited from the new political reality is an enlarged and integrated canon.

In the opening remarks of his famous lecture, *The Concept of Comparative Philosophy*, Henry Corbin[12] expresses regret that

> [T]here are today all too few philosophers capable of simultaneously grasping several complete cultural unities and sufficiently prepared linguistically to be able to cope with the texts at first hand.[13]

Although this remark may seem to set the standard impossibly high, nevertheless Corbin's rare philosophical bird is surely likely to hatch out in reasonable numbers eventually – from within the various diasporas in the West. Within those diasporas there will be some who experience, on the one hand, the same disappointment with the state of philosophy as Corbin does, and to which I shall return. On the other, some experience a sense of invisibility and cultural dispossession, all in the form of that most painful but creative condition, the crisis of identity, as they live out the temptations and the pressures towards assimilation – pressures that reflect precisely the arrogance, incuriousness and self-absorption that they find in an alien philosophy. This is an unconscious arrogance that is naturally met by resentment, so that what emerges is the triumphalism of resentment contending against the triumphalism of arrogance, a state of contention which can also divide the individual psyche. Such states of mind are inimical to philosophy, which degenerates instead into aggressive polemics or defensive apologetics.

Meanwhile, by the criterion Corbin offers here about the ability to "cope with the texts at first hand," most of us in the profession could never be "comparative philosophers." That does suggest that philosophers should see it as a very particular scholarly specialism of which they can at best be the beneficiaries. Even in the case of the canonical writings of their own traditions, most philosophers depend on critical translations and commentaries by scholarly experts and are vulnerable to the familiar pitfalls of such dependence.

But it is worth recalling that Corbin's lecture was given at the University of Tehran. I mention this because, although he regrets the shortage of philosophers who are able to cope with texts at first hand, and, although it is important that scholar-philosophers should make such texts available, it is nevertheless *philosophical dialogue* that is fundamental to philosophy and, *a fortiori*, to comparative philosophy. This may seem a rather obvious remark, but I have already commented that philosophy can descend into aggressive polemic or defensive apologetic, so we need some sense of how philosophical dialogue may be distinguished from these activities. It is also possible to be unconsciously one-sided in one's account of what might be involved in "comparative philosophy," so that one thinks of it as *us over here*, as it were, *availing* ourselves of the resources of *another* tradition. One does this by mediating its texts to our fellow philosophers in the West, in the manner of Schopenhauer, say, who found inspiration as well as confirmation in Indian Buddhist texts and sought to naturalize them into the language of the Kantian philosophy.

The first person plural is very slippery in this kind of context. For most of this paper I have used it to associate myself with a particular position within analytic philosophy. But parallel conversations have been going on in India, for example, in which "we" reflected on our proper relation to the philosophy that was coming out of the West. What we need to attain is a first person plural whose scope covers all those engaged in this kind of dialogue as they come to their common conclusions and discuss their common experience. We best understand comparative philosophy as involving participants on different sides of the dialogue. As in general philosophy, the essential act is one of dialogue, i.e., the sort of dialogue that becomes possible when we become conscious of the presence of different notions of reality – and the interests and the possibilities of appropriation belong to both sides in the conversation. For obvious historical and political reasons, however, the position, if not the interests of the participants, may be different, and this is, again, in familiar ways inimical to the conditions for the possibility of genuine philosophical dialogue.

So, in talking about what I take to be fundamental to philosophy I do so at a particular cultural moment and what I say has the status, not of a pronouncement, but of an overture to someone else who, for current purposes, must be taken to come from a different tradition, and who is now, and this is a matter of both our attitudes, free to respond. I say "both our attitudes" because the demeanour and position of the different parties to a philosophical dialogue can inhibit or promote the freedom to engage in it. But it is worth repeating that we are not dealing with a general notion of dialogue here, but of specifically philosophical dialogue – and in proposing a Socratic conception of philosophy I invoke a form that involves a robust *agon* between the parties to the *elenchus*.

But there is a serious question about what constitutes the freedom to engage in this kind of dialogue. It is one thing to be capable of conducting the *elenchus* and another to be capable of submitting oneself to it. For one thing, there is no assumption of equality between the participants – indeed, it involves an *unequal* relationship, one between a teacher and a pupil, in which the teacher by various means seeks to dislodge the pupil from a condition that obscures their view of reality or of how things really are. But the inequality does not derive from the fact that one person formally holds the role of teacher and the other the role of pupil. Rather it is determined precisely by a more adequate awareness of how things are, by who has something to teach and who something to learn. The premise, to return to the beginning, is that one person can see the obscuring mechanisms and the other cannot. It is vitally important to realize that we are not talking in the *elenchus* simply of changing someone's beliefs. As I also mentioned at the beginning, we are talking about a transformation of the person, of a kind that reflects not greater knowledge but greater understanding reflected in a changed demeanour. But the upshot of this is a curious one that is extensively discussed in the work of Kierkegaard, viz. that communication between the parties represented by the liberated prisoner and those still bound by the mechanisms of bondage has to be artistic and indirect. It is not a matter of telling someone something, or defeating them in argument, and there is, no doubt, to recall a famous Zen story, many a professor whose cup is already full.

Corbin's Tehran lecture gives eloquent expression to a disappointment and alarm about the moral condition of the West, the processes of westernization, and the state of philosophy, which, in his case, is a particular secular direction of post-Hegelianism. But as we have seen, Corbin's sense of danger, which no doubt echoes Heidegger's vigorous warnings, is and has been no less felt by thinkers of different cultures who have seen the engulfing effects of "westernization" on those cultures. Corbin's proposal for comparative philosophy represents a politico-religious agenda, a call as it were to arms to thinkers of affected cultures against the encroachment of an occidental ideology, impelling a conception of philosophy that unconsciously conceals what should be the task of philosophy to reveal.

It seems to me that Corbin's notion of comparative philosophy is that of an essential preliminary to the enlargement of a canon. It is the idea of bringing into contact recognizable philosophical traditions that are relatively unknown to one another, traditions that have diverged at some point in the past and lost contact, or traditions that have developed independently but are capable of a fruitful and challenging engagement with one another. In other words comparative philosophy is always aimed towards a new condition of philosophy itself. I say *preliminary* because it stands at the threshold of the enlargement or expansion of a canon. I do not mean here *our*, as opposed to someone else's, canon, but rather the idea of a shared, global canon – so that, for instance, and to use Corbin's own example, both the Cambridge and the Persian Platonists would feature in a common history of Platonism. Once there is a fruitful engagement and mutual integration, then that particular task of the comparative philosopher is over. There is a mutual incorporation, not a continued comparison, of what constitutes a canon in the first place.

I am already of course using some of the language deployed by Corbin, in particular the distinction, familiar from the work of Heidegger, between concealment and revelation, and a conception of philosophy according to which the philosophical task is by no means to conceal from view but to bring to light, to show what is hidden in and by the appearances. And if we are to take this further with any degree of philosophical seriousness we must surely now turn to the interrogation of the perceived inadequacy to reality and experience of the dominant and threatening condition of philosophy. By putting it in those terms, of course, I am giving less than its due weight to Corbin's sense of the gravity of our predicament. His eschatological Christian Platonism comes out fairly clearly in this passage:

> An agnostic humanity cannot organize the world by giving itself the same goals as does a humanity whose effort goes into projecting an arc the far side of which penetrates beyond this world of ours, a humanity which escapes the perils of history gone mad from losing direction.[14]

Corbin's "agnostic humanity" appears here to be in possession only of values that we would associate with "the world" and his agenda for a comparative philosophy is an appeal to fellow Platonists to help stem the tide of an encroaching nihilism set to overwhelm the approaches of the divine. But as we have seen, the major philosophical task is to re-examine the nature and implications of this intellectual fission.

I should want to see whether one can articulate a middle position between this nihilism and Corbin's eternalism, to see whether an "agnostic humanity" need after all be a humanity entirely lacking *gnosis*. It may be that our philosophical labours are better spent seeking to articulate how we can look back at this world and transcend it in the way that the released prisoner is forced to do, so that we become strangers, and in that sense genuine philosophers, just to the extent that we follow the transformation of being and knowledge without seeking to discern the lineaments of another, higher, world. We can do this, it seems to me, without in any way denying that there could be such a world, a world which is unchangeable and ultimately real.

This is the moment at which I might be expected to introduce the Buddhist philosophical traditions into the discussion, and to do so would be an obvious move towards expanding the terms of Corbin's Comparative Philosophy beyond those of the Platonic traditions that developed within the monotheistic religions. I refrain, however, not simply because I do not have the scholarly or linguistic competence or inclination but because when I started to think of myself as a Buddhist in the mid-seventies it seemed important to conduct an experiment which I think now was a groping attempt to establish an authentic connection between life and philosophy.

My immediate thinking was based on a personal reaction to what Western Buddhist artists of my acquaintance were doing, viz. educating themselves into the traditional techniques of Buddhist artistic forms, especially Tibetan. Though it was hardly for me to say, I thought that they should simply allow their painting to emerge naturally from their practice, to see, in other words, whether there might not be some creative, imaginative response to their Buddhist experience in their seeing and their painting. Simply to copy the forms of traditional art seemed to be analogous to the complaint of Bhattacharya and others about Indians becoming expert in analytic philosophy, say, and allowing this enterprise to overlay the creative currents of their own cultural forms. Perhaps the analogy is misconceived, but nevertheless, rather than making myself familiar with the various Buddhist philosophical texts and the debates between the various Buddhist and Brahmanical schools, which, to be honest, I had no appetite for, I thought that I ought to see to what extent my Buddhist practise impinged upon my thinking, to see whether it made a difference to my seeing and thence to my attempts as a philosopher to articulate that vision. This also excuses me rather conveniently from having an opinion about abstruse disputes between the Buddhist schools. But it was hardly an experiment that could be conducted in a vacuum – the cultural and philosophical background to it was precisely the loss of that faith so vigorously reasserted by Corbin. To put it rather pointedly, I was not about to sit in silence on a meditation mat and become aware of the presence of God, though it was also humbling to discover at last a degree of interior silence that led me to understand a little of the conditions which might have led me to talk just in those terms.

But the underlying premise of Buddhist practice – and the idea implicit in the core Buddhist metaphor of *bodhi* or "awakening" – is the simple human truth that states of consciousness determine the forms and limits of knowledge and experience. Of course, it is a very particular application of an alleged general truth, that very particular states of consciousness do indeed constrain the possibilities of action and experience – possibilities that can be glimpsed when the *kleśa* (defilements) are suspended.

But all this talk of danger and threat is already the expression of a partially suppressed voice and derives from its perspective, a perspective that must, if we are prompted at all by this language of danger, be evanescently present to us. The complication here is that sometimes one is tempted to write as though there were some possibility of *enlargement* or *expansion*, which it is difficult to see how we can discern if our vision is so narrow. It is rather the other way round, that we see a constant danger of a *narrowing* vision because we see it *being narrowed*, again either evanescently or overwhelmingly, both in ourselves and in others. We are in that case all released prisoners, some of us, though, more reluctant than others to acknowledge the truth of our situation.

Notes

1 Pierre Hadot, *Philosophy as a Way of Life: Spiritual Exercises from Socrates to Foucault* (Oxford: Wiley-Blackwell, 1995).

2 Hadot, *Philosophy as a Way of Life*, 57.

3 Ludwig Wittgenstein, *Zettel*, trans. G.E.M. Anscombe (Oxford: Blackwell, 1981).

4 "Der Philosoph ist nicht Bürger einer Denkgemeinde. Das ist was ihn zum Philosophen macht" (Wittgenstein, *Zettel*, §455). For a discussion see my "Wittgenstein's Temple: Or How Cool is Philosophy?" in *Philosophical Investigations* 30, no. 1 (2007): 25–44.

5 Roy Mottahedeh, *The Mantle of the Prophet: Religion and Politics in Iran* (London: Chatto and Windus, 1985).

6 Mottahedeh, *The Mantle of the Prophet*, 296.

7 J.L. Mehta, *Philosophy and Religion: Essays in Interpretation* (New Delhi: Indian Council for Philosophical Research, 1990), 38.

8 Mehta, *Philosophy and Religion*, 38.

9 K. C. Bhattacharya, "Svaraj in Ideas," reprinted in *Indian Philosophical Quarterly* 11, no. 4 (1984).

10 Ibid., 383.

11 Ibid.

12 Henry Corbin, *The Concept of Comparative Philosophy* (Ipswich: Golgonooza Press, 1981).

13 Corbin, *The Concept of Comparative Philosophy*, 3.

14 Ibid., 10.

Locating Intercultural Philosophy in Relation to Religion

TINU RUPARELL
University of Calgary

A central problem for comparative or intercultural philosophy[1] – one that continues to both irritate philosophers interested in the area and elude their attempts at an adequate response – is that of maintaining the authentic voice of the Other. I refer not to the now-famous question of whether the subaltern can speak, though this is a facet of the issue, but rather to the broader problem of the potential incommensurability of "categories in the typology of beliefs crucial to the understanding of [the] side[s] of the symbolic systems being juxtaposed."[2] When the foundations required to understand a philosophical system in one tradition are either absent from or irrelevant to the other being compared, whither comparative philosophy? This is a well-known issue in the field and I need hardly rehearse the problem in full here. Suffice it to say that the fundamental problem, for the business of intercultural philosophy, of the extent and nature of conceptual incommensurability still haunts us. I want to suggest that one way of shedding light on this issue may lie in considering the intended audience for intercultural philosophy, that is for whom is philosophizing "in a comparative mode" done? In what follows, then, I will propose a *location* of intercultural philosophy: its relation to its practitioners and its intended audience.

Of course "location" can refer in many and diverse ways: geographically, socially, professionally, economically, discursively, and so on. One might also consider location as a form of tracking: a snapshot of a moving discourse. I do not here intend to provide a map or history of the field in relation to other forms of philosophy; rather, I wish to consider the question on more pragmatic grounds, namely through the question of who is intercultural philosophy for? If, following Dewey, all rationalization is at the same time a "doing for the sake of," then for whose sake is this practice? What good is it and what does it enable for its intended beneficiaries? Clarifying the target audience of intercultural philosophy will in turn make better sense of its rationalization, its particular form and suitability to its purposes, and thus how it might provide grounds for a response to charges of conceptual incommensurability. To some extent this question leaves aside for the time being the more basic question of what intercultural philosophy is and whether the notion is coherent. The issue of incommensurability arises from this more basic question and will reappear in what follows, but to begin with and for the sake of argument let us allow that intercultural philosophy is indeed a possible and coherent practice. The question, then, is who is its audience?

At least three possible audiences for intercultural philosophy are typically identified – to which I shall add a fourth, non-typical alternative later: (1) society at large, that is the public whose taxes support the academic and other institutions in which most if not all intercultural philosophy is now done – at least in the West; (2) some subset of society as in, for instance, what we might call the philosophical public – namely those who may be both interested in these topics already and have some training and/or expertise in philosophy (and this would include most professional philosophers); and finally, (3) adherents of or believers in the philosophical systems being compared; that is, the members of philosophical schools of thought or religious communities. I will dispense with audience (1) at the outset since, while it may be a laudable aim to educate and enrich the wider society in which one lives with the information and wisdom gleaned from years of study as well as frequent intellectual forays into foreign thought-worlds, it is highly unlikely that many of our neighbours and friends will have the required background or interest in what can be quite abstruse philosophical meanderings for the project of intercultural philosophy to be worthwhile for them. Put in a nutshell, most people do not care to what extent Mencius and Aquinas agree on the nature of our ethical duties or just how Leibniz and Rāmānuja might together supply a metaphysic relevant to quantum theory, and so, if intercultural philosophers are to work for them in any direct way, I fear their efforts will go even less rewarded than at present.

The second potential audience would make intercultural philosophy merely an academic affair. If intercultural philosophers are writing mainly or solely for other philosophers – a distinct possibility given the institutional nature of philosophical and theological social projects – then comparative philosophy risks being a very small and perhaps not very important activity in the academy (already a marginalized institution within most societies). Doing comparative philosophy for other philosophers or theologians is no doubt interesting for its practitioners and, within the field, perhaps a necessary task; however, if philosophic professionals are the only or main audience for such philosophy, then perhaps it deserves its place at the margins of "mainstream" philosophy and theology – comparative philosophy being, after all, a minority practice. This puts intercultural philosophers in a bind to some extent since it is other philosophers and scholars of religion who are their best audience, having among them the requisite understanding, skills, and commitment both to critically judge the ideas and proposals arising from their comparative philosophical experiments and to suggest new and more fruitful avenues for their research. But this gives rise to various problems of over-specialization endemic to the modern academic practice of philosophy. No doubt one of the reasons many philosophers and humanists are suspicious of comparative projects, and I suggest one of the unsaid reasons why religious studies scholars are so as well, is due in part to the culture of training academics that has taken hold in Europe and North America. Where once the doctorate was seen to be the bleeding edge of development in a field, having taken account of all that was done before and thus acquiring a synoptic standpoint from which to speak to a broad range of scholars, the sheer growth of literature now available to scholars, as well as the quasi-professionalization of academia, has meant that such a requirement is now seldom required and much less realized. Rather, it is presently sufficient to corner a small segment of the literature, showing adequate mastery over its languages, concepts, and contours, in order to contribute an increasingly small increment to the conversation. The academy no longer aims to create generalists capable of creatively traversing disciplines but rather rewards those who lay claim to expertise in an increasing variety of small and tightly defined niches.[3] The cliché of academics devoting themselves to knowing more and more about less and less has never been more true, so it should come as no surprise that the broader philosophical and religious community of scholars look to projects such as, for example, a comparative evaluation of Indian and Greek metaphysical systems, with a good deal of suspicion.

Some might argue that these "professional issues" are beside the point: that intercultural philosophy faces substantive questions concerning its very cogency and that issues concerning how philosophy happens to be done in some Western universities are not really germane. While I do not want to dismiss any substantive debate, I would argue, however, that the criticism fails to see philosophy and intercultural philosophy in particular as social projects, embedded within economic, social, and institutional contexts. The biases and rules of propriety implicit within these contexts both guides how philosophy is carried on in a given society and partly determines what gets studied and funded. Nicholas Rescher makes a persuasive case that meta-level assumptions inchoate in social projects are to a large extent the cause for philosophical disagreements among scholarly communities otherwise unified with respect to the theory and methods of their disciplines.[4] Such "orientational pluralism," as he labels it, must be accounted for if we are to understand the basis of disagreement on the value of intercultural philosophy. Context is often the largest determinant of the shape and possibility of discourse and one cannot neglect its effect in evaluating the location of intercultural philosophy.

Various "professional issues" problematizing intercultural philosophy are, I suspect, also at the bottom of much (though not all) of the discourse in religious studies concerning the post-modern valorization of the Other and its concomitant suspicion of any form of constructive metaphysics. The dilettante followers of Derrida, Foucault, Deleuze, and Barthes (among others) have, in the name of the destruction of any and all metanarratives, so demonized metaphysics that even the possibility of strategic comparison between philosophies is now greeted with barely muffled hisses; yet, one wonders just how much of this is little more than guarding the small bit of turf on which philosophers are trying to build an academic career. It is ironic that such a fashion has taken hold to such a degree in religious studies, which itself grew from the nineteenth-century practice of comparative religions. The oedipal battle with their forebears in philology, anthropology, sociology, history, and philosophy in which many contemporary scholars of religion are locked, means that to utter the words "comparative/intercultural philosophy of religion" in academic company is now almost as bad as admitting one's admiration of Fox News. There are, I suspect, a number of mewling infants in the streets along with the remnants of their ablutions and perhaps it is high time to forego any queasiness about tenure applications and go pick them up. Comparison is indeed a fundamental mode of understanding – compare we must[5] – and there is simply too much at stake in comparative/intercultural philosophy of religion to demur for the sake of professional conservation in the guise of post-modern angst. This is not to say that intercultural philosophy is an easy task, but it is, I submit, a necessary one, and I shall suggest a few avenues by which we might move forward later.

But first we still must clarify for whom the practice is done, and we come now to the third typically proposed audience, namely those who belong to the particular schools of thought or religious traditions under comparison. By this category, I do not mean to suggest that philosophers or religionists are non-problematically classifiable into such schools. It will come as no surprise that a philosopher or religionist who categorises him or herself a follower of Wittgenstein, Hume, or Shankara, for instance, or indeed a Christian, Buddhist, or Hindu, may well have many disagreements with aspects of their group's founding beliefs and/or the views of their fellow philosophers and religionists. By isolating this potential audience for intercultural philosophy, I do not wish to impute any necessary degree of homogeneity to them. As with most such communities, the binds that tie are usually quite fluid – in reality, at least, if not by design – and for my purposes here we can safely leave it this way. Such communities are effectively self-policing with respect to their membership so that belonging to these groups is won through a once or continuing series of negotiations. On this view, continuing as a good Wittgensteinian, for instance, is something I would more or less regularly have to demonstrate through my words and actions submitted to the *ad hoc* community of other Wittgensteinians with whom I wish to have fellowship. If I start writing or teaching that Wittgenstein did not in fact repudiate his earlier work in the *Tractatus*, then my error will soon be pointed out to me by other Wittgensteinians, either in the corridors of my university or, more disastrously, in the pages of academic journals. If I subsequently maintain my position and cannot convince my fellow Wittgensteinians of the truth of my views, again my errors will be corrected; however, this time, the methods will be through marginalizing my work through refusing to publish it and/or perhaps personal marginalization in academic and social situations – the invitations to speak at conferences and other venues will dry up.[6] My membership in the group labelled "Wittgensteinians" is thus the result of a continuous series of negotiations between me and relevant others in the group and is impacted by numerous factors directly and indirectly related to its putative raison d'être.

These negotiations, whether straightforward or subterranean, are important to consider at this stage since they effectively remove the spectre of what has been called the insider/outsider problem for comparative philosophy. If what is meant by "insider," in the case of such social groups like "Wittgensteinians" or "Buddhists," is never fully settled but always at least in principle liable to revision through a process of negotiation between the relevant stakeholders, then we need not worry greatly about the issue of whether an outsider comparativist can legitimately carry on his/her work merely due to him/her being an outsider. While the situation is no doubt complicated by particular historic factors, for instance systems of hierarchical power, it is by these very tokens that we can factor them out of our understanding of what makes the group. My point is that we need not be waylaid by the insider-outsider question since upon closer scrutiny this distinction may be found to be quite permeable. No essence hides here and inclusion and exclusion may be due more to extrinsic, non-substantive factors. Comparativists simply need not be "in the group" in order for them to carry on their research because what counts as being "in" is not settled except by rather artificial and quite arbitrary criteria. This leaves the nature of inclusion just too slippery to afford any strong grip to those who wish to close ranks.

I do not expect many disagreements at this stage. On one level, what I have pointed out is quite obvious. Religious as well as philosophical social groups are non-natural and thus cannot themselves uphold any significant barriers to comparison. Claims that Indian thought, for example, is in its fullness open only to Indians are easily defeated by the question "who is an Indian?" But it is important to note here that these kinds of claims are indeed made in the literature critiquing the possibility of intercultural philosophy. The claim is not so much centred on the membership status of the erstwhile philosopher but rather on the requirement that a philosopher be insinuated in the relevant community in order for the meaning of philosophical texts and ideas to be fully appreciated:

> [...] if we were to suppose that each religion is an organic whole and that to that extent a system complete in itself in a way that no part of it can be isolated and considered separately from the other parts, how is comparison possible? If each part had a particular function that could not be explicable outside the system of which it is a part then any assumptions about a "comparable" part in another religion might well be spurious.[7]

The view here is that religions are whole and well-defined, but what is implied, I argue, is that such wholeness and definition are also extended to the social religious group such that one must belong in order to understand properly, one must be nurtured in the faith to avoid taking things out of context, and policed by the discourse in order not to make foolish comparisons. How are these requirements unlike the demand that one be fully contextualized in the language and literature of a tradition before being able to make tentative steps outside that tradition? George Lindbeck's contextual-linguistic model of religion[8] here stretches to a kind of Wittgensteinian fideism where a structural aspect of a religion or philosophy is extended to social groupings to exclude outsider comparativists. The pragmatic picture I sketched above concerning membership in social groups, however, works in the opposite direction. If that view of membership is correct, then one can argue that religions and philosophies are equally ragged unities. The organic wholeness of religion quoted above turns out to be a misleading model. What one needs instead is a kind of structured open-endedness where one can make sense of the connectedness and contextuality of cultural-linguistic units without assuming the same structure holds for the social groups that define or embody this structure.[9]

So where does this leave us with respect to the audience for intercultural philosophy? The general public lacks the requisite knowledge to enter into discussion and the requisite interest to care; other philosophers and religionists may be the best conversation partners and critics, but intercultural philosophy must transcend this group if it is to avoid the Scylla of over-specialization with its concomitant irrelevance and the Charybdis of professional politics and petty turf wars; and those true believers in their religious and philosophical traditions turn out to be difficult to form into coherent groups without either drawing highly arbitrary and artificial boundaries around them or reifying misleading models of their discourses into too-cosy social groups. While admitting that contextual rootedness is essential to intercultural philosophy, the practice still needs a proper audience, and this, I suggest, may in fact be the comparativist him/herself. And if this is the case, that intercultural philosophy is for the person undertaking the comparison, then the practice becomes a vehicle of transformation – a way, to borrow Michael McGee's phrase, for the philosopher to become strange to him or herself.

What I want to argue is that the practice of intercultural philosophy is doing philosophy from a particular standpoint – not a real place in the sense of an objective Archimedean vantage point outside cultures, histories, and languages, but a narrative, ironic locus of intersection sustained through a dialogical redescription. What Michael Barnes labels the space in between traditions.[10] which I call the 'interstitial mode,' is a discourse through which a hybrid or double position is created between traditions in comparison. This is a shifting and evanescent area of intersection or overlap – but not of identity – wherein religions being compared or philosophies in contact are mutually redescribed in the creation of the self as other or stranger. To be the audience for intercultural philosophy is to take up this position and become strange to oneself, to become Other, yet never lose grasp of one's self. There are at least two ways in which one might make sense of the position I am proposing: through the notions of *translation* and *mimesis*.

The business of *translation* will be familiar to many comparative philosophers. Translators insinuate themselves for a time between conversants, texts, or thinkers in order to play[11] double agents. It is a position very clearly between traditions and for this reason has been an obvious model for the comparative philosopher. To the extent that a translator excels at his/her job, they become invisible, and this ideal is of course just the problem critics of intercultural philosophy decry. Ironically, the perfect translators of a text or tradition would have mastered the languages, cultures, and histories of the objects of comparison; yet, by that very mastery , they efface their own biases and prejudices. The perfect translator thus tries, and of course fails, to inhabit the view from nowhere; however, intercultural philosophy as translation is still instructive in its highlighting the piecemeal and subjective nature of its practice. The intercultural philosopher as translator is a *bricoleur* both in respect to the specificity of the elements he or she brings together in comparison as well as the "at-hand-ness" of the tools he or she brings to the job. Moreover it is often the translator him/herself who is best able to judge the quality and elegance of the translations – the members of the translated sets being themselves essentially rooted within their own contexts. Intercultural philosophy as translation, as I am suggesting it, then becomes a practice for the sake of the philosopher as audience. The mutual translation involved in intercultural philosophy is then a piecemeal construction of the self for the immediate requirements of living, a form of temporary philosophical consolation: what Richard Rorty refers to as edifying discourse. By locating its audience as the *bricoleur* him/herself, intercultural philosophy may also avoid the charge of obfuscating its own position since the goal is precisely its opposite – to highlight the position of *bricoleur* as beneficiary. Moreover, in *bricolage*/translation, difference is conserved since every translation is to some extent merely to construct an artifice – one that draws attention to its put-together nature and its rendering of parts-at-hand to effect the job of communication.

The second way in which we might make sense of the claim that the audience for intercultural philosophy is the philosopher him/herself is through the notion of *mimesis*. If one of the central problems of intercultural philosophy boils down to a question of authenticity, the difficulty of speaking in another voice for the sake of the Other, then locating oneself as the proper audience of the practice (inhabiting the "for-the-sake-of" position) makes intercultural philosophy an imitation of one imitating oneself.[12] There is an inherent reflexivity built into intercultural philosophy as mimesis: one "plays" at the foreign philosophical position for the sake of oneself as the audience. In so doing, one makes the foreign position imitative of one's own position so as to make it commensurable and understandable. In order for the foreign position to be known, it has to be interpreted in a hermeneutic of recovery – to do anything else would be to avoid the project of intercultural philosophy entirely[13] and in doing so the foreign position becomes imitative of the home position. In intercultural philosophy, therefore, one is imitating an Other imitating oneself. This would seem to efface the other but for the difference upheld in intercultural philosophy as translation/*bricolage*. The dialectic that ensues between translation and mimesis is, I would argue, at the heart of the transformative power of intercultural philosophy.

Locating intercultural philosophy in this way, with the practitioner as audience, avoids both disingenuousness as well as obfuscation. The twin movements of translation and mimesis ironize and make possible the other. Moreover, translation highlights the specificity and serendipity of intercultural philosophy, while mimesis clarifies its transformative power as well as its potential to open up new options for living. It is this second possibility that I wish to take up briefly here since not only will it help illuminate the notion of intercultural philosophy as mimesis but it will also elucidate one of the motivations for practising comparative philosophy. To illustrate a particular element in the motivation behind comparative philosophy, I shall use a problem in interreligious dialogue, namely that of the reluctant other, where there is an absent or recalcitrant party in a dialogue between religious believers. This example parallels the problem of authenticity for intercultural philosophy through the silent refusal of the other to engage in dialogue. Just so, the compared tradition resists potential amalgamation or integration by erecting a firewall of incommensurability and charges of disingenuousness.

What I propose is that in the face of resistance, when the only options seem to be reversion to monologue or self-imposed silence, one option is for the intercultural philosopher to consciously hybridize their religious or philosophical position with the other's, and, because of their position as audience, hybridize even themselves. Through the use of mimesis – that is, imitation of the other imitating for the sake of oneself - one can consciously and carefully seek to hybridize one's own religious and philosophical commitments, practices, and beliefs with those of the reluctant Other. In so doing, one creates a novel discursive location liminal to oneself and the Other. One also redescribes the Other's and one's own positions in order to contribute new options for living. This is the practice of comparative philosophy as constructive metaphysics.

This is, I believe, a fairly radical proposal. In the context of interreligious dialogue, what I am arguing for is that when the would-be dialogue partner refuses to engage in open, honest conversation, due either to contrary ideological commitments or mere disinterest, it may be one's responsibility to carry on the conversation oneself. This is not simply to play the other part in some perverse pantomime, but something much more significant – through the reflexive double mimesis where the philosopher is the audience, it is nothing less than allowing the Other's tradition to interrogate, supplement, edit, magnify, or significantly change one's own tradition in a hybridizing redescription. It becomes the job of the reflexively mimetic, intercultural philosopher to create an intermediary position between themselves and the compared tradition. And this would not be a mere intellectual exercise but would need to create new options for living/thinking. It is, therefore, not a simple, one-time affair, but rather entering into a process whereby one risks comfortable certainties for the sake of creativity. This brings forth several questions, not least the problem of motivation: why would anyone seek to do this? Surely to loosen one's grip on one's own religious or philosophical commitments for the indeterminacies of a strange hybrid would negate the very reasons one sought comparison in the first place – and for what? – a mutant hybrid of one's own deeply felt religious commitments with those of a silent or reluctant Other? How would one know that what one is hybridizing with is even remotely close to the tradition of one's silent partner? Is this not simply a muddled way of creating even more confusion?

There are, I suggest, religious and non-religious reasons why one would wish to lay oneself open to hybridization. In the context of interreligious dialogue with a reluctant other given above, an example of such hybridization can be seen in the Christian theological idea of kenotic incarnation.[14] The self-emptying required in mimetic hybridization such as I have described has a close analogue, I would argue, in the theological concept of *kenosis*. I should note here that I do not understand kenosis as a form of self-denial in the sense of complete eradication, but rather as a conscious opening up to the Other in order to partially become the Other. The intercultural philosopher becomes a stranger to herself precisely through such openness to transformation just as the God-man is precisely the kind of interstitial hybrid required when one party is trying to communicate a new option for living to an obstinate partner. In kenosis the divine condescension both changes its own nature and creates a new option for its partner – God becomes human in order that humans may discover their divine likeness. A kenoticly inspired intercultural philosophy can thus create the possibility of a new option for the Other – one that may be freely accepted or refused, but one that is required if any progress is to be made beyond the stalemate of a reluctant other.

But what about the problem of religious or philosophical syncretism, or the possibility that one loses one's self altogether? If the locus of intercultural philosophy is the philosopher who undergoes the transformation of becoming strange to herself, is there not a danger of her being overtaken by the other? I suggest that the dialectic of mimesis ensures that neither syncretism nor assimilation becomes a significant problem. Since mimesis, like metaphor, always begins in otherness - indeed *requires* this otherness to be conserved for its redescription to work - the worry that one loses oneself in an interstitial hybrid is groundless. What happens to the self is that it is redescribed, not annihilated, so there is little worry that one becomes something else altogether. Identity is conserved so that the self grows rather than being replaced. The problem of syncretism is also a non-starter since, apart from legitimate analyses of syncretism as primarily a political rather than an ontological issue,[15] mimetic redescription may also be understood to stretch the semantic horizon of one's tradition but not to supplant it. Intercultural philosophy in this mode is not a method of grafting and absorbing the Other onto oneself but a form of re-organization, a re-creation of oneself in a fundamentally artistic or imaginative act. This is wholly appropriate and in keeping with contemporary discussions of identity as "oneself as another." Worries about syncretism ignore the accretions necessary in one's own development and owe more to eighteenth-century fear of impurity than anything else.

There is legitimate worry, however, in the question of whether or not what one is imitating bears any resemblance to the tradition being compared. As the comparativist is also the audience, one might be liable to caricaturing the Other's tradition. To some extent, this is inevitable, but absolute fidelity to the Other's tradition is not necessarily required, nor, it must be said, possible. In any comparison, one may only grasp a similitude of the positions represented – even one's own. Certainly, great care and much time is required when one seeks to represent the Other, but this is the same kind of care and respect shown to one's own tradition, not different. Intercultural philosophy's potential for creating novel, liminal positions may, however, make the risks acceptable.

Let us now move to the non-religious motivations for embarking on comparative philosophy as reflexive mimesis. My example of kenosis above would, obviously, speak most eloquently to Christians, so we need a more "generic" motive if my proposal is to have greater usefulness.

For this I turn to the work of Emmanuel Levinas, whose morality based on the face of the other gives a clarion call for an ethics that makes supererogatory kenosis a first responsibility for all people. While I have too little space to fully develop his thought here, we can focus on the fact that Levinas seeks to ground subjectivity in the Other. Our very being as a subject is construed by Others, and thus we have at the very core of who we are an ethical relationship – nay, an ethical duty.[16] Indeed, this relationship with the "otherness" of the Other – what Levinas calls "the face" – brings me as a subject into being and demands my ethical regard. Levinas writes:

> I am responsible for the Other without waiting for reciprocity.... It is precisely insofar as the relationship between the Other and me is not reciprocal that I am subjection to the Other; and I am subject essentially in this sense.[17]

Levinas argues that the creation of our subjectivity relies on the Other and this constitution entails and demands responsibility to and for the Other in a non-reciprocal way. This is particularly apropos for intercultural philosophy as it is precisely in the redescription of our own subjectivity that the ethical call of the face beckons. Levinas claims more than that we are duty-bound to take on aspects of the Other's selves. He suggests that in authentic ethical behaviour we have already done so. For the intercultural philosopher, Levinas's requirement furnishes not only motivation but also the promise of self-transformation wherein we ironically find ourselves in and through being made strange. Levinas's theory of the ethical construction of the self in the face of the Other parallels the kenotic attitude towards the other: in each case there is a prior call to both recognize and facilitate one's own essential hybridity with those with whom we wish to converse, to understand, and, ultimately, to partially become. This recognition, facilitated through the dialectic of translation and mimesis, is the true *telos* of intercultural philosophy. It is in this *telos* that intercultural philosophy discovers its location.

In conclusion, I have argued that the locus of intercultural philosophy, the "for-whom" it is undertaken may best be understood as the self and that locating the discourse in this way sheds light on some of the problems and critiques regularly levied against its practice. To be consistent with my own pragmatic principles, however, I must admit that my conclusions can only be a temporary pause in a wider discussion concerning the nature of comparative philosophy and that my views must ultimately furnish the materials for other intercultural philosophical *bricoleurs*.

Notes

1 In what follows I shall use the terms 'comparative' and 'intercultural' more or less synonymously. While some will argue that the use of 'comparative' carries too much nineteenth- and early twentieth-century baggage, I see it as a fundamental task to rehabilitate this altogether useful and clear term. While 'intercultural' is somewhat more descriptive of the perspective taken by the research herein under consideration, as well as the resultant product, it lacks the active connotation that 'comparative' so clearly expresses. So while I do not want to draw any hard and fast distinctions between these terms, I shall use 'comparative' when I wish to accentuate the practice of philosophical thinking consciously using and reacting to two or more diverse philosophical traditions or texts, and 'intercultural' when I wish to accentuate the perspective and product of philosophizing in this comparative mode. Needless to say, I intend no pejoratives through my choices in any particular instance.

2 Purushottama Bilimoria, "What is the 'Subaltern' of the Comparative Philosophy of Religion?," *Philosophy East and West* 53, no. 3 (2003): 341.

3 For a useful discussion of the origins of the academic virtue of specialization, see Simon Schaffer and Steven Shapin's *Leviathan and the Air-Pump* (Princeton, NJ; Princeton University Press, 1989).

4 Nicholas Rescher, *The Strife of Systems: An Essay on the Grounds and Implications of Philosophical Diversity*

(Pittsburgh: University of Pittsburgh Press, 1985).

5 I would agree with Jonathan Z. Smith's tenor when he writes of the necessity of comparison as a unique mode of rationality in his "In Comparison a Magic Still Dwells," in K. C. Patton and B. C. Ray, ed., *A Magic Still Dwells* (Berkeley: University of California Press, 2000), 23–46.

6 At this point, it might be possible to resurrect my membership through other means: perhaps I could begin to dress like Wittgenstein and affect an Austrian accent; or maybe I could become extraordinarily taciturn and wave pokers in the direction of my philosophical enemies. Thus, a number of non-philosophical factors might also contribute to my readmission to the society.

7 Bilimoria, "What is the 'Subaltern,'" 350.

8 George Lindbeck, *The Nature of Doctrine, Religion and Theology in a Postliberal Age* (London: SPCK, 1984), 33.

9 Delineation of such a model is beyond the scope of this paper. It seems to me, however, that there is no *necessary* connection between the level of structure found within a particular discourse and that found within the community practising that discourse. While evidence of such mirroring can be found, it would, I submit, be a result of historical accident rather than essential connection between the discourse and its practitioners.

10 See his *Theology and the Dialogue of Religions* (Cambridge: Cambridge University Press, 2002).

11 I use the term *play* very consciously to connote both an activity without a particular goal – that is play as a self-authenticating activity needing no external goal or *telos* for its sensibility - as well as that of performance as in a theatrical production. Both ideas of play are relevant to the practice of comparative philosophy, though I do not have space here to develop them.

12 Wendy Doniger relates a little known fact about the film *Singing in the Rain*. In the story, one of the characters, Lina Lamont (played by Jean Hagen) is a Hollywood starlet during the silent picture era. When her new film is turned into a 'talkie' she has to sing the film's finale, but Lina has been cursed with a voice which, to put it mildly, is perfect for silent films. The decision is made to have her song dubbed by Kathy Selden (played by Debbie Reynolds). All goes well and the movie is a big hit, but it all comes unravelled when the actors Lina Lamont and Don Lockwood (played by Gene Kelly) take their show on the road and Lina is asked to sing the show-stopping finale. Of course hilarity ensues. What most people do not know, however, is that Jean Hagen, the actress playing Lina Lamont, actually dubbed Debbie Reynolds in the final song. So we have the case of Jean Hagen playing Debbie Reynolds playing Kathy Seldon playing Lina Lamont played by Jean Hagen. Such playful mimesis in this reflexive mode is not unlike what I suggest is going on in comparative philosophy and locates the audience of comparative philosophy in the philosopher/translator/actor herself.

13 Donald Davidson's idea of radical translation is apropos here. A necessary charitable imposition of one's own rules of holism and normativity is required for the very possibility of understanding. In this case, the played, foreign philosophical position is so translated.

14 The Buddhist example of a bodhisattva could also be used here.

15 See Rosalind Shaw and Charles Stuart, ed., *Syncretism/Antisyncretism: The Politics of Religious Synthesis* (London: Routledge, 1994).

16 Emmanuel Levinas, *Ethics and Infinity: Conversations with Phillip Nemo*, trans. R. A. Cohen (Pittsburgh: Duquesne University Press), 95–101.

17 Levinas, *Ethics and Infinity*, 98.

The connecting *Manas*: Inner sense, common sense, or the organ of imagination

ARINDAM CHAKRABARTI
University of Hawai'i at Manoa

> Together may your minds know. (*saṃvo manāmsi jānatām*)
> — *Atharva Veda*

> There is always more pleasure to be gained from combinations than from simplicity.
> — St. Thomas Aquinas's Commentary on *De Anima*, 426b7

Quite a few of us had to read both Plato and the *Upaniṣads*, both Aquinas and Udayana, both Kant and Dharmakīrti, both Wittgenstein and Nāgārjuna, Quine and Bhartṛhari, as we were taught how to philosophize. Long before one was aware of the 'dangerous liasons' of international academic politics (where colonialism still rules under the garb of the post-colonial), not just one's thought and talk, but even one's everyday sensibilities had become incorrigibly 'comparative.' Now, when one painfully finds out that in the insular power-enclaves of philosophy even a mention of non-Western theories of mind, knowledge, or truth is punished by polite exclusion, well-preserved ignorance about other cultures, and mono-cultural hubris define the mainstream of professional philosophy in Euro-America, that the discovery of exciting connections, sharp oppositions or imaginable dialogues between some ancient or modern Eastern and ancient or contemporary Western ideas is going to be greeted with condescension or cold neglect, it is already too late. While lamenting the misfortune of our purist (and power-blinkered) colleagues who are missing out on this fun, one of the best ways to deepen the collective celebration of culture-straddling contemplation is to reflect, critically and analytically, on the *sense-organ* or cognitive instrument. It is this organ or instrument with which we compare, connect, imagine, re-arrange, choose to focus on, desire to ignore or investigate, will to change, like and dislike, – or even try to witness without attachment or aversion – disparate traditions of thinking. In this essay, we shall engage in such a paradigmatically philosophical reflexive exercise of thinking about the very idea of a sense-organ for thinking and cross-sensory comparison, comparatively. In a nutshell, that is the agenda of this paper.

In Sanskrit, the cognitive and active instrument or faculty is called "*manas*." That word is standardly and not wholly without justification translated as "mind." But for all sorts of well-known reasons, having to do with a Mind/Self confusion in Western thought, it is safer to translate it as "inner sense." Whatever else it is, the *manas* is never the *ātman* (soul).

In the most ancient *Bṛhadāraṇyaka Upaniṣad* (I. 5. 3), *manas* is functionally defined in terms of desire, resolution, doubt, memory, and introspection. In Sāṃkhya, Vedānta, and Nyāya, it becomes a distinct sense-organ responsible for attention, cross-modal comparison, and reflexive awareness of cognitive and hedonic states. In Aristotle's *De Anima* (425a–426b), such a sixth inner sense is proposed and rejected, but the idea of a "sensus communis" is taken seriously. In Kant, inner sense has a very crucial role to play, but it is distinguished from the common sense that is central to aesthetic reflective judgment. This paper will go through six main arguments for the existence of *manas* and show how it does both the jobs of inner and common sense, suggesting a richer theory of a sixth common sense-organ for imaginatively perceiving possibilities. We shall end with the soteriological role of the inner sense, in binding as well as liberating the embodied self.

Philosophy, in both East and West, is uniquely characterized by this inward reflexivity of noticing its own practice and presuppositions, analytically and phenomenologically. So, that is what we shall do in this paper: *reflect comparatively on the cognitive and motor organ of comparison.*

THE AGENT-INSTRUMENT-OBJECT MODEL OF ACTION

An action performed by an embodied being requires an agent, an instrument, and an object. The very grammar of our thinking about an action seems to demand an answer, initially, to three questions:

- who does it?
- with what?
- to what?

A tailor could be the agent of a particular act of cutting, its direct object – a piece of cloth, and the tool – a pair of scissors. The act of seeing or hearing, thus, requires, besides the self or embodied person who sees or hears and the colours or sounds seen or heard, a visual or auditory organ, distinct from both the seer and the seen, from both the hearer and the heard. This, in brief, could be the conceptual root of the idea of a sense-organ (*indriya*), a central idea of Indian philosophies of mind.

Just like tearing and touching, talking and tasting, even thinking, remembering, imagining, desiring, looking within oneself, attending to the fact that one is tearing or touching, trusting or doubting something, also seem to be cognitive mental acts. They also require an inner instrument or faculty, besides the thinker, or the agent of volition, desire, attention, or introspection. This job cannot be done by the outer senses. Hence, a sixth sense of a different level is postulated.

It is not easy to determine what exactly a sense-organ is, especially if we are seeking to map them onto contemporary neuro-science of perception. Even within the classical Indian metaphysics of the mind, there is considerable disagreement as to what the sense-organs are made of. While everybody agrees that the eyeball or the retina is not the visual sense-organ, but rather the subtle function or power to see which is realized by those organs, Nyāya-Vaiśeṣika postulates that the sense-organ has to be made of the same material element as what it can receive. Thus, the visual organ has to be made of fire/light, olfactory organ out of smelly earth, and the auditory organ out of "*ākāśa*" – the vacuum where sounds can emerge. The Sāṁkhya-Vedānta camp construes sense-organs as (unconscious but) immaterial, having emerged out of the transparency-dominated aspect of the ego-maker (*sāṃvika ahamkāra*). But, about the *manas* – the inner sense that receives qualities and acts of consciousness – both camps agree that it has to be immaterial. Surely, even the grossest materialist will not insist that we can find out with our eyes that we are pleased, or that we can figure out by touching that we are willing or imagining things. So we need an internal sense-organ. This is what is called *manas*, one of the three constituents of the group of faculties collectively called *antahkaraṇa* (inner instrument) in Indian psychologies.

Are we conflating the idea of an "organ" (a body part, e.g., a hand) and the idea of an "instrument" (a tool, e.g., a hammer or an axe) here? Such an objection actually helps us penetrate deeper into the general concept of an *instrument* as something in between the patient of an action. Thus, if we think of the disembodied soul as the agent and the external world as the patient, the body itself is an instrument (like a chariot) which the soul or consciousness (*jña*) wields in order to get things done in the world, but if we think of the embodied organism as the agent and the knife or the brake as the patient, then the hand or the foot is the instrument by means of which the organism moves and uses the tool. If, on the other hand, we regard the hand as the agent and the tree as the patient, then that which mediates the former's action on the latter – the axe, itself becomes the instrument. Thus, an instrument literally is the "means," that which operates in the middle.

On the basis of this concept of the "means," the orthodox (Sāṃkhya) Indian philosophers make deeper and deeper use of the agent-instrument-object model of action. It first generates an external organ (e.g., hands), which is more agentive than the tool (spoon), which we wield to catch, cut, move, or grab an object, and then generates an inner sense that is more agentive than the external organ, which then becomes in a sense an object manipulable by the inner sense. Thus, the instrument in the middle partakes of both the ends. The most abstract notion of an "instrument" (*karaṇa*) seems to be something that is both an agent and an object used by the agent, as well as functions as a connector between them: Thus, between self and external senses, there is the *manas*, and between *manas* and the material tool, there is the external – motor organs, between the external motor senses and the objects, there is, in some cases, a physical tool.

Unlike the Vedānta or Vaiśeṣika metaphysic of the mind, the early Buddhist meditational psychology has a very different conceptual cartography of the sense-organs as well as of the *manas*. In the list of twelve *indriya*-s the *manas* occurs side by side with separate organs for pleasure, for depression (*daurmanasyendriya*), for memory, etc. – a list that would look horribly guilty of cross-division from the Nyāya Vaiśeṣika perspective! The distinctions between *citta* and *caitasikā* dharma-s, and the reflective *mano-vijñāna* are all fascinating research topics for any serious engagement with Indian psychology. Though, as I shall show at the very last section, even the Vedic *āstika* schools study the *manas* with a view to liberation, the Abhidharma psychology is much more closely a phenomenology of meditational practice, and its taxonomies are also openly ethically loaded. Thus, one type of ego-erecting mental function is called: "The sick (*kliṣṭa*) *mano-vijñāna*"! In this chapter, I shall not discuss this complicated and obscure Buddhist theory of *manas*.

From the Sanskrit philosophical texts of the orthodox schools, at least six or seven different arguments can be culled for the existence of an inner sense-organ. Let me state them briefly in what I consider their order of importance.

FIRST: THE ARGUMENT FROM ABSENT-MINDEDNESS

It is empirically well-established that sometimes normal subjects whose eyes and ears are wide open cannot see or hear what is right in front of them. If the well-functioning external sense-organs and their proximity or exposure to *their* appropriate objects were sufficient conditions for sensory perception, then such non-perception would be inexplicable. Hence, there must be an additional faculty or organ, due to the absence or non-operation of which externally stimulated sense-organs also fail to register their given objects. And this additional sense is the *manas*. If the *manas* is disconnected from the appropriate sense-organ where the relevant stimulus strikes, being caught up somewhere else, then even things presented to open healthy eyes or ears are not registered.

This argument occurs for the first time clearly in *Bṛhadāranayakaṣad* (I. 5. 3; ca. 800 B.C.E.; hereinafter "B.U."), where it is immediately followed by a fascinating empirical detail. When a man is touched on his back by another person, the first man is able to tell without looking back whether it is a touch of a hand or a touch of a knee. The tactile organ itself does not make those distinctions since as sheer touch they might feel qualitatively pretty similar. After all, the concept of a knee or the concept of a hand are far richer than merely cutaneous concepts; they require the articulate recognition of different functionally distinguished body parts conceived in a partly first-person fashion. It is the *manas* which, at an imperceptible but now perhaps measurable speed, reflects upon and discriminates between the tactile sensations in terms of remembered and conceptualized body-schema of other people. The direct relevance of this keen observation to the proof of the existence of *manas* may be unclear. But it surely reminds us of the work of Maurice Merleau-Ponty and, more recently, Mark Johnson,[1] which talks about our processing external sensory data through an internalized body schema.

Sāṁkara's commentary here is very succinct: "If the discriminator inner sense-organ were not there, then how could skin (the tactile sense) alone make such discriminations? That which is the cause of knowledge of distinctions is the inner sense" (*yadi viveka-kṛn mano nāma nāsti, tarhi tvan mātreṇa kuto viveka pratipattih syāt? yat tad viveka-pratipatti kāraṇam tan manah*) (Commentary under *B.U.* I. 5. 3).

SECOND: THE ARGUMENT FROM NECESSARY NON-SIMULTANEITY OF ALL COGNITIONS

Sensory data as well as thoughts and acts of imagination come to us necessarily in a successive manner, one after another. This rule of successiveness of all mental representations, shared by Nyāya and Kant, has almost the status of an a priori principle, for untrained introspection seems to claim feeling and perceiving and thinking many things simultaneously. But logically, unless two events are perceived at distinct moments of time, how are we ever going to tell them apart as two distinct events, especially when spatial locations are not relevant? Thus perception of succession is impossible without succession of perceptions. Now, take our hearing of a sentence uttered, even at a great speed. Unless we hear its constitutive phonemes one after another, with proper pauses, it would all get jumbled up as one noise and we would not know where one word ends and another begins. The same is true, as has been shown by Kant, for our visual perception of an extended thing or a long line. Without a sequential perception of different parts of it, we would have no sense of its expanse or length. Now, as far as the visual or tactile sense-organ is concerned, they could easily function together, and a whole range of objects (with colours, textures, sizes, shapes, and perhaps varying temperatures) are simultaneously available to our skin and our visual range. Why is it that we can go through them only one at a time? What breaks up the process to a sequence, so to say? The explanation of this is provided by this additional instrument of focusing attention, the *manas*, a tiny pinpointed organ, which cannot hook up with more than one sense-organ object at a time.

A counter-example is standardly produced to this basic rule of "non-simultaneity of awarenesses." When one eats a long twisty fried pastry (*dīrgha-saskuli*), one may feel that one experiences five sensations at once through the five senses: that it smells good, that it is cold to touch, that it is elongated in shape, that it tastes sharp, and that it even makes a crisp sound as we munch on it! Vyoma Śiva and Jayanta Bhatta takes care of this counter-example by the famous example of a needle going through a hundred petals of lotus. It may look as if the needle goes through all the petals at once. But of course, that is physically impossible. It has to go through them one after another. Thus quick succession of the attention-function of the *manas* switching on and off from one sensory datum to another creates the illusion of a manifold perceptual data all presented at a single time.

Kant spent a very crucial part of his "Transcendental Deduction of Categories" (in the first edition of the *Critique of Pure Reason*) on the three steps of this process of synthesis, including "synthesis of reproduction in imagination." For experience to be possible, the manifolds of intuition have to be run through and bound together in an ordered sequence. And he was also postulating inner sense, parallel to the outer sense, calling time the "a priori given form" of inner sense. But Kant thought that all synthesizing action has to be done by "thinking" or the apperceptive 'I think,' so inner sense could not do the job of binding and ordering. Committed to a sacrosanct distinction between thinking and sensing, Kant would not draw the metaphysical conclusions drawn by the Nyāya phenomenologists from these undeniable facts of subjective synthesis of external data that goes on behind the curtain of our concept-formation and our knowledge of "objects" rich with qualities accessible to multiple sense-organs. What Nyāya philosophers deduce from the same evidence is that there is a fast-moving, constitutionally restless, atomic, unconscious, but immaterial substance, other than the external sense-organs but equally able to control the functioning of all of them. It is non-specific to any particular external sense but unique to each individual conscious body.

Not only is the co-operation of that substance needed for the occurrence of any cognition in a body, the very life of a conscious animal is nothing but this activated contact between the self and the internal organ, thanks to the accumulated karmic residues undergoing the process of natural maturation (*vipacyamāna karmāśya sahita ātmamanha samyogo jīvanam iti vadānti – Nyāyamanjari*, Āhṇikas[2]).

The self in Nyāya is regarded as all-pervasive on systemic ontological grounds. Such an all-pervasive self enjoys and suffers experiences only in those regions of space where a particular *manas*, in touch with the tactile sense-organ spread nearly all over the inside and outside of a specific *karmically* earned body, keeps contact with this individual self.

THIRD: THE ARGUMENT FROM THE PERCEPTUAL CHARACTER OF OUR KNOWLEDGE OF HEDONIC STATES

Our immediate and unerring awareness of our own pleasure and pain is direct and perceptual. Every perceptual awareness requires an appropriate sense-organ as its proximate causal condition, just as visual perception requires the eyes. The inner sense is that special organ through which the self perceives its own pleasures, pains, desires, etc. We cannot say that pleasure is nothing but a mode or intrinsic feature of other external sensations, such as a delightful colour or a pleasant sound or a pleasing taste, so that it is received by other external sense-organs and does not require a special internal sense-organ. Such a reasoning can also reduce external qualities such as colours, textures, and sounds into intrinsic forms or modes of cognition; in that case, there would be no perception of blue colour or of a loud sound but only a bluish cognition or a noisy awareness, all objects becoming merely adjectival to the cognitions, just as pleasure and pain were supposed to be.

Since we cannot tolerate such an adverbial reduction of external perception (e.g., "I see a red patch" to be read as "I am perceiving redly"), we cannot also reduce inner perception of pleasure to having some other external perceptions just in a pleasurable manner. Pleasure must be independently perceivable. So, the need for a sense-organ is parallel in the two sorts of perceptions, outer and inner. And we cannot introspect with our eyes or ears. We need the *manas* to do that (*sukhadi pratītir indriya-jā; sākṣātkāri-pratītitvat, rupādi-pratiti-vat/ na ca śātādyākaro jñānātmā eva iti vācyam, niladi-bodhe 'pi tathābhava-prasangāt*).[3]

FOURTH: THE ARGUMENT FROM CROSS-MODAL COMPARISON BY A "COMMON SENSE"

External sense-organs cannot do the explanatory work done by the inner sense because each of them is limited to a specific kind of quality of physical objects. Eyes cannot smell perfumes, the tongue cannot taste sounds. But we make cross-modal comparisons through very short-term memory such as: "This sound is more interesting than that sight," "The freezing touch of this ice-cream is not as pleasant as its nice flavour," etc. It is on the basis of these quick cross-modal comparison that a subject reflexively takes the decision as it were to switch attention, that is, attach one's *manas* to a particular sensory stimulus to the neglect of another of a totally different modality.

Obviously, this comparison cannot be done through either one of the mode-specific external senses. The ears do not help us remember the colours; neither does the olfactory organ mediate our recall of the touch. So there has to be an over-arching non-specific instrument of such sensory comparison. That is the *manas*: it is *aniyata-visayaka*. It also helps us feel bodily sensations such as thirst and excitement, which are not specific objects of any one of the five external sense-organs.

Karl Potter's description of the function of *manas* is very accurate:

> ... it acts as a sort of secretary for the knowing self, passing on one sensation at a time so that the self will not be swamped

with too many data at once ... the time it takes the self to synthesize its awareness of an object from the data gathered by the senses is due to the time it takes for the internal sense-organ to get into and out of contact with each of the several organs.[4]

In his *De Anima* (Book III, 425a–b), Aristotle argues against a common sixth sense. He first admits that there seem to be "common sensibles" such as motion, number, unity, etc., which are not specific to any particular mode of external sensation. We can count colours as well as sounds, we can even detect a smell to be moving. But the non-specific recognition of these common qualities can be easily explained by a co-operation of several senses, by one external sense, "incidentally" drawing our attention towards the quality accessible to another external sense, as in synaesthesia. The sight of sandalwood may evoke in us an olfactory perception of its fragrance. The sight of a pickle may make our mouth water. Even Nyāya has an account of such incidental non-ordinary contact between the sense of sight and a smell or taste.

We don't need to postulate a "common over-arching inner sense" for the sake of explaining this. But how can the eyes alone, while making us aware that the wall is white, also make us aware that we are seeing that white wall? Surely our cognition of white does not cast an image on the retina as the white wall does! Here Aristotle gives a pretty smart argument, first anticipating the hypothesis of an inner sense-organ and then rejecting it:

> Since it is through sense that we are aware that we are seeing [notice that he is talking about awareness of seeing or *anuvyavasaya* here, and not of seeing] ... it must be either by sight that we are aware of seeing or by some sense other than sight. But the sense that gives us this new sensation must perceive both sight and its object, viz. colour: so that, either (1) there will be two senses both percipient of the same sensible object or, (2) the sense must be percipient of itself. Further, even if the sense, which perceives sight, were different from sight, we must fall into an infinite regress, or we must somewhere assume a sense, which is aware of itself. If so, we ought to do this in the first place.[5]

Thus, he makes each sense-organ self-perceiving, thereby dispensing with the need for a meta-sense-organ like the Indian *manas*. The Nyāya Vaiśeṣika psychologists are very much aware of the difficulty that, if *manas* does the job of a meta-cognition or apperception of the seeing, then it has to grasp both the visual awareness as well as the colour that is the object of the visual awareness. But if the inner sense can "see" colours in this incidental fashion (through a *jñānalakshana* link), why can't we say the reverse, that the outer senses can also perceive cognitive inner events such as seeings and hearings and that the visual sense-organ apperceives itself? But there is a subtle difficulty here in Aristotle's position, which is not there in the Nyāya position. Once we have given an account of a direct normal perception of a kind of sensible object or quality through its own appropriate sense-organ, we can then complicate that story with another sense-organ accessing it in an incidental or associative non-ordinary way. Thus, once sandalwood is smelt through olfactory sense, later on, even visually perhaps, one could perceive its smell. But Aristotle refuses to give us any account of the direct, non-incidental perception of one's own cognitions and expects the special senses to pick up their own cognitive episodes as they are picking up colours and sounds and smells. He himself feels uncomfortable in the very next paragraph about eyes seeing colours as well as seeing *of* colours, but solves it by distinguishing two senses of "seeing," one of which applies even to perception of darkness where we have to be aware that we are not seeing anything. (According to Richard Sorabji, Aristotle does believe in a "common faculty" residing in the heart and asserts this in his short work *On Sleep*.)[6]

The reason why Indian psychology can never admit the external senses to be self-revealing or introspective goes very deep into its Vedic roots: The *Upaniṣads* announce that the Self-born Creator had cut out the sensory holes in such a way that they only open outward but cannot see the self inside or their own functioning. Hence the doctrine that the sense-organs are themselves imperceptible. Only a *manas* can infer its own existence; even the *manas* is not accessible directly to itself. The only self-lit (*svayaṃjyotiḥ*) or reflexively self-aware entity is pure consciousness or Atman. In Nyāya, even the Self is not independently self-luminous; it needs the *manas* to know itself. Aristotle's infinite regress problem does not daunt the Nyāya epistemologist because every act of perception need not be necessarily perceived. But there is a need for an explanation of our direct acquaintance with our own mental states, and Aristotle could not coherently make eyes or ears or the tongue do the work of informing a thinker or a wisher that he is thinking or wishing. So, he too ended up admitting a common sense.

FIFTH: THE ARGUMENT FROM DEEP SLEEP

During deep sleep, we breathe through our nostrils and keep our ears open, and, of course, our skin touches a whole lot of things, yet we neither smell, nor hear nor feel anything. What is missing could not be the self or its occupation of the body, for we are not dead. So it must be a disconnection between another common cause of all sensation which, during such sleep, leaves all the sense-organs and takes rest in a special place. The ancient Indian physiology gave it a name "puritat nadi," and it could be a part of the central nervous system where the *manas* remains in a standby off-line position.

SIXTH: THE ARGUMENT FROM MEMORY AND IMAGINATION

Suppose I am pondering how it would be if we could taste colours or hear textures. Even if the result is to recognize the impossibility of such a perception, we would need a cross-modal over-arching sense-organ to feel this impossibility with. Similarly, intuitively grasping the metaphorical meaning of a statement such as "Van Gogh could feel the golden yellow of the Sunflowers on his tongue like a hot sauce!" would require an organ of knowledge that can provide the sensory support for such a cross-modal imagination. This must be a sixth sense!

Not only does the man who has now gone deaf remember sounds, he is sometimes able to imagine a hitherto unheard combination of notes. We must not forget that Beethoven composed music after going deaf. The hearing organ or faculty, which is absent in those cases, cannot explain such recall and imagination. So we need an inner sense to do the work. Even the somewhat strange list of "nine properties" of the *manas*, found in *Mahābhārata* mentions imagination:

> Holding attention, finding justification or reason, recollection, error (reversing the order of things), imagination, forgiveness, goodness, badness, and swiftness – these are the nine qualities of the *manas.*
>
> (*dhairyopapatti vyakti ścāvisargah kalpanā kṣamā*
> *sad asad cāśuta caiva manaso nava vai gunāh.*)
> (*Mahābhārata* XII.255.9).

When we read or listen to poetry, we have to figure out the meaning of such sentences as:

> At midnight, butchers convene a conference.
> To make sure the proceedings are free from all bias,
> They invite a cow to chair it.
> [Translated from Bengali: Abalupta caturtha caraṇa,
> by Sisir Kumar Das (Calcutta,1986)]

In Navya Nyāya semantics, the resulting understanding of meaning is not classified as knowledge by testimony (*śābdabodha*) or information gathered from words, but a make-believe awareness generated by the *manas* (*āhārya-mānasa bodha*), which can creatively put together a cow and chairing, otherwise thought to be incongruous. The Dvaita school of Vedānta goes to the extent of classifying memory as a kind of inner perception of the past by the internal sense-organ!

SEVENTH: THE ARGUMENT FROM RESOLUTION, INTENTION, AND DESIRE

Close to imagination is another fundamental job of the *manas*: resolution or intending: "*sāṃkalpa.*" The verb for imagination "*kalp*" is present in "*sāṃkalpa*" as well because in order to intend to accomplish a project we have to first imagine it. The assignment of intent to the *manas* is at least as old as the Yajurveda. Even today, in the beginning of a Vedic ritual one must first resolve: "This is the ritual I am going to perform," to prepare the body-mind of the performer for the entire sequence of actions that is to follow. The following mantra from the Yajurveda is called the "*sāṃkalpa-sukta*" – the hymn of resolution – because it tries to focus the internal organ of attention to the task at hand:

> That which goes up and far ahead for a person who is awake,
> That which returns back to him when he is asleep,
> That light of all lights, which travels very far,
> May that *manas* of mine have this good resolve.
>
> – Śukla Yajurveda, XXXIV, 1–6

When the Upaniṣad gives the above-mentioned argument from absent-mindedness, in that context, it also mentions the following processes: "Desire, resolution, doubt, trust, distrust, forbearance, lack of forbearance, shame or modesty, wisdom, fear – all of these are nothing but *manas*" (B.U., 1.5.3). The language of the original is worth noticing here: "*etat sarvam mana eva*," as if these functions themselves constitute the *manas*. This functional concept of the inner organ seems to me to be more defensible in modern terms than the Nyāya concept of a fast-moving atomic substance running around the body hooking up with one sense-organ at a time. Actually, the Sāṃkhya-Yoga and Vedānta concepts of *citta* or *antahkarana* are concepts of a fluid substance capable of assuming the form of objects and also reversing its flow. As the Yoga-bhasya beautifully comments: "The river of *citta* flows both ways, it flows towards evil, it flows towards the good also."[7]

The ancient commentary *Yukti-dīpikā* (YD) on *Sāṃkhya Karika* develops the argument for the existence of *manas* simply on the basis of the function of *sāṃkalpa* or motivating resolution which is after all the mother of desire: *sāṃkalpa-prabhavān kāmān*, the *Bhagavad Gītā* reminds us. In fact YD simply identifies resolve with intention, desire, or thirst, and defines the *manas* as that which does this job. (This will not be approved by the Nyāya where desire is the property of the self, but in Sāṁkhya the self is pure consciousness which cannot have desire or even knowledge of objects, all of that being done by evolutes of *prakṛti*.) Neither singly nor together can the external senses do the work of wishful resolution, since the outer senses can only grasp what is given to them at the present time, "whereas the resolve-making organ has to deal with the future and the past." Next month I intend to present the paper that I wrote last year. In making that resolve, the *manas* has to make both the past and the future its object. Because of this capacity to access the data of all the senses and also the past and the future, the *manas* has to be postulated as a special organ of intention. Even life-sustaining functions like breathing are generally attached to all sense-organs, one may say, why can't they help the special senses to make motivating resolves? YD answers this objection by remarking that breathing, etc., cannot perform the intentional job of resolving because they simply happen in the body but do not take "objects" like a sense-organ does. So we need the inner sense-organ. Even breathing seems to become intentional when you put your *manas* to it by attending to it as in *prāṇāyāma*. But then it is actually the intention of the manas and the breathing is its object. Since most of our resolutions involve both our inner and outer life (these being seamlessly continuous), the *manas* stands in between the so-called self and the body, so much so that in Sāṁkhya it is categorized as both a *karmendriya* and a *jñānendriya*, a motor as well as a sensory organ, an initiator as well as a receiver. The *manas* calls into question a rigidly drawn distinction between the sensory and the motor in neuro-psychology, between receptivity and spontaneity in Kantian psychology.

Of course, many problems remain unsolved. The idea of self-awareness, with or without the inner sense, raises the toughest philosophical problems. How can the self know itself, making itself both the subject and object, agent and patient, of the act of knowing? How can the agent of introspection get passively and empirically affected by itself? And even if that happens, how can it end up only knowing how it appears to itself and not the real self?

CONCLUSION: WHAT WE CAN MAKE THE *MANAS* DO AND UNDO

Let me conclude by pointing at an important eighth explanatory function of the concept of an inner sense. Just as, for fidgety distracted people like us, the *manas* is constitutionally vacillating, restless, and constantly getting attached to and desiring to get attached to this or that external sense-organ, escaping to a distracting stimulus when we are trying to focus on something "*asamsayam mahābāho mano durnigraham calam*"

(*Bhagavad Gītā*, 6.35), there is no doubt that the *manas* is hard to control and perpetually moving – to try to 'contain' it seems as absurd as trying to restrain air; for a Yogin, the *manas* itself *is* an aid to detachment and control. Kaṇāda, the ancient author of *Vaiśeṣika Sūtra*, defines liberation in this fashion:

> When the internal organ abides in the self but not in the senses, there results the absence of pleasure and pain, which is called Yoga. In the absence of *aḍṛṣṭa* which causes transmigration, there is the absence of contact between the internal organ with the self (which results in life), and also non-appearance of another body: this state is liberation.[8]

This brings us to the fundamental spiritual underpinning of Indian psychology. Again, spirituality must not be taken as a denial of the life of the body. Indeed, the *manomayakosa*, the internal organ, along with the cognitive sense-organs, is, after all, a very important body that we need to take care of in order to lead a flourishing spiritual life. The spiritual "use" of the theory of inner sense defies the Cartesian division between mind and body since even the most elementary yogic postures require focusing of the inner sense on parts of the body and on the most spiritually significant bodily function of breathing!

Just as much of Western psychology is proudly applied in nature, being usable in human resource development, management, clinical practice, education, etc., much of Indian psychology too is for the sake of application. But the goal of that application is not utmost exploitation of what is called 'human resources,' as if human beings are like coalmines or oil fields to be harvested for material productivity. The goal is a healthy, unsuffering, ecologically and interpersonally harmonious life, ultimately ending in freedom from frustrating desires. For that purpose, the *manas* is first diagnosed as the cause of distraction, sick desires, doubt and error, and then explored as a possible tool of focused attention that cures those pathological states. There must be such an internal tool of involvement as well as withdrawal, if ultimate tranquility and freedom of the self is possible. And the very restlessness and far-imagining nature of the *manas* shows that the human person seeks such a freedom in the fullness of God or in Omnipresent Self. Since liberation is possible, and concentration is a means to it, the first instrument of concentration, *manas*, must exist.

In this context the words of the *Maitrayani Upaniṣad* clearly bring out the value-orientation of most traditional Indian theories of the inner sense:

> *Manas* is of two kinds: pure and impure. The impure *manas* is filled with resolves to get what is desired. The pure *manas* is content, it has no desire. When, being made waveless without wants and distractions, the *manas* is well-fixed, then it ceases to be a *manas* – and that is the ultimate state to be in. The *manas* has to be held fast in the heart only as long as it is still there. This knowledge is *mokṣa*, all the rest is proliferation of theories and books. The *manas* that has washed away all its dirt with *samadhi* enjoys a bliss which cannot be described in words, only the inner organ can feel it (just as it is about to disappear). Just as water cannot be separated from water, fire cannot be seen apart in fire, sky cannot be distinguished from the sky, an inwardized *citta* vanishes from the sight of the self. It is the *manas* which is the cause of bondage as well as of liberation for human beings. A *manas* addicted to worldly objects makes for bondage and a *manas* that is objectless leads to liberation. (*Maitrayani Upaniṣad*, VI.34: 6–11.)

UNSCIENTIFIC POST-SCRIPT

In his long and middle commentary on Aristotle's *De Anima*, Ibn Rushd (Averroës) was deeply concerned with the nature and unity of such a *sensus communis*, which enables us to see the difference between whiteness and sweetness, and therefore could not be identified with the eye or the tongue. But in his acute argumentation for the unity of the common sense, he brings in a comparison with interpersonal judgments of comparison:

> If it were possible for that which judges two different things to be itself two, then when I perceived a given object as warm and you perceived something else as white, I could determine that the object which I perceived is different from yours without

> having your perception, which is absurd.... Just as it is necessary that one and the same man be the person who says that "a" is different from "b," so it is necessary that the faculty whereby this individual judges that sweet differs from white be one and the same.[9]

What is most uncanny is how intra-sensory comparison is understood in analogy with inter-personal comparison. For, the most controversial original idea that Averroës had about the mind is that there is a single Material Intellect, which is the same for every human being, and individual human intellects and imaginations are parts or fragments of that. Almost no other Hellenistic, Arabic or Christian commentators supported him in this hypothesis. But the concept comes pretty close to that of a common collective inner sense, or cosmic intellect (*virāt* or *mahān*), found in the Vedic, Puranic, and Sāṃkhya-Vedāntic metaphysic of the mind. The following metaphor used by Ibn Rushd resonates deeply with many Sāṃkhya-Vedānta pictures of Divine and human intellects:

> Our bodies are like dew-drops, varying in size and shape. The quantitative differences of the glassy surfaces, observable on the dewdrops, may be compared to the passive intellect, that is, to our different individual dispositions. When the Sun, the active intellect, sends out his rays on the dewdrops, the smooth glassiness of these drops becomes luminous, capable of mirroring external objects, and this luminosity, a common character in every dewdrop, may be compared to the material intellect. The material intellect, in our comparison the sunny luminosity, is not an emergence from the dewdrops, Water can never turn into sunshine. Rather the material intellect is to be conceived as identical with the sun which radiates actively and is luminous passively, although its luminosity can come into existence only in the presence of the dewdrops.[10]

With the de-individuation of the organ of imagination and emotional cognition, *sensus communis* can then re-emerge in the Kantian sense of that common aesthetic sensibility which is the transcendental condition of our claims of taste being compelling across private personal judgments. Such a common inner sense, then, not only tastes the first-order pleasures of contact with desired objects, but it also feels its own free-play of imagination, its sheer purposeless delight in re-arranging possible sensory-motor representations. In this, the inner sense becomes an inter-personal creator and spectator of beauty, and indeed of divinity. And the root "*div*" from which "*deva/devi/devatā*" (deity, divinity) comes, Abhinavagupta reminds us, primarily stands for play or sport (*dīvyati* = krīḍati). When freed from its egoistic individual boundaries and interests, our *Manas* is not only the instrument with which we worship God by sacrificing our breath in sacred speech or sacrificing our speech in meditative silence, but it is also the Divinity whom we worship. Both Sāṁkara and Abhinavagupta tell us, in different contexts, that the deities are just the universalized sense-organs in our bodies. The comparing common sense relishes its own playfulness in a divine spilling and crossing over of its own personal and regional limits.

Notes

1 Mark Johnson, *The Body in the Mind: The Bodily Basis of Meaning, Imagination, and Reason* (Chicago: University of Chicago Press, 1987).

2 *Nyāyamanjari*, of Jayanta Bhaṭṭa, ed. K.S. Vardacharya, 2 vols. (Mysore: Oriental Research Institute, 1983), 412.

3 Nyāyachārya Vallabha, *Nyāya Lilāvatī*, ed. Pandita Vindhyesvari Prasad Dvivedi (Benares Sanskrit Series, n. 151, 1910), 35.

4 Karl Potter, ed., *Encyclopedia of Indian Philosophies*, vol. II: *Indian Metaphysics and Epistemology: The Tradition of Nyāya Vaiśeṣika, Up to Gangesa* (Princeton, NJ: Princeton University Press, 1977), 94.

5 Aristotle, *De Anima*, III, In *Basic Works of Aristotle*, ed. Richard McKeon (New York: Random House, 1971), chap. 2, 425b.2.

6 Sorabji, Richard, *Aristotle on Demarcating the Five Senses.* Reprinted in *Articles on Aristotle*, vol. 4: *Psychology and Aesthetics*, ed. L. Barnes, M. Schofield, and R. Sorabji (London: Duckworth, 1979), 65–75.

7 Swami Hariharananda Aranyaka, *Yoga Philosophy of Patañjali*, trans. P.N. Mukerji (Calcutta: University of Calcutta, 2000).

8 Karl Potter, ed., *Encyclopedia of Indian Philosophies*, Vol. II: *Indian Metaphysics and Epistemology: The Tradition of Nyāya Vaiśeṣika, up to Gangesa*, 217.

9 Averroës, *Long Commentary on the* De anima *of Aristotle*, trans. Richard C. Taylor (New Haven, CT: Yale University Press, 2009), 268.

10 Stephen C. Tornay, "Averroës' Doctrine of the Mind," *Philosophical Review* (May 1943): 270–88.

Studying the "Other": Challenges and Prospects of Muslim Scholarship on World Religions[1]

AHMAD F. YOUSIF

International Institute of Islamic Thought and Civilization, Kuala Lampur, Malaysia

INTRODUCTION

In institutions of higher learning in the Muslim world, in contrast to similar institutions in Western countries, scant attention is paid to the field of comparative religion. This, however, was not always the case. Between the third/ninth and sixth/twelfth centuries, Islamic civilization witnessed the rise – and also eclipse – of the discipline of *'ilm al milal wa n-nihal* (literally, "knowledge of religious groups and sects"). According to Ismail Raji al-Faruqi, interest in learning about other faiths and in interreligious debate and discussion during this period was so high that these areas became subjects of "salon conversation" and a "public past-time."[2]

Among the works written during the heyday of comparative religious studies in Islamic history are: *Ar-Radd 'ala n-Nasara* ("Refutation of the

Christians") by 'Umar b. Bahr al-Jahiz (d. 255/869), *Al-Farq bayna l-Firaq* ("Differences among Muslim Groups") by 'Abd al-Qahir b. Tahir al-Baghdadi (d. 429/1038), *Al-Fasl fi al-Milal wa al-Nihal* ("Decisive Treatise on Religious Sects and Divisions") by 'Ali b. Ahmad b. Hazm (d. 456/1064), *Al-Radd al-Jamil li Uluhiyyat Isa bi-Sarih al-Injil* ("Proper Refutation of the Divinity of Jesus with Clear Evidence from the Bible") by Abu Hamid al-Ghazali (d. 505/1112), and *Al-Milal wa al-Nihal* ("Religious Sects and Divisions") by Abu l-Fath ash-Shahrastani (d. 548/1154). Mention may also be made of such writers as Muhammad b. Jarir at-Tabari (d. 313/926), who wrote about the religion of the Persians; Abu l-Hasan al-Mas'udi (d. 346/958), who wrote two books on Judaism, Christianity, and the religions of India; al-Qadi 'Abd al-Jabbar (d. 415/1025), who devoted part of *Al-Mughni* to Muslim sects and to religions other than Islam; and Abu Rayhan al-Biruni (d. 440/1053), who wrote about religion in India and Persia.

After a lapse of about six to seven centuries, there is, today, renewed interest among Muslims in studying other religions and faiths. Notable works in this connection are: Faruqi's *Christian Ethics*, *Trialogue of the Abrahamic Faiths*, and *Islam and Other Faiths*; Ahmad Shalabi's four-volume *Muqaranat al-Adyan* ("Comparative Study of Religions"); Taha al-Hashimi's *Tara'ik al-Adyan wa Falsafatuha*) ("Religions: Their History and Philosophies"); Muhammad Abu Zahrah's *Muhadarat fi n-Nasraniyyah* ("Lectures on Christianity"); Muhammad 'Abdallah Daraz's *Ad-Din* ("Religion"); and Sulayman Muzhir's *Qissat ad-Diyanat* ("Story of the Religions").

As in the early Islamic period, so today Muslims scholars and students face several challenges in their study of world religions. Some of these challenges are common to Muslim and Western scholarship on the subject, while others are peculiar to Muslim scholarship. They range from the challenge of defining and delimiting the field to those associated with methodology. This paper examines some of these challenges, drawing upon the classical Islamic heritage, the experience of Western comparativists, and the works of modern Muslim scholars in the field. First, however, it will deal with the question, "Why do Muslim scholars need to make a serious study of other major world religions?" To be sure, some Muslims are opposed to such an exercise, arguing that it will do more harm than good. It is, therefore, necessary to ask what led Muslim scholars, especially in the past, to study other religions.

MUSLIM STUDY OF WORLD RELIGIONS: MOTIVATING FACTORS

Historically, several factors have motivated Muslims to undertake study of other religions:

1. *Qur'anic Injunctions.* For a Muslim, the main impetus for studying other peoples and their faiths comes from the Qur'an itself. Numerous Qur'anic verses urge human beings to reflect and ponder on the world around them. In so doing, Muslims cannot help but notice the diversity of belief professed by people. The Qur'an not only affirms such differences but also contains a wealth of information about other religions – both revealed and man-made – including Judaism, Christianity, paganism, and idolatry. Though not a textbook on other religions, the Qur'an encourages Muslims to investigate and study religious differences. For example, 49:13 says: "O Mankind! We created you from a single (pair) of a male and female, and made you into nations and tribes, that ye may know each other (not that ye may despise each other)."

Exposure to different beliefs often contributes to greater mutual understanding and to collaboration among people of different faiths, reducing hatred and suspicion born of ignorance and prejudice. According to Qur'an 4:48, God has created differences among human beings as a means of testing the latter: "To each among you have we prescribed a Law and an open way. If Allah had so willed he would have made you a single people, but [His plan is] to test you in what He hath given you: so strive as in a race in all virtues."

2. *Dialogue and Discussion.* The Qur'an stresses the importance of a healthy exchange of ideas among different religious communities: "Invite [all] to the Way of thy Lord with wisdom and beautiful preaching and argue with them in ways that are best and most gracious, for thy Lord knoweth best, who have strayed from His Path and who received guidance" (16:125). The Prophet Muhammad, whom Muslims regard as the living embodiment of the Qur'an, was on several occasions known to have engaged in religious discussion with both Jews and Christians.

3. *Addition to Knowledge.* In the very early Islamic period, Muslims were sometimes surrounded by, and sometimes had as their neighbours, Jews and Christians, Magians, idol-worshipers, as well as star-, sun-, and moon-worshippers. Inspired by the above-quoted and other Qur'anic verses, classical Muslim scholars studied the beliefs of the various groups they encountered. Initially, they focused primarily on differences between the Muslims and the "People of the Book" – that is, the Jews and Christians. With the expansion of the Islamic State, however, they enlarged the scope of their inquiry to include the new religions they came into contact with, particularly Hinduism. Today, large numbers of Muslims live in multireligious societies. Muslims who live as a minority religious community in a land or region – as in North America – interact with non-Muslims on a daily basis. On the other hand, sizeable non-Muslim minorities exist in many so-called Muslim majority countries. Furthermore, modern systems of communication and transportation have increased interaction among diverse religious groups. Such interaction inevitably raises a question: Why do people hold the beliefs they do or practice their religion the way they do? While some people may choose to ignore the fact of diversity of belief and to associate with like-minded people only, such an attitude of aloofness is becoming more and more difficult to maintain in a world that is becoming increasingly cosmopolitan.

4. *Truth and Falsehood.* Many classical Muslim scholars were motivated to study religious differences out of a desire to compare false religions with Islam – which they regarded as the religion of truth. Frequently, such studies were undertaken with the intention of refuting, either directly or indirectly, un-Islamic beliefs or philosophies – especially those that were perceived to have had a deleterious effect on the Muslims' faith. Such refutation was supposed to make Islam intellectually stronger, and also more attractive to others.[3] According to Faruqi, study of other religions should aim at bringing out the commonalities rather than the differences among the religions. He thinks that it is up to the researcher to determine the extent to which the various religious traditions agree with "*din-al-fitrah*, the original and first religion."[4] Keith Roberts opines that a scientific study of other religions can be beneficial in that it will force one to be rigorous in the search for truth and in that it demands logical coherence in the articulation of faith.[5]

5. *Colonial Powers and Missionary Activities.* Muslim interest in studying other religions peaked in the sixth/twelfth century, declining thereafter. It resurfaced with the arrival of the colonial powers in the Muslim world. Muslims, on the one hand, wished to acquire a sounder understanding of the religion of those who had defeated them – namely, the Christians – and, on the other, hoped to counteract the work of the Christian missionaries who accompanied the colonial powers. Thus, we notice the appearance of such works as the *Mahomedan Commentary on the Holy Bible*, written by Sayyid Ahmad Khan (d. 1898)[6]; among the later works were those written by Abu Zahrah, Faruqi, and Shalabi. Interestingly, many Orientalist works written during this period were prompted by the desire to gain a better understanding of the mores and practices of the colonized people – with the eventual aim of strengthening administrative and political control over those people.

6. *Affirmation of One's Religious Commitment.* Study of other religions and philosophies may serve to increase one's own religious belief and commitment. Those who interact with people of different faiths often feel the need and pressure to find out more about their own faith. It is not uncommon for Muslim students in recent times to express the view that it was only after they had travelled overseas to study in non-Muslim countries that they truly came to understand Islam.

DEFINING AND DELIMITING THE FIELD

A variety of terms have been used, particularly in the Western scholarly tradition, to designate the field under discussion. They have ranged from "comparative religion" to "religious studies" to "history of religion."[7] But first we will take a brief look at the relevant Qur'anic terminology.

The Qur'an uses three main terms for "religion": *din*, *millah*, and *ummah*. Although *din* has a number of meanings, including "obligation, direction, submission, retribution,"[8] it is frequently used to denote religion in the generic sense of the word.[9] In some cases, it refers to the primordial, monotheistic religion that, being one and the same, has subsisted throughout history. In others, it alludes to one of the false or corrupted forms (for example, polytheism) of a once true religion – a falsehood or corruption that may be regarded as *din* by those who accept it as a true and uncorrupted religion. This latter meaning is evidenced 109:1–3, 6: "Say: O you who deny the truth! I do not worship that which you worship, and neither do you worship that which I worship.... Unto you, your moral law (*dinukum*) and unto me mine." Commenting on these verses, the classical scholar Qurtubi says that the religion of the infidels has been referred to as a religion (*din*) because "they believed and adhered to it."[10]

Millah denotes a religious tradition, a worldview, or a faith.[11] The term implies a system of doctrines, creeds, and rituals that is followed by a group of people regardless of whether, from a social and political standpoint, that group does or does not make up an independent polity.

Ummah stands for a religio-moral and socio-political community. Aasi maintains that, although *ummah* sometimes gives "the meaning of a nation, a people, a culture or a civilization, basic to all these groups of people is the idea of one binding religio-moral system of law and values."[12]

Islamic tradition does not assign an official name to the study of religious communities and sects. Faruqi says that the discipline was called *'ilm al-milal wa n-nihal*.[13] But there is no scholarly consensus on the term. According to Shalabi, the discipline of comparative religion, which he calls *muqarant al-adyan*, can be traced back to al-Hasan b. Musa an-Nawbakhti's (d. 202/816) *Ara' wa-d-Diyanat* ("Opinions and Religions"). On this view, the discipline originated about the same time as a number of other Islamic sciences, including those of *Fiqh*, *Tafsir*, and *Hadith*.[14] Shalabi goes on to list a number of reasons for the decline of the discipline in later times. First, since, in Islamic societies, non-Muslims came to occupy high positions in the administrative and political fields, and since many members of the Muslim ruling elite were married to non-Muslim women, comparative works that showed Islam to be superior to other faiths – and the other faiths to be deficient in comparison with Islam – were ill-suited to the political climate of the times. Second, the Crusades, which aimed at wiping out Islam and Muslims by means of the sword, left little hope for religious dialogue and discussion. Third, most of the *fuquha'* ("jurists") developed a fanatical loyalty to their own *madhhabs* ("schools") and had little interest in studying other *madhhabs*, much less other religions. Finally, some scholars refused to acknowledge the existence of other religions and felt that no comparison could be made between them and Islam.[15]

In the modern period, the most commonly used Arabic term to describe the discipline of study of other religions is *muqaranat al-adyan*, which is a direct translation of the Western term "comparative religion." The word *muqaranah* ("comparison") may mean *muwazanah*, *tashbih*, *qiyas*,[16] or *muqayasah*.[17] Generally, however, the word "comparative" in this context refers to comparison of two or more kinds of phenomenon.[18] It is also used to describe the method whereby likenesses or dissimilarities between two or more items are determined through a simultaneous examination of those items.[19]

The classic Western definition of "comparative religion" is that offered by Louis H. Jordon in 1905. According to Jordon, comparative religion is:

> The science which compares the origin, structure and characteristics of the various religions of the world, with the view of determining their genuine agreements and differences, the measure of relation in which they stand one to another and their relative superiority and inferiority when regarded as types.[20]

In the third quarter of the nineteenth century, the German-British philologist F. Max Müller (1823–1900) extended the comparative approach, which he had used in his philological studies, to the study of religion.[21] Central to this conception of comparative religion was application of the comparative – or scientific – method to the data supplied by the world's religions, past and present, in order to discover the laws that are operative in the realm of religion. In Germany, however, the newly developed school had a narrower scope, limiting its research to the background of the Old and New Testaments.[22] The term "comparative religion" remained in use until the end of World War II, even though, by the end of World War I, the discipline had already started to split up into a number of interrelated disciplines, such as history of religion, psychology of religion, sociology of religion, and philosophy of religion.[23] Although, initially, the main discipline involved collecting, in a dispassionate manner, a massive amount of information about other people's religions, there has been, since World War II, a large-scale direct interaction among persons of diverse faiths, both on professional and on personal levels.[24] This has, in turn, led to a shifting of the focus of study. One result of the shift has been that Western scholars have almost entirely ceased to concern themselves with the "relative superiority or inferiority" of religions. A second outcome is that Western scholarship has almost abandoned the term "comparative religion,"[25] replacing it with a wide variety of terms, which reflect both diversity of thought and methodological uncertainty. One of the more popular of these terms is "religious studies," which came into existence in the 1960s, which was a period of growth of higher education in the West.[26] According to Sharpe, "religious studies attempts to study religion not on the basis of one tradition (or a part of a tradition) only, but 'in the round.'"[27] In his view, religious studies can, at best, reveal the principles on which all religious belief and behaviour, viewed from the believer's angle, rests – principles which, once grasped, can be applied in other, separate areas.[28]

It seems, however, that the discipline of religious studies began to lose its focus in the 1980s. Its curriculum has increasingly become "a crazy quilt of courses encompassing many disciplines, areas, regions, languages and methods of inquiry."[29] At the end of the millennium, Juschka argues that "the discipline of religious studies is seen to be void, empty, [or] whimsical at best. Since it lacks an identity it also lacks cultural capital, and lacking cultural capital its survival in the changing world of the university is uncertain."[30]

In light of this overview of the historical origins and development of the terms "comparative religion" and "religious studies," as well as of the status of these disciplines, in the West, the next question to ask is, "Where do Muslim scholars in the field stand in relation to such developments?" The chasm between modern Western and Muslim scholarship in the field is very wide. While in the Western academic tradition the discipline appears to be on the wane owing to a lack of direction and focus, in academic institutions in the contemporary Muslim world the field is still in the early stages of revival.

Western historical experience has demonstrated that each new scholarly attempt to define the field is based upon a new understanding, not only of the goal of the research to be undertaken, but also of the methodology to be employed in the research. While the term "comparative religion" may have gone out of vogue in Western academic circles, comparison is still a valid method in Islamic intellectual circles. This method is frequently used in the Qur'an, and was also used by early Muslim scholars, particularly the *fuquha'*, who were known for their use of *qiyās* ("analogical reasoning"). At the same time, some of the assumptions underlying the new term "religious studies" seem to be questionable from an Islamic point of view. The Western religious studies programs are predicated on the assumption that, epistemic certainty being unattainable, no religion has an exclusive claim to truth. On this view, we are left with three possibilities: (1) all religions are equally true; (2) all religions contain bits of truth; (3) none of the religions contain any truth at all. But while the above-stated assumption is in keeping with modern trends in Western philosophical thought, in which "no form of knowledge can be absolute" and all truth is relative, it would not appeal to a Muslim, since the denial of absolute values in favour of relative ones serves to negate God and the hereafter.[31]

Having said that, we must add that some of the issues that Western scholars in the field have grappled with must be addressed by Muslims as well. For example: "Should study of world religions focus on the external – namely, doctrinal, legal, and social – aspects and manifestations of religion or on the internal – namely, experiential – aspects of religions, or on both?" "To what extent is it possible for an individual who is committed to a given religious belief to make an objective study of another religion?" "Should the study of other religions include an evaluative aspect or should it defer evaluation in light of the difficulty in reaching epistemic uncertainty?" Some of these questions will be dealt with in the following sections.

CHALLENGES OF METHODOLOGY

The classical Greeks, who were critical of the popular native religion, were curious about other religious traditions – and, therefore, open to studying them. In their quest for information and truth, they recorded and described what they saw, read, and experienced; they also compared and contrasted the material thus collected with their own tradition and culture.[32] But, according to Sharpe, the Judeo-Christian tradition, in contrast to the Greek, has been exclusivist and intolerant in the matter of religion. In his view, the New Testament exhibits a total lack of objective interest in other religious traditions and virtually rules out even the possibility of an objective study of other religions.[33]

The classical Muslim approach – insofar as one can speak of one – to the subject is in stark contrast to the Judeo-Christian. It is true that Muslim scholars viewed other religions from the perspective of the foundational sources of Islam, the Qur'an and Sunnah. At the same time, however, they felt free to approach the subject from several different angles. In this connection, we will briefly compare the methodologies of three representatives of the classical period – Biruni, Ibn Ḥazm, and Shahrastani.

Biruni made an extensive and profound study of Hindu civilization, including Hindu religion, philosophy, manners, customs, and scientific achievements. In both *Kitab al-Athar* (English trans.: *The Chronology of Ancient Nations*) and *Kitab al-Hind* (translated as *Al-Biruni's India*), Biruni discusses a total of twelve religions and religious communities and then compares their traits with corresponding features in Islamic and other known cultures.[34] He makes three types of comparisons: interreligious, intrareligious, and intersectarian.[35] This enables him to make use of his knowledge of the Greek and Indian philosophical systems to reach conclusions and make observations that would be understood and appreciated by his fellow Muslims. It is noteworthy that Biruni wrote about Hindu doctrine in a completely detached manner. He quoted Hindu sources verbatim at length when he thought they would contribute to elucidating a subject. Biruni himself confirms that his book "is not a polemical one," and that it is "nothing but a simple historical record of facts."[36] Biruni was highly successful in describing Hinduism in an objective manner, without identifying himself with the religion.[37]

Ibn Ḥazm was the first Muslim comparativist to use a critical analytical approach to study other religions, particularly the Jewish Torah and Christian Gospel.[38] Although both the Christians and Jews kept rejecting his analysis for three-quarters of a millennium, Faruqi states that today some Christians have come to acknowledge the worth of Ibn Ḥazm's study.[39] As far as his methodology was concerned, Ibn Ḥazm would report all the beliefs of the group in question and then critically analyze them with a view to showing their merits and demerits. Using the *Zahirite* methodology, he rejected interpretations of the Old Testament offered by clergymen and Christian theologians, who, he thought, might have committed errors in interpreting that scripture. Ibn Ḥazm preferred to examine the original texts and arrive at new conclusions, taking an approach similar to that taken by the Protestant Reformers in understanding the Bible.[40] He would, however, reject the texts if he found contradictions in them.

Shahrastani's *Kitab al-Milal wa al-Nihal* is a virtual short encyclopedia on all the religions, sectarian groups, and supernatural and philosophical systems known at his time. According to Sharpe, Shahrastani has the honour of having written the first ever history of religion. In his view, Shahrastani's work "far outstrips anything which Christian writers were capable of producing at the same period."[41] In contrast to Ibn Ḥazm, who bases his analysis strictly on a study of original and primary sources, Shahrastani does make use of a number of secondary sources – for which he is severely criticized by A. J. Arberry, who remarks that Shahrastani's *Milal* "is little more than a farrago of quotations from older writers, loosely arranged and inconsequently strung together without the slightest acknowledgment."[42] A. K. Kazi and J. G. Flynn, who are less critical of Shahrastani, argue that, although Shahrastani draws heavily on Asha'ri's *Maqalat al-Islamiyyin*, he does make use of other sources as well and often differs considerably from Asha'ri – especially in terms of arrangement of material and classification of the subsects – and gives a fuller account of some of the sects than Asha'ri. Kazi and Flynn point out, furthermore, that Shahrastani's section on the Isma'iliyyah seems quite independently written.[43] Nevertheless, they admit that Shahrastani rarely mentions his sources, with the exception of Abdallah b. Mahmud al-Ka'bi (d. 319/931), whose name occurs quite frequently.

Unlike Ibn Ḥazm, Shahrastani does not critically analyze the ideas of the groups he discusses. Generally, he reports the views of the sects without elaboration and without comment, though he offers an occasional brief criticism.[44] "I have," he says at the beginning of his book, "stated their beliefs as found in their books without favouring them and without attacking or criticizing them."[45] This approach, however, has not found favour with some Muslim scholars. Mahmoud Ali Himaya, for instance, criticizes Shahrastani for not correcting the mistaken ideas he described. Himaya thinks that the major problem with such an approach is that false ideas may stick in the readers' minds, without these readers knowing whether such ideas are false or wrong. He further says that it is easy to learn about the ideas of another group and report them but that it is more difficult to respond to the wrong ideas.[46]

This brief review of the differing methodologies of three Muslim scholars has shown that there is no such thing as a single "classical Muslim method" for studying other religions. Both Biruni and Shahrastani preferred to take a descriptive approach, but Biruni obtained his information from first-hand field research, while Shahrastani relied more heavily on secondary sources. Ibn Ḥazm, on the other hand, preferred the critical analytical approach and relied exclusively on original religious texts, ignoring second-hand commentaries on those texts.

In the modern era, Western scholars have used an increasingly wide variety of methods to study the field. The so-called Orientalist methodology reigned supreme in nineteenth-century Western Europe. The Orientalists treated the religions of the world as "dead-cold data and static external observables in human behaviour or as enemy territory, which must be reconnoitered in order to be conquered with the least possible effort."[47] In their view, the ideal scholar was a detached academic who surveyed material impersonally, almost majestically, and subsequently reported on it objectively. This detachment meant that the scholar studied the religion without participating in it.[48] In addition, many Orientalists were evolutionists in the sense that they tended to classify religions historically, geographically, and culturally, systematizing them into various "isms," each a rough equivalent of a biological species.[49]

One of the shortcomings of the Orientalist methodology is that it failed to recognize that "religion is not a 'scientific' fact that can be coldly examined in the manner of a geological or biological sample."[50] To be sure, several dimensions of religion are amenable to scientific study, but these may not be religion as such, the heart of a religion consisting of the meaning a religion holds for those who believe in it.[51]

A second shortcoming is that the great majority of the Orientalist writings were prejudiced by Western – if not strictly Christian – categories of thought and analysis.[52] Sharpe says that comparisons frequently involved "undue and conventional selectivity, which chose not what is most important in an exotic tradition, but what is accessible and superficially attractive." In addition, many Western students tended to treat the "other" tradition as a mirror for their own concerns.[53]

As already mentioned, "comparative religion" since World War I was broken down into a number of subdisciplines, each with its own methodology or approach. The anthropological approach examines the role of religion in early or traditional societies – particularly the ways in which religious rites and ceremonies bind a community together – the role of a chief or *shaman* in the life of the people, and the function of myth in revealing a tribe's self-understanding and identity.[54] Anthropologists are also interested in finding out how society's religious beliefs and institutions sanction or elicit acceptance of a certain behaviour and how these factors assist in making that society integrated and cohesive.[55] A favourite method of the anthropologists is that of participant observation, which requires an open, serious, and respectful attitude toward alien ways of life and thought.[56]

Many of those who used the anthropological approach to study other religions were criticized for being arm-chair scholars, in the sense that their methods were skewed by unreliable data obtained at second hand, by unsifted sources, and by inauthentic comparisons and haphazard synthesis in which bizarre phenomena were focused on, or certain types of examples selected, to prove preconceived theories. The latter-day anthropological method – that of undertaking intensive fieldwork – has also been criticized as impressionistic, haphazard, or simply meaningless busywork, while even the technique of "participant observation" has been dismissed as the romantic illusion that one can get an inside view of a foreign culture in a few months or years.[57]

The sociological approach to other religions focuses on group or social behaviour and on the way religion interacts with other dimensions of our social experience.[58] The psychological approach, on the other hand, tends to emphasize the study of such experiences as conversion, prayer, and mystic ecstasy, using such methods as questionnaires, personal interviews, autobiographies, and other empirical data that could be analyzed, classified, and statistically measured.[59] The historical approach is concerned with establishing the role that religious experience and ideas play in the lives of individuals and communities, and also with determining how religion influences the development of larger societies, nations, and whole cultures. In reconstructing a religion's past or by attempting to distinguish historical fact from myth, legend, saga, and religious tradition, the historian draws on a vast range of non-textual sources, including archaeology, numismatics, and geography.[60]

The phenomenological method attempts to supply the deficiencies of the Orientalist approach and of the reductionism of several of the above-noted approaches. It is designed "to portray each religion in its own terms as a unique expression, as a reality that is not to be reduced." In order to achieve this goal, the phenomenologist must remain detached and impartial. But insightful description and interpretation also requires a genuine feel for, and empathy with, religious experience.[61] The phenomenologist must exercise *epoche*, or the suspension of judgment, a state that allows him or her to see through the eyes of those who believe – or of those who are committed.[62]

CONCLUSION

This chapter has critically examined a number of challenges facing Muslim scholars and students of world religions. It commenced with a discussion of why Muslim scholars in both the past and present have undertaken investigations of people of different faiths.

Upon examining the issue of "defining the field," it was revealed that there has never been any agreed upon term for the discipline of studying "other" religions. In the contemporary Muslim scholarship, some such as Faruqi refer to the discipline as *'ilm al-milal wa al-nihal* (knowledge of religious groups and sects). The vast majority of present-day Muslim scholars, however, employ the term *muqaranat al-adyyan*, which is essentially a direct translation of the Western term "comparative religion." It was argued that, although the term "comparative religion" is no longer in vogue in Western academic circles, it can still be considered valid in the Muslim world since the comparative technique is frequently used by the classical Muslim scholars in various fields of study, especially jurisprudence. At the same time, it was also evident that the term "religious studies," which has found a place in Western academic circles since the 1960s, is considered questionable by Muslims due to its epistemological foundations.

The next issue this chapter addressed was the challenge of methodology. It was argued that there was no one classical Muslim method of studying world religions. While some scholars preferred a descriptive approach, others preferred to undertake a critical analysis of the religion in question. Moreover, while some scholars preferred to undertake the investigation directly in the field, others preferred to rely on secondary sources. The common thread between these divergent approaches, however, is that their perception of reality was derived from Islamic epistemology, which is based on the Qur'an and/or the prophetic traditions.

As far as a contemporary methodology for Muslim scholars in the field is concerned, it was maintained that there is no one precise "Islamic methodology" *per se.* Instead, Muslim intellectuals are encouraged to study and investigate different religious beliefs held by people in a manner that is objective and fair to the people under investigation. In fact, it is unacceptable for Muslim scholars to maliciously attack or downgrade "other" religions.

Finally, the third issue addressed by the chapter was the extent to which a Muslim's religious commitment affects his or her objectivity when studying other religions. It was argued that every scholar is committed – either consciously or unconsciously – to certain convictions or presuppositions about what constitutes reality, rationality, or evidence. The key to overcoming any inherent bias is to state one's fundamental presuppositions from the beginning, rather than keeping them unclear, under the claim of being "objective."

While the issues discussed are hardly an exhaustive list of challenges facing Muslim scholars and students of world religions, they do represent some of the greater difficulties in academic institutions of higher learning. While some insight has been offered into a scientific methodology of comparative religion, much more work has to be done to further develop and refine such a methodology.

Notes

1 This paper was originally published in *Studies in Contemporary Islam* 2, no. 1 (2000):1–27.

2 Ismail Raji al-Faruqi, ed., *Trialogue of the Abrahamic Faiths*. (Herndon: International Institute of Islamic Thought, 1991), ix.

3 Mohammad Rafiuddin, "The Meaning and Purpose of Islamic Research," in *Research Methodology in Islamic Perspective*, ed. Mohammad Muqim (New Delhi: Institute of Objective Studies, 1994), 11–12.

4 Ismail Raji al-Faruqi, *Christian Ethics* (Montreal: McGill-Queen's University Press, 1967), 15–16.

5 Keith A. Roberts, *Religion in Sociological Perspective* (New York: Wadsworth, 1995), 35.

6 C. W. Troll, *Sayyid Ahmad Khan: A Re-Interpretation of Muslim Theology* (Karachi: Oxford University Press, 1978–79), 58, 70.

7 "History of religions is an academic pursuit composed of three disciplines: reportage or the collection of data; construction of meaning-wholes, or the systemization of data; and judgment, or evaluation, of meaning wholes." Ismail Raji al-Faruqi, *Islam and Other Faiths*, ed. Ataullah Siddiqui (Leicester, UK: The Islamic Foundation, 1998), 161.

8 L. Gardet, "Din," in B. Lewis, Ch. Pellat, and J. Schacht, eds., *The Encyclopaedia of Islam* (Leiden: E. J. Brill, 1960, continuing), 2:293.

9 Ghulam Haider Aasi, "The Qur'an and Other Religious Traditions," in *Essays on Islam*, Felicitation Volume in Honour of Professor W. Montgomery Watt. Hakim Mohammed Said, ed. (Karachi: Hamdard Foundation Pakistan, 1993), 212.

10 Muhammad Sayed Ahmad al-Masir, *Al-Madkhal li-Dirasat al-Adyan* ("Introduction to the Study of Religions") (Cairo: Dar at-Tiba'ah al-Muhammadyyiah, 1994), 34.

11 Aasi, "The Qur'an and Other Religious Traditions," 226–27.

12 Ibid., 221.

13 Faruqi, ed., *Trialogue*, ix.

14 Ahmad Shalabi, *Muqarant al-Adyan* ("Comparative Religion: Judaism"), 4 vols., vol. 1: *Al-Yahudiyyah* ("Judaism") (Cairo: Maktabat al-Nahdah al-Misriyyah, 1996), 31.

15 Shalabi, *Muqarant al-Adyan*, 32.

16 Magdi Wahba, *A Dictionary of Literary Terms – English-French-Arabic* (Beirut: Librairie du Liban, 1974), s.v. "Comparison."

17 Ahmad F. Yousif, "Al-Nizam al-Ma'rifi 'inda l-Biruni fi Dirasat al-Adyan" ("Al-Biruni's Epistemology for Studying Religions"). Paper presented at the International Seminar on Islamic Epistemology, Amman, Jordan, 1998.

18 Munir Ba'lbakki, *Al-Mawrid: A Modern English–Arabic Dictionary* (Beirut: Dar al-'Ilm li l-Malayin, 1985), s.v. "Comare."

19 *Webster's Third New International Dictionary of the English Language Unabridged* (Springfield, MA: Merriam-Webster, 1993), s.v. "Comparative."

20 In Eric J. Sharpe, *Comparative Religion: A History* (London: Gerald Duckworth, 1975), xii.

21 Seymour Cain, "History of the Study of Religion," in Mircea Eliade, ed., *The Encyclopedia of Religion*, 16 vols. (New York: MacMillan Library Reference, 1995), 13:69.

22 Eric J. Sharpe "Comparative Religion," in Eliade, ed., *Encyclopedia*, 3:578–79.

23 Sharpe, *Comparative Religion*, xiii.

24 W. C. Smith, "Comparative Religion: Whither and Why?," in *The History of Religions: Essays in Methodology*, Mircea Eliade and Joseph M. Kitagawa, eds. (Chicago: University of Chicago Press, 1959), 32.

25 Sharpe, *Comparative Religion*, xii–xiii.

26 Darlene M. Juschka, "The Construction of Pedagogical Spaces: Religious Studies in the University," *Studies in Religion* 28, no. 1 (1999): 86.

27 Eric J. Sharpe. *Understanding Religion* (New York: St. Martin's Press, 1983), 10.

28 Sharpe, *Understanding Religion*, 13.

29 Thomas L. Benson, "Religious Studies as an Academic Discipline," in M. Eliade, ed., *Encyclopedia*, 13:91.

30 Juschka, "The Construction of Pedagogical Spaces," 88.

31 Syed Muhammad Naquib al-Attas, *Prolegomena to the Metaphysics of Islam* (Kuala Lumpur: International Institute of Islamic Thought and Civilization, 1995), 87.

32 Sharpe, *Comparative Religion*, 3.

33 Ibid., 7–8.

34 Jussi Aro, "Encounter of Cultures in the Work of al-Biruni," in Hakim Mohammed Said, ed., *Al-Biruni Commemorative Volume* (Karachi: Hamdard National Foundation, 1973), 319.

35 Kamar Oniah Kamaruzaman, "Early Muslim Scholarship in Religionswissenchaft: A Case Study of the Works and Contributions of Abu Rayhan Muhammad ibn Ahmad al-Biruni." Doctoral dissertation, International Institute of Islamic Thought and Civilization, Malaysia, 1996, 107. See also A. Jeffery, "Al-Biruni's Contribution to Comparative Religion," in Said, *Biruni*, 125–59.

36 *Al-Biruni's India: An Account of the Religion, Philosophy, Geography, Chronology, Astronomy, Custom, Laws and Astrology of India about AD 1030.* Edward C. Sachau, ed. and trans., with notes and indices (London: Kegan Paul, Trench, Trubner & Co., 1910), 7. See also, Ahmad F. Yousif, "A Socio-cultural, Religious Analysis of al-Biruni's Contributions towards the Study of Science, Mathematics and Philosophy," in *Cultural and Language Aspects of Science, Mathematics and Technical Education.* M. A. (Ken) Clements and Leong Yong Pak, eds. (Brunei: University Brunei Darussalam, 1999), 18–19.

37 *Al-Biruni's India*, xxii.

38 Mahmoud Ali Himaya, *Ibn Ḥazm wa-Manhajuhu fi Dirasat al-Adyan* ("Ibn Ḥazm'a Methodology for Studying Religions") (Cairo: Dar al-Ma'arif, 1983), 148–49.

39 Ismail Raji al-Faruqi, *Christian Ethics*, 19.

40 Himaya, *Ibn Ḥazm wa-Manhajuhu fi Dirasat al-Adyan*, 178.

41 Sharpe, *Comparative Religion*, 11.

42 A. K. Kazi and J. G. Flynn, Introduction to Muhammad b. 'Abd al-Karim Shahrastani, *Muslim Sects and Divisions* (London: Kegan Paul International, 1984), 4.

43 Kazi and Flynn, Introduction to Muhammad, 4.

44 Ibid., 7.

45 Muhammad b. 'Abd al-Karim al-Shahrastani, *Al-Milal wa-n-Nihal* ("Muslim Sects and Divisions"), ed. 'Abdul 'Aziz Muhammad al-Wakil (Beirut: Dar al-Fikr, n.d), 14.

46 Himaya, *Ibn Ḥazm wa-Manhajuhu fi Dirasat al-Adyan*, 147–48.

47 Faruqi, *Christian Ethics*, 9.

48 Smith, " Comparative Religion: Whither and Why?", 44–45.

49 Sharpe, "Study of Religion," in M. Eliade, ed., *Encyclopedia*, 13:84.

50 Faruqi, *Christian Ethics*, 3.

51 Smith, " Comparative Religion: Whither and Why?", 35.

52 Faruqi, *Christian Ethics*, 35.

53 Sharpe, *Understanding Religion*, 88.

54 Richard C. Bush et al., *The Religious World Communities of Faith*, 2nd ed. (New York: Macmillan, 1988), 9.

55 James C. Livingston, *Anatomy of the Sacred: An Introduction to Religion* (New York: Macmillan, 1989), 29.

56 Cain, "History of the Study of Religion," 72.

57 Ibid., 73.

58 Livingston, *Anatomy of the Sacred*, 31.

59 Cain, "History of the Study of Religion," 77.

60 Livingston, *Anatomy of the Sacred*, 28.

61 Ibid., 39.

62 Sharpe, *Understanding Religion*, 32.

The Vices of Ethics: The Critique of Morality in Nietzsche, Kierkegaard, and Daoism

KATRIN FROESE
University of Calgary

The call to transcend or go beyond morality is sometimes associated with an amoral relativism or religious exception, with dangerous repercussions for the social order. Nietzsche and Kierkegaard are two thinkers who issue pleas to loosen the constraints of morality. In Nietzsche's case, it is often presumed to clear the way for an untrammelled creativity, while Kierkegaard hopes to provide an avenue for the unmediated relationship between the individual and God. In both cases, there appears to be a profound concern that the authenticity of the individual is hampered by strict moral edifices. Daoist thinkers are also suspicious of moral strictures, and the relentless sarcasm with which Confucian moral pedantry is often treated could easily be interpreted in the West as praise for the virtues of individual creativity. However, upon careful reading, one begins to recognize that in Daoist philosophy, adherence to moral prescriptions not only ushers in the possibility for conflict but is accompanied by a burgeoning egoism as individuals begin to use moral appearances to solicit the admiration of others. Furthermore, it is associated with a rigidity that prevents open adaptation to others, which would allow for genuinely harmonious relationships. From a Daoist perspective, morality does not prevent egoism but rather cultivates it.

A reading of the writings of Nietzsche and Kierkegaard in conjunction with Daoist philosophy helps to shed light on the criticism of egoism that is at the centre of their philosophies as well. According to Nietzsche, morality feeds on egoism while at the same time trying to mask it, and his plea to go beyond good and evil is also an exhortation to unhinge us from the hubris that mars our being. Kierkegaard insists that faith catapults us beyond an engagement with the world in which other human beings become mere extensions of the self. By examining these thinkers' pleas to go "beyond good and evil," it appears that morality may require something other to itself in order to be saved from its own vices.

NIETZSCHE'S "BEYOND"

Nietzsche's attack on Judeo-Christian mores is perhaps one of the most ruthless in the history of philosophy. He insists that it is part of the quest to render human beings knowable and thus ensure that a certain degree of conformity associated with the herd mentality defines our behaviour.

> Our eye finds it more comfortable to respond to a given stimulus by reproducing once more an image that it has produced many times before, instead of registering what is different and new in an impression. The latter would require more strength, more 'morality.' Hearing something new is embarrassing and difficult for the ear; foreign music we do not hear well.[1]

Michael Weston points out that the formation of the herd represents a dramatic shift in our mentality, promoting the abstract, perfect man or the universal individual rather than cultivating a human being embedded in a particular cultural context.[2] The pressure to conform exerted by moral systems of the herd fosters a profound egoism because it is not based on genuine community but rather demands a constant evaluation of the self according to external standards. The narcissism that morality promotes creates a human being obsessed with itself and this eventually destroys it from within. The moral system, in his view, has laid the groundwork for its own destruction.

Nietzsche's account of morality famously begins with the master-slave dialectic, which describes the ebullient energy of the masters, who conceive of the good "spontaneously out of themselves."[3] The *pathos of distance* between masters and their underlings marked the genesis of value judgments such as good and bad: "The pathos of nobility and distance, ... the protracted and domineering fundamental total feeling on the part of a higher ruling order in relation to a lower order, to a 'below' – *that* is the origin of the antithesis of 'good' and 'bad.'"[4] These terms were not yet laden with moral value but simply marked a power dynamic that separated the strong from the weak. Nietzsche is making the point here that value judgments were originally brazen assertions of power and difference, in order to remind us of their relative value.

In an ironic twist of history, Nietzsche suggests that the weaker slaves triumphed by introducing a conceptual revolution that permitted the mind to triumph over the body. The slaves, subjected to the power of the master

> ... with awe inspiring consistency, dared to invert the aristocratic value equation (good = noble = powerful = beautiful = happy = beloved of God) and to hang on to this inversion with their teeth, the teeth of the most abysmal hatred (the hatred of impotence), saying 'the wretched alone are the good; the poor, impotent, lowly alone are the good ... and you, the powerful and noble are on the contrary, the evil, the cruel the lustful, the insatiable, the godless to all eternity; and you shall be in all eternity the unblessed, the accused, the damned.'[5]

The slaves accomplished this by transforming their inaction in relation to the masters into a virtue, suggesting that the masters were incapable of choosing not to act. Furthermore, the shift from good and bad to good and evil denotes a shift from relative values to permanent moral ideals that impute to good and evil an essential nature, inherent in the disposition of human beings themselves.

Nietzsche does not want to repudiate the birth of such moral decorum entirely because he suggests that the self divided in this manner also made possible the birth of the sovereign individual, who could assert conceptual control over her/his own activity by making promises and thereby planning her or his future:

> If we place ourselves at the end of this tremendous process, where the tree at last brings forth fruit, where society and the morality of custom at last reveal what they have simply been the means to: then we discover that the ripest fruit is the *sovereign individual*, like only to himself liberated again from morality of custom, autonomous and supramoral.[6]

However, this came at a tremendous price, namely the festering *ressentiment* against an outside world which is then negated:

> … slave morality from the outset says No to what is 'outside,' what is 'different,' what is 'not itself'; and *this* No is its creative deed. This inversion of the value-positing eye – this *need* to direct one's view outward instead of back to oneself – is of the essence of *ressentiment*: in order to exist, slave morality always first needs a hostile external world."[7]

A schism is established between human beings and their environs, and, unlike the self-affirmation of the master, which is spontaneous, this affirmation is secondary, and derived from contempt: "he has conceived 'the evil enemy,' '*the Evil One*,' and this in fact is his basic concept, from which he then evolves, as an afterthought and pendant, a 'good one' – himself!"[8] For Nietzsche, the propensity to judge others is an automatic outgrowth of morality. Egoism in his view is an obsession with the self that is always looking to others for its assessment of itself.

According to Nietzsche, the irony of this development is that the sovereign potential of the individual is undermined almost as soon as it is born, for the success in asserting control over the masters depends upon a remarkable degree of assimilation amongst the slaves. The herd mentality that ensues is solidified as measurable external standards are used to evaluate the self. It is important to reiterate that the herd is *not* a community but rather each individual is left to conform to abstract and external standards of morality and justice. According to Nietzsche, the creditor-debtor relationship contributed to the development of this relationship, and he highlights the etymological connection in German between guilt (*Schuld*) and debt (*Schulden*).[9] The monetary relationship between creditor and debtor made it easier for one person to measure himself "against another."[10] Monetary debts are easy to measure, and a strange notion of equivalence developed whereby gruesome punishment was exacted based on the debt that was owed.

However, this system was not as effective at obtaining the internal repression of the debtor. For this, the invention of God was necessary, whose debts could never be repaid. The Christian God "as maximum god attained so far, was therefore accompanied by the maximum feeling of guilty indebtedness on earth."[11] According to Nietzsche, the moral system that we ascribe to has its roots firmly anchored in religion, and, with the decline of faith, it too begins to crumble. Christian values in his eyes cannot survive the death of the Christian God. This god, in relation to whom we always fall short, exacerbates individual self-contempt that impels us to direct our rage against our own bodies and nature itself. However, in Nietzsche's view, the humility that we experience is false, for it also masks the enormous hubris that underlies it. God is a metaphor for what we would like to be, namely omnipotent and omniscient, while at the same time reminding us of what we are not.[12] Eventually our resentment is directed against this God himself, symbolized in Nietzsche's work by the ugly man in *Thus Spoke Zarathustra* who announces that he has murdered God: "You could not endure him who saw you unblinking and through and through, you ugliest man! You took revenge upon this witness."[13] Furthermore, the constant self-deprecation that Christian humility demands also fosters a narcissistic obsession with the self and is matched by a readiness to quickly cast judgment on others. The love of our neighbour, which Christianity extols, in reality manifests our attempt to solicit from others not companions but wellsprings of approval:

> You invite in a witness when you want to speak well of yourselves; and when you have misled him into thinking well of you, you then think well of yourselves.... One man runs to his neighbour because he is looking for himself, and another because he wants to lose himself. Your bad love of yourselves makes solitude a prison to you.[14]

In *Thus Spoke Zarathustra*, Zarathustra becomes an unwilling witness to this perverse form of Christian love, when a tightrope walker who manifests his courage is sent plummeting to his death by a buffoon, who, knowing only scorn, deliberately destroys his concentration by calling him lamefoot.[15] The dead tightrope walker is simply abandoned by the community and nobody makes any effort to provide him with the proper burial that is owed to him by Christian standards. Only Zarathustra remains by his side and buries him with his own hands.

Nietzsche seeks redemption from Christian morality by trying to infuse life into the very sentiments Christianity purports to espouse, namely universal love, but a love which is based on affirmation. It is significant that Nietzsche chooses the figure of Zarathustra, who represents the Zoroastrian religion that demarcated good and evil in the first place, to journey beyond it. This indicates that Nietzsche wants us to take his desire to overcome resentment seriously by making the perpetrator of morality an agent of its renewal. While Zarathustra is often seen as the epitome of the sovereign individual, trying to create new worlds in a sea of conformity, what is ignored is that he is on a voyage to become humble to the extent that he can recognize that he is only one part of an infinite universe that he will never control. This humble attitude, however, is self-affirming rather than deprecating because it is without guilt in the face of an omnipotent god. Undoubtedly Zarathustra has difficulty with this mission. He must descend from his heights on the top of the mountain and go into the valley. He struggles with his arrogance but is in search of companions, refusing to be "herdsman and dog to the herd."[16] Zarathustra is constantly on a quest to find friends who will interrupt the lonely dialogue within himself and enable him to reach new heights:

> I and Me are always too earnestly in conversation with one another: how could it be endured, if there were not a friend. For the hermit the friend is always the third person: the third person is the cork that prevents the conversation of the other two from sinking to the depths.[17]

Zarathustra hopes that his friends will also be enemies, indicating that self-overcoming demands a kind of sparring that catapults one to new horizons: "In your friend you should possess your best enemy. You should feel closest to him when you oppose him."[18] Furthermore, no attempt should be made to reduce the friend to oneself for the friend should be a master of "keeping silence: you must not want to see everything."[19] Although Zarathustra appears to long to redeem himself from the treadmill of his own egoism, the friend is still an intermediary that provides new fodder for his conversation with oneself. This demonstrates how wedded Zarathustra is to egoism, even in spite of his genuine desire to escape its clutches.

The transformation beyond the ego requires an openness of spirit that is represented by the three metamorphoses of the camel, the lion, and the child. The camel or weight-bearing spirit simply takes upon itself all the loads that are bequeathed upon it but in so doing wanders into the lonely desert. The camel takes pride in the burdens it carries and its ability to comply with demands. Ironically, this gives birth to the ego, for the camel must resist his own impulses in order to do its duty. The split self allows for its transformation into the lion who rebels against the commands imposed upon it, wanting to be the master of its own desert. Against the "thou shalt" that the camel has simply accepted, it roars "I will" and bellows "no" to all external imposition. All that is sacred is profaned by the lion who "finds illusion and caprice even in the holiest." Nietzsche ingeniously demonstrates the close connection between subjection and domination. But Nietzsche's story does not end with this thunderous rebellion of the lion but rather with the child, who is "innocence and forgetfulness, a new beginning, a sport, a self-propelling wheel, a first motion, a sacred Yes."[20] The metaphorical child is able to affirm life without judgment, playing with things to transform them into something new, without asserting its dominion over the world. Above all, the child is not poisoned by resentment; it loves the world without conditions or presuppositions. In fact, throughout his journey, Zarathustra is in search of these children whose arrival he still awaits as he exclaims at the end of the book: "My children are near my children."[21] Yet, in the end, Zarathustra is unable to make the movement beyond egoism: "And once more Zarathustra became absorbed in himself and sat himself again on the great stone and meditated."[22] He greets the world as *his* own while he still waits in vain for his children to come: "This is *my* morning, *my* day begins: *rise up now, rise up great noontide*."[23]

Perhaps there is only one moment in the text that provides a glimmer of what a movement beyond egoism would look like. The metaphor of the eternal recurrence of the same is an illuminating parable that offers the possibility of affirmation without ego attachments. As human beings, we are suspended between the lane running into the future and the lane running into the past.[24] All things that will happen have already happened and we are but an infinitesimal threat on this tremendous wheel of recurrence, which binds all things together. Everything lies along these paths that eventually meet: the good and the evil, as well as the ugly and the beautiful. While Zarathustra is contemplating this phenomenon, a dog calls his attention to a peasant with a serpent coiled in his throat. The wheel of recurrence that goes on forever also can easily claim our lives. Zarathustra sees the peasant choking and tries to help him but fails to release the grip of the serpent. Eventually, he tells the peasant to bite and the peasant takes his advice and is able to spit out the head of the serpent. He is completely transformed as a result: "No longer a shepherd, no longer a man – a transformed being, surrounded with light, laughing. Never yet on earth had any man laughed as he laughed."[25] The shepherd had both taken his life seriously and fought to hold onto it, but in the very same breath recognized the fragility of his own existence. This is a laughter of affirmation that regales in the paradoxes of existence and is freed from the fetters of his own ego and resentment. He affirms eternity, even though it has almost cost him his life. This is very different from the mocking laughter of the herd watching the tightrope walker. The peasant has accepted existence in its entirety: the good and the evil, his death and his life. He can laugh at the cosmos and can laugh at himself, realizing both the significance and insignificance of his existence.[26] Zarathustra himself fails to achieve this level of awareness.

FAITH ECLIPSES MORALITY: KIERKEGAARD

While Nietzsche's exhortation to go beyond good and evil demands that we jettison the chains of the Christian religion, Kierkegaard maintains that faith in God alone can not only eclipse morality but throw it into question. Like Nietzsche, he detests the abstract levelling of the crowd, lamenting the absence of individual authenticity and the complete lack of commitment that typifies it: "Not only in the business world but also in the world of ideas our age stages *ein wirklicher Ausverkauf.* Everything can be had at such a bargain price that it becomes a question of whether there is finally anyone who will make a bid."[27] In Kierkegaard's view, only faith can resuscitate a moribund particular and elevate it above the universal in such conformist environs. However, it is important to recognize that Kierkegaard is not suggesting that we dispense with morality altogether to make room for faith but rather suggests that, without faith, morality may become too closely wedded to an attachment to one's own. In other words, morality may undermine the community spirit that it is supposed to foster.

The paragon of bourgeois morality in Kierkegaard's philosophy is Judge Wilhelm, who is very proud of his propriety and exemplary position in society. He does everything a bourgeois citizen is supposed to, working hard and extolling the virtues of the married life. As the mouthpiece of bourgeois values, he appears to waver between Hegelian and Kantian ethical philosophies. On the one hand, he maintains that the purpose of the ethical individual is to transform the "self into a universal individuality,"[28] thereby shielding it from a kind of heteronomous wandering that Kant also regards with suspicion. However, his Hegelian voice comes forward when he suggests that the concrete individual is not simply supplanted by the universal but mediated by it for he must do this without "taking off his concretion," instead "interpenetrating it with the universal."[29] However, unlike the Hegelian, the ethical individual cannot subsume all possible outcomes into the progressive dialectic of history. The ethical individual must show himself capable of making a decision, recognizing that he cannot waver between "either/or" but rather must choose between them and take responsibility for the consequences. According to Judge Wilhelm, he "is transparent to himself" and does not "allow vague thoughts to rustle around inside him or let tempting possibilities distract him with their juggling."[30]

This certainty and self-assurance that characterizes the ethical sphere is laden with problems in Kierkegaard's view. Enjoying the "outside himself within himself,"[31] the ethical individual feels completely at home in the world and is not infected with the insatiable yearning for the infinite nor plagued with the sentiment that he does not belong. Judge Wilhelm's God does not impose strain on the individual in the form of value collisions, nor does he contribute to the soul's torment: "It takes away from him the vain joy of being out-of-the-ordinary in order to give him the true joy of being the ordinary. It brings him into harmony with all existence, teaches him to rejoice in it, because as an exception as an out-of-the-ordinary person he is in conflict."[32] Even one's erotic and sensual fantasies are ministered to by God, who would select a "young and beautiful wife."[33]

While Kierkegaard recognizes the need of having a comfortable abode in the ethical sphere, we must also be shaken out of our slumber, if ethics is to have meaning. Like Nietzsche, he implies that if values are simply repeated, they eventually grow hollow. Faith, in Kierkegaard's view, disrupts the bourgeois ordinariness of experience in dramatic fashion. It fills the individual with an insatiable yearning for the infinite. However, it is important to recognize that faith does not supplant the ethical but rather is engaged in its "teleological suspension." This term in itself is replete with irony, for a veritable teleology does not allow for suspension but rather progressively moves towards its ultimate goal. A suspension suggests that ethics is put on hold, perhaps temporarily. It is a rupture in the ethical fabric but does not replace it.

The most dramatic rendition of such a suspension of the ethical is the story of Abraham and Isaac that Kierkegaard retells in *Fear and Trembling*. Abraham, a stalwart member of a community and founder of a people, is asked by God to sacrifice Isaac, his progeny. He does so without questioning God's word, in spite of being a thoroughly ethical individual: "In ethical terms, Abraham's relation to Isaac is quite simply this: the father shall love the son more than himself."[34] Kierkegaard reminds us repeatedly that Abraham's act is not comprehensible and cannot be reasoned away in Sunday sermons. The pseudonymous teller of the tale is so perplexed by the story that he imagines four alternate beginnings, which render Abraham's behaviour more comprehensible. For example, in one story, Abraham begrudgingly complies with Abraham's request but loses his faith in God. In another, Abraham assumes that God cannot really be asking this of him and refuses to go through with the dreadful act.

The tale of Abraham is absurd because, in Kierkegaard's view, Abraham becomes himself at the moment where he is prepared to relinquish that which he holds most dear, namely his own son. In this he is utterly alone, and he cannot make sense of his mission to others in ethical terms and therefore is forced to remain silent. The command that he faces is issued to him by a God who is radically other, and he must respond as an individual without having recourse to the support of the community. According to Kierkegaard, only the complete alterity of a transcendent God can break the shackles of self-interest, while at the same time speaking to Abraham most intimately. God, in this story, is both infinitely distant and intensely close.

Abraham's situation transcends the rational for another reason. His faith impels him to follow through with God's wishes but also leads him to believe that his son will be returned to him. However, this is not meant to diminish the impact of sacrifice. Ironically, Abraham believes both that he will lose his son and, against all logic, that his son will be returned.[35] To make this clear, Kierkegaard contrasts this story with the account of the knight of resignation who has let love infiltrate every fibre of his being, but then surrenders it. The example he gives is of a young swain who is in love with his princess but cannot have her due to the constraints of custom. He feels blissful delight in letting love palpitate in every nerve.[36] He gives up his princess but transforms his love into an eternal as opposed to a temporal love. She becomes a recollection, and he needs no finite occasion "for the growth" of his love.[37] In so doing, he becomes sufficient unto himself and resides in the eternal sphere, cutting his ties to the temporal realm. The princess is metamorphozed into an abstraction: "In infinite resignation there is peace and rest; every person who wills it can discipline himself to make this movement, which in its pain reconciles one to existence."[38] He consoles himself with the thought that what he has achieved is on a higher plane than the finite sphere and therefore his sacrifice is worth it.

The knight of faith is not like the knight of infinite resignation for he does not give up the finite:

> He does exactly the same as the other knight did: he infinitely renounces the love that is the substance of his life he is reconciled in pain. But then the marvel happens; he makes one more movement even more wonderful than all the others, for he says: nevertheless I have faith that I will get her – that is by virtue of the absurd by virtue of the fact that for God all things are possible.[39]

The real courage for Kierkegaard lies in making this sacrifice and yet fully embracing the finite world: "But it takes a paradoxical and humble courage to grasp the whole temporal realm now by virtue of the absurd and this is the courage of faith. By faith Abraham did not renounce Isaac, but by faith Abraham received Isaac."[40] The Isaac that he receives is an individual in his own right, who is not simply an extension of himself. In short, Abraham recognizes that the infinite is in the finite and that the infinite is difference, not assimilation.

In the story of Agnes and the merman, also recounted in *Fear and Trembling*, Kierkegaard demonstrates that in some situations, faith may be necessary in order to embrace the universal. The merman seduces Agnes "and in wild lust seizes and breaks the innocent flower standing on the seashore."[41] When he is on the verge of carrying her to the depths of the sea, her faith breaks his resolution:

> Agnes looks at him once more, not fearfully, not despairingly, not proud of her good luck, not intoxicated with desire, but in absolute faith and in absolute humility, like the lowly flower she thought herself to be, and with this looks she entrusts her whole destiny to him in absolute confidence.[42]

The merman cannot "withstand the power of her innocence," which amounts to a kind of radical openness to another, and ceases his seduction, refusing to whisk her away to her certain death in the sea. Because he is a merman, who is precluded from belonging to the universal, only faith will allow his entry into its port:

> When the single individual by his guilt has come outside the universal, he can return only by virtue of having come as the single individual into an absolute relation to the absolute.... The merman, therefore, cannot belong to Agnes, without, after having made the infinite movement of repentance, making one movement more: the movement by virtue of the absurd.[43]

If difference is to be accommodated in the universal, it also requires a tremendous leap of faith. What Kierkegaard is describing here is a radical openness that transcends ethics in order to make ethics possible. The open acceptance of the other who is not reduced to the same is necessary if ethics is to function. Kierkegaard's tale is about the importance of including difference and the leap of faith that is required in order to do so.

NOTHING IS VIRTUOUS: DAOISM

Daoist philosophy, like that of Nietzsche, espouses an ethical philosophy that is not dependent on moral values, going so far as to spurn them. The word *dao* (道) signifies process, way, and movement, but it can also signify language. The opening line of the text of the *Daodejing* begins with a paradox. The English translation of this line is "the way that can be spoken of is not the constant way."[44] The Chinese text reads *dao ke dao fei chang dao* (道可道非常道).[45] This could be translated as follows: "the *dao* that can be *dao*'d is not the constant *dao*." To speak of the *dao*, or to "*dao* the *dao*" is both a part of the process of the *dao*'s movement and is, at the same time, inadequate to convey what the *dao* is. Language is part of the rhythm of the *dao*; it does not transcend it. Both the beauty and limits of language are conveyed here. The *dao* is beyond each particular thing; yet, it is in each particular thing and thus is always close and far at the same time, like Kierkegaard's God. This is why it must be spoken of, even though it cannot be spoken of. The *dao* does not speak, nor does it issue decrees like Kierkegaard's God. It moves constantly because all living things are part of it, coming into being and passing away, but because it comprises the movement of everything, it is also motionless.

> There is a thing confusedly formed,
> Born before heaven and earth
> Silent and void
> It stands alone and does not change
> Goes round and does not weary
> It is capable of being the mother of the world.
> I know not its name
> So I style it 'the way.'[46]

Value judgments are rooted firmly in the trappings of language, which tries to fix impermanent things into permanent categories. In fact, morality is necessary when "the great way falls into disuse" and this marks the birth of the Confucian values of "benevolence and rectitude."[47] Moral language also fixes dualities, which cannot make sense except in relation to each other, and therefore, according to the text, the good and the bad as well as the beautiful and the ugly are one: "The whole world recognizes the beautiful as the beautiful, yet this is only the ugly; the whole world recognizes the good as the good, yet this is only the bad."[48]

Daoist thinkers point out that the attempt to fix categories by means of language and morality is akin to a kind of desire for possession, and all possession is linked to the pursuit of personal advantage or *li* (利). Even the good and the bad are united in the one. Both hold onto the *dao* and the *Daodejing* uses wordplay to underline their similarity. The good man treasures the *dao* (*shan ren zhi bao*; 善人之寶), while the bad man tries to hold onto it and preserve it (*bu shan ren zhi suo bao*; 不善人之所保).[49] The phonetic *bao* links these phrases. In one case, it means to treasure, and, in the other case, it means to hold onto or preserve. Evil is thus a derivative of goodness. The bad man does not repudiate the *dao* but rather tries to contain it and in so doing reduce it to a possession:

> The Tao [*dao*] is the innermost recess of all things
> It is what the good man cherishes
> As well as what the bad man wants to keep.
> With the Tao, beautiful words can buy respect;
> Beautiful deeds can be highly regarded.
> How can the bad man desert the Tao.[50]

The last line in this passage reads somewhat differently in Chinese, namely *ren zhi bu shan he qi zhi you* (人之不善, 何棄之有),[51] which asks "how can the bad man abandon having."

The similarity between the bad and the good man in terms of possession is also illustrated in the *Zhuangzi*, which is a more iconoclastic text than the *Daodejing*. Robber Zhi is the brother of Liu Xia Ji, a friend of Confucius. This link is symbolically indicative of the link between the alleged "good" and "bad." Confucius berates his friend for not raising his brother properly in accordance with the laws of ritual propriety. When his friend responds that nothing can be done when one's brother resists this education, Confucius sets out to see Robber Zhi and lecture him on proper behaviour and the cultivation of virtue. His hopes are soon crushed for Robber Zhi flies into a rage and berates Confucius:

> The more you say the more ridiculous it is. You eat yet you do not plough, wear without ever weaving. You wag your lips and use your tongue like a drumstick. You just decide what you think is right and wrong and lead the rulers astray, preventing scholars from studying the roots of the whole world. You establish notions of filial piety and fraternal duty just as you fancy, yet you also want to wriggle your way into favour with the princes, the wealthy and the nobility.... Get off home now, for if you don't then I will take your liver and add it to this meal.[52]

Furthermore, Zhi points out that the emperors who are so revered create a "great walled city." This is in marked contrast to the time of Shen Nong, when the people lay "down in peace and rose in serene security."[53] The Yellow Emperor could not sustain this era of virtue because he established kingdoms and ministers. The only difference between a criminal and an emperor inheres in the difference of scale. Robber Zhi has maligned all the heroes of the Confucian tradition.

The Daoist antidote to morality is the cultivation of nothingness. Nothingness does not refer to simple absence but rather is the kind of openness that makes presence possible. The opening lines of the *Daodejing* make reference to the centrality of *wu* (無), which is the beginning of heaven and earth:

> ... 'non-existence' I call the beginning of Heaven and Earth. 'Existence' I call the mother of individual beings. Therefore does the direction towards non-existence lead to the sight of the miraculous essence, the direction towards existence to the sight of spatial limitations.[54]

Some commentators, such as Wang Bi, argue that nothingness is central to the text arguing that non-being is a point of origin:

> ... all being originated from nonbeing. The time before physical forms and names appeared was the beginning of the myriad things. After forms and names appear, 'dao' develops them, nourishes them, provides their formal shape and completes their formal substance, that is, becomes their Mother.[55]

It is also clear that nothingness and being interact in a complementary manner and that one is not independent of the other. We must learn to cultivate nothingness because as one of the "ten-thousand things" we are not as attuned to the beginning of heaven and earth and tend to venerate existence rather than nothingness.

In the *Zhuangzi*, the value of diversity is much more pronounced than in the *Daodejing*. Nothingness is no longer simply associated with the beginning of heaven and earth but is clearly linked to the celebration of multiplicity. The habit of issuing moral judgments is very much connected to the desire to "wait for one voice to bring it all together," which Zhuangzi asserts is "as pointless as waiting for no one"[56] Morality contains and tries to limit the diversity of things. Zhuangzi brings up the relationship between being and nothingness or being and not-being as a response to questions of right and wrong:

> With regard to what is right and wrong, I say not being is being and being is not being. But let us not get caught up in discussing this. Forget about life, forget about worrying about right and wrong. Plunge into the unknown and the endless and find your place there.[57]

Nothingness reminds us that all things are undifferentiated and thus interrelated. Yet, at the same time, they are differentiated from each other. Nothingness is an openness that allows things to connect, and, yet, it is the space between them that allows them to be different. This is why it is also being. Furthermore, only things that are different can connect to each other and thus become one. Oneness does not make sense without difference and difference does not make sense without oneness. The sage is able to navigate amongst this multiplicity of perspectives and thus "manages to harmonize right and wrong" rather than ensuring that right triumphs. More often than not, right is a matter of upholding one's own interest: "Imagine that you and I have a disagreement, and you get the better of me, rather than me getting the better of you, does this mean that you are automatically right and I am automatically wrong?"[58] Right and wrong are defined against one another, and this is why Zhuangzi reminds us that being and not-being are connected. Those things that we assume are our opposites are in reality closely intertwined. Harmony as a goal is more important than the cultivation of moral virtue. Moral virtues step in where harmony has failed.

Nothingness also offers a kind of formlessness that is necessary for the flourishing of form. This interaction is personified in a dialogue between the outline and the shadow. The outline is frustrated with the undecidability and fidgety nature of the shadow: "first you are on the move, then you are standing still; you sit down and then you stand up. Why can't you make up your mind?"[59] The last line of this section in Chinese could read: "Why don't you hold on in a distinctive way" (何其無特操).[60] The shadow responds:

> Do I have to look to something else to be what I am? Does this something else itself not have to rely upon yet another something? Do I have to depend upon the scales of a snake or the wings of a cicada? How can I tell how things are? How can I tell how things are not?[61]

The shadow recognizes that each being is dependent upon another and does not care about maintaining its own form. Rather, it adjusts its shape to whatever being it encounters. Nonetheless, it could not do so if other things did not have form. While the shadow is formless, it too has an outline and therefore has form in the midst of its formlessness.

The sage in Daoist texts is someone who is able to cultivate nothingness within himself and thus has no need for morality: "the perfect man has no self. The spiritual has no merit; the holy man has no fame."[62] The Chinese expression for "the perfect man has no self" is *zhi ren wu ji* (至人无己).[63] *Ji* is used when a more egotistical conception of the self is being referred to, while the other term for self, *shen* (身), refers to an interconnected being. This is why the sage cultivates his *shen* but not his *ji*. Ironically, the cultivation of *shen* has little to do with constructing a self-identity because it refers to the interconnected aspect of one's being. This does not mean that we deny ourselves but rather that we live an embodied existence that is always already connected to other beings. Zhuangzi points out that we "go around telling everybody 'I do this, I do that' but how do we know that this 'I' we talk about has any 'I' to it?"[64] Wang Youru points out that Zhuangzi, in arguing for the elimination of the distinction between subject and object, self and other, also makes the distinction between right and wrong irrelevant.[65] If self and other are not perceived of as distinct, there is no need for morality.

Cultivating nothingness is also closely connected to the art of *wuwei* (無為) or "actionless action":

> The sages are quiescent, not because of any value in being quiescent, they simply are still. Not even the multitude of beings can disturb them, so they are calm.... The sage's heart is stilled! Heaven and Earth are reflected in it, the mirror of all. Empty, still calm plain, quiet silent, non-active, this is the centredness of heaven and Earth and of the Dao and of Virtue.[66]

Actionless action does not mean that one is indolent but rather implies that one acts without prior preconceptions or a will that one brings to one's activities. Openness allows one to remain responsive to other beings. This means not only that one allows them to be but one must recognize their uniqueness in order to act upon it. The sage must be an astute judge of character and situation. The sage is non-active because through his action he does away with the subject-object dichotomy. Instead, he provides an opening through which the diversity of other beings can thrive, which is why his heart is like a mirror. Confucian rituals are assumed to be demonstrative and thus cannot be associated with the art of *wuwei*.

> A man of the highest virtue does not keep to virtue and that is why he has virtue. A man of the lowest virtue never strays from virtue and that is why he is without virtue. The former never acts yet leaves nothing undone. The latter acts but there are things left undone.[67]

In Chinese, the opening line of the text reads: "*shang de bu de, shi yi you de*" (上德不德 是以有德),[68] which suggests that the virtuous man has virtue because he is not virtuous. Once again, the multivalent nature of the language is played upon. *De* (德) can be translated as virtue but is also associated in Daoist thought with the flourishing of particular characteristics of each things. Each thing is assumed to have its own *de*. Thus, he may cultivate difference, while rejecting moral virtue. Unique characteristics can only emerge in interaction with other beings, and thus differentiation and oneness are revealed in the title of the text *Daodejing* (道德經) through the juxtaposition of the terms *dao* and *de*. Everyone has a different *de* that must be cultivated: "The Dao begets all creatures, the virtue rears them, promotes them, nurtures them."[69] The importance of *de* in its title is often underestimated.

In order to stress that the cultivation of virtue takes on many forms, texts like the *Zhuangzi* offer some very unconventional models of the sage. In contrast to the Confucian sage, who plays a very traditional role within the social order, the Daoist sage is often a social or even political rebel. This contrast comes to the surface in a dialogue between an old fisherman and Confucius. The old fisherman remarks about Confucius: "so benevolence is benevolence, yet he won't escape without harm to himself. Exhausting the heart and wearing out the body puts his true nature in jeopardy. Sadly, I believe he is far removed from the Dao."[70] Although Confucius is ridiculed in this interaction, he nevertheless treats the fisherman with a respect that surprises his disciple: "Now this old fisherman stood tall before you with his pole, while you bent double like a musical chime bar, and you always bowed twice before speaking to him."[71] Confucius is not represented as a complete fool, only a partial one. He recognizes the sagacity of the fisherman but ironically turns this into a lesson on moral virtue and cannot dispense with his exaggerated display of deference:

> If you meet a person who is older than you and are not respectful, then this is a failure of etiquette. If you meet a worthy person and fail to offer respect, this is a lack of benevolence.... Now the old fisherman most certainly has the Dao, so how can I not offer respect to him.[72]

Confucius has received the message of the fisherman and recognizes the power of the *dao* but at the same time is deaf to the fisherman's advice to abandon moral virtue. Even a fool like Confucius cannot help being receptive to the *dao* at some level, but at the same time its message falls on deaf ears. Confucius is both mocked and respected in this passage. No one, not even the most hardened Confucian, can be completely unaware of the *dao* even if he perverts its message. In the spirit of openness, the Daoist text embraces even those it mocks.

CONCLUSION

According to Daoist thinkers, morality operates on the basis of a profound dualism that fosters egoistic tendencies that it aspires to keep in check. It is based on an attachment to concepts that are often reified and inextricably woven into the social fabric. Because good needs its opposite, namely the bad or evil to define itself, morality often becomes a line dividing insiders from outsiders, or the noble from the base. This gives rise to rituals of performance surrounding morality, which are often less concerned with virtue than they are with occupying the proper rung on the social hierarchy. For Daoist thinkers, hypocrisy is a natural companion to morality and not merely an unfortunate side effect. Confucius is often presented in Zhuangzi's parables as a pedant who tries to curry favour with government officials, albeit to no avail. Both morality and its opposite are linked to the desire to possess or *you* (有), which means that one tries to bring others into the fold of the self or one's community rather than opening oneself up to spontaneous interaction with them. An egoistic mindset sees the self as a kind of walled entity that thrives on the approbation of others and tries to avoid disapproval or scorn. However, even in so doing, it does not let others penetrate its boundaries.

Instead of promoting codes of moral conduct, Daoist thinkers recommend cultivating openness and nothingness that would allow one to connect to others based on their particular virtues or dispositions (namely, *de*). Oneness and difference are not seen as mutually exclusive in the Daoist canon but rather as correlated, since oneness is based on the interconnection of different beings. The Daoist sage is blissfully unconcerned with her own identity, which is fluid and changes from moment to moment, depending upon who surrounds her.

Both Kierkegaard and Nietzsche would concur with Daoist thinkers that morality often breeds conformity and self-righteous judgment. Kierkegaard acknowledges that ethics cannot be dispensed with altogether since the need for a comfortable abode wherein parameters are clear and behaviour is routinized holds much appeal. Nietzsche's invective against morality is somewhat more acerbic, for he insists that it develops out of a resentment on the part of the weak against the strong and is intended to make the behaviour of others more palatable and predictable. The focus on predictability suggests that Nietzsche, like Daoist thinkers, links morality to the desire to know the world.

Nietzsche and Kierkegaard both argue that it is important to try to shed the chains of egoism, but this process is very much centred on feats of self-overcoming. In Kierkegaard's case, it demands faith in God, who is radically other, to wrench one away from the hold of self-interest. In his view, only this will allow one to treat the other as a particular other, who is irreducible to the self. This is in marked contrast to the thought of Daoist philosophers, who remark that the *dao* is never completely other. No intermediary between self and other is necessary because they are always already connected. The *dao* does not bellow commands from the outside. In fact, its presence is hardly noticed. There is no problem of the other in Daoist thought because all others are linked to one's self in the *dao*.

For Nietzsche, the journey beyond egoism is toilsome, as he illustrated by his metaphor of the three metamorphoses, which celebrates the child. It is extremely difficult to return to the openness of the child who plays with things without prior presuppositions. Furthermore, it is not clear that, according to Nietzsche, egoism can ever be overcome completely. The peasant must assertively defend himself to protect his life and yet, at the same time, overcome this defensiveness in peals of laughter. Zarathustra himself has more trouble with this since he is constantly agonizing about the opinions of his foes and his enemies.

Perhaps the most marked difference between these approaches is that the issue of self-identity and authenticity is very much a concern for Nietzsche and Kierkegaard, whereas the Daoist sage or genuine person is freed from the desire for self-identity. This is most poignantly depicted in the famous butterfly dream of Zhuangzi, who cannot decide whether he is a man dreaming he is a butterfly or a butterfly dreaming he is a man. On one level, this is irrelevant to him. Yet, at the same time, he pronounces that there "must be some sort of difference between Zhuangzi and a butterfly. This is the transformation of things."[73] Zhuangzi and the butterfly are one and the same because they are part of the movement of things that constitutes the *dao*. If they were not different, they could not be connected this way. What this passage reveals is the beauty of celebrating diversity without clinging to one's identity. Thus, according to Daoist thinkers, one cannot cling to one's identity and be liberated from the fetters of egoism. Kierkegaard and Nietzsche, on the other hand, are very much preoccupied with the task of self-making and self-overcoming, and they excoriate moral systems that attempt to undermine this process. Nietzsche and Kierkegaard's authentic individuals are never satisfied with who they are at a particular moment since they strive to go beyond it while the Daoist sage is always satisfied with his current state and for this reason undergoes constant transformation almost painlessly. He has no need for morality because his contentment with himself ensures that he has no reason for doing others harm.

Notes

1 Friedrich Nietzsche, *Beyond Good and Evil*, trans. Walter Kaufmann, in *Basic Writings of Nietzsche* (New York: Modern Library, 1968), Sect. 192.

2 Michael Weston, *Kierkegaard and Modern Continental Philosophy: An Introduction* (London: Routledge, 2003), 67.

3 Friedrich Nietzsche, *Genealogy of Morals*, trans. Walter Kaufmann in *Basic Writings of Nietzsche* (New York: Modern Library, 1968), Sect. I:11.

4 Ibid., I:2.

5 Ibid., I:7.

6 Ibid., II:2.

7 Ibid., I:10.

8 Ibid., I:11.

9 Ibid., II:4.

10 Ibid., II:8.

11 Ibid., II:20.

12 Robert Solomon remarks that Nietzsche often directly adapted the views of Feuerbach: "Nietzsche's case against Christianity depends in large part on his basic acceptance of Feuerbach's view that human beings invented God by divesting themselves of any sense of their own powers." This suggests that human powers are displaced and imputed to God. Robert Solomon, *What Nietzsche Really Said* (New York: Schocken, 2000), 88.

13 Friedrich Nietzsche. *Thus Spoke Zarathustra*, trans. R.J. Hollingdale (Middlesex: Penguin, 1968), 276.

14 Ibid., 87.

15 Ibid., 48.

16 Ibid., 51.

17 Ibid., 82.

18 Ibid., 83.

19 Ibid., 83.

20 Ibid., 53.

21 Ibid., 334.

22 Ibid., 336.

23 Ibid., 336.

24 Ibid., 178.

25 Ibid., 180.

26 Mark Weeks offers a different conception of Nietzsche's laughter. He suggests that Nietzsche's notion of laughter is hierarchical and differentiates the laughter of the height and the laughter of the herd. He makes note of Nietzsche's repeated allusions to "higher laughter" or supra-laughter. Mark Weeks, "Beyond a Joke: Nietzsche and the Birth of Super Laughter," *Journal of Nietzsche Studies* 27 (Spring 2004): 14. However, I argue that the peasant's laughter is different from that of Zarathustra, which is why he cannot comprehend it.

27 Søren Kierkegaard, *Fear and Trembling*, trans. Howard V. Hong and Edna Hong (Princeton: Princeton University Press, 1983), 5.

28 Søren Kierkegaard, *Either/Or*, trans. Howard V. Hong and Edna Hong (Princeton: Princeton University Press, 1987), 256.

29 Ibid., 256.

30 Ibid., 258.

31 Ibid., 259.

32 Ibid., 304.

33 Ibid., 44.

34 Kierkegaard, *Fear and Trembling*, 57.

35 Mark Taylor points out that in Kierkegaard's philosophy, God and human beings are *not* one and remarks that the absolute paradox is due to their absolute antithesis. In this, Kierkegaard's thought differs dramatically from that of Hegel, for whom God and human beings are synthesized. Mark Taylor, *Journeys to Selfhood: Hegel and Kierkegaard* (Berkeley: University of California Press, 1981), 131.

36 Kierkegaard, *Fear and Trembling*, 42.

37 Ibid., 44.

38 Ibid., 45.

39 Ibid., 36.

40 Ibid., 49.

41 Ibid., 94.

42 Ibid., 94.

43 Ibid., 98–99.

44 Laozi, *Tao Te Ching*, trans. D.C. Lau (London: Penguin, 1963), Sect. 1.

45 Laozi, *Daodejing* (Beijing: Beijing University Press, 1995), Sect. 1.

46 Laozi, *Tao Te Ching*, Sect. 25.

47 Ibid., Sect. 18.

48 Ibid., Sect. 2.

49 Laozi, *Daodejing*, Sect. 62.

50 Laozi, *Tao Te Ching*, Sect. 62.

51 Laozi, *Daodejing*, Sect. 62.

52 Zhuangzi, *The Book of Chuang-tzu*, trans. Martin Palmer (London: Arkana Penguin, 1996), chap. 29, 262.

53 Zhuangzi, *The Book of Chuang-tzu*, chap. 29, 262.

54 Laozi, *Tao Te Ching*, Sect. 1.

55 Wang Bi, *Commentary on the Lao-Tzu*, trans. Arianne Rump with Wing-tist Chan (Honolulu: University Press of Hawaii, 1981), 13.

56 Zhuangzi, *The Book of Chuang-tzu*, chap. 2, 20.

57 Ibid., chap. 2, 19.

58 Ibid., chap. 2, 19.

59 Ibid., chap. 2, 20.

60 Zhuangzi, *Zhuangzzi duben* (Taipei: Sanminshu, 1988), chap. 23, 23.

61 Zhuangzi, *The Book of Chuang-tzu*, chap. 2, 20.

62 Ibid., chap. 1, 3.

63 *Zhuangzi duben*, chap. 1, 5.

64 Zhuangzi, *The Book of Chuang-tzu*, chap. 18, 80.

65 Wang Youru, "Philosophy of Change and the Deconstruction of Self in Zhuangzi," *Journal of Chinese Philosophy* 27, no. 3 (2000): 358.

66 Zhuangzi, *The Book of Chuang-tzu*, chap. 13, 106.

67 Laozi, *Tao Te Ching*, Sect. 38.

68 *Daodejing*, Sect. 38.

69 Laozi, *Tao Te Ching*, Sect. 51.

70 Zhuangzi, *The Book of Chuang-tzu*, chap. 31, 286.

71 Ibid., chap. 31, 286.

72 Ibid., chap. 31, 286.

73 Ibid., chap. 2, 20.

Comparative Philosophy of Religion and Modern Jewish Philosophy: A Conversation

MICHAEL OPPENHEIM
Concordia University

The guiding question for this exploration is: What might a conversation between comparative philosophy of religion and modern Jewish philosophy contribute to each participant? The suggestions that follow intimate that, while this conversation is just at its beginning, there are important insights that each side can bring to the other. This is just a single episode in a series of conversations with particular philosophic traditions that comparative philosophy of religion must embark on, but I believe that this step provides one type of model for this lengthy and important process. I will begin with reflections on the nature of philosophy and Jewish philosophy from a comparative perspective, as well as on comparative philosophy of religion itself. This will be followed with an examination of some problem areas in comparative philosophy of religion and Jewish philosophy, and I conclude with discussions about the potentialities for each side to address these problem areas in the terrain of the other. I want to add that certainly at this stage in the development of the discipline of the comparative philosophy of religion no effort can possibly be inclusive enough, *c'est à dire*, we are all learning from each other.

An important lesson in the repertoire of feminist philosophers is that the ways that a philosopher identifies, defines, and approaches philosophic issues reflects a host of conditions. These conditions would include: culture, language, class, age, religious tradition, ethnicity, academic training, conscious and unconscious preferences, and, of course, gender.This understanding, termed "feminist standpoint epistemology," reminds us that each philosopher has a particular horizon with its attendant strengths and weaknesses. These factors both enable and limit the vision of the thinker.[1] A thinker's approach is like a road; it both facilitates travel and restricts possibilities of movement. Consequently, no person is allowed to offer proposals in the name of objectivity or the universal. It is in the context of this understanding that this male modern Jewish philosopher proceeds.

REFLECTIONS ON PHILOSOPHY, JEWISH PHILOSOPHY, AND COMPARATIVE PHILOSOPHY OF RELIGION[2]

The vast majority of philosophers trained in Europe and the Americas assume that the discipline of philosophy is universal. However, what they have in mind is a particular tradition of philosophy rather than an understanding of the plurality of its traditions. While this problem also dramatically haunts the early history of comparative philosophy, many contemporary comparative philosophers of religion recognize that there is more than one tradition of philosophy. Usually scholars identify three major philosophic traditions, although such identifications are not uncontested.[3] These are discussed in terms of South Asian philosophies, Chinese philosophies, and Western philosophies. Each of these has particular concerns and emphases, reigning questions and issues, including such foci as: logic, mathematics, epistemology, ontology, aesthetics, religion, ethics, and political thought. They exhibit a variety of notions of what constitutes reason (and perhaps even logic), the self or non-self, knowledge, the world, and the appropriate methods and *tele* of philosophy. There is also a great amount of internal diversity,[4] since each philosophic heritage has multiple currents, shows changes over time, and waxes and wanes over a period of at least fifteen hundred years. In general, the major currents of South Asian or what is often termed Indian philosophy are linked to Hinduism and Buddhism, which have come to influence not only India but also the other countries of South Asia. Chinese philosophy includes Confucian, Taoist, Buddhist, and Neo-Confucian philosophy, and the countries of China, Japan, and Korea. Western philosophy encompasses the period from the ancient Greeks to the contemporary era and includes those traditions that drew upon Greek philosophy, utilizing its nomenclature, definitions, and issues. There are Christian, Jewish, and Islamic traditions of philosophy, as well as modern Western or what might be termed post-Christian philosophy.

Some scholars even contest the use of the term 'philosophy' to cover such diversity, or suggest alternative designations, such as Ninian Smart's term *darsanas* or worldviews.[5] Still, one can generalize, with much circumspection, about those phenomena that we usually group under the term 'philosophy.' In this case, philosophy is a discipline that addresses some of the widest and most profound human questions: the nature of the human, the universe, the true and the beautiful, as well as what constitutes authentic existence, communal life, and relations with others. What is distinctive to each of the three major traditions of philosophy is the culture(s) and history(ies) or the experiences out of which these streams of philosophy arise, the questions that are most prominent, and the methods used to address these questions. In terms of the prominent questions or fields, a number of scholars have noted the Indian philosophical concern with religion, psychology, and dialectics; Chinese philosophical interests with ethical, political, and social thought as well as aesthetics; and Western philosophical considerations about ontology, epistemology, logic, and mathematics.[6]

In light of the above, it is difficult to suggest a single method or pursuit inclusive enough to do justice to the variety of philosophies. A tentative suggestion might be that these are approaches characterized by reflection that is *articulate*, *sustained*, *critical*, and *self-critical*. The notion of 'articulate,' which I am borrowing from the work of Charles Taylor, is tied to language itself.[7] The word 'articulate' is from the Latin *articulat-us* meaning jointed. The *Oxford Dictionary* includes such additions as: "distinctly jointed or marked; having the parts distinctly recognizable," and in reference to sound; "Divided into distinct parts (words and syllables) having each a definite meaning; as opposed to such inarticulate sounds as a long musical note, a groan, shriek, or the sounds produced by animals."[8] To speak of 'articulate' highlights clarity, meaningful distinctions, and connections. Philosophers use language to examine issues and to present arguments and counter-arguments. Issues are addressed by breaking questions into distinct components, looking into relations, and insisting on providing the maximum appropriate clarity and meaning. The term 'sustained' just reinforces the tenacity or persistence of the process of examination. The word 'critical' refers to uncovering presuppositions and implications of positions and statements. Ideas are not just explored, but, in particular, what both grounds them and leads from them is traced. Finally, philosophy is 'self-critical.' The philosopher not only presents arguments but continually reflects on her or his own position, presuppositions, and implications.[9] Philosophy, and this has special relevance to Indian philosophy,[10] is sometimes taught and performed through debates, where one invites or welcomes the other to critically examine one's own position as part of the process of doing philosophy.[11] The Jewish philosopher Emmanuel Levinas has said that, despite all of Western philosophy's lapses, it is the feature of being self-critical that is both outstanding and redeeming. In his words, "what I am interested in is precisely this ability of philosophy to think, to question itself, and ultimately to unsay itself."[12]

The histories of philosophy are filled with self-critical statements about the nature of philosophy. One of the most compelling contemporary Western positions, which reflects the importance of the "linguistic turn"[13] in many disciplines, is expressed by Richard Rorty. Rorty's much cited essay, "Pragmatism and Philosophy," describes a shift in how Western philosophy itself is seen. He distinguishes between "Philosophy" and "philosophy." Thinkers who believe in "Philosophy" search for ultimate truths that transcend cultures, languages, and particular discourses. Adherents of "philosophy" "compare and contrast cultural traditions" and find that "in the process of playing vocabularies and cultures off against each other, we produce new and better ways of talking and acting."[14] These post-Philosophical philosophers study "the comparative advantages and disadvantages of the various ways of talking that our race has invented."[15] The relevance of this definition of philosophy to comparative philosophy of religion is obvious.

There are multiple and divergent understandings of the nature and scope of Jewish philosophy. As will be discussed later, some thinkers suggest that Jewish philosophy utilizes the methods of [Western] "philosophy" to explore or interpret specific Jewish issues, while others propose a broader understanding of Jewish philosophy. In harmony with the earlier discussion, coming out of a comparative perspective, of the foci of the discipline of philosophy, Jewish philosophers also explore, again, some of the widest and most profound human questions: the nature of the human, the universe, the true, and the beautiful, as well as what constitutes authentic existence, communal life, and relations with others. One of the best examples of this understanding of the scope of Jewish philosophy is found in Franz Rosenzweig's *The Star of Redemption*. The *Star* looks at nothing less than God, humans or "man," and the world, through the integral categories – and Jewish understandings of these categories – of creation, revelation, and redemption. Additionally, in "narrating" a Jewish philosophical view of these topics, Rosenzweig also explores such matters as: mathematics, logic, aesthetics, philosophy, theology, world history, Western intellectual history, world religions, psychology, sociology, political theory, biblical literature, and linguistics.[16]

In addition, Jewish philosophy has always been seen to include, and some even limit it to, the philosophic exploration of specific Jewish topics or issues.[17] For example, in the modern period, Jewish philosophers have addressed such issues as: the essence or character of Judaism, the nature of Jewish identity or what it means to be a Jew, what role Judaism has in the modern world, how continuity with the Jewish past can be maintained or re-established, the importance of Halacha (Jewish law) for individual and communal life, the challenges to religious faith by secularism and the Holocaust, and the impact of both feminism and religious pluralism on Jewish life and thought.

In terms of the broader conception of Jewish philosophy, one of the defining characteristics of this discipline is that its resources emerge out of Jewish history or Jewish experiences. Jewish religion, literature, culture, and history provide the experiences and categories out of which Jewish philosophy is done. Some speak of Jewish experience or Jewish memory,[18] but these terms must always be put in the plural, reminding us of the multiplicity of experiences of Jewish communities and individuals, including the importance of cultural, economic, and social groupings as well as gender. Religion points to Jewish beliefs, practices, and worldviews. Literature might include such sacred texts as the Hebrew Bible, Mishna, and Talmud, as well as the halachic and aggadic commentaries and reflections, and liturgy that arise out of these religious sources. Literature would also include other writings, such as poetry, stories, and novels that may be religious or "secular." The term 'culture' would include the huge variety of cultural productions including such things as folkways, music, dance, and art. Diachronically, Jewish experiences range from the biblical period to the present, and particularly relevant for contemporary Jewish philosophy are the Holocaust, the establishment of the state of Israel, and the Jewish communities in North America. Jewish philosophy reflects out of these foundations and, following an earlier definition, proceeds in ways that are articulate, sustained, critical, and self-critical.

Two fundamental features are deeply embedded within the history of Jewish philosophy and continue to be prominent in the modern period. These are the themes of *community* and *responsibility*. The solitary individual is never a topic in itself. The view that the individual must always be understood in relation to others, in the midst of community is pervasive in Jewish philosophy and in Judaism overall.[19] A full or authentic human life is lived with others. Classically, the relationship to the transcendent is treated within the context of covenant, the covenant between the transcendent and the Jewish people. In more secular positions, the individual is always seen within the umbrella of the people, Israel. Thus, whether the understanding of Judaism reflects a religious, cultural, or national viewpoint, the web of relationships between persons is a central matter of reflection. As the twentieth century Jewish philosopher Martin Buber wrote: "There is no I as such," but only the I in relation.[20]

A second theme is that of responsibility. That web of relationships that links persons together is constituted by responsibilities or obligations. Classically, once again, the covenant is a love relationship delineated through obligations. Halacha was the instrument to live out these obligations, to the transcendent, to the people, and to the neighbour, stranger, poor, orphan, and widow. The philosophical rubric for this concern is, of course, ethics, and many Jewish philosophers have insisted that the centrality of ethics continually distinguishes Jewish philosophy from others streams of Western philosophy.[21]

My own work as a Jewish philosopher has focused on a tributary that includes those twentieth-century Jewish philosophers of the interhuman: Franz Rosenzweig, Martin Buber, and Emmanuel Levinas. The notion of relationship, characterized primarily by responsibility, is the keystone of their thought. Born into relationships with others, into a community and communities, they speak of how one begins as chosen rather than as choosing. They mean by this that to understand the individual one must first see her or him in terms of obligations that both precede one's freedom and define one's uniqueness. This astonishing insight is not only in contrast to the usual notions of the person in the modern West in terms of autonomy and autarchy but is almost an affront to the reigning stream of philosophy of that time and place.

The beginning of the discipline of comparative philosophy of religion is often traced to those three pivotal modern European philosophers who are credited with founding the philosophy of religion in the West. These are the philosophers Hume, Kant, and Hegel, whose contribution to a truly comparative endeavour is being reassessed today.[22] While this is one way to narrate its origin, in my view, comparative philosophy of religion should not be seen as the property of, and thus not beginning within, any one philosophic tradition. To be comparative it requires the dialogue or conversation among philosophers who are looking at religious phenomena from a variety of philosophic traditions and perspectives.[23] In this sense, despite its limits, comparative philosophy of religion properly begins with the First East-West Philosophers' conference of 1939, which took place in Honolulu.

There are two main foci, one constructive and one critical, for comparative philosophy of religion. First, it seeks to introduce and explore comparative definitions, methods, and categories, problems and solutions through conversations and studies about the diverse traditions, communities, and experiences located within the heuristic category of religion. It ultimately seeks to provide philosophic understandings of the variety of ways that humans express the religious meanings and dimensions of their lives. The second focus follows upon the self-critical feature of philosophy discussed above. Comparative philosophy of religion seeks to uncover the "forces of power, domination, resentment, racism, inferiority, prejudice, and a host of other human characteristics [that] are very much a part of our world views, ideologies, philosophies, and conceptual frameworks."[24] It is precisely the comparative aspect, that of dialogue or conversation among thinkers of diverse traditions, that provides the best means for uncovering these distortive and repressive features in all "our world views, ideologies, philosophies, and conceptual frameworks." Additionally, as critics continually insist, just as the impact of these forces is perennial, the process of illumination and correction is interminable. There is a famous admonition in the Mishnah's *Pirke Avot* or *Sayings of the Fathers* (11:21): "You are not required to complete the work, but neither are you free to desist from it."

The following sections of this text will provide an example of the philosophic dialogue between comparative philosophy of religion and particular religious traditions, in this instance modern Jewish philosophy. This treatment will highlight the irreplaceable power of conversation to illuminate specific aporia within and possible correctives for both comparative philosophy and Jewish philosophy.

SOME BASIC PROBLEMS IN COMPARATIVE PHILOSOPHY OF RELIGION AND JEWISH PHILOSOPHY

As indicated above, prior to the 1939 Philosophers' Conference, one may say that the proto-origins of the discipline of philosophy of religion coincides with the beginning of modern Western philosophy. The abjects in the latter haunt the history of the former. The list of these rejected others is well known. Among them include the primitive, "racial" others, women, Jews, and often religion or the religious itself. In various ways, these others stood for the backward and irrational, those bereft – often constitutionally – of the full endowment of reason that defined both man and civilization.[25] The ethno- or euro-centrism of these origins enshrined through various ideologies of phylogenetic development, colonialism, racism, sexism, and anti-semitism bequeathed practices, definitions, norms, and categories that still mitigate against comparativist tasks.[26] For example, Western philosophy of religion has, in the main, failed to respond to contemporary feminist philosophy, to include Jewish philosophy (as well as Islamic philosophy) as having historic and ongoing roles in its own narrative, and often regards "religious belief" as an unproven presupposition, with Western secularism playing the part of the universal and objective.

Some current efforts in the comparative philosophy of religion retain the same monothetic categories and questions, even if the data has been widened.[27] Those classical issues concerning God's existence, evil, the afterlife, the soul, and the relationship between philosophy and "religion" continue to have currency. The task of "justification,"[28] that is, the examination of the phenomenon of religion in order to decide whether it ought to have a place or value in human life has not been abandoned. Religion is still discussed in terms of a variety of myths of origin, seeing it as an inauthentic projection or an irrational response to particular crisis situations.

Finally, while many of the overt ideologies listed above are rejected, and an open, dialogical quest for multi-factor definitions and more inclusive categories is being pursued, there is an alarming void in terms of the impact of feminist philosophy on comparative philosophy of religion. Some of the most critical and inclusive articles seem to see no need for an examination of the contributions of feminist philosophy to the comparative effort.[29] Ten years ago, Marilyn Thie, in an article that was published as part of a group of essays dedicated to feminist philosophy of religion in the journal *Hypatia*, spoke of feminist philosophy of religion as a "field that does not yet exist."[30] While this field has been developing in the past decade, it has left little or no imprint on comparative philosophic work.

A preliminary discussion of the nature of feminist philosophies will illuminate some of the ramifications of this lack. My point of departure will be Thie's article. The title, "Prolegomenon to Future Feminist Philosophies of Religions," emphasized the plurality of feminisms, feminist philosophies, and feminist philosophies of religions. She begins with a definition of feminism:

> Feminist refers to mindsets, consciousness, and so on, which are aligned with liberation struggles that a) take into account the complex interconnections among the various ways peoples' lives are concretely defined, for example, race, class, age, sexual orientation, religion, and ethnicity interacting with gender; b) recognize the structural and institutional nature of interconnected oppressions; and c) acknowledge that only by beginning with the lived experience of multiply-marginalized women

(and those dependent on them) will liberation agendas be sufficiently inclusive, radical, and transforming.[31]

Thie uses the alliteration of adjectives of "political, practical, pluralistic, passionate, and partial," to characterize feminist philosophies of religion.[32] Drawing on her explanation and the work of other feminist philosophers, I would suggest that some of the most distinctive and important features of feminist philosophy include a (political) commitment to justice, the salience of gender as a category of experience and an analytic category, and heightened sensitivities for concrete experiences, especially the experiences and voices of those marginalized. There are also other features that are often prominent in feminist philosophy and feminist thought overall. These would include an understanding of humans as embodied, relational, and part of the natural order of living creatures and the environment.[33] In terms of all of these characteristics, the lives and voices of women are central.

While some philosophers may be "gracious" enough to allow the focus on gender to prove itself over time as a central philosophic category of analysis, it might well be the feature of a prior commitment to justice that is the most problematic for those trained (whether men or women) in traditional Western philosophy. For them, philosophy is a love for or commitment to truth that allows the concern for justice at most and only secondarily as ethics. However, many feminist philosophers hold, in Hava Tirosh-Samuelson's words, that "the act of philosophizing and the telling of the history of philosophy are always political acts,"[34] and thus that the issue of justice is always at play and cannot be ignored or deferred. Similarly, Emmanuel Levinas, who has had great impact on contemporary philosophy, insisted on "ethics as first [the beginning and foundation of] philosophy,"[35] and defined philosophy as; "the wisdom of love at the service of love."[36] Levinas saw this love in terms of responsibility and believed that it was precisely the heritage of Judaism that could bring this imperative, in its full priority and urgency, forward.

In terms of Jewish philosophy, I would like to highlight two problem areas: the way the relationship between [Western] "philosophy" and Jewish philosophy is usually depicted, and the failure, once again, to recognize and enter into a dialogue with feminist Jewish philosophy. As noted earlier, there is a great diversity of views concerning the nature and scope of Jewish philosophy.[37] An influential and diagnostic definition was provided in Julius Guttmann's 1936 classic, *Philosophies of Judaism*. He wrote that: "Since the days of antiquity, Jewish philosophy was essentially a philosophy of Judaism."[38] Some decades later, there was a statement of goals of the Academy for Jewish Philosophy (AJP) in 1979, which saw the task of Jewish philosophy as "enabl[ing] individuals actively involved in some form of Jewish religious life who have professional training in philosophy to think about contemporary Jewish faith in new ways."[39] What is understood by philosophy in this regard is clarified by one of the leaders of the AJP in his statement that Jewish philosophy "should use the tools of analytic philosophy in order to rethink and reformulate all of the traditional religious issues of Judaism as well as the new kinds of questions that arise from Jewish secularism."[40] Philosophy, that is, Western philosophy, provides the methodologies and categories to elucidate Jewish philosophy. In this guise, the history of Jewish philosophy is narrated in terms of series of encounters between the leading systems of Western philosophy, whether Platonic, Aristotelian, Cartesian, Kantian, Hegelian, Existentialist and Phenomenological, and Jewish experience and thought. What is characteristic of this "encounter" is that the direction of inquiry is one way. Philosophy provides the categories and Jewish thought the material, or, in other words, philosophy is the subject and Judaism the object. In this case, Jewish philosophy seeks to understand itself and to explain itself to the other through those purported universal categories of reason[41] that philosophy proffers. The model of a mutually transformative dialogue between the two sides, where each can learn from the other, is not regarded as desirable or even possible.[42] The lack of recognition of Jewish philosophy by Western philosophy referred to above is here reflected in the way Jewish philosophers see themselves, which is a familiar feature in the dynamics exposed by postcolonial thought.

In terms of another possible dialogue, between Jewish (male) philosophers and feminist Jewish philosophy, the situation is not dissimilar. It has been a little over ten years since the appearance of an important article on feminist Jewish philosophy, Hava Tirosh-Samuelson's "'Dare to Know': Feminism and the Discipline of Jewish Philosophy."[43] Recently, Tirosh-Samuelson supplemented her original appeal with the publication of *Women and Gender in Jewish Philosophy*, a book that contains both historical studies of and constructive essays about Jewish philosophy by a variety of authors.[44] Both works challenge contemporary Jewish philosophers, the first by affirming that Jewish philosophy has been impervious to the writings of feminist theorists and philosophers and the second by providing a forum for feminist Jewish philosophers to "re-read" and "re-think" the tradition of Jewish philosophy. While Tirosh-Samuelson's efforts to initiate a "conversation between feminist philosophy, Jewish philosophy, and Jewish feminism,"[45] and the critical writings of a growing group of feminist Jewish philosophers and historians of Jewish philosophy require responses, very few to date have been forthcoming.

Feminism and feminist philosophies have deeply influenced feminist Jewish philosophy. Feminist Jewish thinkers demonstrate the commitment to justice, and the attention to gender, as well as perspectives that highlight humans as embodied, relational, and within the natural order, which were discussed earlier. They speak of some of the most important issues of human life out of the resources of Jewish experience or memory, especially the experiences and memories of Jewish women. Their commitment to justice would include the critical feature of the recognition of the historical ways that Jewish women have been oppressed, repressed, and marginalized in the Jewish tradition. Feminist Jewish philosophers feature a responsibility to transform those elements within the Jewish experience that have caused this oppression, repression, and marginalization, as well as to bring forgotten and silenced Jewish women's voices of the past forward and to create room for such voices in the present and future. There is a growing list of those who define themselves as feminist Jewish philosophers, feminist Jewish thinkers, and feminist theologians.[46] Some of those whose work has been especially helpful to me include: Hava Tirosh-Samuelson, Susan Shapiro, Susannah Heschel, Judith Plaskow, Heidi Ravven, Randi Raskover, Claire Katz, Leora Batnitzky, Laura Levitt, and Rachel Adler.

THE DIALOGUE BETWEEN COMPARATIVE PHILOSOPHY OF RELIGION AND JEWISH PHILOSOPHY

What contributions can comparative philosophy make to Jewish philosophy? In a number of ways, some already foreshadowed, looking at Jewish philosophy in the context of comparative philosophy alters its usual portrayal. First, enigmatically, it sets the stage for a true dialogue, rather than a dictation, between modern Western philosophy and Jewish philosophy. Since the tradition of Western philosophy is only one branch or exemplar of the wider phenomenon of philosophy, the encounter between it and Jewish philosophy is an encounter of particularities. Modern Western philosophy is no longer allowed to portray itself, or to be regarded by Jewish philosophers, as a universal enterprise, the single paradigm of "Philosophy." Modern philosophy can longer be seen as synonymous with reason or the rational. Modern philosophy is the heir of a tradition and of an ongoing community of thinkers, with their particular practices, presuppositions, definitions, categories, and issues. It is as important for Jewish philosophy to dialogue with, learn from, and critique Western philosophy as it is for Western philosophy to proceed similarly. Since both speak out of histories, experiences, and resources that are at the same time specific to each and overlapping, this dialogue should be fascinating and productive.

Second, Jewish philosophy is now open to more than one dialogue partner in this conversation between philosophic traditions. This will deeply influence its self-understanding, as well as multiply its possibilities for development. In addition to the renewal of the medieval discussion with Islam, encounters with different tributaries of Indian and Chinese philosophy should prove rewarding. For example, the centrality of ethics for Jewish philosophy, over ontological and epistemological concerns, may now be seen, not as a break with "Philosophy," but as a legitimate option taken by others. It might be compared with the role of *mokṣa* in many Indian philosophies. The valence given to community within Jewish philosophy might, once again, no longer be seen as a deviation from the single defining norm, but as comparable to the sophisticated treatments of social and political thought within Chinese philosophies.

What contributions can Jewish philosophy make to comparative philosophy? First, the encounter of Indian and Chinese philosophies with Jewish philosophy will reinforce the lesson about the plurality of traditions even within the three main philosophic heritages. Western philosophy will no longer be taken as a single stream of Greek, Christian, and post-Christian philosophy, but one of three traditions coming out of Greek roots. Equally, this recognition will further an understanding of the diversity (of experiences, histories, communities, practices, presuppositions, definitions, categories, and issues) within Indian and Chinese philosophy.

Second, the emergence of feminist Jewish philosophy should prove to be a very significant development for other traditions of philosophy. This might well problematize the notion that feminist philosophy is but a single stream with Christian and post-Christian foundations. Feminist philosophies can not just be dismissed as another colonial effort, synonymous with a homogeneous and dominant West. The critical and creative projects of feminist Jewish thinkers may encourage similar still nascent undertakings. Their commitment to justice, unearthing the historical ways that Jewish women have been oppressed, repressed, and marginalized in the Jewish tradition, should stimulate and contribute to comparable efforts. Their dedication to bringing forward forgotten and silenced Jewish women's voices of the past and to create room for such voices in the present and future should further motivate both female and male philosophers in other traditions to similar questioning and commitments.

Finally, the possible contribution of Levinas's insight about ethics as the foundation for philosophy is intriguing. How would one discuss and what would be the consequences of thinking about "Ethics as First Comparative Philosophy"? How is the new discipline changed when responsibilities and obligations to the other replace the quest for knowing the other – the other as object – as the point of departure for the comparative philosophic endeavour? How does one translate this wisdom in the service of love into specific theoretical breakthroughs and methodological practices?

The conversation between comparative philosophy of religion and modern Jewish philosophy promises to be fruitful for both sides. It stands as an important effort in itself, as well as a model. It reminds us of the vast difficulties in doing justice not only to major philosophic traditions but to the plurality of histories and communities that participate in each one: daunting on the one hand, yet hinting at a plethora of creative possibilities on the other.

Notes

1 The modern Jewish philosopher Franz Rosenzweig provided a colourful rendition of this idea. I would not use the terms "objective" and "subjective" as he does, but the overall meaning is clear. He wrote: "To achieve being objective, the thinker must proceed boldly from his own subjective situation. The single condition imposed upon us by objectivity is that we survey the entire horizon; but we are not obliged to make this survey from any position other than the one in which we are, nor are we obliged to make it from no position at all. Our eyes are, indeed, only our own eyes; yet it would be folly to imagine we must pluck them out in order to see," *Franz Rosenzweig: His Life and Thought*, ed. Nahum N. Glatzer (New York: Schocken, 1961), 179.

2 Portions of this and the following sections have been adapted from my earlier article, "Feminist Jewish Philosophy: A Response," *Nashim* 14 (2007): 209–32.

3 Discussion about great philosophic traditions as well as "world religions" are always problematic in terms of their exclusivity and disparagement of the expressions of other traditions and communities. For a discussion of the attempt to widen understandings of philosophy's traditions, see: Thorsten Botz-Bornstein, "Ethnophilosophy, Comparative Philosophy, Pragmatism: Toward a Philosophy of Ethnoscapes," *Philosophy East and West* 5, no. 1 (2006): 153–71.

4 A number of writers have alluded to Western philosophy's dominant narrative, which falsely portrays its history as unitary. See the two chapters, Daya Krishna, "Comparative Philosophy: What It Is and What It Ought to Be," 76, and Ninian Smart, "The Analogy of Meaning and the Tasks of Comparative Philosophy," 176, both in the volume *Interpreting across Boundaries*, edited by Gerald Larson and Eliot Deutsch (Delhi: Motilal Banarsidass, 1989).

5 Ninian Smart, *World Philosophies* (London: Routledge, 2000), 7.

6 See Smart, *World Philosophies*, 1–11, and also Ben-Ami Scharfstein, "The Three Philosophical Traditions," in *A Comparative History of World Philosophy: From the Upanishads to Kant* (Albany, NY: SUNY Press, 1998).

7 Charles Taylor has two fine essays on the role of articulation in philosophy in "The Person," in *The Category of the Person*, edited by Michael Carrithers, Steven Collins, and Steven Lukes (Cambridge: Cambridge University Press, 1985), 272, 275, 280; and "Comparison, History, Truth" in *Myth and Philosophy*, edited by Frank E. Reynolds and David Tracy (Albany, NY: SUNY Press, 1990), 41, 48.

8 *The Compact Edition of the Oxford English Dictionary*, vol. I (Oxford: Oxford University Press, 1971), p. 118. By the way, I am uncomfortable with the example of animals for a variety of reasons.

9 These reflections on the nature and methods of philosophy share a number of features with

two twentieth-century Chinese philosophers, Hu Shi and Feng Youlan, discussed in Carine Defoort, "Is 'Chinese Philosophy' a Proper Name?: A Response to Rein Raud," in *Philosophy East and West* 56, no. 4 (2006): 625–60. The former defined philosophy as; "In general, a discipline that studies the most important questions of human life, a fundamental reflection that wants to find a fundamental solution to these questions: this is called philosophy," 634. Defoort paraphrases the latter's definition as: "something to do with a rational, systematic, original, subdivided inquiry into fundamental matters of human life and the world," 635.

10 Scharfstein, "The Three Philosophical Traditions," 31.

11 Rosenzweig spoke of a philosophic "New Thinking," that is "in need of the other," *Franz Rosenzweig's "The New Thinking,"* edited by Alan Udoff and Barbara E. Galli (Syracuse: Syracuse University Press, 1999), 87.

12 Emmanuel Levinas, "Dialogue with Emmanuel Levinas," in *Face to Face with Levinas*, edited by Richard A. Cohen (Albany, NY: SUNY Press, 1986), 22.

13 See Terry Eagleton, *Literary Theory: An Introduction* (Minneapolis: University of Minnesota Press, 1983), 60.

14 Richard Rorty, "Pragmatism and Philosophy," in *After Philosophy: End or Transformation?*, edited by Kenneth Baynes, James Bohman, and Thomas McCarthy (Cambridge, MA: MIT Press, 1987), 54.

15 Rorty, "Pragmatism and Philosophy," 58.

16 See Franz Rosenzweig, *The Star of Redemption*, trans. Barbara E. Galli (Madison: University of Wisconsin Press, 2005). This understanding of Jewish philosophy is also discussed by Heidi Ravven in her "Observations on Jewish Philosophy," *Judaism* 46, no. 4 (1997): 422–38. As I read her essay, she speaks of the two aspects of Jewish philosophy as "philosophical exploration and Jewish elaboration," 425, or "Philosophical accounts that explore universal aspects of a shared humanity as well as cultural particularities," 427.

17 See author's article, "Some Underlying Issues of Modern Jewish Philosophy," in *Truth and Compassion: Essays on Judaism and Religion in Memory of Rabbi Dr. Solomon Frank*, edited by Howard Joseph, Jack N. Lightstone, and Michael D. Oppenheim (Waterloo, ON: Wilfrid Laurier University Press, 1983), 91–109.

18 Heidi Ravven, in an insightful and nuanced discussion, describes the resources for Jewish philosophy in terms of Jewish memory. Memory has the advantage of including Jewish identity and allowing for the continual reassessment and reconfiguration of the Jewish past. See "Observations on Jewish Philosophy," 196–200.

19 Israeli philosopher Eliezer Schweid has argued that the individual's ties to her or his family, people, culture, and history provide the platform for both authenticity and creativity, in *The Solitary Jew and His Judaism* [Hebrew] (Tel Aviv: Am Oved, 1974), 17.

Also see the article "Community," by Everett E. Geller, *Contemporary Jewish Religious Thought: Original Essays on Critical Concepts, Movements, and Beliefs*, edited by Arthur A. Cohen and Paul Mendes-Flohr (New York: The Free Press, 1987), 81–85.

20 Martin Buber, *I and Thou* (New York: Charles Scribner's Sons, 1970), 54.

21 Steven S. Schwarzschild has expressed the centrality of ethics throughout the history of Jewish philosophy as: "The view held here ... is that philosophy is Jewish by virtue of a transhistorical primacy of ethics," in "Modern Jewish Philosophy," *Contemporary Jewish Religious Thought*, 629.

22 See David Tracy, "On the Origins of Philosophy of Religion: The Need for a New Narrative of Its Founding," in *Myth and Philosophy*, ed. Frank E. Reynolds and David Tracy (Albany, NY: SUNY Press, 1990), pp. 11–36.

23 Krishna's definition of comparative studies, the attempt to look at what "is 'another reality' from the viewpoint of that which is not itself," underscores the significance of dialogue, "Comparative Philosophy," 72.

24 Gerald Larsen, "Introduction: The 'Age-Old Distinction between the Same and the Other,'" in *Interpreting across Boundaries*, 16.

25 Celia Brickman traces a parallel history in her treatment of psychoanalysis, in *Aboriginal Populations in the Mind: Race and Primitivity in Psychoanalysis* (New York: Columbia University Press, 2003). Additionally, Morny Joy examines the similar dynamics of the "othering" of non-Western cultures and of women, when she writes: "For, as many women authors have indicated, the process of 'othering' that has been inflicted by dominant Western values on other cultures, is similar to the way women (in both Western and many other societies) have been judged and found wanting according to the prevailing standards of masculinity and/or rationality," in "Beyond a God's Eyeview: Alternative Perspectives in the Study of Religion," in *Perspectives on Method and Theory in the Study of Religion*, edited by Armin W. Geertz and Russell T. McCutcheon (Leiden: Brill, 2000), 112.

26 Larsen sees the core of "ethnocentricism" as a Hegelian legacy through which the non-West is either assimilated or surpassed, "Introduction: The 'Age-Old Distinction between the Same and the Other,'" 8.

27 See, for example, Joseph Runzo, *Global Philosophy of Religion: A Short Introduction* (Oxford: Oneworld Publications, 2001). His book also has some helpful innovations, including a chapter on "Love and the Meaning of Life."

28 See David Tracy's article, "On the Origins of Philosophy of Religion," 14–15.

29 For example, two fine articles on critical problems in comparative philosophy of religion fail to introduce any discussion of feminist issues in the study of religion: Gerald Larson's "Introduction: The 'Age-Old Distinction between the Same and the Other,'" and Daya Krishna's "Comparative Philosophy: What It Is

and What It Ought to Be." On a more positive note, Morny Joy, in "Beyond a God's Eyeview: Alternative Perspectives in the Study of Religion," explores the challenges and insights that feminists, particularly through the voices and perspectives of non-Western women, contribute to the contemporary study of religion.

30 Marilyn Thie, "Epilogue: Prolegomenon to Future Feminist* Philosophies of Religions," *Hypatia* 9, no. 4 (1994): 229.

31 Thie, "Epilogue," 229.

32 Ibid., 231.

33 A number of feminist philosophers could be cited who show the integration of all of these features, one of the most important is the French feminist philosopher Luce Irigaray. Additionally, Hava Tirosh-Samuelson provides an excellent description of central characteristics of feminist philosophy in [Hava Tirosh-Rothschild] "'Dare to Know': Feminism and the Discipline of Jewish Philosophy," *Feminist Perspectives on Jewish Studies*, edited by Lynn Davidman and Shelly Tenenbaum (New Haven, CT: Yale University Press, 1994), 85–96.

34 Hava Tirosh-Samuelson, "Editor's Introduction: Jewish Philosophy in Conversation with Feminism," *Women and Gender in Jewish Philosophy*, edited by Hava Tirosh-Samuelson (Bloomington: Indiana University Press, 2004), 7.

35 One of Levinas's most famous essays is titled, "Ethics as First Philosophy," in *The Levinas Reader*, edited by Sean Hand (Oxford: Basil Blackwell, 1989), 75–87.

36 Emmanuel Levinas, *Otherwise Than Being Or Beyond Essence* (The Hague: Martinus Nijhoff, 1981), 162.

37 See the discussion of the nature of Jewish philosophy in *Studies in Jewish Philosophy: Collected Essays of the Academy for Jewish Philosophy, 1980–1985*, edited by Norbert Samuelson (Lanham, MD: University Press of America, 1987).

38 Julius Guttmann, *Philosophies of Judaism* (London: Routledge and Kegan Paul, 1964), 4.

39 Norbert Samuelson, "The Death and Revival of Jewish Philosophy," *Journal of the American Academy of Religion* 70, no. 1 (2002): 117.

40 Samuelson, "The Death and Revival of Jewish Philosophy," 121. Although the lack of consensus about the nature of this topic is highlighted in Tirosh-Samuelson's "Editor's Introduction," this description seems to cover many of the viewpoints that she identifies. In "Dare to Know," she defines Jewish philosophy as: "a systematic reflection about Judaism by means of philosophical categories and in light of philosophical questions," 98.

41 For example, Tirosh-Samuelson speaks of "the secular, universal truth-claims of philosophy," in "'Dare to Know'," 98.

42 Emil Fackenheim is one example of those who see the possibility and necessity for a more balanced dialogue. In the essay, "Jewish Philosophy in the Academy," in Emil Fackenheim, *Jewish Philosophers and Jewish Philosophy* (Bloomington: Indiana University Press, 1996), 189–92, he discusses three contemporary areas where Jewish philosophy might

critique or contribute to (Western) philosophy, which are tied to the Holocaust, the establishment of the state of Israel, and the nature of Jewish identity.

43 Tirosh-Rothschild, "'Dare to Know'."

44 Tirosh-Samuelson, *Women and Gender in Jewish Philosophy.*

45 Tirosh-Samuelson, "Dare to Know," 85.

46 At this time, such titles as feminist Jewish philosopher, feminist Jewish thinker, and feminist Jewish theologian have no consistent usage.

Philosophy, Medicine, Science, and Boundaries

DAN LUSTHAUS
Harvard University

The *Caraka-saṃhitā* is widely accepted as the earliest extant Indian medical text. Its founding ideas are attributed to an ancient preceptor named Ātreya and his disciple Agniveśa, about whom we know very little that is not deeply drenched in conflicting hagiographia. The core redaction of this text is attributed to someone named Caraka, whose historical identity is equally soaked in conflicting hagiographical details.[1] In this text, however, we find, along with a plethora of medical information about sundry physical and mental illnesses, symptoms, drugs, herbs, diagnostic theory, and principles, methods of prognosis, treatments, anatomical theory, and so on, what is usually considered to be the first appearance of the theory of *pramāṇa*, the instruments or means by which knowledge is acquired. Medieval Indian philosophy – after the *Nyāya-sūtra* (which appears to have been influenced by the *Caraka-saṃhitā* [hereafter *CS*] in its own treatment of the *pramāṇas*), and especially after the innovations in epistemology and logic developed by the Buddhist philosophers Dignāga and

Dharmakīrti – devoted much of its energy and attention to arguments and refinements of *pramāṇa* theory.

For centuries, *pramāṇa* theory was the grounding discipline for all Indian philosophy, no matter which school or tradition one belonged to. Why did it first appear in India in a medical text? Does that make the *CS* a philosophical text or a medical text with some philosophical sections? Is this a question for comparative philosophy or for comparative "history" of science? I will try in this paper to both complicate and clarify those questions.

COMPARED TO WHAT?

This essay will be a departure from my usual approach, which would be to focus on a careful reading of a text or limited range of texts. Instead, here, I will raise more general issues gathered from some of the thoughts I have had over the years as a practitioner of what could be called comparative philosophy, ideas raised by working on a variety of materials in a variety of religious and philosophical traditions. For the most part, what will be offered are, not so much conclusions, but possible research directions or considerations for myself and other practitioners of this sort of philosophy, though, as I will suggest in a moment, in some very important sense, *all* philosophy is comparative.

All thinking is comparative: *X* and non-*X*, *X* and *Y*, *Q* implicating *R*; all thinking presupposes notions of identity and difference. In what ways are *X* and *Y* the same or different? All relations presuppose at least two things must be different from each other, and at the same time united in a common relation. When we wish to test whether our students can think rather than regurgitate, we ask them to write essays that "compare and contrast" one idea, or system, or theory, etc., with another. Rubbing things together creates mental friction, which can, under the right conditions, ignite insightful and even innovative thinking – a type of creative *tapas* in the Ṛg Vedic sense.[2] A contemporary philosopher tackling Plato, or Aquinas, or Descartes, or Hegel, or Frege, or Whitehead, or Derrida is, in effect, doing comparative philosophy, comparing the thought of another time and/or place, often in another language, with one's own. Even when philosophizing strictly within one's own contemporaneous idiom with one's contemporaries, one is thinking comparatively of one idea with another, or one theory with another, though obviously within a much more restricted horizon of comparative possibilities. Hence, there is a risk of ideational sterility unless new ideas, imported from elsewhere, can revivify the ideational pool. That "other" source can be a foreign philosophy, a system from another time, or simply the appearance of someone with new ideas that stem from bringing some new factor or permutation into the current discourse.[3]

Someone wrestling with Plato or Aristotle is engaged in something very much like what someone wrestling with medieval Indian or ancient Chinese philosophy encounters, i.e., an encounter with a foreign language that 'thinks' and expresses itself differently than we do today. This involves systems of thought embedded in alien cultural and conceptual horizons whose meanings and orientations must be recovered through whatever means available or devisable. At the same time, translating the ideas in these alien texts into our thinking patterns often requires negotiation with a complicated set of texts, commentaries, divergent interpretations, and hermeneutic challenges. These in turn may be riddled with painful lacunae in terms of missing pieces, unknown opponents, and multiple contexts, often indistinct (or less distinct than we might imagine them). These texts and their contexts all remain moving targets that are re-imagined and re-configured by every generation that attempts to think through these text-sets afresh. All of this is wrapped in an ever-increasingly dense accrual of baggage and assumptions requiring discriminative weeding. The encounter can engender a massive oedipal confrontation, or a minor re-arrangement of trivial details, or a refashioning to suit current tastes and needs. Of these last three alternatives, the first is likely to produce philosophy; the second, some form of scholasticism or doxography; and the last, revisionism or fundamentalism.[4]

Yet we tend to think of Greek, or Christian, or German philosophy, and so on, as part of *our* "tradition," *our* history, while *Caraka-saṃhitā*, Dignāga's *Pramāṇa-samuccaya*,[5] *Cheng weishilun* 成唯識論 (Treatise Establishing *Vijñapti-mātra*),[6] and Zhu Xi's 朱熹 *Jinsi lu* 近思錄 (Reflections on Things at Hand[7]) are not. Some Western philosophers still insist that non-Western philosophy is not philosophy at all, but even if generously granted the label of "philosophy," they don't practice *our* philosophy, i.e., what we consider to be philosophy proper. In a more ambiguous status are works by Islamic and Jewish philosophers such as Ibn

Sīnā, Ibn Rushd, Maimonides, Gersonides[8] and Crescas.[9] Their ambiguity is due to the fact that, while they are rarely part of the curriculum of Western philosophy, it is recognized that important figures in Western philosophy, such as Aquinas and Spinoza, were aware of and were influenced by them. Buber and Levinas have impacted the academy, but Rosenzweig and Hermann Cohen still remain primarily "tribal" reading. One obvious goal of comparative philosophy would be to expand the horizons of our sense of "our" tradition. Laozi and Zhuangzi now *are* part of *our* tradition. One could even argue, without too much inaccuracy or perversity, that making the *Upaniṣads* a metonymy for Indian thought was an invention of *our* tradition more than a fair appraisal of the actual history of Indian philosophy, one with which certain factions in India became complicit. Nonetheless, the status of such divisions between "our" and "their" tradition has become increasingly ambiguous over the last century, as texts such as the *Bhagavad Gītā*, the *Daodejing*, and the *Zhuangzi* have become staples of humanities programs (and even popular reading), while, in Asia, Western fare has taken firm root in standard curriculums. The East-West divide is more imaginary than real these days – more a question of identity politics than a characterization of styles of thinking.

We are situated in a very privileged place. Rarely has such a large segment of the world had such access to so much of the world's philosophical literature.

It is an historical truism that philosophies are at their innovative best when located at the intersection of competing systems. Philosophical xenophobia leads to stagnation, as the results of the largely successful efforts by Anglo-American philosophers to expel even the philosophy of their European contemporaries from the curriculum of philosophy departments sadly illustrates. Rorty sneaking Heidegger in through the backdoor has proven insufficient to revitalize the analytic project. He failed partly because so much of what made the German and French philosophies of the twentieth century vital was lost or distorted in reductionistic translation.[10]

Philosophy is not just any thought on something novel but a disciplined form of thought, at once tradition- and rule-bound, and yet seeking new discoveries or insights. Different philosophical traditions assume different rules and rhetorical styles. Some prize exhaustively detailed prose exposition in formalized univocal syntax – e.g., a syllogism – while others prefer evocative, poetic multivocality designed to say more with fewer words. Some seek to express their syllogisms and rigorous method in the pithiest of verses. Whatever its style, philosophy seeks to reason, i.e., to apply reason methodically to a topic or agenda.

My interest at the moment, however, is not to argue for some sense of the universality of comparison. (As soon as universals become sufficiently restricted to allow comparison with other universals or particulars, they lose some of their presumed universality.) Neither is it to essentialize some notion of philosophy, but rather to think about what 'reasoning' means in different philosophies, and what sorts of typical gestures and characteristics reasoning exhibits in various philosophies. I am not proposing a definition of "reason" beforehand in order to remain open to possible suggestions offered by the different traditions.

QUESTIONING PARAMETERS

To advance more quickly, let me throw out some questions.

Is there something that makes Chinese philosophy – if there is any such unitive discipline as opposed to multiple, divergent philosophical and religious traditions that we lump together on the basis of a common historical and geographical proximity – distinctively a Chinese philosophy? And so on for Indian, Islamic, Jewish, etc., philosophies. Deciding this is important if we wish to know what is being compared to what when we propose to do comparative philosophy. As we will see, this also entails the question of where our centre of gravity lies: *From where* do we begin to compare? What sets the agenda? Is comparative philosophy done from a home base looking out at the "others"? Or do we try to locate ourselves in some privileged neutral or lofty position from which we look down at the objects being compared, as if implicated by or committed to none of them? Is there any viable standpoint upon which a comparative philosopher can take his or her stand?

Might it be the case that so-called Western philosophy is also distinctively "Christian" philosophy, even when practised by non-Christians (such as Spinoza, Aristotle, Nietzsche, modern secularists, etc.), such that Hegel – despite coining the phrase "death of God" – is after all at bottom a Christian thinker? Does his *Encyclopedia* – consisting of the tripartite *Logic, Nature, Spirit* – bear only a superficial structural and conceptual parallel with the Trinity, or is there something more fundamental at play?

Has Spinoza become a Buddhist when he identifies the three primary affects – the affects from which all other affects are derived by permutational combinations – as pleasure, pain, and desire? In Buddhist jargon pleasure-pain is called *vedanā* while desire in a primary sense is called *tṛṣṇā*. *Vedanā* and *tṛṣṇā* are two of the most important *nidānas* in the twelve-fold chain of *pratītya-samutpāda* (conditioned co-arising), often considered Buddhism's premier doctrine. Pleasure, pain, and desire in Spinoza's system of affects play a similar primary role as do *vedanā* and *tṛṣṇā* in Buddhist discourse. Or is this model Jewish, since Spinoza partly draws on Crescas' ethical philosophy for these and other components of his own?[11] What else would Spinoza have to include or exclude before we see his philosophy as Buddhistic, in the same way that Pure Land, Huayan, or Tantra are seen as, at one and the same time, deeply similar yet profoundly dissimilar to the Buddhist teachings of the early Pali canon? Might Spinoza be closer to, for instance, Pali Buddhism or Huayan Buddhism, than either is to Pure Land or Tantra?

What makes these distinctive types of philosophy distinctive? What, aside from their different narrative histories and accidental differences (language, socio-political factors, institutional support or suppression, changing fashions in styles and rhetoric, etc.), makes them distinctive from each other *as philosophies*? Are there characteristic factors that can be enumerated? How do we bracket our expectations of what is properly "philosophy" in order to inquire fairly into such a question? Even more problematically, how do we circumscribe what counts as "religion"?

It is axiomatic in Indian philosophy that a definition must be sufficiently restricted so as to exclude anything that is not the case, and broad enough to include everything that is the case. Western scholars will quickly recognize that this is rarely as simple as it seems, especially when trying to find a stable referent for a term as famously difficult to define adequately as "religion." Christian or so-called Western presuppositions concerning what counts as a "religion" quickly exclude many of the world's leading religions, such as Buddhism, Confucianism, Mīmāṃsa, Sāṃkhya, Jainism, etc. This is because these either reject or give short shrift to deities and especially deny a central role to a Divinity with a capital "D." These are major religions explicitly devoid of "God." Responding to that by enlarging the definition of religion into something as inclusive as Tillich's "man's ultimate concern" fails to exclude Marxism, health care, sports, romance, ego-gratification, and a host of other -isms and human pursuits. Similarly, the Western notion that religion is grounded in faith and belief rather than reason and logic would be anathema to many Indian traditions (and even some pre-Renaissance Western religions). If the essence of religion requires neither God nor belief, such that these are contingent properties appropriate only for describing *some* religions, then what essentially marks a religion as a religion? We partially run into such problems because we start within the assumptions and "evidence" of our Western traditions and then try to explain the "other" traditions in terms of how well or adequately they mirror our own. In this way, we set the agenda and prioritize the importance of issues based on what our religions claim is important. Since other religions revolve around different centres of gravity, inconvenient anomalies invariably emerge. If we believe that "our" religion is paradigmatic for all religions, then its concerns must also constitute the paradigmatic underpinnings of *any* proper religion. Consequently, when faced with the aforementioned anomalies, if "our" concerns and definitions render other traditions marginal or insufficient relative to what we deem the "ultimate" and most essential concerns, the fault lies with them, not us.

What would this look like if, instead of taking Christian assumptions as the baseline, we let other traditions formulate their own consensus among themselves as to what counts as central concerns? What if Christianity was deemed marginal or insufficient by that exercise? What if, for example, one places ethical canons (*halakhah*, *shāri'a*, *dharma-śāstra*, *vinaya*, Confucian codes, even Daoist ethical treatises) at the core of what would constitute a religion? Then Christianity becomes the odd religion out. Christianity emits a great deal of moralism (much of it centred on "bedroom ethics"), but it lacks a foundational ethical canon that plays a comparable role to *shāri'a* in Islam, or *halakhah* in Judaism, or *dharma-śāstra* in Hinduism, *vinaya* in Buddhism. These ethical canons are typically more important than "belief" in determining the degree of one's participation in these religions. This is not merely an ethnographic question but has immediate philosophical import. For instance, is it, as some have conjectured, due to the strong emphasis on the ethical in Judaism that Jewish philosophers predominantly embraced Aristotle – rather than Plato or explicit forms of Neo-Platonism – during medieval times, and Kant in modern times? What is lacking, in the Western study of religion or in Western philosophical method, is a well-formed discipline that deals with the canons and reasoning styles of religious jurisprudence. (This is in contradistinction to such well-worn and traditionally Christian disciplines as ontology, myth, epistemology, and exegesis.) As such, this lack is a symptom of an evident myopia, and thus a potentially fatal challenge that is presently threatening to render Western scholars irrelevant to the growing religious confrontations. Such confrontations are occurring not only abroad but within our own shores (despite however relevant we may feel ourselves to be from within our own frameworks). For instance, we become reduced to mouthing questionable ideological, ahistorical claims when we insist that Islamists in Somalia are misusing the term *jihad* as they declare Holy War on their government and suspected Ethiopian (which, in their eyes, means Christian) interference. As a result, we fail to explain adequately to our students how jurisprudential reasoning works. At the same time, while searching for alternatives to military confrontation, we lack a commonly respected language and the recognized disciplined reasoning skills to address the holders of such worldviews on their own terms. This is very obvious in discussions of the role of women in Islam, caste inequities with Hindutvas, or abortion rights with evangelical and fundamentalist Christians. (In contrast, e.g., Palestinians and Iranians have demonstrated deft command of *our* rhetorical polemics of rights, self-determination, post-colonial *ressentiment*, etc.) One might ask therefore whether Kant's Practical Reason (and its spawn) include or occlude jurisprudential thinking? Is his ethical thinking the same or different as ethical thinking within religious traditions?

In a lighter but equally serious vein, as one surveys the religions of the world one finds in every religion – except Christianity – a sacred humour tradition. Midrashic and Hasidic tales in Judaism, Zen anecdotes and kōan collections in Buddhism, the ironic parodies in *Zhuangzi*, the tales of Mullah Nasruddin in Islam, Śiva's *līlā* (play), and so on, are best known, but only the tip of a largely unexplored iceberg. For most religions, sacred humour is an important component of the spiritual path, an attunement to the Cosmic Giggle, as some have called it. In contrast, Christians, as Umberto Eco's *Name of the Rose* highlighted, have often condemned comedy, laughter, humour, and even smiling as sacrilegious.[12] This was not merely a medieval predilection but still influences contemporary Christianity. When, in the 1950s, inspired by Aldous Huxley's

Doors of Perception,[13] the British scholar of Indian and Iranian religion, Richard Zaehner, decided to experiment with mescaline under clinical supervision, he subsequently declared the experience "profane" rather than "sacred." This was largely because all of his attempts to have a "sacred" experience while under the influence of mescaline (visiting his favourite cathedral, looking at pictures of the Virgin Mary, etc.) resulted in laughter, either an urge within himself, or "hallucinations" of the figures in the stained glass windows laughing at him, etc. The book he wrote on this is in two parts.[14] The second part is an abridged but still lengthy transcript of his "trip," in which one needn't be a clinical psychologist to discern that his experiences were concertedly advising him to lighten up and enjoy the humour – a message he not only resisted but found shocking and disturbing. The result was the book's first part in which, clothed in the guise of objective scholarly discourse, he laid out a hierarchic typology of religious mysticisms, with such labels as "pantheism" and "panentheism."[15] The obvious purpose was to reaffirm the superiority of the Roman Catholic variety to which he had converted, deeming the mysticisms of other religions less sacred and even profane. His typology was influential in the field for some time, but, as an example of bald apologetics, should stand as a cautionary tale for all comparativists.

Such assumptions concerning what counts as a religion or as legitimate philosophy lead us to become selective about which literature we pay attention to, and even what parts to focus on in the literature we do select. What is Buddhist or Hindu ontology? Is there a Daoist theory of language? What are Neo-Confucian metaphysics? Such are our typical questions, but are they typical, much less prominent features of these traditions, as our sustained and narrow attention to them would seem to imply?

If a Hindu and an observant Jew begin to converse, they would quickly discover that *dharma-śāstra* and *halakhah* – which are more constitutive of each's sense of identity and practice within their own traditions – speak the same language. They share similar concerns about proper and improper foods, business affairs, daily behaviour, hygiene, familial and social obligations, ways to celebrate, etc. However, a Christian observer of that discussion might wonder what the bulk of their discussion had to do with "religion." He may be envious of the poignant traditional humour tales they trade. And the Christian would likely overlook or resist that for the

Jew and the Hindu, what you *do* is infinitely more important religiously than what you personally *believe*. A Hindu can believe in one, many, or no gods, and still be a good Hindu; what he or she cannot do is violate the specific dictates and mores of his or her caste and still be deemed a "good" Hindu. At the level of *dharma-śāstra* and *halakhah*, such matters are no longer ad hoc or sociological (or even ethnographic). They are instead philosophical, to be attended to with all the rigour of a system of detailed, rational jurisprudence, one which has for millennia pervaded every facet of social, personal, and spiritual life.

BOUNDARIES

The boundaries between "philosophy" and "religion" (and science, medicine, physics, grammar, linguistics, astronomy, rhetoric, hermeneutics, etc.) are unclear, and the separations between such disciplines that we take for granted today were less clear even in the West a century or so ago. Philosophers and scientists, for instance, were often the same people during the Middle Ages in Islamic and Jewish circles. Ibn Sīnā (Avicenna), Ibn Rushd (Averroës), Maimonides (Rambam),[16] Gersonides (Ralbag), etc., all made major scientific contributions,[17] and, with the exception of Gersonides,[18] all were practising physicians esteemed for their medical skills during their day.[19] Kant may have been the last of this breed of scientist-philosophers, at least in the Western tradition, since he is credited with discovering the existence of galaxies. (Similarly, all except Ibn Sīnā and Kant were prominent jurisprudents of their day. Maimonides, for example, in his *Mishneh Torah*, was the first to organize the full gamut of Jewish law into a systematic code. This, along with his Responsa and other halakhic works, continues to be influential and studied today.)

Nor were such scientific endeavours done in isolation. While certain Islamic and Jewish religious matters may have been primarily in-group matters, scientific knowledge was shared and common. Maimonides (1135–1204) and Ibn Rushd (1126–1198) – contemporaries born in Cordoba, Spain – drew from the same medical well-springs. (This occurred even though Maimonides' family had to flee Spain due to the persecution of Jews by the Almohades; he completed his secular education at the famous University of Al-Karaouine in Fez, Morocco.) And such knowledge was far more globally disseminated than is usually recognized.

"The greatest tribute paid to the Indian [medical] system came from Avicenna [Ibn Sīnā], who categorically acknowledged in *Al Qanun* (*The Canon*) that he had benefited tremendously from the Indian *jogis* he used as one of his sources."[20]

The convergence of philosophy and medicine was not a creation of the Middle Ages. In the West, philosophy and medicine have been intimately related at least since Diocles of Carystus (fourth century BCE) and Aristotle. As van der Eijk states: "the relationship between Aristotelianism and medicine has long been a neglected area in scholarship on ancient medicine."[21] One might add that the same neglect is evident in scholarship on ancient philosophy. While the present essay cannot substantially remedy that neglect, a few of van der Eijk's observations about Greek medicine and philosophy – which have striking parallels in the case of India – may help bring some attention to what it is we have been neglecting.

> … more recently there has been a greater appreciation of the fact that Greek medical writers did not just reflect a derivative awareness of developments in philosophy – something which led to the long-standing qualification of medicine as a 'sister' or 'daughter' of philosophy – but also actively contributed to the developing concepts and methodologies for the acquisition of knowledge and understanding of the natural world. (Philip J. van der Eijk, *Medicine and Philosophy in Classical Antiquity*, p. 8)
>
> Moreover, it would be quite misleading to present the relationship between "doctors" and "philosophers" in terms of interaction between "science" and "philosophy," the "empirical" and the "theoretical," the "practical" and the "systematical," the "particular" and the "general," or "observation" and "speculation." To do this would be to ignore the "philosophical," "speculative," "theoretical," and "systematic" aspects of Greek science as well as the extent to which empirical research and observation were part of the activities of people who have gone down in the textbooks as "philosophers." Thus Empedocles, Democritus, Parmenides, Pythagorus, Philolaus, Plato, Aristotle, Theophrastus, Strato, but also later thinkers such as Sextus Empiricus, Alexander of Aphrodisias, Nemesius of

Emesa, and John Philoponus took an active interest in subjects we commonly associate with medicine, such as anatomy and physiology of the human body, mental illness, embryology and reproduction, youth and old age, respiration, pulses, fevers, the causes of disease and of the effects of food, drink and drugs on the body. (p. 10)

... Galen ... wrote a treatise advocating the view that the best doctor is, or should be, at the same time a philosopher.... It is no coincidence that Aristotle's comments on the overlap between "students of nature" and "doctors" are made in his own *Parva naturalia*, a series of works on a range of psycho-physiological topics – sense-perception, memory, sleep, dreams, longevity, youth and old age, respiration, life and death, health and disease – that became the common ground of medical writers and philosophers alike. (p. 11)

... interaction... also took place in the field of methodology and epistemology. As early as the Hippocratic medical writers, one finds conceptualizations and terminological distinctions relating to such notions as a "nature" (*phusis*), "cause" (*aitia, prophasis*), "sign" (*sēmeion*), "indication" (*tekmērion*), "proof" (*pistis*), "faculty" (*dunamis*), or theoretical reflection on epistemological issues such as causal explanation, observation, analogy, and experimentation. This is continued in fourth-century [BCE] medicine, with writers such as Diocles of Carystus and Mnesitheus of Athens, in whose works we find striking examples of the use of definition, explanation, division and classification according to genus and species relations, and theoretical reflection on the modalities and the appropriateness of these epistemological procedures, on the requirements that have to be fulfilled in order to make them work. (p. 12)

Some [philosophers] are known to have put their ideas into practice, such as Empedocles, who seems to have been engaged in considerable therapeutic activity, or Democritus, who is reported to have carried out anatomical research on a significant

> scale, or, to take a later example, Sextus Empiricus, who combined his authorship of philosophical writings on Scepticism with medical practice. (p. 13)

> It is interesting in this connection that one of the first attestations of the word *philosophia* in Greek literature occurs in a medical context – the Hippocratic work *On Ancient Medicine.* (p. 19)

Comparable observations could be made concerning the early Indian medical literature, such as *Caraka-saṃhitā* and the slightly later *Suśruta-saṃhitā*, as a survey of those texts, or even their tables of contents, would quickly show. Space limitations preclude documenting that here in detail, but one example should suffice. The core of chapter 8 of part 3 (*Vimāna-sthāna*) of the *CS* consists of a rigorous, detailed description of the components of "debate" (*vāda*). This includes a full discussion of the parts of a formal inference, the *pramāṇas*, distinguishing sound from unsound arguments, and the value and protocols of argument.[22] Passage 68 lists ten topics a physician should explore by the three *pramāṇas* of authoritative tradition, perception, and inference. (Here, unlike in part 1, chap. 11, where *āpta-pramāṇa*, 'authoritative tradition,' is given great weight, several indications place *āpta-pramāṇa* in a subservient, even expendable position in relation to perception and inference.[23]) The ten topics are: *kāraṇa* (the cause or agent initiating action, i.e., the physician), *karaṇa* (instrument assisting the agent's action, e.g., pharmaceuticals), *kāryayoni* (the matrix from which the action emerges), *kārya* (what is being done), *kāryaphala* (the result or purpose of the action), *anubandha* (what the action is bound to entail), *deśa* (the locus of the action, viz. the place and the patient), *kāla* (time, viz. seasonal factors and the state of progress of the disease), *pravṛtti* (the process), and *upāya* (procedure or device, i.e., proper preparations and initiation of proper actions). All students of Indian philosophy will instantly recognize these ten terms are central, pervasive categories of Indian philosophy. Here, where a patient's life or death (not to mention the reputation of the physician, an issue the *CS* also takes very seriously) hang in the balance, these terms acquire not only concreteness but a sense of urgency. This list could serve as the program for virtually any Indian religion or philosophy. That the first five items are conceptually and etymologically[24] linked to the term *karma* underlines this.

Are we failing to produce philosophers of the stature and acuity of Ibn Sīnā and Maimonides because philosophy departments do not require their majors or graduate students to attend medical school, much less seriously practice the hard sciences?

What then are the limits or horizons of philosophy proper? Some styles of philosophy strive for univocality. Thinking can only be clear, goes the claim, when words are drained of all ambiguity or multivocality. Today the implications of the desire to reduce all voices to one, to eliminate alternatives, or to reduce a word to a single meaning, strike many of us as disconcerting. We learn more from exploring different styles of philosophy, different ways of accounting for the human condition, than we benefit from silencing alternatives.

Are there meaningful lines to be drawn between philosophy and religion? Let me suggest two:

(1) Borrowing Neitzschean vocabulary, we might say that religion is a will to meaning, while philosophy is a will to knowledge. These two types of wills may converge, when either meaning is understood as equivalent to knowledge or vice versa. Yet there are conceivably meaningful endeavours that do not rest on knowledge per se, e.g., romance.[25]

    Religion thus seeks to make life meaningful, to provide purpose and meaning to one's existence and one's life experiences. Philosophy, in contrast, seeks to know, to understand, and to make life comprehensible through evidence and reason. When meaning and knowledge converge, the line between religion and philosophy blurs.

(2) Religious thinking is ultimately tautological (e.g., "I am that I am"; Being is; scripture is true because it is scripture). Tautology can be a handmaiden to authoritarianism ("It's so because I say so!"). Philosophy, however, considers tautology a logical error, and thus it prefers (i) reasoning from premises to conclusions. This is Aristotle's preferred method (derived from the third

segment of Plato's divided line) and is a cornerstone of scientific method. Even more importantly and radically, however, philosophy prefers (ii) reasoning from premises to their presuppositions (as in recovering the *archē*; the fourth segment of Plato's divided line). Such a procedure can be found in Nāgārjuna's quieting of all presuppositions (*prapañcopaśama*) and perspectival attachments (*dṛṣṭi*). He undertakes this in order to expose the absurdities masquerading as reasoned positions to which we attach and with which we construct our identities (*ātma-dṛṣṭi*). It is also found in Husserl's search for a presuppositionless philosophy in order to ground the sciences, *Wissenschaften*.

With such considerations in mind, we might ask the following questions:

(1) Does Hegel's teleological view of history, as a rediscovery of the self by itself through the other, finally only reaffirm a Christian tautological *telos*? (The result here is that history's destiny is already decided before it has begun, the alpha in the omega, so that the eschaton is prefigured in the creation. One moves all the way from one end of history to the other only to rediscover what was already there at the beginning: *A* = *A*. History and time become nothing more than the working out of the = that declares tautological self-coincidence as a discovery upon which all history awaits.)

(2) What significance or insight lurks in the tension between his Being vs. Nonbeing sublating into Becoming, i.e., his famous *Aufhebung* offered in the *Logic*? On the one hand, Hegel seems to suggest that a dynamic process necessarily arises from, and then supersedes static contraries. On the other, he posits Becoming, seen as *Geist*'s search for itself, as ultimately terminating in a static *telos* of authentic self-realization at the end of

> history. Does this result in a terminus in which the movement of mind, spirit, and history itself comes to a stop once reaching its actualized self-recognition? Does Becoming emerge from the tension of two static contraries only to culminate eventually, with historical and ultimate finality, in a new stasis where the contraries have been replaced by a tautological self-coincidence? (This self-identity will have *aufheben*-ed all contrastive tensions.)

Becoming stops becoming. In what way, then, might this terminal historicism of Hegel be compared with the Kashmiri Shaivite idea of *līlā*, as a game Śiva plays with himself? In this game, Śiva repeatedly, even eternally, alienates himself from himself, multiplying himself into "others" into which he forgets himself in order to find himself again. He thus continually engenders and wanders through various realms of existence that are the forgotten aspects of himself. Eventually, he rediscovers himself as the source of the game of forgetfulness, only to forget himself again once he is found, in order to keep the game in play. Each of us is nothing more than moves in this game of hide-and-seek, mere facets of Śiva's forgetfulness. For Hegel, History becomes a finite search by Spirit for itself consisting of a series of logical predictable moves with a guaranteed climax. The notion of Becoming with which Hegel reintroduced Western thought to time and historicality finally leads to its own static culmination. No such finite limits restrict Śiva's *līlā*. The divine's game of hide and seek with himself not only plays out perpetually, restarting once completed, but time and temporality are byproducts of the game. The game is not only a temporal narrative conceived chronologically, but synchronically *all* levels of the game are at play simultaneously, so that remembering and forgetting happen simultaneously as well as sequentially. History plays out, but full realization is always available and instantaneous. It is a *telos* that is forever culminating because it never really culminates. The joy of realization is only one more joyous moment in a joyous game. The game and the joy continue nonetheless. The cosmic cards are reshuffled. Śiva forgets once again, and the game continues.

LOGICAL STYLES: ROOT METAPHORS

Let me suggest a quick rubric for differentiating Western philosophy from Indian philosophy, and each from Chinese philosophy, though I will not expand this here into a full analysis. Each is grounded in certain root metaphors, basic models or disciplines which become, from the beginning, fundamental and constitutive of what follows and thereby counts as philosophy in each of these traditions.

For the Greeks (and still in the West), the foundational disciplines were physics and mathematics. For India, the root models were grammar and medicine. For China, it was the family viewed, on the one hand, as hierarchical relations (parents over children, elder sibling over younger sibling, etc.), and, on the other hand, as dialectical relations between family members (the give and take between a couple, parents and children, etc.). Family relations, combined hierarchically and dialectically, yield a pattern in which individuals both change and keep roles through a stable system: The youngest daughter, starting out life at the bottom of the family hierarchy, can gradually raise her status until she is matriarch of the family, overlording her sons and their wives. Social order, the web of correlative thinking into which all natural and artificial entities and forces – including medical theories – were plotted, and ascension through the stages of the spiritual path followed that model.

For the West, then, we think we are at our most profound when engaged in questions of infinity, ontology, and the translation of time and space into mathematical equations. This fosters the illusion that soft sciences become hard once they adopt a mathematical method, etc. The sense of profundity that wells up in us when such topics are broached is our inheritance from the Greek presuppositional foundation of mathematics and physics. The word *meta-physics* resonates. "Infinity," for instance, has had neither the prominence nor the emotional affect in other cultures that it has held in ours. Kant, having completed the three critiques, still thought his philosophy unfinished, "or else a gap will remain in the critical philosophy."[26] In a letter to Kiesewetter, Kant explains what remains to be done: "The transition from the metaphysical foundations of natural science to physics must not be left out of the system.... [W]ith that work the task of the critical philosophy will be completed and a gap that now stands open will be filled."[27] He died before completing this task that the

Western tradition tacitly insisted he address. It is like a voice of conscience or internalized imperative that had become categorical, unavoidable, an urgent need that now defined him and his system. Conversely, Nathan Sivin has to argue, in his treatment of Chinese science,[28] that Chinese scientists did not deal with "Nature" in the sense of *phusis*. Understanding what they have been concerned with thus becomes a conceptual stretch for the "Western" mindset.

For Indians, grammar disclosed the structure of reality. Just as words are means to apprehend referents (*artha*), so does perception apprehend objects (*artha*). The detailed relations and variations denoted by Sanskrit grammatical inflections mirror and reveal the relational realities, variations, and even the eternal verities of the operations of the cosmos. Medicine is about saving beings from sickness, illness, and suffering, restoring them to health. Buddha's famous four Noble Truths[29] is taught these days, in an expanded form, in medical schools throughout the West under the label "Pathological Model," i.e., symptom, diagnosis, prognosis, and treatment. When early Buddhist texts spoke of the Buddha as the "Great Physician," one who turns poison into medicine, etc., they were not speaking metaphorically. Buddhism itself, these texts explain, is "medicine," consisting of specific therapeutic devices designed to cure dis-ease (*duḥkha*). Like all-powerful medicines, it is forged from toxic materials specifically designed to treat specific illnesses; when the medicine has done its task one should stop taking it, or else it also can make one sick.

Hence, that we should find *pramāṇas* (means of knowledge) being introduced in the medical text, the *CS*, should not surprise us.

THE *CARAKA-SAṂHITĀ*, INSANITY, AND THE *PRAMĀṆAS*

I came to the *CS* as a result of work on the *Mano-bhūmika* section of Asaṅga's encyclopedic *Yogācārabhūmi*. Asaṅga is the nominal founder of the Yogācāra school of Buddhism, one of the two Mahāyāna systems in India. The *Yogācārabhūmi*'s first chapter, on the five bodily consciousnesses (*pañca-vijñāna-kāya-bhūmi*), discusses the sense organs, perception, karma, and related topics. For the second chapter, the "mental stage" (*mano-bhūmi*), Asaṅga makes the transition from physical, bodily processes to more exclusively mental conditions through a medical survey of psycho-somatic topics, specifically physical conditions that affect mental states, such as intoxication (*mādhyati*) and insanity (*unmādyati*). Insanity or mental disorders is a topic to which the *CS* and Indian medicine generally devote great attention.[30] Asaṅga gives us a list of possible causes, which includes such things as physical and mental trauma (*uttrāsa-bhayata*), strikes to vital spots (*marmābhighāta*), and other external factors such as attacks from ghosts (*bhūta-samāveśatayā*). He explains the causes of sleep and the causes for awakening from sleep (e.g., a loud noise, bodily discomfort, etc.). He takes this into a somewhat detailed discussion of medical conditions, employing the three *doṣa* model and various other clearly medical concerns.[31] This leads to a discussion of the causes of health and longevity, and the causes of the shortening of life span and death (food, digestive processes, and moral habits are cited as critical factors). Asaṅga even provides a description of how death occurs, how consciousness leaves the body.

Interested to discover how typical Asaṅga's treatment was of Indian medical theory at that time, my search for Buddhist medical literature of that period revealed that there is precious little available today on the Buddhist medical theories and practices of his day. As a result, I turned to the next best thing, the text considered to be the oldest of the Hindu medical texts, the only extant medical treatise generally considered to predate Asaṅga.[32] While, unfortunately, it quickly became apparent that the Hindu medical theories were a closely related but different system (enumerations and models differed), the *CS* provided charms of its own.

As mentioned above, the *CS* is usually considered to be the first text to introduce the idea of *pramāṇa*, the means of acquiring knowledge. This should not come as a surprise, since medicine requires not only a disciplined method of observation to observe symptoms, to take account of treatments and experiments that work or do not work, etc., but it also requires a method by which what is unobserved and even potentially unobservable, namely the cause of a disease, can be inferred and known in order to be treated. The present symptoms displayed by an ill person may have an etiology that lies in the past, and diseases often progress through stages. Thus the physician must be able to infer from what presents at the moment to what likely has transpired in the past, just as one would infer a past fire from ashes and smoke. As the *CS* itself argues, one also has to be able to infer predictability, i.e., from the present to the future, in order to make an accurate prognosis and to have some confidence in the effectiveness of specific treatments. The current popularity of forensic medicine on television shows such as the CSI-style programs illustrates the power still inherent in such approaches. To the chagrin of idealists and solipsists, physical remainders of past actions can provide definitive evidence of what happened – evidence sufficient to convict a perpetrator "beyond the shadow of a doubt."

Various Indian schools proposed different *pramāṇas* as viable means of acquiring certain knowledge. Virtually all agreed that perception and logical inference were *pramāṇas*. For example, I know that the table is there because I can see it, feel it, etc. I know it can hold a certain weight, because when I place objects of a certain weight on it, it doesn't collapse, and I have this knowledge even when nothing is presently on the table. As the *CS* states, the fact of pregnancy compels one to infer that sexual intercourse has occurred (unless one is a certain type of theologian).

To these two *pramāṇas*, some Indian schools wished to add reliable testimony, meaning testimony from a respectable witness, as in a court proceeding, or a respectable authority, i.e., an expert. In addition, and more importantly, this *pramāṇa* includes the testimony of scripture. Curiously, the first school to challenge *śabda-pramāṇa* (reliable testimony) as a viable source of knowledge was the Vaiśeṣika, a Hindu school that eventually merged with Nyāya. Buddhists, rejecting the validity of Hindu scriptures, also eventually dismissed the validity of *śabda-pramāṇa* as a *pramāṇa* (at least after Dignāga, although Asaṅga in his *Abhidharmasamuccaya* already makes it subsidiary to perception and inference). This was because they argued that claims made by testimony or scripture must themselves be subjected to test by inference and/or perception to be deemed valid. The reliability of a witness must be tested, as must the truth-value of claims made in scripture. Such tests would examine whether the claims conform to what is evident to the senses or to what is reasonable. Thus, Buddhists insisted, it is perception and inference that guarantees the validity of knowledge, not the testimony itself. Additional *pramāṇas* proposed by others included "comparison," "analogy," and even "absence," but for Vaiśeṣikas and Buddhists these too are either fallacious or subordinate to perception and inference.

Pramāṇa-theory first appears in the eleventh chapter of the first part (*Sūtra-sthāna*) of the *CS*. Here the *CS* intriguingly proposes, along with the three *pramāṇas* one would expect (perception, inference, and authoritative testimony), a fourth not found anywhere else: synthetic inductive reasoning (*yukta-pramāṇa*). Discussion of *pramāṇa* occurs in two other parts of the *CS*: part 3, *Vimāna-sthāna*, chap. 4 and chap. 8, but the unique *yukta-pramāṇa* is absent from those discussions, a sign of the stratified nature of the text.

The discussion in chap. 11 of the *Sūtra-sthāna* is interesting because it offers some explanation for why a discussion of *pramāṇas* should appear in a medical text. It begins by stating that for humans there are three basic desires or impulses (*eṣaṇa*): (1) desire for life itself (*prāṇaiṣaṇā*), (2) desire for material possessions (*dhanaiṣaṇā*), and (3) desire for (happiness in) the next world (*paralokaiṣaṇā*) (11:3). Of these, the first, the impulse for longevity, is most basic since "when life departs, all departs" (11:4). Since life without adequate means is miserable, the second impulse comes next.

As to the third impulse, the desire for the next life, *CS* states that some have doubts whether such a thing is real. To disabuse its readers of such skepticism, *CS* launches into an attack on all sorts of skepticism (those who disbelieve in gods, sages, *siddhis*, efficient and material causes, the necessity for examination and investigation, etc.). He argues, for instance, that non-perception does not entail non-existence. There are numerous reasons why something real may be imperceptible. It may be too far way, too close, too small, obstructed by something else, a sense-organ defect, and so on. *CS* admits that the scriptures are also in conflict on the question of afterlife. Such conflicts, it recommends, should be resolved by reason (*yukti*).

After arguing for the existence of the self (*ātman*) despite its being perceptually unobservable, and for a world created by purposeful causes, and denouncing the nihilist (*nāstika*) as "the worst of the sinful,"[33] *CS* states that everything falls into one of two categories: *sattva* and *asattva*, i.e., real or unreal, or, perhaps, true and false (11:17). Then the four *pramāṇas* are introduced, starting with *āpta*, traditional authority. This, the *CS* informs us, is knowledge passed on by the experts (*śiṣta*). Instead of *śabda-pramāṇa*, *CS* calls this *āptopadeśa*, "teachings of the Respected ones," and a list of the types of people this includes is given (passages 18–19). These people are indubitable because they lack *tamas* and *rajas*,[34] and thus are incapable of lying. Next comes perception (*pratyakṣa*), which is described as contact between the self and what is present. This is followed by inference (*anumāna*), which *CS* says is based on having previously perceived or learned something. *CS* explains that there are three types of inference, corresponding to inferences about the past, present, and future. "Fire is inferred from smoke, and sexual intercourse from pregnancy" (present and past, respectively), and a future fruit can be inferred from a seed, based on having previously observed, i.e., perceived, that process (11:21–22).

The fourth *pramāṇa*, *yukta*, is explained with the following examples (11:23–24):[35]

> Growth of crops from the combination of irrigation, ploughed land, seed and seasons; formation of embryo from the combination of six *dhātus* (five *mahābhūtas* and *Ātman*); Production of fire from the combination of the lower-fire-drill, upper-fire-drill and the act of drilling; cure of diseases by fourfold efficient therapeutic measures.

Yukta here means something like: the coordination of multiple factors converging into a trajectory in which something is changed or transformed. It is taking into account the coordination of multiple causes, a process with contributive factors that might affect the outcome, as in crops or medical treatments. To plant a crop requires attention to multiple factors, from the time of planting, the type of seed, properly working the land, fortuitous seasonal conditions, and so on. If all the factors work properly, the seed turns into a plant that produces the desired crop. Any of the contributing factors (e.g., amount of rainfall) can alter the outcome. There is no strict one-to-one cause-effect relation between the seed and the fruit. The additional factors mediate it. Similarly, an embryo becoming a human undergoes a process requiring multiple factors in addition to the sex act that initiated it. Any of these factors could terminate the pregnancy or inflict permanent damage on the embryo. Producing fire by coordinating fire sticks similarly illustrates the coordination of multiple factors. Treating illness, likewise, requires coordinating conditions across a trajectory in time in order for the person's condition to change from sickness to health. The physician must recognize and coordinate those conditions: what to watch for in the disease's progress; what types of treatments are most effective, and when to administer them; what habits and regimens, such as diet and exercise, contribute to health or maladies; etc.

Inference (*anumāna*) was treated (vs. 21–22) as inferring from a specific condition or cause to a specific effect, i.e., a fruit from a seed. And *CS* also insists that inference requires previous perception (*pratyakṣa-pūrva*). One recognizes the relation between the fruit and seed on the basis of prior observations of this process, and so one can predict a future fruit is likely from a present planted seed. Although *CS*'s account is terse, the claim, I believe, is not simply that a seed will become a plant, but the fact that we recognize by looking at a certain type of seed what *type* of plant it will produce. One sees an acorn and knows that it will produce an oak tree, not a weeping willow. This type of knowledge would be important in medicine, since it is important to know that certain types of treatments, medicines, bodily conditions will become or change into something else. But this does not necessarily happen automatically. Additional contributory causal factors must play a role as well. An acorn sitting on a table does not become an oak; it must be planted, and it must receive nutrients from the soil, heat, water, etc. None of these factors is sufficient alone. Each must contribute for the seed to progress along a trajectory in which it changes into something else.

Yukta (= *yukti*), which literally implies to tie together, or connect, and later comes to be one of the numerous terms for "reasoning" or "logic," is used in *CS* specifically to denote combining a group of factors that, together, produce a result. A doctor cannot diagnose a disease on the basis of a single symptom but must weigh multiple symptoms together, many (such as headaches, nausea, etc.) that could be shared by numerous diseases. This multitude of factors must be taken into account in order to determine correctly the specific disease affecting a particular patient. Diagnosis is inductive, not purely deductive, so, to the old debate about whether Indian logic is strictly deductive or includes induction, *CS* at least provides a case for inductive reasoning.

Unfortunately, *yukta-pramāṇa* never underwent further development in India, appearing nowhere else than in this text. It is rich in analytic possibilities, and one wonders what Indian philosophers, as deeply concerned as most were with causal analyses, might have created had they explored further possibilities of this inductive tool.

Since the *CS* arrived here by attempting to refute skepticism about after-lives, it is not surprising that, having now established a basis for knowledge, the *CS* next turns to arguing for the validity of rebirth, the issue that instigated this excursion into epistemology in the first place. To do this, it offers arguments from each of the *pramāṇas* in turn, i.e., arguments from authority, perception, inference, and *yukta*. A modern reader would not find the arguments very convincing, and apparently neither did the ancients, since we do not find them repeated, or improved upon, in subsequent literature. In fact, one of the striking things about the *CS*'s attempt to provide arguments supporting the idea of rebirth and reincarnation is the fact that it does so at all, since such arguments are surprisingly rare in Indian philosophical texts. Indian philosophers seem to have understood that it would be very difficult to mount a reasonable argument for the validity of the theory of reincarnation, and thus largely chose to avoid embarrassing themselves with such attempts. Thus the *CS*'s boldness in this regard is refreshing, even if the arguments themselves are far from compelling.

This *CS* chapter has explained that the *pramāṇas* can help resolve doubts about the objectives of one of our basic impulses, the desire for the next life. It also demonstrates that, in addition to the *pramāṇas* employed by some other Indian schools, the physician requires a *pramāṇa* suited to the needs of his profession. This is *yukta-pramāṇa* that deals inductively with synthetic judgments about changes and alterations (*pariṇāma*, etc.) affected, in temporal phases, by multiple contributory causes. Illness is a transformation of bodily factors from a healthy balance to imbalance; restoring health is a transformation back to proper functioning. Birth, life, health, sickness, old age, and death are transformations involving multiple factors that the physician must learn to recognize and manipulate. The physician is a philosopher who lacks the luxury of indulging in speculation. Either his knowledge is true, or the patient dies.

But this matter, along with such other fascinating topics in the *CS* as its use of the idea of "intellectual blasphemy" (*prajñā-parādha*[36]) as an explanation for some diseases, must await another occasion.

CONCLUDING SUMMARY

So what does it mean to do comparative philosophy of religion? Since all thinking is comparative, comparative philosophy of religion draws its strength from expanding the range of philosophies and religions it "compares." Expanding the horizon of our exploration provides more than additional data; it enriches the possibilities of thinking. For a Western philosopher to think about Indian or Chinese or Arabic or Jewish philosophies, etc., is basically no different from a North American philosopher thinking about Plato, Spinoza, Hegel, or Wittgenstein. Each task requires looking at the other through similarities and differences of language, culture, context, foundational categories, historical developments, and a host of other factors. For a Chinese, Indian, Jewish, etc., philosopher to think, philosophically, about Western philosophy is no different. Starting from a different standpoint, however, might entail that different priorities and categories set the agenda. The basic differences are not between East and West, as is often assumed, but between styles of philosophizing and the root metaphors from which different traditions take their orientation. Similarly, philosophy, religion, and medicine have always been intertwined, especially in ancient and medieval philosophy.

As Thomas H. Huxley, the biologist, noted:[37] "The only medicine for suffering, crime, and all the other woes of mankind, is wisdom."

Notes

1 Some attempt to date Caraka to as early as the sixth century BCE, though most date the bulk of the *Caraka-saṃhitā* to ca. the first century CE, with some obvious later interpolations and additions. Our received edition is based on an eleventh-century CE commentary and redaction by Cakrapāṇi.

2 *Tapas* eventually came to mean the heat of austerities that burn off bad karma, thus, like the fire of sacrifice, purifying the practitioner; but its earlier meaning in the *Ṛg Veda* is the heat from friction produced in the sex act, which is creation *par excellence*. Cf. *RV* 10.129.3: "*tuchyenābhvapihitaṃ yadāsīt tapasastanmahinājāyataikam*" ("that One which had been covered by the void, through the heat of desire [*tapas*] was manifested," trans. Antonio de Nicolas).

3 This is easier to assert once a dominant paradigm or theory has run its course, marked by the repetition, reiteration, and refinement of previous insights rather than the inspirational introduction of truly novel ones, as some view the situation today for both analytic and postmodern styles of philosophy. When caught in the throes of the creative possibilities that are being opened by a new paradigm, the mere implementation of its directives, or putting into motion permutations merely implied by the new paradigm – analogous to Frege's indication that all of mathematics springs from 1 + [i.e., a unit and a function] – may give the feeling of opening onto limitless horizons with boundless future potential. Hence the exuberance and heady feeling of having brought something new and momentous into the world that often accompanies "movements" in their early phases.

4 "Living adherents," i.e., old traditions that have modern-day exponents, introduce other sorts of problems, since modern exponents typically are not transplants from another time, but instead embody all sorts of permutations and sensibilities derived from centuries of changing interpretations that become embedded in the transmission. And the modern exponent's motivations are, consciously or unconsciously, geared toward accommodating modern issues and modes of expression that a careful researcher would have to take into account and isolate.

5 Interest has recently been rekindled in Dignāga's foundational Buddhist work on *pramāṇa*-theory. Until a few years ago *Pramāṇasamuccaya* was only available in two poor Tibetan translations. Jinendrabuddhi's Sanskrit commentary, found in Tibet, which contains much of Dignāga's original text, is now coming out. The first volume has appeared – Ernst Steinkellner, Helmut Krasser, and Horst Lasic (eds.), Jinendrabuddhi's *Pramāṇasamuccayaṭika*, chap 1, part 1: *Critical Edition*; part 2: *Diplomatic Edition* (Beijing: Österreichischen Akademie der Wissenschaft, 2005) – with more to follow.

6 This is the only "translation" by Xuanzang (600–664) – the famous Chinese pilgrim who travelled to India and, on his return to China, became the most prolific translator

of Buddhist texts – that is *not* a strict translation of a single text but instead a redacted compendium based on a number of Sanskrit commentaries on Vasubandhu's *Triṃśikā* (Thirty Verses). This "translation" incorporates a host of other materials as well, resulting in an encyclopedic work on the Buddhist Yogācāra system as it was debated in India in the seventh century. Louis de la Vallée Poussin's French translation, *Vijñaptimātratāsiddhi: Le Siddhi de Hiuan-tsang* (Paris: Geuthner, 1928, 2 vols.), is overly interpretive, transforming the text into a tract on idealism, an interpretation that has largely stuck. Wei Tat published a bilingual edition, *Cheng Wei-shih lun: The Doctrine of Mere-Consciousness* (Hong Kong, 1973), that contains an English rendering of Vallée Poussin's French (minus Vallée Poussin's extensive annotations) on facing pages with the original Chinese. Swaty Ganguly, *Treatise In Thirty Verses on Mere-Consciousness* (Delhi: Motilal Banarsidass, 1992), offers an abridged translation. Francis Cook, *Three Texts on Consciousness Only* (Berkeley: Numata, 1999), is sometimes an improvement over Vallée Poussin but too frequently follows his misinterpretation. On the philosophy of Yogācāra as reflected in *Cheng weishi-lun*, see my *Buddhist Phenomenology: A Philosophical Investigation of Yogācāra Buddhism and the Ch'eng Wei-shih lun* (London: Routledge Curzon, 2002).

7 This has been translated by Wing Tsit-Chan, *Reflections on Things at Hand* (New York: Columbia University Press, 1967). Zhu Xi's name may be more familiar to some Western readers by its older transcription: *Chu-hsi*. This is only one of the many works of Zhu Xi (1130–1200), the most prominent Neo-Confucian thinker.

8 A number of Gersonides' (i.e., Rabbi Levi ben Gershon, whose name in acrostic is Ralbag; 1288–1344) works have been translated. His major work, *The Wars of the Lord*, is available as: (1) Levi ben Gershom (Gersonides), *The Wars of the Lord: Book One: Immortality of the Soul*, trans. Seymour Feldman (Philadelphia: Jewish Publication Society, 1984); (2) Levi ben Gershom (Gersonides), *The Wars of the Lord: Book Two: Dreams, Divination, and Prophecy*; *Book Three: Divine Knowledge*; *Book Four: Divine Providence*, trans. Seymour Feldman (Philadelphia: Jewish Publication Society, 1987); a third promised volume to complete the work has not yet appeared. Book Five of the *Wars* includes treatises on trigonometry (which sparked the development of trigonometry in Europe); a description of the *meguleh 'amuqot* ("revealer of profundities"), a device Gersonides invented to measure the angular distances of heavenly bodies (this also circulated as an independent text); astronomical tables and critiques of astronomical theories. An alternate translation, with analysis, of Book Three of the *Wars* is Norbert Samuelson, *Gersonides on God's Knowledge* (Toronto: Pontifical Institute of Mediaeval Studies, 1977). His style as a Biblical commentator is displayed in Menachem Kellner (trans.), *Commentary on Song of Songs: Levi ben Gershom (Gersonides)* (New Haven, CT: Yale, 1998).

9 Harry Wolfson's translation of Book One of Crescas' *Or Adonai*

(Light of Our Lord) – *Crescas' Critique of Aristotle: Problems of Aristotle's* Physics *in Jewish and Arabic Philosophy* (Cambridge, MA: Harvard University Press, 1929) – is a classic treatment of a work that deeply influenced Spinoza and moved Western thought closer to the end of the Middle Ages. Crescas' critique is comparable to al-Ghazzali's *Tahafut al-falsifa* (The Incoherence of Philosophy) in that its motive is to purge Aristotelian contamination from religious thought, though it is very different in style and conclusion. Crescas (Ḥasdai ben Abraham Crescas, ca.1340–1410/11) delves deeply into Aristotle's arguments and principles and concludes they are *not scientific enough*, i.e., they are merely reified speculations that inadequately and incorrectly interpret the physical world.

10 Defenders of analytic philosophy may contend that it is still going strong, but what is practised under that name today would be unrecognizable to its practitioners of only a couple of decades ago. The label "analytic" philosophy was supposed to signal above all that only the quality of arguments (propositions sequentialized into logical entailments) counted, not personalities or the authors of the arguments. The cult of personality was considered a serious error committed by philosophies of the past. A proper essay, they believed, should begin with a rational exposition accessible to all that subsequently would be developed into more technical implications. The essay's merit rested in the cogency of the argument, not the weight of its author. Citing others was to be largely avoided, unless the essay's purpose was an analysis of a particular philosopher, and reverence for a philosopher instead of appreciation for an argument was simply bad taste. Today not only must one recite and acknowledge a pantheon of analytic philosophers to make even the most trivial argument, but publishers are producing an endless stream of books with simple titles such as *Quine*, *Ayer*, *Strawson*, etc., typically with a photo or drawing of that person adorning the cover. The cult of personality is now embraced. While analytic philosophers of the past would find all that shocking, it is perhaps a belated recognition that philosophy without philosophers is a platonic fantasy, as well as a curious attempt to breathe new life and sustainability into the analytic project. Others would object that even with these changes, unlike philosophers of the past who wrestled with the "big issues" of perennial interest to all thinking individuals, the issues that analytic philosophy engages and the parameters within which it permits what it accepts as legitimate analysis have become so restricted and narrow that few outside the ranks of the analytic philosophers themselves find their discussions pertinent or even interesting.

11 "Spinoza's distinction between attributes and properties is identical with Crescas' distinction between attributes subjectively ascribed and their objective reality in God. The connection between Spinoza's views on creation and free will, on love of God and of others, and those of Crescas has been established by [Manuel] Joël in his '[Spinoza's Theologisch-Politischer Tractat auf

Seine Quellen Geprüft] Zur Genesis der Lehre Spinoza's' (Breslau, 1871)." From the article, "Crescas, Ḥasdai ben Abraham," by Kaufmann Kohler and Emil G. Hirsch, in *JewishEncyclopedia.com*, http://www.jewishencyclopedia.com [square brackets added]. See also Harry Wolfson, *Crescas on the Problem of Divine Attributes* (Philadelphia: Dropsie College, 1916); Warren Zev Harvey, *Physics and Metaphysics in Ḥasdai Crescas* (Amsterdam: J.C. Gieben, 1998).

12 Umberto Eco, *The Name of the Rose*, trans. William Weaver (Boston and New York: Harcourt, 1983). While Church complicity in suppressing Aristotle's lost work on comedy remains speculative, the medieval debates between Dominicans, etc., on whether laughter is permitted or sinful are grounded in history.

13 Aldous Huxley, *The Doors of Perception* and *Heaven and Hell* (New York: Harper & Brothers, 1954, 1956).

14 R.C. Zaehner, *Mysticism: Sacred and Profane* (Oxford: Clarendon Press, 1957. Reprint: London: Oxford University Press, 1961).

15 The term "panentheism" was coined by the German philosopher, Karl Christian Friedrich Krause (1781–1832), a student of Fichte, Hegel, and Schelling, and one of Schopenhauer's teachers.

16 Jewish tradition often uses acrostics of the names of prominent figures as their official nicknames. Hence Maimonides, e.g., Rabbi Moshe Ben Maimon, becomes RaMBaM; Gersonides, Rabbi Levi Ben Gershon, becomes RaLBaG, and so on. For an overview of Maimonides' works on medicine, including a translation of two of his treatises, see Ariel Bar-Sela, Hebbel E. Hoff, and Elias Faris, "Moses Maimonides' Two Treatises on the Regimen of Health: *Fi Tadbir al-Sihhah* and *Maqalah fi Bayan Ba'd al-A'rad wa-al-Jawad 'anha*" (Philadephia: Transactions of the American Philosophical Society, New Series, v. 54, 4, 1964), 3–50. Also cf. Gerrit Bos (trans.), *Medical Aphorisms: Treatises 1–5* (Provo, UT: Brigham Young University, 2004) (the first of six volumes on Maimonides' summary of Galen); and Fred Rosner, *Medicine in the Mishneh Torah of Maimonides* (Northvale: NJ: Aronson Press, 1997).

17 On Ibn Sīnā, see note 19. As Hamed Abdel-reheem Ead, Professor of Chemistry at the Faculty of Science, University of Cairo, Giza, Egypt, and director of the Science Heritage Center, states on a web page (http://www.levity.com/alchemy/islam21.html) devoted to Ibn Rushd's medical contributions (slightly modified):

- Ibn Rushd … spent a great part of his fruitful life as a judge and as a physician. Yet he was known in the West for being the grand commentator on the philosophy of Aristotle, whose influence penetrated the minds of even the most conservative of Christian Ecclesiastes in the Middle Ages, including men like St. Thomas Aquinas. People went to him for consultation in medicine just as they did for consultation in legal matters and jurisprudence.
- Ibn Rushd's major work in medicine, *al-Kulliyyat*

("Generalities"), was written between 1153 and 1169.

- Its subject matter leans heavily on Galen, and occasionally Hippocrates' name is mentioned. It is subdivided into seven books: *Tashrih al-a'lda'* ("Anatomy of Organs"), *al-Sihha* ("Health"), *al-Marad* ("Sickness"), *al-'Alamat* ("Symptoms"), *al-Adwiya wa 'l-aghdhiya* ("Drugs and Foods"), *Hifz al-sihha* ("Hygiene"), and *Shifa al-amrad* ("Therapy").
- Two Hebrew versions of *al-Kulliyyat* are known, one by an unidentified translator, another by Solomon ben Abraham ben David.
- The Latin translation, *Colliget*, was made in Padua in 1255 by a Jew, Bonacosa, and the first edition was printed in Venice in 1482, followed by many other editions.
- Ibn Rushd wrote an (abstract) of Galen's works, parts of which are preserved in Arabic manuscripts.
- He showed interest in Ibn Sīnā's *Urjūzah fi al-ṭibb* ("Poem on Medicine," *Canticum de medicina*), on which he wrote a commentary, *Sharh Urjuzat Ibn Sina*.
- It was translated into Hebrew prose by Moses ben Tibbon in 1260; a translation into Hebrew verse was completed at Beziers (France) in 1261 by Solomon ben Ayyub ben Joseph of Granada.
- Further, a Latin translation of the same work was made by Armengaud, son of Blaise, in 1280 or 1284, and a printed edition was published at Venice in 1484.
- Another revised Latin translation was made by Andrea Alpago, who translated Ibn Rushd's *Maqala 'l-tiryaq* ("Treatise on Remedies," *Tractatus de theiaca*).
- Ibn Rushd's unsuccessful attempts to defend philosophers against theologians paved the way for a decline in Arabic medicine.
- The great image of the Hakim (physician-philosopher), which culminated in the persons of al-Razi and Ibn Sīnā, has been superseded by that of *faqih musharik fi 'l-ulum* (a jurist who participates in sciences), among whom were physician-jurists and theologian-physicians.
- The German physician Max Meyerhof remarked that: "In Spain, the philosophical bias predominated among medical men. The prototypes of this combination are the two Muslims, Ibn Zuhr (Avenzoar) and Ibn Rushd (Averroës)."
- According to Draper, Ibn Rushd is credited with the discovery of sunspots.

18 Gersonides' main scientific contributions were in mathematics, astronomy, and logic. For a collection of essays detailing his scientific achievements, especially his innovative astronomy which influenced the astronomical revolution we usually associate with Galileo and Copernicus, see Gad Freudenthal, ed., *Studies on Gersonides: A Fourteenth-Century Jewish Philosopher-Scientist* (Leiden: E.J. Brill, 1993).

19 The Wikipedia entry on Avicenna (Ibn Sīnā) correctly summarizes his contributions thus <http://en.wikipedia.org/wiki/Avicenna>:

Ibn Sīnā ... was a Persian polymath and the foremost physician and philosopher of his time. He was also an astronomer, chemist, geologist, logician, paleontologist, mathematician, physicist, poet, psychologist, scientist, soldier, statesman, and teacher.

Ibn Sīnā wrote almost 450 treatises on a wide range of subjects, of which around 240 have survived. In particular, 150 of his surviving treatises concentrate on philosophy and forty of them concentrate on medicine. His most famous works are *The Book of Healing*, a vast philosophical and scientific encyclopaedia, and *The Canon of Medicine* [in fourteen volumes], which was a standard medical text at many medieval universities. *The Canon of Medicine* was used as a text-book in the universities of Montpellier and Louvain as late as 1650. Ibn Sīnā developed a medical system that combined his own personal experience with that of Islamic medicine, the medical system of the Greek physician Galen, Aristotelian metaphysics (Avicenna was one of the main interpreters of Aristotle, and ancient Persian, Mesopotamian and Indian medicine. He was also the founder of Avicennian logic and the philosophical school of Avicennism, which were influential among both Muslim and Scholastic thinkers.)

Ibn Sīnā is regarded as a father of early modern medicine, and clinical pharmacology, particularly for his introduction of systematic experimentation and quantification into the study of physiology, his discovery of the contagious nature of infectious diseases, the introduction of quarantine to limit the spread of contagious diseases, the introduction of experimental medicine, evidence-based medicine, clinical trials, randomized controlled trials, efficacy tests, clinical pharmacology, neuropsychiatry, risk factor analysis, and the idea of a syndrome, and the importance of dietetics and the influence of climate and environment on health. He is also considered the father of the fundamental concept of momentum in physics and is regarded as a pioneer of aromatherapy for his invention of steam distillation and extraction of essential oils. He also developed the concept of uniformitarianism and law of superposition in geology.

Also, from http://www.isesco.org.ma/pub/Eng/Architects/P20.htm:

Ibn Sīnā mastered medicine in particular. He made new discoveries in this field; he was the first to describe a worm that he called the "round worm," currently known as "anklestoma." He also studied neurological dysfunctions and was able to reach certain pathologic and psychological facts through psychoanalysis. He believed in the existence of an interaction between psychology and physical health. He also described the brain's apoplexy resulting from excess in the blood flow.

Ibn Sīnā made original contributions in medicine, based on his own observations. He founded his conclusions on experiments and was able to reach new observations, including the contagious nature of tuberculosis and the propagation of diseases through water and soil. He also described at length dermatological and sexually transmitted diseases. Moreover, he described the pharmaceutical preparation of some medicines.

Ibn Sīnā was also the first to describe the irritation of the brain's envelope, distinguishing it from other chronic irritations. He elaborated the first clear diagnostic of neck's scleroses and of meningitis He also described the facial paralysis and its causes. He made the distinction between the paralysis caused by a dysfunction in the brain and that resulting Scientific contributions in other fields.

Ibn Sīnā made important contributions in physics, through the study of several natural phenomena such as motion, force, vacuum, infinity, light and heat. He made the observation that if the perception of light is due to the emission of some particles from a luminous source, the speed of light must be finite.

Ibn Sīnā made contributions in geology with a treatise on the formation of mountains, precious stones and metals. In this treatise, he discussed the effect of earthquakes, water, the degree temperature, sediments, fossilisation and erosion.

Ibn Sīnā was also an outstanding mathematician and astronomer. He studied infinite bodies from religious, physical, and mathematical perspectives. His findings helped Newton and Leibniz to develop infinite numerals in the seventeenth century.

20 Mansura Haidar, "Medical Works of the Medieval Period from India and Central Asia," *Diogenes* 55, no. 27 (2008): 28.

21 Philip J. van der Eijk, *Medicine and Philosophy in Classical Antiquity* (Cambridge: Cambridge University Press, 2005), 15.

22 This chapter is important, not only because of its description of debate and its epistemological elements, but because it also informs us that debate (between different physicians as well as between physicians and others) was a professional obligation of physicians. It was part of their pedagogy, how they learned, how they defended their theories and practice, and how they practiced medicine.

23 When we think of "authoritative tradition" in a medical context, rather than, as is more usual, in a religious or philosophical context, the value and indeed necessity of a respect for tradition becomes obvious, since, if every physician had to re-invent the full inventory of medical lore and acquired knowledge all over again, everyone's health would be at greater risk. Medicine learns from the trial and error of preceding generations; its accumulated knowledge can be supplemented and modified by fresh observations and discoveries, but accumulated traditional knowledge can only be ignored at the peril of the physician and his patients.

24 Deriving philosophical categories by inflecting a key verb, in this case the verbal root of "action," *karma* (from the root √kṛ), is an inheritance from the other great influence on Indian philosophy, the grammatical tradition. See below under "Logical Styles." For an example in a decidedly philosophical context that draws on the same root, compare the following *kārikā* from Nāgārjuna's *Mūlamadhyamakakārikā* (8:4): "If a cause [for an action] does not actualize (*asat*), the enacted (*kārya*) and activator (*kāraṇa*) are not found. | Those not having come

to be (*abhāva*), activity (*kṛiya*), actor (*kartā*), and acting (*karaṇa*) are not found." (*hetāvasati kāryaṃ ca kāraṇaṃ ca na vidyate | tadabhāve kriyā kartā karaṇaṃ ca na vidyate*)

25 The *Tevijja sutta* of the Dīgha Nikāya of the Buddhist Tipiṭaka gives a humorous, satirical parody of religious devotionalism, comparing it to someone who proclaims he is in love with the most beautiful woman in the world, but when asked what does she look like, what type of hair, eyes, and so on does she possess, what is her caste, etc., he replies: "I don't know." Devotionalism, Buddha concludes, is as ineffective as someone who, wishing to get to the other shore of a river, builds a fire and sits down, chanting to the other shore to "come here," rather than building a raft and making his way across.

26 Kant, in a letter to Christian Garve. Quoted in Immanuel Kant, *Opus postumum*, ed. Eckart Förster; trans. Eckart Förster and Michael Rosen (Cambridge: Cambridge University Press, 1993), "Introduction," p. xvi.

27 Ibid.

28 Geoffrey Lloyd and Nathan Sivin, *The Way and the Word: Science and Medicine in Early China and Greece* (New Haven, CT: Yale University Press, 2003).

29 (1) *Duḥkha* (dis-ease, a.k.a. "suffering"), (2) *samudaya* (identifying the causes of *duḥkha*), (3) *nirodha* (assurance that the causes can be eliminated), and (4) *mārga* (the way to eliminate the causes).

30 For instance, it is the topic of chap. 7 of part 2 (*Nidāna-sthāna*) of the *Caraka-saṃhitā*.

31 The three *doṣas* – *vāta*, *pitta*, and *śleṣman*, based respectively on the three elements wind, fire-heat, and water – are fundamental categories of Indian medicine into which diseases, symptoms, pharmaceuticals, foods, etc., are classified and analyzed. For a general discussion that includes Buddhist usages, see Hartmut Scharfe, "The Doctrine of the Three Humors in Traditional Indian Medicine and the Alleged Antiquity of Tamil Siddha Medicine," *Journal of the American Oriental Society* 119, no. 4 (1999): 609–29.

32 The next oldest Indian medical text, *Suśruta-saṃhitā*, contains materials roughly contemporaneous with Asaṇga (4th century) but is recognized to also contain much later material in the redaction that has come down to us.

33 *Pātakebhyaḥ paraṃ caitat pātakaṃ nāstikagrahaḥ*. I have consulted two editions of the *Caraka-saṃhitā*, both containing the original text in devanagri and an English translation: (1) *Caraka-saṃhitā: Agniveśa's treatise refined and annotated by Caraka and redacted by Dṛḍhabala: text with English translation*, Priyavrat Sharma (editor-translator) (Varanasi: Chaukhambha Orientalia, 1981–83), 4 vols.; and (2) *Agniveśa's Caraka saṃhita: text with English translation & critical exposition based on Cakrapāṇi Datta's Āyurveda dīpikā*, Ram Karan Sharma and Bhagwan Dash (trans. and ed.) (Varanasi: Chowkhamba Sanskrit Series Office, 1976–2002), 7 vols. The translation above is from passages 14–15 of chap. 11, vol. 1, p. 209 of Sharma and Dash.

34 The *CS* in its available redaction is heavily steeped in Sāṃkhyan theory, which holds that the world consists of varying proportions of three constituent factors: *sattva* (light, pure, etc.), *rajas* (passionate, active), and *tamas* (dark, dull, inert). By implication, *CS* is claiming that someone devoid of *rajas* and *tamas* (skewering passions and stupidity) must be *sattvic* (pure, enlightened), and thus constitutionally incapable of lying.

35 Sharma and Dash, vol. 1, 213.

36 *Prajñā-parādha* is translated by Sharma and Dash as "intellectual blasphemy" and "intellectual error" by P.V. Sharma. It literally means "an offense to reason," i.e., acting unreasonably. The *CS* uses the term in a number of ways, but what they seem to have in common is acting or having an attitude that is unreasonable, i.e., endangering one's health in ways that one should know better than to engage in. E.g., *Sūtra-sthāna*, chap. 38: 39-40 states: "Due to *prajñāparādha*, he indulges in unwholesome sense objects, suppression of natural urges and taking up risky jobs. The ignorant one is attached to temporarily pleasing objects but the learned is not so because of his understanding having been clear" (P.V. Sharma, vol. 1, 231).

37 Reflection #90, *Aphorisms and Reflections*, selected by Henrietta A. Huxley (London: Macmillan, 1907).

Religious Intellectual Texts as a Site for Intercultural Philosophical and Theological Reflection: The Case of the *Śrīmad Rahasyatrayasāra* and the *Traité de l'Amour de Dieu*

FRANCIS X. CLOONEY, S. J.
Harvard Divinity School

I. REFLECTIONS

Introduction

I propose that religious texts – considered seriously, in depth – constitute a most appropriate and fruitful place for reflection on philosophical and theological issues in an intercultural context. This is because such texts provide access to worlds of thought that are invariably complex and diverse terrains, partly accessible and partly particular, insider discourse, branching off in various diverse and elusive ways. Such texts are often particularly rich in style and in reader expectations. Two such texts from two traditions, read together, create an array of intercultural possibilities that can generate a considerable range of philosophical and theological reflection. This kind of reflection on complex texts that are both philosophical and theological, highly rational and richly imaginative, is superior to thematic comparisons; for the texts resist conclusive generalizations and keep introducing cultural and religious specificity back into generalizing discourses.[1]

I thus reaffirm my long-term interest in the close study of texts as productive of religious and philosophical insight in part because of what I have learned from a more generalist and generalizing project I was part of from 1995 to 2000: the Comparative Religious Ideas Project (CRIP) directed by Robert Neville at Boston University, a five-year venture that involved only fifteen participants and led to three edited volumes, *The Human Condition*, *Ultimate Realities*, and *Religious Truth*.[2] CRIP was a very fine effort to bring together theorists and philosophers of comparative work (such as Neville himself) and tradition-specific specialist scholars (such as myself, in this instance), for the sake of creating a more integral conversation that would be both theoretically satisfying and responsible in particular disciplinary detail. Our hope in CRIP was to bridge the gap between the theoretical frameworks for comparative work and the highly professionalized detailed scholarship of the specialist, rooting the former in detail and liberating the latter from the control of narrow groups of specialist experts.

My impression, however – shared by others both in the project and observing it – has been that the volumes arising from CRIP did not achieve the integration that was hoped for. Rather, they less successfully placed specialist studies between meta- reflections on traditions and themes, and even on particularities. Readers have tended to read selectively, without having to engage the whole project. From the particularities of the conversation, the participants sought a common ground in general thematic issues, but this thematic generality failed to keep up with the particularities of what had been learned; we would have been better off, I decided, in more particularity and less generalization.

In the course of CRIP, I had been stressing specific Hindu traditions' claims about truth and the accessibility of truth to those willing to reason coherently, and all of this was related to my own book, *Hindu God, Christian God.*[3] But after that I wrote that book and was aware of the complexity of my own production, I ended up reaffirming the view that learning across traditional boundaries takes a very long time and cannot be speeded up by swifter theorizing – and is best mediated by long reflection on carefully studied texts. So now I am again interested in the possibility of gaining help from richly variegated texts that afford multiple points of access but also connect one to the other points of access.

The rest of this reflection has to do with an intercultural reading project that I finished recently, dealing with a Tamil Hindu text and a French Catholic text.[4]

BY WAY OF EXAMPLE, TWO TEXTS

I wrote about two extraordinarily rich and complex religious texts: first, the *Śrīmad Rahasyatrayasāra* [*Essence of the Three Mysteries*; henceforth *Essence*] by the fourteenth-century Hindu theologian Vedānta Deśika (Veṅkaṭanātha), a work that is an exegesis of the three holy mantras [rahasyas] of his tradition and argument for radical surrender to God; second, the *Traité de l'Amour de Dieu* [*Treatise on the Love of God*; henceforth *Treatise*] of the seventeenth-century French Catholic theologian (and bishop of Geneva) Francis de Sales, a text that argues that the deep pleasure and satisfaction of "Nothing but God" is the only true destiny of the human person.[5] The *Essence* is a key work for the Śrīvaiṣṇava tradition (dedicated to the worship of the deities Nārāyaṇa with his consort Śrī), and a kind of *summa* of spiritual theology; it was written at the end of Deśika's life, intended to provide a full and correct framework in which to understand and practice of surrender to God. Francis de Sales's most famous work is the *Introduction to the Devout Life*, but the *Treatise* offers his full vision of the mystical life of the Christian – toward unity with God in love – with its philosophical grounding.

Both the *Essence* and the *Treatise* are classic religious texts offering philosophical starting points that are, at least in theory, accessible to any intelligent and attentive reader. They can be read and understood, and they are forceful enough to provoke reactions, and then possible empathy and intentional engagement. Both move from philosophical starting points to increasingly tradition-specific assertions that require insider belonging and loyalty. Both respect reason but push on to engage more mystical claims that can be partly understood, while possibly remaining in significant ways inaccessible to those who have not participated in the life and practices of its tradition. The *Essence* and *Treatise* are complex texts including varied kinds of discourse, which Deśika and Sales claim to be successfully melded into whole texts.

Because the *Essence* and *Treatise* are reasoned treatises that make philosophical claims that then open into theological and mystical claims, they can be read in a distanced and speculative fashion, they can be thought about, but they can also be appropriated in an increasingly engaged way by those who would take them to heart and even pray with them, through them.

For the sake of an example to accompany this brief paper, I have paired the third chapter of the *Essence* with Book I, chapters 15–17 of the *Treatise*, and appended both sections in translation. I urge readers to spend some time with them since there is really no other satisfactory way to understand what I mean. Reading carefully is the substance and the point. These sections are early in each work, part of the foundations intended to prepare for their later arguments in favour of complete surrender to God; for it is necessary, they believe, to make the case that the higher ideals and sentiments of divine love are, not merely unexpected or miraculous graced events, but also completions to human existence even as ordinarily understood. Let us now consider each text in turn.

ESSENCE OF THE THREE MYSTERIES, CHAPTER 3: ON THE PRIMARY AND DISTINCTIVE DOCTRINE OF THE ŚRĪVAIṢṆAVA TRADITION

Here is an outline of *Essence*, chapter 3, "On the Distinguishing Doctrine of Our Tradition":

a. Opening verse
b. The meaning of "distinctive doctrine"

c. The distinguishing feature of our Vedānta: the lord as possessor of all as his body, as support of all, and as the one on whom all depends
d. The analogy of beings and their qualities and defining characteristics
e. The Lord supports all by his proper form and his will
f. The Lord upholds nature by his proper form and by will
g. The relationship of depending and being depended on
h. This knowledge of dependence as fruitful and exclusive
i. The distinctive teaching is revealed in the three holy mantras
j. The traditional teaching of Appuḷḷār on the *Tiru Mantra*
k. The *Tiru Mantra* and the freedom distinctive to humans
l. Concluding Tamil and Sanskrit verses

In ways that cannot be adequately detailed here, Deśika is setting up the entirety of his *Essence* – all thirty-two chapters – in this chapter. The theme of the human's utter dependence and the divine's utter intent to protect the human appears regularly and variously in the chapters to follow, and, as the title of the work suggests, in the regular reference to the truths of self and God as inscribed in the three mantras. A basic philosophical point about finitude is played out in a variety of theological and devotional ways.

Deśika does not discuss where Rāmānuja might have gotten the idea of the *body–possessor of the body* (*śarīra-śarīri*) relationship, although we know that the *dependent–depended upon* (*śeṣa-śeṣi*) relationship of utter dependence is most easily traced to the *Mīmāṃsā Sūtras* of Jaimini and notions of ritual utility. In Rāmānuja's usage (in the *Vedārtha Saṃgraha*, for instance)[6] both the *body–possessor of the body* and the *dependent–depended upon* relations are allied with a more elaborate theory of denotation, toward a striking conclusion about how language works and words mean: all words refer, not only to bodies and possessors of those bodies in our world, but ultimately to the Lord who is the inner support of all dependent realities.

But it is key that, at the start of the process, there is nothing in particular about this distinctive (*pratitantra*) idea that requires one to be a Śrīvaiṣṇava to understand it. Much of the middle of chapter 3 (sections e–h) is about the divine presence and intention that keep the universe in working order, and Deśika is very interested in how God supports all things by his simple existence and also by the divine will.

It is only in the latter part of the chapter that Deśika turns to the religious/spiritual meaning of the body–possessor of the body and dependent–depended upon relationship he has explained philosophically, by now turning to the liberative fruitfulness of knowing this relationship to God, and, for conscious beings, by choosing to affirm what is already ontologically the case; utter dependence (*śeṣatva*) counts as a distinctive religious position that is nonetheless first presented as a philosophical position that does not require faith or a learning of tradition. Later, it becomes a matter of ethics – service (being a servant, slave: *dāsatva*) – which then too is a matter of a spiritual life lived entirely in accord with dependence on God. One cannot end as a philosopher, but certainly one can begin as a philosopher.

When we get to the reflections on the *Tiru Mantra* (and other mantras) and the inner truths of the tradition (sections i, j, k), it is obviously the case that we have now become involved in insider discourse that requires respect for the mantras and a willingness to listen to and accept the traditional oral teaching of Appuḷḷār, Deśika's own teacher. These points are ostensibly inaccessible to non-Śrīvaiṣṇavas, and of little interest, and yet – this is the key point – for Deśika there is a natural and inevitable flow from the philosophical explication to the scriptural and mantric analyses, and to reflections drawn from the oral tradition.

Finally, the opening and closing verses of the chapter seem intended by Deśika to reach a wider audience that may find Deśika's arguments hard going, but can still appreciate the loveliness and devotion of such verses. Appreciative readers can thereby begin to appropriate, simply on the basis of beautiful words that "happen" to be rich in potent meaning, the underlying insight into dependence on God as a life-transforming reality. But I suggest that the verses are *more* accessible to readers when they understand the philosophical and linguistic and exegetical arguments in the chapter; for here, too, the boundaries are not fixed, and what is true easily shifts into what is beautiful.

TREATISE I.15–17: ON THE NATURAL LOVE FOR GOD AND THE FRUSTRATION OF THAT LOVE BY SIN

In the *Treatise* I.15–17 we do not see so dramatic a shift from philosophy to traditional wisdom, but there is still a very imaginative diversity to Sales's discourse, which includes philosophical grounding and a variety of spiritual claims. Here is my outline of the three chapters:

Treatise I.15, "Of the affinity there is between God and man"

a. The testimony of Aristotle; indications from ordinary experience
b. Human Pleasure in God is natural, but also known from scripture
c. The analogy of human and divine natures and ways of being and knowing
d. The reciprocal fulfillment of God and the human
e. Analogies: mother's milk; erotic affinity; wine and breasts
f. An appetite satisfied only in God

Treatise I.16, "That we have a natural inclination to love God above all things"

a. The inclination to God is both natural and supernatural
b. The desire for God persists even in the current state of things
c. The analogy of a partridge seeking its true mother
d. The instinct for God is never lost

Treatise I.17, "That we have not naturally the power to love God above all things"

a. The inclination toward God diminished by sin
b. The testimony of the philosophers
c. The failure of the philosophers to follow through on their knowledge
d. Imperfect love and the weakness of the will

Sales first (section I.15.a) stakes out a philosophical starting point, when he begins chapter 15 with reference to Aristotle's teaching on the proclivity of humans toward the celestial realm, in their search for happiness.[7] What philosophy declares, scripture confirms (section I.15.b)

Enlisting Aristotle as an ally, Sales echoes the classical Christian theological view – of Augustine and Aquinas, for instance – that humans are both innately oriented to God, happy only in that relationship, but also, in the current condition of original sin, unable ever to complete and satisfy that desire for union with God. Strikingly, he then (section I.15.c) takes up in a rather matter of fact fashion the analogy between the nature of the soul's self-knowledge and the Trinity's own knowledge of itself. While the latter is of course a specifically Christian doctrine, it is here presented in a rather matter of fact fashion, as accessible in reason to audience members willing to think about this truth that they already know.

Similarly, the reflection (in section I.15.d) on the joys of giving and receiving – the wondrous exchange of God and humans, by which both are fulfilled – does not at first demand any particular Christian insight – until Sales rather definitively determines that giving is better, because Jesus so indicated by his words and example. But clearly Sales is hoping to achieve more by turning (in section I.15.e) to the *Song of Songs*, and then to the images of breast feeding and erotic affinities; he wants to awaken the minds and desires of his readers, to make real his point on the natural intimacy of the self and God.

I.16 is at its core another affirmation of Catholic doctrine: sin damages and diminishes the innate human inclination toward God, but cannot destroy it. Yet here too, Sales offers a variety of reasons and analogies and does not depend simply on doctrine. Thus, just as a partridge chick raised by a partridge other than its mother instinctively seeks out its own mother, even a wandering soul inevitably and by instinct seeks for its true source, mother, God. The whole of I.16 is at once a careful analysis of the natural realm, which Sales wants to preserve, and a meditation on the role of grace, which for Sales is everywhere in nature.

I.17 is notable also because of its mention of philosophers. Here Sales employs another classic Christian apologetic strategy, both calling the pagan philosophers as witnesses to the truth of the one God and as examples of those who know what is true but do not follow up on it. This reading of the philosophers – sweeping, undocumented in the *Treatise* – is all about applying the judgment of *Romans* 1 to them, a move that requires confidence that Greek philosophers can be thus judged according to the New Testament. But two further points can be made. First, Sales is serious that the testimonies of the philosophers count for something; they do testify to the truth, and reading them illumines the truth of the one true God. Second, attacking the philosophers is not itself a goal. Sales's point (like that of Deśika later on, in chapter 7 of the *Essence*),[8] is that knowledge by itself is of no profit; an honest knower must recognize and live out the implications of what one has found to be true and change one's life. Sales's claim, correct or not, is that many a great philosopher had the right ideas but failed in courage and virtue when it came to stating forthrightly and living honestly what he (or she) had understood to be the case.

Together, the three chapters, with their inscribed references to scripture, the Greek philosophers (and Augustine's views on them), offer an intellectual terrain that is accessible as text and a set of ideas, and yet too an entrée to Christian-specific insights, apologetic and mystical. As one picks up the *Treatise* and begins to read it, one also begins to understand each of the elements Sales brings together, and all of them as interwoven, from the generally accessible to the more specifically Christian insider discourse.

READING DEŚIKA AND SALES TOGETHER, AS THE FOUNDATION FOR AN INTERCULTURAL REFLECTION

Against the background of a careful reading of the two excerpts – a reading merely suggested here, not fully practised – we can now engage in an additional and also complex operation of intercultural philosophical and theological reflection.

Each text affords access to a reasonable and intelligent reader but draws that reader into more particular and less comfortable modes of insight peculiar to each tradition itself. Reading the *Treatise* as a Roman Catholic, I am reminded of familiar themes, beliefs, and values, and I am taught to see them a little differently and more deeply; reading the *Essence* as a Roman Catholic, I begin to understand the unfamiliar, getting drawn into the ideas and then to beliefs and affective connections of the Śrīvaiṣṇava community. Reading them both together, both become both more and less familiar as expositions of ideas and beliefs and practices, and together create new combinations for consideration in a variety of ways. We can consider in turn issues of content, method, and the transformation of the reader. *Essence* 3 and *Treatise* I.15–17 read together as an intensely interesting and provocative, but also unruly and open-ended, site for an intercultural philosophy or theology that is *philosophical* and *religious* and possibly *mystical* too, if the individual texts and their combination do their work.

CONTENT

Reading the selected *Essence* and *Treatise* passages together allows us to reflect on the nature of the human in relation to the divine, beginning with basic anthropological and theological notions about human and divine beings. Both Deśika and Sales have strong and similar views about the orientation of all beings to God, and about how humans are in a position to observe this dynamism in nature and in themselves, making a choice to affirm the dynamism and live in accord with it. In a way that is not reducible to theses or general concepts, but which nonetheless is not overly encumbered with tradition-specific claims, these texts, read together, provide for us a site for an intercultural reflection on human nature and related matters; for they are written as if philosophy and faith rest on a continuum.

If one chooses, one can use these texts as a basis for arguing that there are universal – or at least universalizing – patterns to "the human" and its relation to "the divine"; for both Sales and Deśika argue for the same general pattern of human dependence on the divine, the finite on the transcendent, despite the vast differences in their religious and cultural locations and the utter lack of any shared historical context. However interesting such claims may be, they ought not to replace attention to the texts, since both authors want to do more than make claims about human nature, and their texts are always saying more than any set of claims drawn from them.

Both write with passion, and both put forward affective and imaginative claims and insights about desire and instigative of desire, as a physical and spiritual reality, about the natural and unexpected ways in which desire is fulfilled, and thus too thereby opening paths into the two traditions' positive religious and even mystical claims. In terms of ethical implications, both point to the ideal of a life entirely dedicated to God, and lived with a sense of not belonging to oneself, and then specify these implications in terms of more articulate communal religious values.

It is still more elusive to think about whether we also find in the *Essence* and the *Treatise* deeper mystical resonances lending credence to the view that mystical experiences are at least similar across religious and cultural boundaries. But one could just as easily accentuate differences in emotion or affect, noticing for instance that Sales's appeal to the *Song of Songs* and "the kisses of the mouth," is quite apart from Deśika's intense but restrained reflections on the graciousness of the divine teacher or the steadfastness of Rāma, Sītā, and Lakṣmaṇa in their forest travels.

METHOD

Each text "works" on multiple levels and makes connections among linguistic, philosophical, theological, mystical, and other tradition-based resources. When the texts are read together, the possibilities are maximized and intensified. Taken seriously, the continuum of traditional, religious, and rational insights written into the *Essence* 3 and *Treatise* I.15–17 facilitates a new conversation that can be philosophical and about human nature and finitude, or theological and about dependence on God, or pious and tradition-specific, or even a matter of rhetoric, related to the deeper and more particular ways by which writers touch the hearts of attentive readers who are open both to ideas and to religious sentiment. All of this can be thought and written through comparatively, perhaps beginning with the rhetoric of such texts.

This shared reading provides a complex starting point – reference, foundation, directions – for an intercultural reflection, philosophical or theological. Each text is itself a synthesis compounded by its author; together, the paired texts constitute a still more complex conversation in which the reader who is philosophically or theologically inclined reads his or her way back and forth across the spectrum of matters philosophical and theological, or rational and affective.

CHOICES BY THE AGENT OF AN INTERCULTURAL REFLECTION

If one then reads more widely in the whole of these texts, and then in other texts as well, there will be no end to what can be imagined and understood, philosophically or religiously, by a careful and dedicated reader. If so, the reader has to make choices about how to read and what to privilege, but also can never do so in a way that forecloses other such choices.

All of this then depends on the authors of each text, on the scholar who brings the hitherto unconnected texts together, and on subsequent readers (including the intercultural scholar) who read the two together and manage to shape meanings for them. There is no sure way to prescribe how such readers – from one tradition or the other, or from neither – is to begin to decipher either the *Essence* or the *Treatise* – for example, by preferring historical or philosophical analysis, or instead by plunging more directly into the more "interior" moments of tradition-specific and mystical language. So too, it is up to such readers to decide whether to follow the texts as far as they go, or to stop with any segment of their analysis. And finally, it follows that the various combinations open for an intercultural reflection – stressing the philosophical or the theological or the mystical, highlighting differences or similarities, speaking on a distanced and meta-level or deciding to become autobiographical – are up to the reader.

In all these moments, no particular choices by any given reader can foreclose other such possible choices; and no determinations, however forcefully made, can succeed in stipulating *the* meaning of the reading practice or the consequences to be drawn from it. My approach thus requires attention again to the agent – author, intercultural scholar, reader – and the capacities of that agent to cross boundaries and to learn with agility in the new framework, beginning with what he or she finds more accessible but then also moving to what is less so because of genuine or seeming demands on the agent to decide how and whether to be also a participant. This kind of intercultural theology or philosophy of religion is an inherently provisional practice that one cannot ever be quite finished with. The reading goes on – to great profit – but nonetheless is never done with.

I suggest that this entire process, in which the reader is intensively and continually over time faced with two (or more) potent texts which can be read in various ways but in no way that successfully ends the reading of them, can make the reader into a philosopher or theologian or even mystic, with an openness and selectivity that are appropriate to our times, and with a hopeful openness to the mysteries of which such texts, still and continually available, continue to speak.

ON THE LIMITS OF MY APPROACH

This is an approach that plays to my strengths and interests, but I would not seriously expect all intercultural work to proceed in this way. It is an approach that has its limits too. It is time-consuming, exhausting, and very slow-moving. However interesting this interplay is, it occurs only on a very small scale. The intercultural conversation is reduced to two cultural and religious traditions, and within that to the writings of specific thinkers and, often enough, as here, to specific manageable sections of such texts. It cannot seriously be justified as merely starting small; at such a pace as I am suggesting and illustrating here, not even a very large section of the engaged traditions could ever be covered. There would be no question of dealing with four or five or six such traditions, even if under ideal circumstances an energetic and learned person might deal with a number of texts, and possibly with a third tradition.

But then the more complex problems I have noticed with regard to the CRIP project re-emerge, should we try to figure out how to streamline things, for the sake of those who want to compare on a grander scale and without the patience to read very carefully over a very long period of time.

But, for now, the proof is in the reading: the following, larger part of this essay is not merely an appendix. Rather, it is the essential site where the work of an intercultural reading takes place, as readers seek to make sense philosophically and religiously of the claims and values proposed by Francis de Sales, Vedānta Deśika, and myself as a writer who has drawn them into my own project.

II. TEXTS

ESSENCE OF THE THREE MYSTERIES, CHAPTER 3, "ON THE DISTINGUISHING DOCTRINE OF OUR TRADITION"
by Vedānta Deśika

a. Opening verse[9]

"All this world –
what is and endures, its activity and results –
is the first maker's body,
in accord with rules regarding what it is to be depended
upon, and the rest:"
when one sees all this,
the Lord is seen in the mirror of the "pervasive" mantras,
and
one plumbs the workings of the minds
of those deep, uncreated peaks [our teachers].

b. The meaning of "distinctive doctrine"[10]

"Distinctive doctrine" (*"Pratitantra"*) indicates some idea that is not commonly shared; it distinguishes one's *siddhānta* (firm, core position), such as is not accepted by proponents of other such *siddhāntas*.

c. The distinguishing feature of our Vedānta: the lord as possessor of all as his body, as support of all, and as the one on whom all depends

If you ask what is that primary and non-common meaning belonging to our Vedānta system (*darśana*), it is the relationship of body and self between the lord and conscious and non-conscious beings. In this regard, the Lord is the possessor of the body (*śarīri*) – he is he who supports (*dhāraka*), in terms of restriction regarding things that are conscious or non-conscious; he is the controller (*niyanta*) and the one to whom all belongs (*śeṣi*). Conscious and non-conscious beings are the *śarīra* – things which are supported (*dhārya*) with respect to the lord, and also controlled (*niyamya*), and dependent (*śeṣa*). He is the support and controller for conscious and non-conscious beings, by his proper form and will, as prompting their existence, continuation, and activity.

d. The analogy of beings and their qualities and defining characteristics

How? Just as the dharmas defining the Lord's proper form and the *guṇas*, specifying his defined proper form [depend entirely on him but remain distinct], similarly, with respect to all those things that are separate from him, he is the support, without interruption and by his proper form.

He is also the support, as substance, for the *guṇas*, etc., that rely on other substances. Some-say that it is by way of the living selves (*jīvas*) that the Lord is the support for the bodies carried by those living souls. Other teachers (*ācāryas*) say that he is support by his proper form, though using the living selves as the means to that.

e. The Lord supports all by his proper form and his will

Thus, all things are inseparable specifications with respect to the Lord's proper form, and so their existence, etc., are dependent on the existence of that [divine] abode.

Yet the existence of all things depends on his will; that is, things that are impermanent arise by impermanent wishes, permanent things by his permanent wish. The discerning have distinguished this by the *śloka*,

> By your wish alone is the existence of all things.
> [Those which are eternally pleasing to you are eternal,
> eternally by their own proper form exclusively dependent
> on you –
> thus your auspicious *guṇas* are examples for us.]
> (*Vaikuṇṭa Stavam* 36 of Āḻvāṉ)

And so, their continuation – continuance in existence – dependent on the Lord's will – and so it is said that all depends on the Lord's will.

f. The Lord upholds nature by his proper form and by will

> That heavy things are carried by his will is stated in scripture,
> The heavens, moon, sun, stars, sky, directions, earth, great oceans – by the manly power of Vāsudeva, the great self, are held in order.
> [Mahābhārata, Anuśāsana Parva 254.136]

Thus they are rooted in their specific places, so that they don't fall.

If you ask what the proper form of the highest self does for such things that have being, continuation, and activity dependent on his will, it is the will of the highest self that makes it happen that all these various things depend on the proper form of the highest self. Thus, all things depend on the proper form of the Lord and also depend on the Lord's will.

In ordinary life, we see that the body depends on the proper form of that one that possesses the body, and on that one's will. After the time of that self's [living in that body], the body perishes when that living self leaves it. That this is a dependence on the proper form, and not on the will, is clear in the states of deep sleep, etc.

In the waking state, it abides by the will lest it fall – and so one can say that it is dependent on the will. It is said to be founded on (*adheyatva*) when it is dependent on the proper form; it is said to be controlled by (*niyamya*) when dependent on the will.

g. The relationship of depending and being depended on

The Lord is the one on whom all depends; as it says,

> He established the conscious and the non-conscious in their existence,
> enduring, and restriction, and so forth,
> indicating them as his own – thus the word of the Upaniṣads.
> Being the means and the goal – such is your Reality, not merely your qualities;
> and so, Lord of Śrī Raṅgam, I take you as my refuge, without pretext.
>
> – [*Śrīraṅgarājastava* II.87]

All these things exist for his purpose, and their sole proper way of being is to be for the sake of this Other; he has control of them, and by them he has his glory.

h. This knowledge of dependence as fruitful and exclusive

What is the fruit for the conscious being of this support–supported relation? We respond: By this support–supported relation, there is the acquisition of a proper form that definitely is not separable – just as is the case with his knowledge, power, etc. By this dependent–depended upon way of being, in accord with that settled human goal which is in keeping with the self's own understanding, there develops a taste for that human goal that is in keeping with his proper form. By the dependent–depended upon way of being and by the controller–controlled way of being, in accord with that human goal which is in keeping with his proper form, there is that specific means which has no need [for anything else]. It is this knowledge that is the fruit. By these, that conscious being becomes one who has no other foundation, no other purpose, no other refuge.

i. The distinctive teaching is revealed in the three holy mantras

If you ask how this meaning is present in the first mystery [*rahasya* mantra, the *Tiru Mantra*, *aum namo Nārāyaṇāya*, Om, reverence to Nārāyaṇa]: In the word "Nārāyaṇa," by the *tatpuruṣa* and *bahuvrīhi* forms of compound, we have both his being the support and the fact that he pervades all. Thus we grasp his proper form as specified by having no other foundation, etc. By the latter two words [in the mantra] which are the source for "being for the sake of the other" and "depending on the other," we find "having no other purpose" and "having no other refuge."

As for the jewel of a mantra [the *Dvaya Mantra*] that illumines the practice of taking refuge (*prapatti*), in its first clause, we find "having no other refuge," and in its latter clause, "having no other purpose." By both parts, [the *Dvaya Mantra*] illumines having no other foundation. These points are made in the *Carama Śloka* too, explicitly and implicitly.

Thus too, in the *Carama Śloka*, in order to win over the *siddha* means (the existent means, the Lord), we find the specification of the means that is to be accomplished [*sādhya* means, the means to be accomplished, taking-refuge]. By the *Dvaya Mantra*, we learn what needs to be meditated on at the time of performance; the *Tiru Mantra* illumines succinctly, as a small mirror show great forms, all the things that are needed.

j. The traditional teaching of Appuḷḷār on the Tiru Mantra

In the first word [*aum*], one sees the meanings found in the chariot of Arjuna, and in the verse,

> Rāma went in front, [Sītā, whose waist is lovely, in the middle; behind, with bow in hand, follows Lakṣmaṇa.][11]
>
> [*Rāmāyaṇa*, *Arāṇya Kāṇḍa* 3.11.1]

In the second word [*namo*], by the word itself, and by the proper-being [*svabhāva*] underlying that meaning, one knows the meanings that pertain to [the other brothers], Śrī Bharata and Śrī Śatrughan.

The meaning of the word "Nārāyaṇa" is in accord with [what the *a<u>l</u>vār* says]:

> "I am not, without you; but see, Nārāyaṇa, you without me are not," [*Nā<u>n</u>mukа<u>n</u> Tiruvantāti* 7]

This is seen when one takes as an example the people of the Kośala land and the emperor's son.[12]

The main thrust is seen in the first two words [*aum* and *namo*] – that is, respectively, the highest meaning that is reaching the goal, and dependence; that desired service – in which the one on whom all depends delights – lies in the meaning of the third word [Nārāyaṇa] in its dative form. All this is clear in the activity and cessation of activity that belong respectively to Lakṣmana and to his special *avatāra* that is Tiruvaṭi (the serpent Śeṣa[13]).

All this is Appuḷḷār's way that occasions meditation on the *Tiru Mantra*'s meaning. In the same way, the meanings of the *Dvaya Mantra* and *Carama Śloka* are clear.

k. The Tiru Mantra and the freedom distinctive to humans

In all this, the Lord's being the one on whom all depend is illumined as a characteristic common to both the conscious and the non-conscious. But this must be reflected on, particularly regarding his being Lord with respect to conscious beings. That is, being-dependent is common to both [conscious and non-conscious beings], but now [with respect to the conscious beings], this is to be meditated on with the conclusive, additional specification of being-a-servant. The dependent–depended upon relationship is common to both and is to be illumined by the dative [implied] in the first syllable.[14]

[With respect to the Lord and the self], being a servant and being a master are both specified here; this is manifest in the meaning [of Nārāyaṇa].[15] Thus both the general and the specific are found in "Nārāyaṇa." The general state of dependence here further indicates that [human] state of being a servant and of doing service that pertain to the conscious being. By this specification, the human goal has the form of service.

Similarly, by being the one on whom all depends, the lord is connected to abundance; this specification insures that his goal will come to fruition. With respect to the protection of conscious beings, the Lord is [self-]established and powerful; aside from their behaviour that depends on him, conscious beings have no foundation and remain impotent; such is the connection. The Lord's being the one on whom all depends is non-adventitious and so too his being the controller is non-adventitious; likewise, [individual selves'] total dependence is non-adventitious and so too their being-controlled is non-adventitious. The "one who possesses" [that is, God] thus protects "what he possesses" [that is, living beings]; the "potent one" protects "those who are not potent." When he protects, the Lord protects selves controlled by karma, making them focus on the means [by which they can see the Lord's protection]. This restriction [to dependence on their karma] has to do with his own will.

L. CONCLUDING TAMIL AND SANSKRIT VERSES

"He gave us our foundation,
he supports us,
he is the lord controlling us,
there is nothing that is not his,
he is our father, all is his,
there is no equal to him –
this one who wears tulasi leaves in his hair;
we are at his feet that are of inestimable value":
those learned in the Veda know this as its true content. (Tamil)

If in this final age someone most wise
knows this unique doctrine taught by the king of ascetics [Rāmānuja],
a dawn dispelling the darkness of ignorance,
then right there right then
the tumultuous waves of chattering arguments,
the caprice of those establishing their own various views,
will subside at once. (Sanskrit)

TREATISE I.15: OF THE AFFINITY THERE IS BETWEEN GOD AND MAN by Francis de Sales[16]

a. The testimony of Aristotle; indications from ordinary experience

As soon as man thinks with even a little attention of the divinity, he feels a certain delightful emotion of the heart, which testifies that God is God of the human heart; and our understanding is never so filled with pleasure as in this thought of the divinity, the smallest knowledge of which, as says [Aristotle], the prince of philosophers, is worth more than the greatest knowledge of other things,[17] just as the least beam of the sun is more luminous than the greatest of the moon or stars, yea is more luminous than the moon and stars together. And if some accident terrifies our heart, it immediately has recourse to the Divinity, protesting thereby that when all other things fail him, it alone stands his friend, and that when he is in peril, It only, as his sovereign good, can save and secure him.

b. Human Pleasure in God is natural, but also known from scripture

This pleasure, this confidence that man's heart naturally has in God, can spring from no other root than the affinity there is between this divine goodness and man's soul, a great but secret affinity, an affinity that each one knows but few understand, an affinity that cannot be denied nor yet be easily sounded. *We are created to the image and likeness of God* [*Genesis* 1]: what does this mean but that we have an extreme affinity with his divine majesty?

c. The analogy of human and divine natures and ways of being and knowing

Our soul is spiritual, indivisible, immortal; understands and wills freely, is capable of judging, reasoning, knowing, and of having virtues, in which it resembles God. It resides whole in the whole body, and whole in every part thereof, as the divinity is all in all the world, and all in every part thereof. Man knows and loves himself by produced and expressed acts of his understanding and will, which proceeding from the understanding and the will, and distinct from one another, yet are and remain inseparably united in the soul, and in the faculties from whence they proceed.

In the same way, the Son proceeds from the Father as his knowledge expressed, and the Holy Ghost as love breathed forth and produced from the Father and the Son, both the Persons being distinct from one another and from the Father, and yet inseparable and united, or rather one same, sole, simple, and entirely one indivisible divinity.

d. The reciprocal fulfillment of God and the human

But besides this affinity of likenesses, there is an incomparable correspondence between God and man, for their reciprocal perfection: not that God can receive any perfection from man, but because as man cannot be perfected but by the divine goodness, so the divine goodness can scarcely so well exercise its perfection outside itself, as upon our humanity: the one has great want and capacity to receive good, the other great abundance and inclination to bestow it. Nothing is so agreeable to poverty as a liberal abundance, nor to a liberal abundance as a needy poverty, and by how much the good is more abundant, by so much more strong is the inclination to pour forth and communicate itself. By how much more the poor man is in want, so much the more eager is he to receive, as a void is to fill itself.

The meeting then of abundance and indigence is most sweet and agreeable, and one could scarcely have said whether the abounding good has a greater contentment in spreading and communicating itself, or the failing and needy good in receiving and in drawing to itself, until Our Savior had told us that *it is more blessed to give than to receive.* [*Acts* 20. 35]. Now where there is more blessedness there is more satisfaction, and therefore the divine goodness receives greater pleasure in giving than we in receiving.

e. Analogies: mother's milk; erotic affinity; wine and breasts

Mothers' breasts are sometimes so full that they must offer them to some child, and though the child takes the breast with great avidity, the nurse offers it still more eagerly, the child pressed by its necessity, and the mother by her abundance.

The sacred spouse wished for the holy kiss of union: *O*, said she, *let him kiss me with the kiss of his mouth*. [*Song of Songs* 1.2]. But is there affinity enough, O well-beloved spouse of the well-beloved, between thee and thy loving one to bring to the union which thou desirest? Yes, says she: give me it; this kiss of union, O thou dear love of my heart: *for thy breasts are better than wine, smelling sweet of the best ointment* [*Song of Songs* 1.2–3]. New wine works and boils in itself by virtue of its goodness and cannot be contained within the casks; but thy breasts are yet better, they press thee more strongly, and to draw the children of thy heart to them, they spread a perfume attractive beyond all the scent of ointments.

f. An appetite satisfied only in God

Thus, Theotimus, our emptiness has need of the divine abundance by reason of its want and necessity, but God's abundance has no need of our poverty but by reason of the excellence of his perfection and goodness; a goodness which is not at all bettered by communication, for it acquires nothing in pouring itself out of itself; on the contrary, it gives: but our poverty would remain wanting and miserable, if it were not enriched by the divine abundance. Our soul then seeing that nothing can perfectly content her, and that nothing the world can afford is able to fill her capacity, considering that her understanding has an infinite inclination ever to know more, and her will an insatiable appetite to love and find the good; – has she not reason to cry out:

> Ah! I am not then made for this world, there is a sovereign good on which I depend, some infinite workman who has placed in me this endless desire of knowing, and this appetite which cannot be appeased!

And therefore I must tend and extend towards Him, to unite and join myself to the goodness of Him to whom I belong and whose I am! Such is the affinity between God and man's soul.

TREATISE I.16: THAT WE HAVE A NATURAL INCLINATION TO LOVE GOD ABOVE ALL THINGS

a. The inclination to God is both natural and supernatural

If there could be found any men who were in the integrity of original justice in which Adam was created, though otherwise not helped by another assistance from God than that which he affords to each creature, in order that it may be able to do the actions befitting its nature, such men would not only have an inclination to love God above all things but even naturally would be able to put into execution just such an inclination.

For as this heavenly author and master of nature co-operates with and lends his strong hand to fire to spring on high, to water to flow towards the sea, to earth to sink down to its centre and stay there – so having himself planted in man's heart a special natural inclination not only to love good in general but to love in particular and above all things his divine goodness which is better and sweeter than all things – the sweetness of his sovereign providence required that he should contribute to these blessed men of whom we speak as much help as should be necessary to practice and effectuate that inclination.

This help would be on the one hand natural, as being suitable to nature, and tending to the love of God as author and sovereign master of nature, and on the other hand it would be supernatural because it would correspond not with the simple nature of man but with nature adorned, enriched and honoured by original justice, which is a supernatural quality proceeding from a most special favour of God. But as to the love above all things that such help would enable these men to practice, it would be called natural because virtuous actions take their names from their objects and motives, and this love of which we speak would only tend to God as acknowledged to be author, lord and sovereign of every creature by natural light only, and consequently to be amiable and estimable above all things by natural inclination and tendency.

b. The desire for God persists even in the current state of things

And although now our human nature be not endowed with that original soundness and righteousness which the first man had in his creation, but on the contrary be greatly depraved by sin, yet still the holy inclination to love God above all things stays with us, as also the natural light by which we see his sovereign goodness to be more worthy of love than all things; and it is impossible that one thinking attentively upon God, yea even by natural reasoning only, should not feel a certain movement of love which the secret inclination of our nature excites in the bottom of our hearts, by which at the first apprehension of this chief and sovereign object, the will is taken, and perceives itself stirred up to a complacency in it.

c. The analogy of a partridge seeking its true mother

It happens often amongst partridges that one steals away another's eggs with intention to sit on them, whether moved by greediness to become a mother, or by a stupidity which makes them mistake their own, and behold a strange thing, yet well supported by testimony! – the young one which was hatched and nourished under the wings of a stranger partridge, at the first call of the true mother, who had laid the egg whence she was hatched, quits the thief-partridge, goes back to the first mother, and puts herself in her brood, from the correspondence which she has with her first origin. Yet this correspondence appeared not, but remained secret, shut up and as it were sleeping in the bottom of nature, till it met with its object; when suddenly excited, and in a sort awakened, it produces its effect, and turns the young partridge's inclination to its first duty.

d. The instinct for God is never lost

It is the same, Theotimus, with our heart, which though it be formed, nourished and bred amongst corporal, base, and transitory things, and in a manner under the wings of nature, notwithstanding, at the first look it throws on God, at its first knowledge of him, the natural and first inclination to love God, which was dull and imperceptible, awakes in an instant, and suddenly appears as a spark from amongst the ashes, which touching our will gives it a movement of the supreme love due to the sovereign and first principle of all things.

TREATISE I.17: THAT WE HAVE NOT NATURALLY THE POWER TO LOVE GOD ABOVE ALL THINGS

a. The inclination toward God diminished by sin

Eagles have a great heart, and much strength of flight, yet they have incomparably more sight than flight and extend their vision much quicker and further than their wings.

So our souls, animated with a holy natural inclination towards the divinity, have far more light in the understanding to see how lovable it is than force in the will to love it. Sin has much more weakened man's will than darkened his intellect, and the rebellion of the sensual appetite, which we call concupiscence, does indeed disturb the understanding, but still it is against the will that it principally stirs up sedition and revolt: so that the poor will, already quite infirm, being shaken with the continual assaults that concupiscence directs against it, cannot make so great progress in divine love as reason and natural inclination suggest to it that it should do.

b. The testimony of the philosophers

Alas! Theotimus, what fine testimonies not only of a great knowledge of God, but also of a strong inclination towards him, have been left by those great philosophers, Socrates, Plato, Trismegistus, Aristotle, Hippocrates, Seneca, Epictetus?

SOCRATES

Socrates, the most highly praised amongst them, came to the clear knowledge of the unity of God, and felt in himself such an inclination to love him that, as Saint Augustine testifies,[18] many were of opinion that he never had any other aim in teaching moral philosophy than to purify minds that they might better contemplate the sovereign good, which is the simple unity of the Divinity.

PLATO

And as for Plato, he sufficiently declares himself in his definition of philosophy and of a philosopher, saying that to do the part of a philosopher is nothing else but to love God and that a philosopher is no other thing than a lover of God.[19] What shall I say of the great Aristotle, who so efficaciously proves the unity of God[20] and has spoken so honourably of it in so many places?

c. The failure of the philosophers to follow through on their knowledge

But, O eternal God! those great spirits which had so great an inclination to love it were all wanting in force and courage to love it well. By visible creatures *they have known the invisible things of God*, yea even *his eternal power also and divinity*, says the Apostle, *so that they are inexcusable. Because that, when they knew God, they have not glorified him as God, or given thanks.* [Romans 1. 20ff.] They glorified him indeed in some sort, attributing to him sovereign titles of honour, yet they did not glorify him as they ought; that is, they did not glorify him above all things, not having the courage to destroy idolatry, but communicating with idolaters, *detaining the truth* which they knew *in injustice*, prisoner in their hearts, and preferring the honour and vain repose of their lives before the honour due unto God, *they grew vain in their knowledge.*

SOCRATES

Is it not a great pity, Theotimus, to see Socrates, as Plato reports, speak upon his deathbed concerning the gods as though there had been many, he knowing so well that there was but one only?[21] Is it not a thing to be deplored that Plato who understood so clearly the truth of the divine unity should ordain that sacrifice should be offered to many gods?[22]

HERMES TRISMEGISTUS

And is it not a lamentable thing that Mercury Trismegistus should so basely lament and grieve over the abolition of idolatry,[23] who on so many occasions had spoken so worthily of the divinity?

EPICTETUS

But above all I wonder at the poor good man Epictetus, whose words and sentences are so sweet in our tongue, in the translation which the learned and agreeable pen of Jean de Saint-François Goulu, Provincial of the Congregation of the Feuillants in the Gauls, has recently put before us.[24] For what a pity it is, I pray you, to see this excellent philosopher speak of God sometimes with such relish, feeling, and zeal that one would have taken him for a Christian coming from some holy and profound meditation, and yet again from time to time talking of gods after the Pagan manner! Alas! this good man, who knew so well the unity of God and had so much delight in his goodness, why had he not the holy jealousy of the divine honour, so as not to stumble or dissemble in a matter of so great consequence?

d. Imperfect love and the weakness of the will

In a word, Theotimus, our wretched nature spoilt by sin, is like palm-trees in this land of ours, which indeed make some imperfect productions and as it were experiments of fruits, but to bear entire, ripe, and seasoned dates – that is, reserved for hotter climates.

For so our human heart naturally produces certain beginnings of God's love, but to proceed so far as to love him above all things, which is the true ripeness of the love due unto this supreme goodness, – this belongs only to hearts animated and assisted with heavenly grace, and which are in the state of holy charity. This little imperfect love of which nature by itself feels the stirrings is but a will without will, a will that would but wills not, a sterile will, which does not produce true effects, a will sick of the palsy, which sees the healthful pond of holy love, but has not the strength to throw itself into it. [*John* 5.7][25] To conclude, this will is an abortion of good will, which has not the life of generous strength necessary to effectually prefer God before all things. Whereupon the Apostle speaking in the person of the sinner, cries out: *To will good is present with me, but to accomplish that which is good I find not.* [*Romans* 7.18]

Notes

1 On the problem of reading carefully and the resistance of texts to selective readings, see my recent essay, "Augustine, Apuleius, and Hermes Trismegistus: The City of God and Advice on How (Not) to Read Hindu Texts," in Kim Paffenroth, ed., *Augustine and World Religions* (Lanham, MD: Lexington, 2008), 141–72.

2 *The Human Condition; Ultimate Realities; Religious Truth.* 3 vols. The Comparative Religious Ideas Project. Edited by Robert C. Neville (New York: SUNY Press, 2000).

3 Francis X. Clooney, S.J., *Hindu God, Christian God: How Reason Helps Break Down the Boundaries Between Religions* (New York: Oxford University Press, 2001).

4 *Beyond Compare: St. Francis de Sales and Śrī Vedānta Deśika on Loving Surrender to God* (Washington, DC: Georgetown University Press, 2008).

5 See "Forms of Philosophizing: The Case of Chapter 7 of Vedānta Deśika's *Śrīmad Rahasya Traya Sāra*," Satya Nilayam and "Passionate Comparison: The Intensification of Affect in Interreligious Reading – A Hindu-Christian Example," *Harvard Theological Review* 98, no. 4 (2005): 367–90.

6 See, for instance, Paragraphs 13–17 (SS Raghavachar tr.).

7 In the *Treatise*, de Sales mentions Aristotle by name fourteen times, Plato six times, and other philosophers occasionally in the *Treatise*. See also XI.10, in which he attacks pagan virtue as self-indulgence.

8 See Clooney, "Forms of Philosophizing: The Case of Chapter 7 of Vedānta Deśika's *Śrīmad Rahasya Traya Sāra*," *Satya Nilayam: Chennai Journal of Intercultural Philosophy* 8 (August 2005): 21–33.

9 I have consulted the Ayyangar translation (1956), but the translation here is my own. In both the *Essence* and *Treatise*, subtitles are my additions.

10 In his recent commentary on this chapter, the Ahobila Math Jeer Swāmi indicates that Deśika explains his use of pratitantra in the *Nyayapariśuddhi*, but I have not been able to discern which passage he means.

11 The *Sārāsvadinī* says that the example of Arjuna indicates the śeṣa-śeṣi relation, and the *Rāmāyaṇa* verse indicates, with Rāma, Sītā, and Lakṣmaṇa, the respective components of the a-u-m sequence.

12 That is, the inability of the people of Ayodhyā to live without Rāma.

13 *Śeṣa* is thus a "totally dependent being" and also "the serpent entirely at the service of Nārāyaṇāya."

14 That is, the "a" in Aum stands for the Lord and is in the dative, as is "Nārāyaṇaya."

15 Understood to mean, "He is the support [*ayana*] for all beings [*nara*]."

16 I have used the Mackey translation. See Clooney's letter of correction. *Treatise on the Love of God by St. Francis de Sales*. Translated by Henry Benedict Mackey, OSB. Rockford, Illinois: Tan Books and Publishers Inc. 1997 [1884].

17 By Aristotle, *On the Parts of Animals* 1.5 [part] "Of things constituted by nature some are ungenerated, imperishable, and eternal, while others are subject to generation and decay. The former are excellent beyond compare and divine, but less accessible to knowledge. The evidence that might throw light on them, and on the problems which we long to solve respecting them, is furnished but scantily by sensation; whereas respecting perishable plants and animals we have abundant information, living as we do in their midst, and ample data may be collected concerning all their various kinds, if only we are willing to take sufficient pains. Both departments, however, have their special charm. The scanty conceptions to which we can attain of celestial things give us, from their excellence, more pleasure than all our knowledge of the world in which we live; just as a half glimpse of persons that we love is more delightful than a leisurely view of other things, whatever their number and dimensions. On the other hand, in certitude and in completeness our knowledge of terrestrial things has the advantage. Moreover, their greater nearness and affinity to us balances somewhat the loftier interest of the heavenly things that are the objects of the higher philosophy." Sales refers to but does not quote the text.

18 *City of God*, VIII, 3. The editor of the *Treatise* notes that the references to *The City of God* are noted by de Sales himself.

19 *City of God*, VIII, 9.

20 *Metaphysics*, 12.10; *The World* (near the end).

21 *City of God*, VIII, 12.

22 *City of God*, VIII, 12.

23 *City of God*, VIII, 23–24.

24 In his *Les propos d'Épictète, recueillis par Arrian, Auteur Grec, son disciple* [1609].

25 With reference to the pool of water at Siloam, able to heal after being touched by an angel.

Phenomenology of Awakening in Zhiyi's Tiantai Philosophy

CHEN-KUO LIN
National Chengchi University

> Buddhism can be paralleled only with the highest formations of the philosophical and religious spirit of our European culture. From now on it will be our destiny to blend that Indian way of thinking which is completely new for us, with the one which for us is old, but which in this confrontation becomes alive and strengthened.[1]
>
> — *Edmund Husserl*

I. INTRODUCTION

In this chapter, I will explore the Buddhist phenomenology of awakening as exemplified in the philosophical writings of Zhiyi (智顗, 538–597), the founder of the Tiantai School of Buddhism. The phrase "phenomenology of awakening" was deliberately coined in contrast to "phenomenology of mundane experience." In the Buddhist context, the former may be referred to as "phenomenology of insight," whereas the latter is classifiable as "phenomenology of consciousness." In both forms of phenomenology, method is required for the disclosure of truth. However, there are different articulations of truth through different methods employed in different religious and philosophical systems. This chapter will be mainly concerned with how the truth of awakened experience is disclosed through the meditative method in the Buddhist phenomenology of Zhiyi.

Before delving into the discussion proper, I would first like to highlight several preliminary methodological notes. In complying with the formative ideas of this volume, which attempts to investigate the ways in which Western philosophy and religion can be rethought through non-Western categories, I would like to raise two questions. First, in what sense can Zhiyi's Tiantai philosophy be characterized as a form of phenomenology? Second, in what way can Husserlian phenomenology be further developed into a phenomenology of awakening as envisioned in the Buddhist tradition? For the first question, I would argue that Buddhist philosophy in general can be characterized as phenomenological and that Zhiyi's philosophy is no exception. Viewing Buddhist philosophy in terms of phenomenology has been the trend in recent decades, and the compatibility of the Buddhist and Western ways of philosophizing has been brilliantly explored by several leading scholars, such as J. Mohanty, Iso Kern, Dan Lusthaus, Plamen Gradinarov, and Ni Liangkang. Most of them are interested in teasing out from Yogācāra Buddhism its phenomenological elements, such as the intentional structure of cognition. They insist that the mode of philosophizing with regard to our understanding of Buddhist philosophy needs to shift from metaphysics to epistemology, and then from epistemology to phenomenology. According to the phenomenological approach, both the object of cognition and the act of cognition are seen as two poles in the same structure of consciousness for the reason that consciousness is always conscious of both itself and something else. For both Husserl and Yogācāra, the structure of consciousness consists of three parts: in addition to the object and act of cognition, there also exists the *self-awareness* of consciousness. It is in the domain of consciousness that all experience occurs, including the experience of "things themselves" in both the Buddhist and Husserlian senses. Things themselves should not be regarded as something separate from our conscious experience. Hence, all we need concern ourselves with is *how* things appear in our experience of consciousness, and what we should *not* concern ourselves with is metaphysical speculation. This is the phenomenological attitude shared by Zhiyi and Husserl.

And as we begin to appreciate the similar phenomenological trends in non-Western philosophies, including especially Buddhist philosophy, we should, however, be cautious not to fall into one-sided readings. To gloss over substantive differences in doing comparative philosophy will inevitably result in miscategorizations, such as, for example, picturing Mencius as Kant, or Zhuangzi as Heidegger. Taking hermeneutical directives from Ricoeur and Gadamer, I prefer to adopt the method of dialogical reading, hoping that the "other" can be brought into critical conversation. For this essay, therefore, I would like to see in Zhiyi's philosophy the possibility of a contribution to the mainstream of phenomenology. And here arises the second question: Is it possible for phenomenologists to learn anything new from Zhiyi's Buddhist philosophy? What exactly can be added to the diversity of the phenomenological legacy from the canons of Buddhist philosophy?

In order to clearly address these questions, this study has been divided into two sections. The first section will attempt to lay out the Buddhist distinction between mundane experience and awakened experience. The two forms of knowledge, mundane knowledge (識; *vijñāna*) and trans-mundane insight (智; *prajñā*) will be closely examined. For convenience, I use "knowledge" to mean "mundane knowledge" and "insight" to mean "trans-mundane knowledge."[2] In the second part, I will focus on Zhiyi's soteriological phenomenology with special attention given to the problems of truth, meditation, and insight.

II. KNOWLEDGE AND INSIGHT

A possible contribution to Husserlian phenomenology might be best found by way of exploring the Buddhist distinctions of *enlightened experience* and *non-enlightened experience*. The former arises from the realization of non-discriminative knowledge (*nirvikalpa-jñāna*), whereas the latter, mundane experience, results from discriminative knowledge (*vijñāna*). Through this distinction, we see the inseparability of experience and knowledge.

But before fully fleshing out the distinctions in Buddhist theory, let us look into Husserl first, who was not completely ignorant of Buddhism as religion and philosophy. In a book review written in 1925 for Karl Eugen Neumann's German translation of the *Suttapitaka*, Husserl praised Buddhism as "a religiosity which looks purely inward in vision and deed – which, I should say, is not 'transcendent', but 'transcendental' – enters the horizon of our religious and ethical as well as of our philosophical consciousness."[3] Although Husserl's remark is very brief, it nonetheless demonstrates that he did view Buddhist philosophy from the perspective of transcendental phenomenology. Here the term "transcendental" is used by Husserl to mean the attitude that is "directed itself to the life of consciousness – *in which* the 'world' is for us precisely that, the world which is present *to us* – we find ourselves in a new cognitive attitude [or situation]," whereas in the natural attitude "the world is for us the self-evidently existing universe of realities which are continuously before us in unquestioned givenness."[4] Husserl seemed quite excited to learn that this "transcendental" insight has long been seen as the guiding principle of Buddhist meditation; that is, the constitution of the world is taken as the object of consciousness in meditative contemplation. Unlike the natural attitude in which the existence of the external world is uncritically assumed, in Buddhist meditation, a practitioner is trained to withdraw from all metaphysical assumptions about the world and reside in solitude for sober contemplation. The practitioner believes that, unless metaphysical assumptions about the existence of the world have been methodically "bracketed," she will be unable to clearly discern the way that objects appear in consciousness. This mode of thinking may be properly regarded as a shift from the "natural attitude" to the "phenomenological attitude."[5]

As mentioned above, the distinction between the enlightened experience and the non-enlightened experience is central to Buddhist philosophy. This distinction can be understood either in terms of ontology or of epistemology. As an ontological distinction, it involves the notion of two *realms* of existence. In view of epistemology, however, the distinction is rather seen as two ways of knowing, i.e., enlightenment and ignorance. According to the Buddhist theory of two truths, these two aspects are inseparable. Methodologically speaking, we should proceed from epistemological analysis to ontological exposition, asking: How does our knowledge of the world become discriminated and concealed? Conversely, what are the conditions for the possibility of unconcealed or non-discriminated knowledge? The Buddhist answer can be found in the various analyses of cognition. Briefly, ignorance (concealment) appears as the result of discriminated knowledge, whereas enlightenment (non-concealed knowledge) is realized by non-discriminated insight. Unless fundamental transformation from the cognitive state of discriminated knowledge to the cognitive state of non-discriminated insight has been accomplished, salvific liberation remains impossible.

Regarding the Buddhist theory of cognition, which is systematically elaborated in the *Abhidharmaśabhāsya* of Vasubandhu, *vijñāna* and *jñāna* are taken as synonymous with cognition/knowledge. *Vijñāna* is defined as cognition relative to each object (*viṣayaṃprativijñapti*).[6] It is also understood as *upalabdhi* (apprehension), which is etymologically derived from the root *labh*, meaning "to seize, get possession of, acquire, receive, obtain, or find."[7] In the usage of epistemology, *vijñāna* (consciousness) refers to cognition that *seizes* something as its object (*viṣaya*) and *makes it known* to the one who cognizes. Accordingly, cognition never exists in itself; it must be the cognition *of* something. For instance, visual-consciousness never exists without form as the visual object. By the same token, visual-consciousness also needs the visual faculty as the condition for its arising. However, knowledge cannot be explained by the function of sensory *vijñāna* only. It requires *prajñā* (understanding) in conjunction with sensory perception for the conditions of knowledge to obtain. In this respect, *prajñā* is defined as the discernment/examination of objects.[8] In contrast to the longstanding misconception of *prajñā* as "mystical wisdom," interpreting it rather as the "source of true knowledge" better coheres with the actual usage of the term in the literature. Instead of alluding to something mysterious, most Buddhist philosophers employ the notion of *prajñā* in the epistemological sense. Keeping this in mind, we should resist the tendency to mystify the notion of "insight" in Zhiyi's philosophy.

Historically, the distinction between "insight/correct knowledge" (*samyagjñāna*) and "discriminated knowledge" (*vijñāna*) as two forms of knowledge seems to make its first appearance in Yogācārin literature. In the *Yogācārabhūmi*, "insight/correct knowledge" is defined as "intuitive knowledge of things themselves (*tathātā*)" in contrast to "discriminated knowledge," which is embedded in conceptualization and verbalization. Three kinds of insight are listed: (1) trans-mundane insight, (2) mundane insight, and (3) trans-in-mundane insight. The first refers to intuitive knowledge of the non-existence of external objects. The second refers to *abstract* knowledge of things in themselves, which is acquired through conceptual thinking (*vikalpa*). The third one refers to the trans-mundane knowledge that is realized within the context of the mundane.[9] In the *Mahāprajñāpāramitāśāstra*, we find another account of three forms of insight (correct knowledge) similar to those elaborated in Yogācārin literature. They are (1) insight of all phenomena (一切智; *sarvajñatā*), (2) insight of paths (道種智; *margajñatā*) and (3) insight of all modes of phenomena (一切種智; *sarvākārajñatā*).[10] As we shall see below, this theory of threefold insight plays an important role in Zhiyi's philosophy.

The distinction between knowledge and insight was also further elaborated in the Yogācārin theory of the eightfold consciousness and fourfold insight. Briefly speaking, in Yogācāra's transformative phenomenology, the eightfold consciousness (five sensory consciousnesses, apperceptive-consciousness, ego-consciousness, and storehouse-consciousness) must be transformed into fourfold insight (all-accomplishing insight, intellectual discerning insight, equality insight, and mirror insight).[11] That is, the five sensory consciousnesses are transformed into all-accomplishing insight, apperceptive-consciousness to intellectual discerning insight, self-consciousness to equality insight, and storehouse-consciousness to mirror insight. A brief outline of the theory of fourfold insight found in Xuanzang's *Vijñaptimātratāsiddhi* is provided below (T.31.56.a):[12]

(1) *Mirror Insight* (大圓鏡智; *ādarśajñāna*): "The mind associated with this insight is dissociated from conceptual constructions (*vikalpa*). Its objects of cognition and their characteristics are too subtle and difficult to be discerned.... It is pure and free of impurity.... Like a great mirror, it reflects the images of all physical objects."

(2) *Equality Insight* (平等性智; *samatājñāna*): "The mind associated with this insight sees the nondiscrimination of all existents, including self and other sentient beings. It is always associated with great compassion.... It is also the special support for intellectual discerning insight."

(3) *Intellectual Discerning Insight* (妙觀察智; *pratyavekṣāṇājñāna*): "The mind associated with this insight perfectly sees the particular (*svalakṣaṇa*) and

the universal (*sāmānyalakṣaṇa*) of existence. It functions without any hindrance."

(4) *All-accomplishing Insight* (成所作智; *kṛtyānuṣṭhānajñāna*): "The mind associated with this insight is capable of performing actions of body, speech, and thought for the benefits of all sentient beings."

The above theory of insight in Yogācārin philosophy can be summarized as follows: Insight is freed from conceptual construction. Following the Abhidharma usage, the Yogācārin notion of insight refers to the cognitive function of understanding (*prajñā*), which is always associated with various forms of cognition (*vijñāna*). The key factor responsible for the distinction between insight and knowledge is conceptual construction (*vikalpa*) in association with cognition. Insight is freed from conceptual construction, whereas ordinary knowledge is embedded in conceptual construction. In most Buddhist texts, *vijñāna* and *vikalpa* are often taken as synonyms, with the latter being more appropriately understood as the "constitution of meaning" in the structure of noesis and noema. In addition to epistemic meaning, *vikalpa* also connotes a sense of psychological attachment. For Buddhism, knowing something is not merely a cognitive act. It is always associated with, or even dominated by, various non-cognitive or ideological factors. This is the reason why the fundamental form of insight is referred to as "insight freed from conceptual/ideological construction." With insight, one is capable of correctly cognizing the aspects of the object: the particular and the universal. As Dignāga argues, these two aspects of the object are known by perception and inference respectively. Aside from this, there is nothing else one can know. According to Abhidharma, however, a yoga-practitioner is capable of directly perceiving the universal character of the object.[13] With insight one also cognizes the equality of all existents, i.e., the truth that all existents are *equally* empty of permanent essence.

There is another crucial issue left for further investigation: Is insight, which is said to be freed from the act of conceptual construction, intentional? If the answer is affirmative, what then is the intentional structure of insight? Can we find the same threefold intentional structure (noesis, noema, self-awareness) in insight? If insight has the same intentional structure of consciousness, then the difference between the two forms of knowledge requires an explanation. Historically, this issue was debated in the Chinese Yogācāra School. Three theories were given in response to this issue in Xuanzang's *Siddhi* (T.31.49.c-50.a): (1) Insight is void of the structure of noesis (the part of seeing) and noema (the part of the seen); (2) insight is structured in noesis and noema; and (3) in insight noesis exists only, but not noema. The last theory, held by Dharmapāla and Xuanzang, was considered the orthodox view.[14] In regards to the debate, however, it should be noted that fundamental insight is generally characterized as being devoid of subject as the grasper (*grāhaka*) and object as the grasped (*grāhya*). The duality of subject as the grasper and object as the grasped is merely a mental construction, which can be eliminated due to its being void of permanent essence. However, the noesis-noema structure in insight remains without change, even if the duality of subject-object is eliminated.

In sum, the difference between mundane knowledge and insight rather lies in the function of the objectivating act, i.e., cognitive construction (*vikalpa*).[15] In mundane knowledge, noesis (the seeing) is objectivated as the subject-as-grasper and noema (the seen) is objectivated as the object-as-grasped. In contrast, the act of objectivation ceases to function in the enlightened experience while the structure of noesis and noema remains intact in regard to insight. This interpretation can be justified by the Yogācārin theory of the three natures (*trisvabhāva*), although it differs somewhat from the orthodox position held by Dharmapāla and Xuanzang. According to the theory of three natures, the duality of grasper and grasped belongs to discursive constructions (*parikalpita*), whereas the structure of consciousness is seen as the ground of phenomena in dependent-arising (*paratantra*). This theory concludes that it is discursive construction, instead of phenomena themselves, that should be eliminated.

III. ZHIYI'S PHENOMENOLOGY OF AWAKENING

Let us now turn to Zhiyi. What is the enlightened experience disclosed in Zhiyi's philosophy? What is Zhiyi's conception of mind/consciousness? And what is Zhiyi's response to Yogācāra and Mādhyamika? Before addressing these questions in detail, I would like to first point out that Zhiyi was more eager than his contemporaries to take on a phenomenological approach for disclosing the experience of "things themselves (*shixiang;* 實相; real phenomena)." However, he was not content with Yogācāra's epistemological approach and also rejected the metaphysical idealism prevalent in certain Chinese Yogācāra sects. As to the Mādhyamika approach, Zhiyi was largely sympathetic. Unlike Indian Mādhyamika thinkers, however, he was not interested in doing logical and epistemological justification for the "thesis" of emptiness. For Zhiyi, the most important issue was the direct realization of "things themselves" through meditation (cessation and contemplation). Zhiyi maintained that, without the direct realization of "things themselves" in meditation, truth would remain abstract and speculative, and thus completely useless for realizing enlightenment. As a devoted Buddhist practitioner, Zhiyi held meditation to be the only genuine path to awakening.

Mind and Worlds

Let us now examine Zhiyi's theory of mind/consciousness, which he holds to be the first object of meditative contemplation. In contrast to Abhidharma and Yogācāra's dualistic conceptions of mind in two aspects (deluded mind and enlightened mind), Zhiyi urges us to return to the *experience* of mind before the metaphysical categorizations of mind as either deluded or pure. For Zhiyi, the practical implication of the dualistic conception of mind is that a certain period of *time* is required as metaphysical assumption for accomplishing the soteriological task of transformation from the deluded state of mind to the pure state of mind. Zhiyi clearly rejects metaphysical speculation about time, which, as he believes, will in the end take us nowhere. On the contrary, Zhiyi contends that the problem of time should be treated *within* the context of meditative practice. That is, time is pragmatically conceivable only in terms of the evolving process of consciousness in meditation. For both Zhiyi and Husserl, one should methodically bracket metaphysical assumptions about the existence of mind and world in order to make the experience of worlds-in-mind fully manifested. Just like Husserl, Zhiyi asks us to turn to "contemplation of mind" (*guanxin;* 觀心) in which all worlds are manifested. Let us see how Zhiyi presented his phenomenological description of mind in the famous passage on "three thousand worlds in one-instant mind"[16]:

> A single thought exists along *with* the ten realms. A single realm exists along *with* the [other] ten realms, so there are one hundred realms. One realm exists along *with* thirty types of worlds [i.e., each of the ten realms are included in each of the three types of worlds: the world of sentient beings, the worlds of the five skandhas, and the worlds of lands]; multiplied by one hundred realms. This results in the existence *with* three thousand types of worlds. These three thousand [worlds] exist along *with* a single momentary thought. If there is no mind, that is the end of the matter. If there is even an ephemeral mind, it exists *with* three thousand [realms]. [emphasis added]

In Paul Swanson's translation, "one mind" is rendered as a "single thought" in order to "avoid the implication of a reified 'mind' as separate from mental functioning and 'objects' that are experienced."[17] This clarification is quite helpful. However, I take issue with his translation of *ju* (具) as "include." Instead, I render it as "exist along with," indicating the simultaneous correlativity of mind (as intentional act) and worlds (as intentional objects). That is, whenever a single thought/mind arises, there simultaneously arises the realm of objects to which it correlates. This description ties in with the classic insight of phenomenology that holds that mind is always conscious of something as its intentional object. Hence, if we follow Swanson in translating the first sentence as "A single thought *includes* the ten dharma realms," the interpretative results will be in opposition to Zhiyi's own phenomenological intent.

How should we then interpret Zhiyi's famous statement, "Three thousand worlds exist *with* a single momentary thought"? It would be pretty easy to understand this statement if Zhiyi had claimed that a single thought arises with a single world. However, the theory of one-to-one correspondence between mind and world is subject to Zhiyi's criticism because it contradicts the Buddhist teaching of emptiness. For there is nothing called "one single thought," neither is there anything called "one single world." Everything, including mind and world, exist inter-relatively and inter-penetratively within the net of existence. Instead of being taken as an empirical description, Zhiyi's fundamental maxim should be read as a description of "real phenomena" that have been realized through phenomenological reduction. In other words, this statement should be understood in view of insight, instead of in view of empirical knowledge. As a result of this phenomenological reduction, all phenomena are themselves shown as the objects inter-relatively constituted in the non-objectivating consciousness.

Zhiyi continues to clarify what is and what is not the proper understanding of the relation between mind and worlds. It is important to note that for Zhiyi the phenomenon of *being-with* cannot be explained by any form of metaphysics. Among various forms of metaphysics, Zhiyi rejects metaphysical idealism in particular, which includes the idealisms of both the pure and the deluded mind. In Zhiyi's own words,

> If all phenomena arise *from* a single moment of mind, this is a vertical [relationship]; if a mind in one moment *encompasses* all phenomena, this is a horizontal [relationship]. But these are neither [merely] vertical nor [merely] horizontal. It is just that mind *is* all phenomena, and all phenomena *are* mind. Therefore [the relationship of mind and phenomena] is neither vertical nor horizontal; they are neither the same nor different. This is mysterious and subtle, profound in the extreme; it cannot be grasped conceptually, and cannot be verbalized. This is what is called [contemplating] "realms of experience as inconceivable." [emphasis added]

Zhiyi concludes that the only alternative way for disclosing the meaning of *being-with* is the method of meditation, but not through any metaphysical speculation. For Zhiyi clearly rejects two forms of metaphysics, namely transcendental idealism (of pure mind) and empirical idealism (of deluded mind). The former is characterized by Zhiyi as the "vertical" way of thinking by which phenomena is explained as being transcendentally grounded in the absolute (pure) mind, and the latter as the "horizontal" way of thinking, which explains phenomena through epistemological analysis. Zhiyi argues that since both forms of metaphysics are rooted in representational thinking, which is also called "conceivable thinking," they are incapable of making real phenomena (things themselves) fully manifest. In this respect, we find that Zhiyi, Husserl, and Heidegger exploit similar lines of reasoning in formulating their rejection of metaphysics. For Zhiyi in particular, the truth of "real phenomena" is concealed within the conceivability of metaphysics.

Truth and Method

The motif of Zhiyi's philosophy is the disclosure of the truth of real phenomena through meditation. Ontologically speaking, truth exists prior to method. Practically, truth needs to be disclosed through method. Thus, in the Buddhist tradition, truth can be realized only through the method of meditation. Though quite complicated, Zhiyi's system of meditation can be divided into two paths: the gradual and the sudden. The sudden path of meditation is often considered the key to producing the experience of perfect and sudden awakening, while the gradual path is regarded as the preparatory step to the final goal of meditation, i.e., the aforementioned perfect and sudden awakening. Some contend that the difference between the two paths is merely pedagogical. Regarding this issue, I rather see in Zhiyi's system of meditation the gradual path as the necessary training for the superior practice of perfect and sudden awakening.

In Zhiyi's system, a practitioner aims to disclose the experience of awakening by taking threefold truth as the object of threefold contemplation. The fruit of practice is called "threefold insight." Therefore, in regard to the architectonics of meditation, Zhiyi's system consists of the structure of threefold truth, threefold contemplation, and threefold insight:[18]

(1) Threefold Truth (san-di; 三諦)

Truth can be viewed from three aspects, consisting of: (i) the truth of emptiness, stated as "all phenomena are empty," (ii) conventional truth, i.e., truth of phenomena, and (iii) truth as the middle way, i.e., truth as the full disclosure through double negation of the two truths. In contrast to the Mādhyamikan theory of truth, Zhiyi develops a dialectical hermeneutic to make reality fully disclosed in each aspect. That is, the enlightened experience will not disclose itself in the truth of emptiness and the conventional truth respectively; it must also be disclosed in the truth of the middle way. No aspect of truth should be separated from the other two aspects because truth can never be exhausted from a single perspective. Truth shows itself only through the holistic and dialectical contemplation. According to this pattern of threefold truth, part and whole are dialectically interrelated and holistically integrated, wherein the whole can be manifested only through the dynamic dialectic of the parts.[19]

(2) Threefold Meditation (san-guan; 三觀)

For Zhiyi, the meditation of cessation and contemplation is instrumental for the realization of truth. This is witnessed in Zhiyi's magnum opus, *Mohezhiguan* (*Great Calming and Contemplation*). The method of meditation is further divided into threefold cessation and threefold contemplation with correspondence to threefold truth and threefold insight. However, it must be noted that this system of meditation does not function mechanically. That is, the first contemplation does not merely take the truth of emptiness as the object of meditation. By the same token, the second contemplation does not merely take the conventional truth as the object and the third contemplation does not take the middle way as the object. For Zhiyi, one should practice contemplation dialectically and dynamically. The first step of meditation is to enter into emptiness from the conventional, which will lead to an insight that reveals the conventionality of all phenomena, i.e., the emptiness. This methodic move is similar to Husserl's shifting from the natural attitude to the phenomenological attitude. The second move is then a return to the conventional from emptiness through a reverse dialectic. Driven by salvific compassion, a practitioner takes this move to return to the mundane world (conventional world) from the state of emptiness, which results in skillful command of the knowledge of the mundane world. In comparison, the second move in Tiantai dialectical meditation is rather similar to the call for returning to the life-world in Husserl's later writings. The third move is thus to realize that the previous two moves are merely provisional for the final realization of things themselves. When one arrives at this final stage, there will be attachment to neither the first truth nor the second. The practitioner will rather be illuminated by the three truths simultaneously. This final move is called the "contemplation of the middle way," which manifests the highest form of insight, namely, the insight of all modes of phenomena.[20]

(3) Threefold Insight (san-zhi; 三智)

According to the *Prajñāpāramitāśāstra*, the text from which Zhiyi's theory of threefold insight is borrowed, (i) "insight of paths" (*margajñatā*) refers to all kinds of mundane knowledge which are required for the fulfillment of religious goals, and (ii) "insight of all phenomena" (*sarvajñatā*), or "omniscience," refers to the *abstract* truth of all phenomena gained by the elimination of ignorance, and (iii) "insight of all modes of phenomena" (*sarvākārajñatā*) refers to the *concrete* truth that is realized in all aspects of phenomena.[21] The sequence of practice is stated as follows: Insofar as one has obtained the knowledge of the paths beforehand, one can be said to know the *abstract* truth of all phenomena. Next, one progresses to the *concrete* knowledge of all aspects of phenomena and then proceeds to cut off all habitual defilements in the final enlightenment.[22]

Thus, in view of the gradual path, the three forms of insight are taken as independent of one another. On the other hand, threefold insight can be attained within a single instant of mind via the sudden path. It is in a single instant mind that threefold truth arises simultaneously with threefold insight and threefold contemplation. Now, how could all of these occur *simultaneously*? The answer to this conundrum is found in Zhiyi's conception of mind. In addition to the intentionality of mind as *being-with*, a notion that we have already explained above, everyday mind is also characterized as both deluded *and* pure. In Buddhist parlance, everyday mind has been in ignorance (*avidyā*) from the very beginning, which is equivalent to saying that mind is the function of mental construction (*vikalpa*). According to the Buddhist theory of emptiness, however, everything, even including ignorance, is empty in itself. Since ignorance is empty of itself, it follows that mind as ignorance is also empty of itself. Hence, mind should be conceived as both ignorance and emptiness. As a consequence, if mind as ignorance is taken as the phenomenological ground of phenomena, mind as emptiness, i.e., *prajñā*, must also be taken as the groundless ground of phenomena. Thus, in view of ignorance, mind functions in the act of objectivation, whereas in view of emptiness, mind is able to function as non-objectivating insight. Finally, in view of the middle way, mind is characterized *neither* as ignorance *nor* as emptiness. It is characterized as "inconceivable" in the sense that any form of metaphysics will fail to account for the dialectical paradox of mind. As the correlates of mind, all phenomena (the three thousand worlds) also manifest themselves as the inconceivable infinity of mutual penetration. This is the reason why Zhiyi always summarizes his system as "threefold truth within an instant mind," "threefold contemplation within an instant mind," and "threefold insight within an instant mind."[23]

IV. CONCLUDING REMARKS

Summing up the above exegetical analysis in response to the questions raised at the beginning: (i) In what sense can Zhiyi's Tiantai philosophy be characterized as a phenomenology of awakening? (ii) What can be added to the diversity of the phenomenological legacy when we bring Zhiyi into philosophical dialogue with Husserl? To begin with, Zhiyi and Husserl belong to different traditions. Zhiyi is religion-oriented, and all of his philosophizing is directed toward a soteriological goal. Husserl's philosophical enterprise, on the other hand, is science-oriented, a fact attested by his dream of establishing phenomenology as the most rigorous science. Although in his later years Husserl became more devoted to ethics and religion, he rarely considered his philosophical task as a path to spiritual liberation. In spite of the historical differences, however, we do see similarities in the two philosophical systems. On the one hand, Husserl contends that truth consists in two aspects: truth as proposition and truth as evidence. The truth as proposition is based upon truth as evidence "where objects and states of affairs are given intuitively as they themselves are or as given in person."[24] On the other side, Zhiyi placed the theory of threefold truth within the methodical context of meditation. Truth manifests itself only in the mental experience of contemplation. Hence, Zhiyi's famous dictum, "threefold truth in an instant mind," might now be better understood in light of Husserl's theory of "evidence as the experience of truth, i.e., as an intentional act in which the intended object is presented intuitively, though in different degrees of fulfillment."[25]

In view of Zhiyi's "classification of teachings," on the other hand, Husserl's phenomenology belongs to the gradual path, whereas Zhiyi considered his own system as the perfect and sudden path that leads to a final realization of the truth of inter-relativity and inter-penetration of phenomena, i.e., the three thousand worlds in one single thought. At the final moment of awakening, one realizes that the world of the rich, the world of the poor, the world of humanity, the world of animals, the world of plants, the world of gods, and the world of ghosts are all interrelated. And as far as any one world is manifested in the mind, all other worlds are also simultaneously manifested. As a result, the experience of awakening is never exclusionary. True awakening, which manifests the enlightened world, must be experienced *along with* all other worlds that have yet to be enlightened. True liberation must be experienced *along with* all other worlds that are still in suffering. This is the core spirit of Zhiyi's phenomenology of awakening.

Notes

1 Cited in Karl Schuhmann, "Husserl and Indian Thought," in D. P. Chattopadhyaya, Lester Embree, and Jitendranath Mohanty, eds., *Phenomenology and Indian Philosophy* (Albany, NY: SUNY Press, 1992), 26.

2 Since the term *vijñāna* has different usages depending upon context, I have translated it in various ways in this chapter. To avoid confusion, I have inserted the Sanskrit term after the translation.

3 Schuhmann, "Husserl and Indian Thought," 25.

4 Edmund Husserl, "Phenomenology," in Peter McCormick and Frederick Elliston, eds., *Husserl: Shorter Works* (Notre Dame, IN: University of Notre Dame Press, 1981), 27. Regarding the term "transcendental" in Husserl's usage, scholars have varying interpretations. Dan Zahavi insists that "the specific and unique *transcendental*-phenomenological question is: What are the conditions of possibility for appearance as such?" See Dan Zahavi, *Husserl's Phenomenology* (Stanford, CA: Stanford University Press, 2003), 54. According to D. W. Smith's interpretation, the term applies to "pure consciousness in abstraction from its connection with natural or cultural objects or activities." See D. W. Smith, *Husserl* (London and New York: Routledge, 2007), 447.

5 In spite of the above "insight," Husserl's "oversight" can be seen in his characterization of Buddhism as "transcendental [subjectivity]," a notion which would seem to contradict the Buddhist doctrinal position of no-self. Historically, the Husserlian notion of "transcendental subjectivity" has been more or less compatible with the Mahāyāna Buddhist doctrine of mind-only (*citta-mātra*) or consciousness-only (*vijñapti-mātra*), though not of course with Early Buddhism.

6 *Abhidharmakośabhāsya of Vasubandhu*, chap. 1: *Dhātunirdeśa*, ed., Yasunori Ejima (Tokyo: Sankibo Press, 1989), 17; Bhikkhu K L Dhammajoti, *Sarvāstivāda Abhidharma* (Hong Kong: Center of Buddhist Studies, University of Hong Kong, 2007), 293.

7 Monier Monier-Williams, *Sanskrit-English Dictionary*, 205.

8 Cf. Bhikkhu Dhammajoti, *Abhidharma Doctrine and Controversy on Perception* (Colombo: Sri Lanka:

Center for Buddhist Studies, 2004), 18–19.

9 *Yogācārabhūmi*, T.30.696.a.

10 In contrast to Abhidharma epistemology, *prajñā* and *vijñāna* are rather placed in opposition to each other in the Prajñāpāramitā literature. True knowledge (*prajñā*) is attainable only when one comes to realize that no knowledge is attainable. According to Prajñāpāramitā thought, just like magic, emptiness can be known through non-apprehension (*anupalabdhi*). In this regard, *prajñā* obtained through *anupalabdhi* (= *nirvikalpa*) is opposed to *vijñāna*, which is obtained through *upalabdhi* (= *vikalpa*). In other words, Prajñāpāramitā thinkers stand for "negative epistemology" instead of "positive epistemology." The problem of "non-apprehension" or "negative cognition" was taken up again via the positive understanding by the later Buddhist philosophers such as Dignāga and Dharmakīrti. The historical development of negative epistemology does not concern us at this stage. For *anupalabdhi* in the Prajñāpāramitā literature, see Edward Conze, "The Development of Prajñāpramitā Thought," in *Thirty Years of Buddhist Studies* (New Delhi: Munshiram Manoharlal, 2000), 127.

11 Louis de La Vallee Poussin, translated and annotated, *Vijñaptimātratāsiddhi: La Siddhi de Hiuan-tsang* (Paris: Librarie Orientaliste Paul Geuthner, 1928), 685f; also cf., Maitreyanatha/Aryāsaṇga, *The Universal Vehicle Discourse Literature (Mahāyānasūtrālaṁkāra)* (New York: American Institute of Buddhist Studies, 2004), 98–101. For analysis of *nirvikalpajñāna*, see Leslie S. Kawamura, "Nirvikalpa-jñāna: Awareness Freed from Discrimination," in Koichi Shinohara and Gregory Schopen, eds., *From Benares to Beijing: Essays on Buddhism and Chinese Religion* (Oakville, ON: Mosaic Press, 1991), 41–67.

12 For Xuanzang's *Vijñaptimātratāsiddhi*, also see Wei Tat's English translation: Hsuan Tsang, *Ch'eng Wei-Shih Lun: The Doctrine of Mere-Consciousness*, trans. Wei Tat (Hong Kong: The *Ch'eng Wei-Shih Lun* Publication Committee, 1973), 766–81.

13 See Bhikkhu K L Dhammajoti, *Sarvāstivāda Abhidharma* (Hong Kong: Center of Buddhist Studies, University of Hong Kong, 2007), 358–60.

14 Shunkyo Katsumata, *Bukkyo in okeru Shinshiki-setsu no Kenkyū* (Tokyo: Sankibo, 1961), 172–84, 278–80.

15 Iso Kern renders "*dharsanabhāga*" (the act of seeing) as "objectivating act" and "*nimittabhāga*" as "objective phenomenon." For Yogācāra, there are two levels of objectivation, one on the mental (*paratantra*) level, the other on the discursive (*parikalpita*) level. The latter is grounded in the former. Husserl himself takes "objectivation," which is defined as "outward experience form" as the condition of objectivity of science. See Eugen Fink, *Sixth Cartesian Meditation* (Bloomington: Indiana University Press, 1995), 104. For Kern's interpretation, see Iso Kern, "The Structure of Consciousness according to Xuanzang," *Journal of the British Society for Phenomenology* 19, no. 3 (1988): 282–95.

16 Zhiyi, *Mohezhiguan*, T.46.54.a. I adapt Paul Swanson's English translation with some modifications. Swanson's translation is available at http://nirc.nanzan-u.ac.jp/welcome.htm

17 See Paul Swanson, 64n94.

18 "Threefold truth refers to the object which is illuminated by the one instant mind. Threefold contemplation refers to the act which is initiated by the one instant mind. Threefold insight refers to that which is accomplished by [threefold] contemplation." See *Mohezhiguan*, T.46.55.c.

19 Zhiyi, *Fahua Xuanyi*, T.33.705.c; also cf., Paul Swanson, *Foundations of T'ien-t'ai Philosophy: The Flowering of the Two Truths Theory in Chinese Buddhism* (Berkeley, CA: Asian Humanities Press, 1989), 252–53; Mou Zongsan, *Foxing yu Boruo* (Taipei: Xuesheng Shuju, 1977) 2:647–71.

20 Zhiyi, *Mohezhiguan*, T.46.24.b.

21 Cf., Fa Qing, *The Development of Prajñā in Buddhism: From Early Buddhism to the Prajñāpāramiāā System*, PhD diss., University of Calgary, 2001, 92–95.

22 T. 25.258.c–260.b.

23 Zhiyi, *Weimojing Xuanshu*, T.38.524.c–529.b.

24 Dieter Lohmar, "Truth," in Lester Embree et al., *Encyclopedia of Phenomenology* (Dordrecht: Kluwer, 1997), 708.

25 Ibid.

Ibn Rushd or Averroës? Of Double Names and Double Truths: A Different Approach to Islamic Philosophy

TAMARA ALBERTINI
University of Hawai'i at Manoa

Unlike other non-Western traditions explored in contemporary comparative philosophy, Islamic thought stands out as a "hybrid" with both an "Eastern" and a "Western" face. It is partly a continuation of Greek and Hellenistic philosophy, partly an intellectual tradition defined by its own very distinct questions and concerns, whether they are of a religious, legalistic, cosmological, epistemological, or ethical nature. This unique property is not always rightly appreciated by Western scholars, in particular specialists of the Middle Ages, who may focus excessively on the "reflection" of the Western face in medieval sources. As a result, the medievalist's approach often fails to recognize questions, intentions, and methodologies specifically developed in and for a Muslim context. In particular, it does not see that the so-called Western face is "Easternized."

To be sure, some Muslim philosophers may have more Greek traits than others. However, as with the Hellenistic Buddha-figures, the blend is harmonious – there is but one face.

To enhance the appreciation of "nativeness" of philosophy in Islam, the present paper will regularly point out features that are characteristic of Muslim forms of inquiry, or, sometimes, merely to Arabic Islamic culture such as the actual significance of the personal name, which helps with the assessment of Muslim authors in their own historic context. More importantly, attention will be given to titles of works carefully crafted to guide the interpretive efforts of the reader, elements of debate typical of the *Kalām* tradition (dialectical theology) that – although originally developed for oral exchange – are reflected in writing as well, and, finally, the import of jurisprudential terminology and the use of reasoning techniques developed by Islamic Schools of Law that are in no way derived from Greek sources.

Basically, the purpose is to help readers interested in the field to understand that just in the same way as Muslim philosophers did not wear cloaks or togas but robes, their ideas too are "clothed" in a different fashion. The fact that their ideas bear cultural, or even ethnic, features does not make these ideas less relevant to other philosophical traditions. There is no need of a new tailoring for a more "Western" look. Quite to the contrary, these features wrap ideas and concepts in ways that can, if appreciated, enrich the dialogue between the traditions.

It is with this possibility in mind that the following examines a text generally referred to as *The Decisive Treatise* (*Faṣl al-Maqāl*), written by the Andalusian Muslim philosopher Ibn Rushd (520–595 A.H./AD 1126–1198), the famed Averroës of the Latin tradition. This text, the legalistic reflections of which clearly marked it as a work written for an Islamic audience, was deemed of no consequence to a Christian philosophical and theological world view. As a result – and unlike Ibn Rushd's commentaries on Aristotelian works – it was never translated into Latin during the Middle Ages. In Europe, the history of the reception of this text begins with the printing of the original Arabic text in 1859 (a revised version came out in 1942). A German translation appeared in 1875, a French one in 1905, and a Spanish one in 1947. The first English version was published by Muhammad al-Jamil al-Rahman in 1921. The two currently most widely used English translations are by George F. Hourani and Charles E. Butterworth. The first appeared in 1961; the latter in 2001.

To help discover the "native" design of this text, this paper will explore four questions:

1. what's in a name?
2. what's in a title?
3. what's in a question?

   and

4. what's in an answer?

As the following will show, major lessons may be drawn from addressing precisely these questions, no matter how unrelated they may at first appear to a Western sense of philosophical relevance. Indeed, all four questions will contribute to the uncovering of the strong influence of Islamic jurisprudential tradition, language, and methodology on Ibn Rushd's thought. The last two, will, furthermore, open up an interpretive path entirely defined by legal directives.

WHAT'S IN A NAME?

From a Western perspective, Ibn Rushd's life-long career as a magistrate, crowned with a position as Chief Justice in his native Andalusia, is usually considered to be unconnected with his philosophical and scientific research. Quite in contrast to assessments made in Muslim biographical sources, the underlying assumption is that what is essential about Ibn Rushd's work are his additions to and further elaborations on Greek-based sciences and thought. Accordingly, most medievalists discuss him to this day under his latinized name "Averroës," strengthening thereby his status as the extraordinary philosopher who contributed to the advancement of Christian-European culture. What is missing in their otherwise highly appreciative profile is Ibn Rushd the theologian and expert of Islamic Law (*sharī'a*), and, more generally, Ibn Rushd the philosopher-scientist whose primary intention it was to contribute to his own culture. Little did Ibn Rushd know that his latinized name would eventually be both glorified and vilified in the Christian West. Unfortunately, the same fate – albeit for different reasons – was to befall his name in the Islamic world as well.

But what was his *full* name? In his own world the Andalusian philosopher was known as Abū al-Walīd Muḥammad ibn Aḥmad ibn Muḥammad ibn Rushd. This is, for instance, how he signed his manuscripts. How to explain this name, or rather this sequence of names? In Arabian culture individuals are perceived as links between past and future generations. Their very names identify them as links in family chains. The first part of a name thus signals whether an individual has fathered or mothered offspring, i.e., whether he or she is already acting as a link between the generations. This part of the name is called the "*kunya*." Ibn Rushd's *kunya* informs us that his oldest son was al-Walīd (*abū* = father of), while his own *ism*, i.e., first name, was Muḥammad. We are further given the first names of his father and grandfather, Aḥmad and Muḥammad, respectively (*ibn* = son of). This part of an individual's name is the "*nasab*" (lit. "lineage"). 'Ibn Rushd,' the name by which our Andalusian philosopher is mostly referred to in Islamic sources, is actually the name of his family clan, i.e., the Banū Rushd. This part of the name is called the "*nisba*." The fact that Ibn Rushd was referred to by his *nisba*, is no minor piece of information. It helps us understand that in his own culture Ibn Rushd's fame (or "infamy" depending on who judged him) did not belong to him alone but to all of the Banū Rushd, a family mostly remembered for having produced a great number of prominent lawyers. There is no indication that *our* Ibn Rushd ever had the intention to break with that family tradition and stand out as the radical and lonely rationalist often portrayed in Western scholarship. In the same way as his ancestors, in particular his father and grandfather, had traced his life path by preceding him as Andalusian magistrates, he himself placed the burden of an intellectual life dedicated to the well-being of the city on the shoulders of his own sons who continued being judges – and physicians. And yet, there was room for "individuality" of a Western type in that many Arabs also enjoy a nickname, called "*laqab*." Ibn Rushd's *laqab* was al-Ḥafīd, i.e., the grandson, to distinguish him from his grandfather who had also been a Chief Justice. Clearly, the nickname he was given identifies him as the heir of a jurisprudential family tradition.

Considering the ethnic and cultural connotations present in Ibn Rushd's name, it should be clear by now that the only acceptable reference to our Andalusian philosopher is by the name that correctly renders his *nisba*. This is not just a matter of proper scholarly transliteration, or, more generally, of linguistic "correctness." It entails an entire change of perspective, since it signals to Western readers that, despite all common traits (such as Aristotelian rationalism) and sources (mainly from the ancient Greek and Hellenistic period), the philosopher they are about to be informed about emerged from a culture that is not only religiously but also intellectually distinct from their own. Does this mean that the name "Averroës" is to join the debris of a discontinued (or, more likely, never truly engaged) dialogue between Muslim and Christian philosophers? No, there does remain a legitimate space for the use of 'Averroës,' provided that one is aware that this name bears the marks of a specific historic context, i.e., Western medieval culture, in which, to put it mildly, some intellectual positions of Ibn Rushd have been interpreted in most peculiar ways. Positively connoted, 'Averroës' refers to "*the* commentator" (of Aristotle). This is the language one encounters, for instance, in the works of Thomas Aquinas, the champion of Christian philosophy and theology. Unfortunately, in the same works one also finds a negatively coloured use of Ibn Rushd's latinized name. It then connects to a long controversy known as the "Averroistic heresy," which played a critical role in challenging both ecclesiastical and political authorities in medieval (and Renaissance) Europe and, as a result, was dealt with most harshly by those same authorities. However, as will be pointed out towards the end of this paper, Averroistic theses are of Western origin and sprung mostly from a misreading of Ibn Rushd's philosophy, which in turn was due to medieval Christians' being entirely unaware of there being a theological basis for many of Ibn Rushd's ideas – albeit an Islamic theological basis.

WHAT'S IN A TITLE?

What better way then to acquaint oneself with Ibn Rushd the Arab, the Muslim, and the Chief Justice than to explore the work commonly known as *The Decisive Treatise*, a text in which the Andalusian philosopher focuses on the relation between Philosophy and Law, not the Greek *nomos* (which he, of course, knew from both Plato's and Aristotle's works) but *sharī'a*, Islamic sacred law? This relation could never have been a central issue to a Christian philosopher-theologian in the Middle Ages. The big controversy in that culture and period was whether reason and faith clashed – not philosophy and law. The founder of Christianity left no instructions as to what Christian Law might be. Besides, as Christian religion moved away from its Jewish roots and spread within the Roman Empire, it found a highly sophisticated legal system in place that it ultimately incorporated. It comes, therefore, as no surprise that the work called *The Decisive Treatise* found no audience in Christian medieval Europe.

But what exactly is the wording in the original title? The full Arabic title says *Kitāb faṣl al-maqāl wa taqrīr mā bayn al-sharī'a wa al-ḥikma min al-ittiṣāl.* George F. Hourani renders the title as *On the Harmony of Religion and Philosophy*, while Charles E. Butterworth remains *prima facie* more faithful to the original by calling it *The Book of the Decisive Treatise Determining the Connection between the Law and Wisdom.* In fairness, one must add that Hourani does offer a correct and complete rendering in the introduction to his translation where he calls Ibn Rushd's work: "The book of *the decision (or distinction) of the discourse*, and a determination of *what there is* of connection between religion and philosophy." The passage clarifies three important points:

1. The original title does not presume to give the ultimate answer in respect to the subjects to be explored. It is not a "decisive treatise" but a book dealing with "the *decision* (or *distinction*) of the discourse";
2. The work in question is not a treatise but a *discourse* (*maqāl*) indicating that it is designed as a piece of *Kalām*; and
3. Ibn Rushd was not investigating *whether* there is a connection between "religion" and "philosophy" but rather *what the nature* of the connection is.

Butterworth's translation, however, is not without merit. Its appeal lies in that it names with greater precision the subjects the relation of which is to be investigated in the text: Law and Wisdom. By comparison, while Hourani's 'religion' covers Islamic law and 'philosophy' and is a valid equivalent for the original *ḥikma*, the English title gives no indication of there being a jurisprudential context. The term '*ḥikma*' also signals that Ibn Rushd has given precedence to the native Arabic term for wisdom. It is as if Ibn Rushd had wanted to remind his fellow Andalusians that the pursuit of wisdom is not solely the domain of the ancient Greeks. Isn't one of Allah's names *al-Ḥakīm* (= The Wise)? The term '*ḥikma*' has, in addition, the advantage of being etymologically related to a number of words that belong semantically to the legal field such as *aḥkām* (= legal categories of human acts; plural of *ḥukm*), which will be discussed in the following section, *ḥakam* (= judge), and, of course, *ḥukm* (= judgment). One may now realize how ingenious it was of Ibn Rushd to opt for *ḥikma* over *falsafa*, the Arabized word for 'philosophy:' The notion of *ḥikma* carries through its root '*ḥ-k-m*' an unmistakable legal connotation. Its very semantic texture suggests its vicinity to Law, which is precisely what Ibn Rushd wished to further demonstrate in his discourse. A careful discussion of the discourse's title suggests that for Ibn Rushd Philosophy and Law are united in a common pursuit. Not surprisingly, he ends up calling them "milk-sisters" for having drank from the same source of knowledge and "companions by nature and lovers by essence and instinct" (p. 70).

It is to be hoped that the analysis of the exact wording of the title was no futile exercise in the reader's mind. As the contemporary Tunisian scholar El Ghannouchi comments, referring to Ibn Rushd's *Faṣl al-Maqāl* as *The Decisive Treatise* makes the Andalusian philosopher appear to be "pedantic and pretentious," as if he had wanted to present "in a peremptory fashion the definitive and decisive solution to the secular question of the accord between religion and philosophy" (my translation). What is one to do after over a century in which this erroneous title has been circulating? Rather than trying to impose a new standardized title, it seems best to use the Arabic original: *Faṣl al-Maqāl*.

WHAT'S IN A QUESTION?

According to most historians *Faṣl al-Maqāl* was composed around 575 A.H./1179 CE, i.e., some seventeen years before Ibn Rushd and his younger son 'Abdallah were denied access to the great mosque of Cordova, Ibn Rushd's works burned and he himself eventually sent into exile. And yet, *Faṣl al-Maqāl* already shows the marks of a text written by an author under siege.

Faṣl al-Maqāl begins by addressing the subject under investigation: "The purpose of this treatise [*sic*] is to examine, from the standpoint of the study of the law, whether the study of philosophy and logic is [1] allowed by the Law, or [2] prohibited, or [3] commanded – either by the way of recommendation or as obligatory" (p. 44). In other words, the question is whether it can be made legally binding to allow, study, or reject (Greek derived) philosophy and logic. In order to fully appreciate the strategy at work in the question Ibn Rushd designed, one needs to know the *aḥkām* mentioned previously, i.e., human acts as defined by Islamic jurisprudence.

There are five *aḥkām*, traditionally discussed in the following order: 1) obligatory (*farḍ*); 2) not obligatory but recommended (*mustaḥabb* or *mandūb*); 3) neutral or permitted (*mubāḥ*); 4) not forbidden but discouraged (*makrūh*); and 5) forbidden (*ḥarām*). By comparison, in his listing of the legal options open to investigation Ibn Rushd begins with the middle – neutral – category that he also calls "*mubāḥ*." After, he moves on to the last two categories that he addresses together as "*maḥẓūr*." Finally, he also conflates the first two categories as commanded (*ma'mūr*). This new category he then divides into "*mandūb*" and "*wājib*." One wonders about the reasoning behind the reshuffling of the *aḥkām*. The juxtaposition of the two lists is revealing:

	Categories of human acts (by divine decree)	**Ibn Rushd's categories (by legal decree)**
1	obligatory (*farḍ*)	obligatory (*wājib*)
2	not obligatory but recommended (*mustaḥabb* or *mandūb*)	commanded (*ma'mūr*)
3	neutral or permitted (*mubāḥ*)	recommended (*mandūb*)
4	not forbidden but discouraged (*makrūh*)	allowed (*mubāh*)
5	forbidden (*ḥarām*)	prohibited (*maḥẓūr*)

It becomes clear now that the language of the strong categories "obligatory" (*farḍ*) and "forbidden"(*ḥarām*) has been softened. No matter how high the status of a magistrate, he does not have the authority to declare an act either obligatory or forbidden in the scriptural sense. The legal obligation the jurisconsult extrapolates is mandatory but to a lesser degree than the divinely decreed obligation. It can never be *farḍ*, only *wājib*. In other words, if it turns out that the study of philosophy is to be declared mandatory, the obligation may never become comparable to the necessity of fulfilling one's ritual prayers, incumbent upon all believers regardless of their predisposition and intellectual abilities. However, if the finding is negative and the study of philosophy is doomed, it shall not end up becoming forbidden in the way adultery or the consumption of pork is (these are unnegotiable prohibitions), but will instead be "*maḥẓūr*," which, according to Ibn Rushd's own legal manual, corresponds to the fourth *ḥukm*: "*makrūh*," meaning "not forbidden but discouraged."

The precise phrasing of the opening question in *Faṣl al-Maqāl* unravels the investigative strategy pursued by Ibn Rushd, which is aiming at preventing the full loss of philosophy. The Andalusian is, in fact, telling his opponents that, while every jurisconsult has, of course, the power to issue a *fatwā* (a legal ruling) forbidding "the reflection on beings," as Ibn Rushd defines philosophy (see following section), there is no scriptural basis to do so, which is the only means by which philosophy could be definitively banned from Muslim lands. Ibn Rushd's own ruling is that the available legal basis could only lead to preventing some groups of fellow Muslims from "reflecting on beings." Thus individuals lacking appropriate intellectual disposition and/or preparation are not to take upon themselves the burden of true *ḥikma*, since the level of reasoning required for this task may put their faith at risk (cf. p. 61).

WHAT'S IN AN ANSWER?

Ibn Rushd's answer closely follows the discourse's introductory question. To the reader somewhat familiar with Islamic theological training, the answer is ingeniously clear and simple: "We say: if the activity of philosophy is nothing more than study of existing beings and *reflection* on them as indications of the Artisan ... and if the Law has recommended and urged *reflection* on beings, then it is clear that what this name signifies is either obligatory or recommended by the Law" (ibid., my emphasis).

The middle term of what appears to be a syllogism is *reflection*. *Prima facie*, this is the structure that presents itself:

> Philosophy is *reflection* on existing beings, and
> The Law recommends and urges *reflection* on beings (= God's creatures),
> Therefore, philosophy is either obligatory or recommended.

This first glance reading led some commentators to think of this being a case of flawed reasoning. Butterworth, for instance, notes "the first premise is not evident; and the second stretches the Qur'ānic verses cited as evidence." I beg to differ: *First*, the initial premise as it emerges in Ibn Rushd's answer is carefully preceded by an 'if.' The Andalusian philosopher was obviously aware of many more ways to define philosophy. The 'if' is an invitation to accept a somewhat narrow notion of philosophy, narrow enough to be compatible with scriptural injunctions, which, as a note in his commentary on Aristotle's *Metaphysics* suggests, may actually reflect Ibn Rushd's genuine understanding of philosophy. *Second*, as for the "stretching" of the Qur'ānic verses, Ibn Rushd is following a tradition that began in Andalusia with the philosopher-mystic Ibn Masarra (d. 310 A.H./AD 931) and can actually be found throughout Islamic philosophy. In his *Treatise on Inference* (*Risāla al-I'tibār*), the older Andalusian philosopher invokes dozens of verses enjoining the rational and scientific investigation of the universe. We are dealing here with a matter of the "inner-cultural evidence" of a statement. Passages such as *"Have they not studied the kingdom of heavens and the earth, and whatever things God has created?"* (VII, 185) – coincidentally quoted both in *Faṣl al-Maqāl* (p. 45) and in Ibn Masarra's *Treatise on Inference* (p. 6) – have been taken by the earliest Muslim commentators to mean that the Qur'ān urges believers to make sense of God's creation by rational means. By invoking the verse, Ibn Rushd is simply reminding his conservative opponents that Islamic theology has long accommodated the need for rationality and sciences. *Third*, and more importantly, Ibn Rushd has a different conclusion from the one read by Butterworth. Here is the content of the actual conclusive statement in context:

> If philosophy is *reflection* on existing beings, and
> *If* the Law recommends and urges *reflection*,
> Then *what this name signifies* is either obligatory or recommended by the Law (my emphasis).

Drawing conclusions by focusing on the meaning of a central term is a characteristic trait of Ibn Rushd's Mālikī training (Malikites belong to one of four Sunni Schools of Law). To give a practical example: in his courtroom Ibn Rushd once used this procedure to determine that a student who had done great damage to the reputation of a teacher in Cordova by insinuating that the teacher was infatuated with one of his pupils was to be punished in the same way as the slanderer who accuses a woman of adultery. Qur'ānic Law provides flogging as the appropriate punishment for the unjustified attack brought against a woman's honour (*qadhf*). Ibn Rushd decided that the student who had defamed the teacher in question should be subjected to the same corporeal punishment. There was no formal syllogism involved in Ibn Rushd's ruling. All he did is reason by using a procedure his school of jurisprudence called "*qiyās al-ma'nā*," analogy by meaning. This is not a case of flawed reasoning, it is just a different type of reasoning. It may not be Aristotelian, but it is all the same logical, according to the criteria afforded by Mālikī methodology.

This type of "semantic reasoning," as I call it, is also at work in Ibn Rushd's philosophical work. For instance, in *Faṣl al-Maqāl*, Ibn Rushd refers briefly to how he countered al-Ghazālī's attack on the Aristotelian theory of the eternity of the world in his *Incoherence of the Incoherence*:

> Concerning the question whether the world is pre-eternal [*qadīm*] or came into existence [*muḥdath*], the disagreement between the Ash'arite dialectical theologians [such as al-Ghazālī] and the ancient philosophers is in my view almost resolvable into *a disagreement about naming....* For they agree that there are three classes of beings: two extremes and one intermediary between the extremes. *They agree also about naming the extremes, but they disagree about the intermediate class.* (p. 55)

The first class refers to "originated" beings, the opposite of which are "pre-eternal" beings. Applied to the world, the world, inasmuch as it comes into existence, i.e., has a beginning in time, is an originated being. Translated into theological terms, the world was created by God (who is, of course, the only pre-eternal Being). Ibn Rushd resolves the contradiction between Aristotle and Islamic scripture (and generally biblical tradition) by claiming that the notion (but not necessarily the term) "pre-eternal" may be safely applied to God's creation, provided one takes the term in its intermediary meaning. It then signifies "the world as a whole"(*al-'ālim bī asrihi*), neither fully eternal (since it has needs of an agent cause) nor perishable the way the single beings in it are. Leaning on Plato and his school, Ibn Rushd ends up calling the world "originated *ab aeterno*" (*muḥdath azalī*; my translation).

What is most striking about this finding is that Ibn Rushd reveals himself to be much more a Muslim lawyer than the strict Aristotelian logician that Western scholars like to project situated in a context dealing precisely with a Greek-derived problem. This does not mean that Ibn Rushd abandoned his beloved master Aristotle altogether, only that he felt at liberty to choose when to apply what form of reasoning. As it turned out, "semantic reasoning" was the better strategy to pursue both, in harmonizing Aristotle's theory of the eternity of the world with scripture and declaring reflection on beings a legal obligation.

Aristotle's logic remains, however, integrated in the remaining obligations Ibn Rushd extrapolates in his discourse. Thus, another obligation says "The Law, then, has urged us to have demonstrative knowledge of God" (p. 45). And to clarify that by "demonstration" he, indeed, means Aristotelian demonstration. Ibn Rushd asserts in the preparation to a further conclusion that "it is difficult or impossible for one man to find out by himself and from the beginning all that he needs" (p. 46). Therefore, there is a legal obligation to follow a more knowledgeable authority "regardless of whether this other one shares our religion or not" (p. 46ff.). The Andalusian philosopher then specifies: "By 'those who do not share our religion' I refer to those ancients who studied these matters before Islam" (p. 47). Without any question, the non-Islamic authority on demonstration to include in one's endeavour to reflect upon beings is Aristotle.

Among the possible objections Ibn Rushd addresses in *Faṣl al-Maqāl* is one of particular interest. It will allow us to close the circle that began by distancing ourselves from the Averroës of the Latin medieval tradition. To the opponent who may resentfully declare that not everyone can follow the intricacies of intellectual reasoning and that, therefore, demonstration cannot be made incumbent upon all believers, Ibn Rushd gladly concedes:

> The natures of men are on different levels with [their paths] to assent [*taṣdīq*; my addition]. One of them comes to assent

> through *demonstration*; another comes through *dialectical arguments* just as firmly as the demonstrative man through demonstration, since his nature does not contain any greater capacity; while another comes through *rhetorical arguments*. (p. 49)

This is precisely the kind of assertion that gave rise in medieval Europe to the "theory of double truth." While Averroism propagated this theory to maintain that one and the same position could contain different truth values, i.e., one for philosophy and another for theology, Ibn Rushd himself never did propose two (or, as the quotation above would rather suggest, three) "Truths." Quite to the contrary, he actually emphasized that "truth does not oppose truth but accords with it and bears witness to it" (p. 50). To understand his position, one need take into account the theological frame within which he developed his ideas. Thus when Ibn Rushd affirmed that one and the same truth may be expressed in multiple ways, he was concerned with how that truth could be accessible to members of a religious community who are naturally different from each other in terms of their reasoning abilities. In this, the Andalusian philosopher thought as a Muslim theologian and applied an important requirement of Islamic faith that ensures that both prospective believers and adherents already in the faith be able to give their consent (*taṣdīq*) to their religion on the basis of personal persuasion. The reasoning is as follows: since certainty in one's religious beliefs is an essential tenet of Islam, it would be unfair to expect an intellectually diverse pool of believers to agree with doctrinal issues in uniform terms. As a result, Ibn Rushd envisaged society divided into what one might call "epistemic classes." Like many of his Muslim predecessors who were inspired by Plato's tripartition in *The Republic*, Ibn Rushd ended up defining three classes: the masses who reason through the use of images (*rhetorical arguments*), the rational theologians who elaborate on their religious knowledge within a pre-defined frame (*dialectical arguments*), and the philosophers who expand on religious knowledge (*demonstrative arguments*). Thus, while all groups have access to the same scriptural truth, they differ in the means that permits them to make sense of scripture. The assignment of different types of arguments to different epistemic classes is to be read as an entitlement given to each of these classes. The masses, for example, are like the theologians and philosophers under the obligation to reason, except that Ibn Rushd the magistrate grants them the privilege of reasoning according to their very capabilities.

How ironic it was to call Ibn Rushd's theologically motivated epistemic tripartition a heresy becomes particularly evident when one realizes that the entire Christian tradition of biblical exegesis rests on the same understanding of scripture holding different levels of meaning. St. Augustine's distinction between "historical, etiological, analogical, and allegorical" has thus been discussed and refined for more than a millennium of Christian theology. And Thomas Aquinas (whom the Middle Ages credited for having crushed "Averroistic heresies") seems to be echoing precisely Ibn Rushd when he writes in his *Summa Theologica*: "It is … befitting Holy Scripture … that spiritual truths be expounded by means of figures taken from corporeal things, in order that thereby even the simple who are unable by themselves to grasp intellectual things may be able to understand it" (Part One, q. I, art. 9)! Thomas Aquinas never suspected that, rather than being an offender, Ibn Rushd was actually an ally in promoting as he did the belief in the existence of one Truth.

In conclusion, there has never been a Rushdian theory of multiple truths. All there was was an understanding that individuals with different intellectual capabilities should be permitted to reason according to the means naturally available to them. And there never has been a "decisive treatise," rather a "discourse" in the best tradition of *Kalām* examining the intrinsic relation between Wisdom (*ḥikma*) and Law (*sharīʿa*). More importantly, wisdom and law were understood to be rational disciplines dealing both with beings, which to the strongly Almohad-influenced Ibn Rushd meant that they had to be compatible. That wisdom and law were "milk-sisters" was his genuine conviction. In his mind, wisdom guided law and law protected wisdom. It would, therefore, be a gross error to assume that Ibn Rushd had advanced this view only to give Greek-derived philosophical pursuit (*falsafa*) a simile of legitimacy in an Islamic context. He did not mean to safeguard the place of *falsafa* in Islamic culture but *ḥikma*, a pursuit more broadly defined to accommodate Muslim intellectual needs that may or may not include Greek expertise and methodologies. No matter how great Ibn Rushd's admiration for Aristotle was, ultimately the object of his intellectual pursuit was wisdom itself. Depending on circumstances and the nature of a problem to be solved, reasoning techniques and/or concepts could be borrowed from the Greeks or from an Islamic school of thought. While demonstration was understood to be a classical Greek tool, reasoning itself was not perceived as the monopoly of ancient Greece.

Without any question, the historic Ibn Rushd was a radically different thinker from the Averroës created by the medievals and perpetuated by the later Western tradition. Before the West knew of Ibn Rushd the "Commentator," there existed in Islamic Andalusia Ibn Rushd the "Magistrate," which is how the Islamic world remembers him to this day. While one should like to tell contemporary Muslim theologians that Ibn Rushd the *qāḍī* should not be separated from the disciple of *Arisṭū* (Aristotle), the West ought to realize that it is the Commentator who must not be separated from the Magistrate.

APPENDIX

Visually speaking, my move away from the Western medieval setting can be conveyed by contrasting Filippino Lippi's "The Triumph of Saint Thomas Aquinas over the Heretics" (1488–92) with Raphael's "School of Athens" (1510/11). Lippi's "The Triumph" is located at the Carafa Chapel in Santa Maria sopra Minerva, Rome. It is one of many works commissioned by the Dominican order to celebrate Thomas Aquinas's victory over Averroës and other heretics. Not only does it feature a crushed Averroës at the feet of the Christian philosopher-theologian but also it shows him holding a Latin inscription saying "*sapientia vincit malitiam*" ("wisdom defeats malice"). Considering what a lover of wisdom – or *ḥikma* – the Andalusian philosopher himself was, the inscription is rather ironic, not to say malicious.

By comparison, one can tell that Raphael had no intention to perpetuate the image of an Averroës solely to be remembered for his commentaries on Aristotelian works and the controversy these sparked in the West. If that had been the intention, surely the Andalusian would have been placed in the vicinity of Aristotle. Instead, one finds him lovingly depicted as the Muslim he was, clothed with a turban and a green kaftan, leaning over the shoulders of the writing Archimedes (3rd century B.C.), in a posture expressing deep humility, but not humiliation, before a respected and admired predecessor. To fully appreciate the inclusion of Ibn Rushd in

"The School of Athens," one need realize that he is the only non-ancient author in this august assembly of Greek, Roman (and Persian) philosopher-scientists. No one else from a later period was considered worthy enough to be included in Raphael's "School of Athens." Ibn Rushd with his great love for the Greeks would not have minded being associated with them. Nevertheless, to use an Aristotelian term, it is doubtful that he would have thought of the "School of Athens" as his *natural place*. In his mind, he most certainly would have felt that – notwithstanding the many differences in opinion – he belonged to the philosopher-scientist-theologians of the Islamic tradition of thought such as al-Fārābī, Ibn Sīnā (Avicenna), and al-Ghazālī.

Notes

1 For the history of this text, manuscripts, editions, and translations see ʻAbdurraḥmān Badawi, *Histoire de la philosophie en Islam* (Paris: Vrin, 1972), I:751–52.

2 *The Philosophy and Theology of Averroës*, trans. Muhammad al-Jamil al-Rahman (Baroda: A. G. Widgery, 1921); George F. Hourani, *On the Harmony of Religion and Philosophy* (London: Luzac & Co., 1961); Averroës, *Decisive Treatise and Epistle Dedicatory*, trans. with introduction and notes by Charles E. Butterworth (Provo, UT: Brigham Young University Press, 2001).

3 Among the exceptions one should list R. Brunschvig's "Averroès juriste," in *Études d'orientalisme dédiées à la mémoire de Lévi-Provençal* (Paris: G.-P. Maisonneuve et Larose, 1962), I:35–68, an essay that focuses on Ibn Rushd's manual of jurisprudence *Bidāyat al-Mujtahid wa Nihāyat al-Muqtaṣid*; and Dominique Urvoy's "Ibn Rushd," in *History of Islamic Philosophy*, edited by Seyyed Hossein Nasr and Oliver Leaman (London and New York: Routledge, 1996), pp. 330–45, in which the impact of Ibn Tumart's "doctrine of thought" on Ibn Rushd's both philosophical and legal positions is repeatedly discussed. One should also commend Roger Arnaldez for dedicating an entire chapter to Ibn Rushd the jurist in his *Averroës: A Rationalist in Islam*, trans. David Streight (Notre Dame, IN: University of Notre Dame Press, 2000).

4 Islamic biographic sources mention that several of his sons had served as judges. No precise information is

available for al-Walīd, his eldest son. It is recorded, however, that among his other sons Abū al-Qāsim Aḥmad was a *qāḍī* (= judge), while Abū Muḥammad 'Abdallah had become physician to Muḥammad al-Nāṣir, the son of the Almohad caliph whom Ibn Rushd had served. See Charles Burnett, "The 'Sons of Averroës with the Emperor Frederick' and the transmission of the philosophical works by Ibn Rushd," in *Averroës and the Aristotelian Tradition*, ed. Gerhard Endress and Jan A. Aertsen (Leiden: Brill, 1999), 263.

5 This is very much in contrast to the Jewish scholarly community that – like Islam – was and continues to be marked by an equally legalistic religious tradition. For a reference to a Hebrew translation, see Badawi, *Histoire de la philosophie en Islam*, 751.

6 George F. Hourani, *On the Harmony of Religion and Philosophy*, 1 (emphasis added). A. El Ghannouchi who is right to criticize the many erroneous titles given to *Faṣl al-Maqāl*, in particular those influenced by Léon Gauthier's French translation beginning with *Le Traité décisif*... (1905), does not appear to be aware of Hourani's note ("Distinction et relation des discours philosophique et religieux chez Ibn Rushd: *Faṣl al-maqāl* ou la double vérité," *Averroës (1126–1198) oder der Triumph des Rationalismus* (Heidelberg: Universitätsverlag C. Winter, 2002), 39–147.

7 This explains Ibn Rushd's reference to it in his *Kitāb al-Kashf* as a "speech" (*qawl*). For a different view, see Averroës, *Decisive Treatise and Epistle Dedicatory*, xix.

8 For the many terms used in Islamic tradition to cover the kind of thought and intellectual pursuit that is called philosophy in a Western context, see Seyyed Hossein Nasr, "The meaning and concept of philosophy in Islam," in *History of Islamic Philosophy*, edited by Seyyed Hossein Nasr and Oliver Leaman (London and New York: Routledge, 1996), 21–26.

9 Butterworth points out some more legal terms in the title of Ibn Rushd's *Faṣl al-Maqāl*: "The term *faṣl* literally means 'separating' but also has a legal significance and can thus suggest something like 'decisive [rendering of] judgment.' *Taqrīr* is also a legal term, one denoting a decision set down by a judge, or an assignment or stipulation" (Averroës, *Decisive Treatise and Epistle Dedicatory*, xix).

10 Unless indicated otherwise, English quotations are from Hourani's translation, while the original Arabic terms are gleaned from Butterworth's bilingual edition.

11 A. El Ghannouchi, "Distinction et relation des discours philosophique et religieux chez Ibn Rushd: *Faṣl al-maqāl* ou la double vérité," 139.

12 Ibn Rushd, *The Distinguished Jurist's Primer – Bidāyat al-Mujtahid wa Nihāyat al-Muqtaṣid*, trans. by Imran Ahsan Khan Nyazee (Reading, UK: Garner Publishing, 1994), xlviii.

13 Averroës, *Decisive Treatise and Epistle Dedicatory*, xxiii.

14 "... the *law* that is particular to philosophers is that of examining closely the totality of beings, because there is no nobler way to worship the Creator than by knowing His works"; quoted after Roger Arnaldez, *Averroës: A*

Rationalist in Islam, trans. David Streight (Notre Dame, IN: University of Notre Dame Press, 2000), 5.

15 Joseph Kenny, O.P., "Ibn Masarra: His *Risāla al-iʿtibār, Orita." Ibadan Journal of Religious Studies* 34, nos. 1&2 (2002): 1–26.

16 This is essentially no different from the ancient Greek cultural (and probably also religiously motivated) assumption that the beauty of the cosmos can be explained rationally and that what makes it rational are the mathematical structures and proportions underlying it. While the supposed "mathematicity" of being became, indeed, the driving force of Western sciences and thus proved to be "correct," many accompanying assumptions such as the perfect luminosity and sphericity of heavenly bodies and circularity of orbits turned out to be flawed. A Qur'ānic statement may be read as the same incentive for rational investigations without itself necessarily complying in all respects with scientific findings.

17 Arnaldez, *Averroës: A Rationalist in Islam*, 17.

18 Ibid., 22.

19 Butterworth translates "everlastingly generated" (Averroës, *Decisive Treatise and Epistle Dedicatory*, p. 15), while Hourani says "originated and coeval with time" (174).

20 *Basic Writings of Saint Thomas Aquinas*, ed. by Anton C. Pegis (London: Random House, 1945).

21 For the impact of Ibn Tumart's "doctrine of thought" (which is at the basis of Almohad-supported theology) on Ibn Rushd's both philosophical and legal positions, see Dominique Urvoy, "Ibn Rushd," in *History of Islamic Philosophy*, 330–45.

The Use of *Lakṣaṇā* in Indian Exegesis

CHRISTOPHER G. FRAMARIN
University of Calgary

INTRODUCTION

Lakṣaṇā is an Indian exegetical principle that permits an interpreter to revert to a less literal reading of a textual claim when the literal reading is sufficiently implausible. If the literal reading implies a contradiction or absurdity, for example, an interpreter is often permitted – and sometimes required – to understand the claim figuratively. Contemporary interpreters of Indian philosophy employ this strategy extensively, but often without acknowledging its limitations.

In this paper I argue that the application of the principle of *lakṣaṇā* by contemporary interpreters of Indian philosophy is appropriate only if at least two criteria are met. First, the premises of the argument that demonstrates that a contradiction or absurdity follows from a literal reading of the claim must be plausibly attributed to the text, author, or tradition of which the text is a part. Second, the inference from the premises to the conclusion of the argument must be plausibly attributed to the text, author, or tradition. In short, contemporary interpreters of Indian philosophy should adopt and utilize the principle of *lakṣaṇā*, but only in accord with the criteria set forth by classical Indian philosophers.

THE PRINCIPLE OF *LAKṢAṆĀ*

One of the most common exegetical strategies among contemporary scholars of Indian philosophy is to argue that their own interpretations avoid absurd or inconsistent consequences that competing interpretations do not. This kind of strategy assumes from the outset that an interpreter should attempt to avoid contradictions of at least three kinds: (1) contradictions within the text, (2) contradictions with the broader tradition of which the text is a part, and (3) contradictions with so-called common sense.

On the one hand, there are certainly circumstances under which this strategy is justified. The alternative of simply letting apparent contradictions lie seems to amount to a denial of the original author's ability to recognize these contradictions. That is, the alternative seems to be the Orientalist interpretation *par excellence*.

In the introduction to her English translation of the *Manusmṛti*, Wendy Doniger makes this point.[1]

> Many scholars believe that the text of Manu is a hotchpotch of inconsistency.... This attitude has been characterized by followers of Edward Said as 'Orientalist'; it is based upon an arrogant Western assumption that 'Orientals' are radically alien even in their basic cognitive processes, that, unlike us, they do not recognize or understand contradictions when they encounter or generate them.[2]

Edward Said, quoting Cromer, further illustrates this assumption: "logic is something 'the existence of which the Oriental is disposed altogether to ignore'."[3]

Even if these texts are the result of numerous authors and redactions, or attempts to reconcile competing, inconsistent worldviews, and so on, to take apparent contradictions at face value seems to amount to a denial of the tradition's ability to recognize contradictions. The *readers* of these texts, both within and without the intellectual milieu, "regard the product as a single text"[4] and hence as a roughly unified document.

Arindam Chakrabarti makes this point in the context of the *Manusmṛti* and *Mahābhārata*. One might attempt to explain the apparent inconsistencies in these texts by mentioning the historical convergence of violent Vedic culture and non-violent post-Vedic culture during the period of their compositions.

> But such an 'explanation' does not solve the moral puzzle that the *Dharmaśāstras* [a broader class of texts that includes the *Manusmṛti*] and *Mahābhārata* present. How could a Dharma-obsessed self-critical hermeneutically meticulous society internalize both of these attitudes within the same moral framework at the same time?[5]

It is difficult to see how the tradition's interpretive and analytic competence can be acknowledged without at least attempting to explain how it reconciles the tensions that characterize its historical background and which might manifest in its texts.

Consider, for example, Rajendra Prasad's interpretation of *niṣkāmakarma* (desireless action) in the *Bhagavadgītā* (*Gītā*). Prasad argues as follows:

> Kṛṣṇa [an incarnation of God in the *Gītā*] also speaks of giving up all desires.... As per common experience, [however,] an intentional action *X* is possible without any desire for doing *X*, if there is another desire for doing something else.... To do an intentional action, therefore, I must have at least some desire for something, or for doing something. But if I have no desire at all, if I am completely desireless, I cannot do any intentional action. Therefore ... all of Kṛṣṇa's exhortations to [Arjuna] for doing actions without any desire ... [are] infructuous [that is, useless].[6]

Prasad argues that desireless action, taken literally, is an obvious contradiction. Since Kṛṣṇa endorses desireless action, Kṛṣṇa's advice is simply nonsense.

If we assume that Prasad is correct that desireless action is an obvious contradiction (although see below), then we should at least consider the possibility that Kṛṣṇa's endorsement of desireless action is qualified in some way. The alternative is to say that the author of the *Gītā* was incapable of recognizing this fact of "common experience."

Perhaps the advice could be taken as an endorsement of action performed without certain desires, rather than without any desire at all. Sarvepalli Radhakrishnan, among others, draws the same initial conclusion as Prasad – that the advice, taken literally, is a contradiction – but then infers that "[w]e are not asked to uproot all desires; for that would imply the cessation of all activity."[7] That is, in Radhakrishnan's view, since the literal reading of Kṛṣṇa's advice entails an obvious contradiction, the literal reading must be abandoned in favour of a less literal one.[8]

Additionally, the Indian traditions themselves see this strategy of adopting a figurative interpretation under certain circumstances as absolutely indispensable. Many of the earliest texts in the Indian philosophical tradition (the *Yogasūtra*, *Nyāyasūtra*, *Sāṃkhyakārika*, and so on) were written with the expectation that a student would hear the text from a teacher, who would explain the extremely concise, ambiguous *sūtras* orally. Commentaries on these texts reflect this oral tradition and often read like the words of one's guru, explicating each term or claim with synonyms, examples, and analogies, considering alternative interpretations and objections, and dismissing them. Without employing some form of the contemporary strategy outlined above, however, it is difficult to see how one interpretation is more plausible than another. Put simply: the commentarial tradition in India has always admitted consistency as a fundamental interpretive constraint. The commentators themselves presumably thought that their own work would be interpreted in accord with this constraint as well, and wrote accordingly.

Indeed, Indian philosophers and literary critics explicitly defend this interpretive principle and outline – albeit sometimes in disagreement with one another – guidelines for its use. In these traditions, the principle of *lakṣaṇā* states that when there is an obstruction (*bādha*) of the primary meaning (*mukhya*, *abhidhā*) of a word or sentence, a secondary meaning (*lakṣaṇā*, also *upacāra*, *gauṇi*, *vṛtti*, *bhakti*) must be adopted.[9] The principle also states that when there is no obstruction to the primary meaning of a word or sentence, it is impermissible to revert to a secondary meaning.[10]

The primary and secondary meanings of a word are generally explained in terms of ordinary established usage. The referent that most immediately comes to mind when the word is heard is that to which the word refers directly and primarily. The referent that comes to mind, although not immediately – usually in part as a result of an obstruction (*bādha*) of the primary meaning – is that to which the word refers indirectly or secondarily.

The term *bādha* can refer to either an immediate breakdown in comprehension or a contradiction of some sort. An immediate breakdown in comprehension might occur when a person hears, for example, that "food is life" or "he is the family."[11] In these cases, it is not clear how one might so much as form a consistent image from these utterances, since food and life are clearly different – someone might die with a full stomach! – and an individual and his family are numerically distinct. Hence the first sentence means food is essential to life, and the second means that he is the head or most prominent member of his family.

In contrast, a contradiction might occur when a person hears that "the village is on the Ganges." In this case, it is not as if it is impossible to construct an image of a village floating atop the Ganges – there is no immediate breakdown in comprehension. It's just that villages cannot in fact be constructed upon rivers.[12] That is, the utterance, taken literally, contradicts common sense. Hence the sentence states that the village sits on the bank of the Ganges.

The examples that are most widely discussed in the literature on *lakṣaṇā* are of the relatively straightforward sort just outlined. They are usually isolated utterances of a single speaker and face a *bādha* in virtue of their own content. In the context of textual exegesis, however, the strategy is extended, so that a secondary meaning can be adopted even if the claim being interpreted is perfectly sensible on its own.

The prevalence of this strategy among classical Indian philosophers cannot be overstated. Consider, for example, the opening passages of the most well-known and influential commentaries on the *Bhagavadgītā* – those of Śaṅkara and Rāmānuja. Śaṅkara begins his commentary with verse 2.12, which reads:

> Certainly I never did not exist, nor you, nor these lords of men /
> And never will we not all exist henceforth //[13]

He explains that the word 'we' (*vayam*) should not be taken literally to refer to an actual multiplicity of selves because this is inconsistent with the non-dualism of both the *Gītā* and the *Upaniṣads*. Instead, 'we' refers to the merely apparent multiplicity of selves. Śaṅkara argues that the primary meaning of the claim should therefore be abandoned for a less literal one.[14]

Rāmānuja begins his commentary with the same verse, only to dispute Śaṅkara's argument for the non-literal reading. He insists that the word 'we' must be taken literally, since Kṛṣṇa uses the word 'we' "at the time of teaching the eternal, ultimate truth, as a means to eliminating the error due to ignorance."[15] If Kṛṣṇa's goal is the elimination of ignorance, then why would he speak in a way that, taken literally, reinforces what Śaṅkara takes to be the fundamental error that results from ignorance – namely the error of believing that there are a multiplicity of selves? Instead, according to Rāmānuja, in order to avoid further confusion, Kṛṣṇa surely speaks literally and means to imply an actual multiplicity of selves.[16]

So this fundamental metaphysical disagreement between Śaṅkara and Rāmānuja amounts, in large part, to a disagreement over which authoritative claims should be taken literally. Rāmānuja in turn must interpret less literally claims that, taken literally, seem to endorse non-dualism.

Elsewhere, Śaṅkara and Rāmānuja agree to dismiss more literal readings of passages that imply that determinism is true. *Gītā* 3.33, for example, reads:

> Even the wise acts according to his material nature /
> Beings follow [their] material nature. What will resistance do? //[17]

Both authors point out the contradiction between the literal reading and scriptural injunctions. Scriptural injunctions imply free will. If it is true that I ought to act in a spirit of devotion towards God, for example, then presumably I am free to do so if I choose. Free will and determinism are inconsistent. Hence *Gītā* 3.33 does not state that determinism is true. Instead, *Gītā* 3.33 should be taken to say that agents are determined by desire and aversion (*rāga* and *dveṣa*), unless they resist their force.[18]

In some cases, the defence of one interpretation over another amounts to a circuitous argument. The Naiyāyikas, for example, take the Upaniṣadic claim that *mokṣa* (liberation) is eternal *sukha* – literally: happiness – in its secondary sense, to mean that *mokṣa* is eternally (and entirely) devoid of pain. They argue against the Vedāntin, who takes the claim literally, to mean that in *mokṣa* the eternal bliss of the true self is manifested. This means that, when a person attains *mokṣa*, he or she becomes aware of the bliss of *mokṣa*. If this is right, then some explanation must be given for what causes the awareness of bliss to arise. One option is to say that there is no cause of the awareness of the eternal bliss of *mokṣa*. It is simply eternal. If the awareness were eternal, however, then everyone would always experience it, and there would be no difference between the liberated person and the unliberated person. This, the Naiyāyikas claim, is absurd, however. If, on the other hand, the awareness of the bliss of *mokṣa* is caused, then it cannot be eternal because whatever is caused is non-eternal.[19] Anything that comes into existence inevitably ceases to exist.[20] Instead, then, the claim that *mokṣa* is eternal *sukha* means *mokṣa* is perfectly devoid of *duḥkha* (pain).[21]

The point of this kind of example is to show that the standards for consistency can be extremely high. Prasad charges the author of the *Gītā* with saying something that directly contradicts a supposedly obvious truth. If he is right, then, at least according to the classical Indian traditions, an interpreter is not only justified in reverting to a less literal reading but is required to do so. Commentators on the *Nyāyasūtra*, in contrast, charge the Vedāntins with saying something the falsehood of which is discerned only through careful, extensive, and perhaps obscure reasoning (if it is at all). Nonetheless, in this case too, the classical Indian traditions say that the interpreter is justified in reverting to a less literal reading.

While all of this suggests that the contemporary strategy of avoiding contradiction is justified, and even unavoidable, there are also reasons for hesitation. It might be objected, for example, that the use of the exegetical principle of *lakṣaṇā* by contemporary scholars amounts to a different form of Orientalism, since it licenses the interpreter to impose her own concepts, values, and truths on Indian texts.[22] As Doniger and Smith warn, "there is always the danger that the coherence is in the eye of the beholder, that we project upon the text a pattern that is not of its making."[23]

It seems that, if contemporary scholars apply the principle of *lakṣaṇā* as rigorously and extensively as classical commentators do, they will mistakenly conclude that the Indian Law Books are consistent with liberalism, that Indian ethics is a species of utilitarianism (or deontology, or virtue ethics), that Indian metaphysics is realist, and perhaps physicalist, and so on, just because they take some of these positions as obviously correct. Indeed, the analyses of *niṣkāmakarma* that I mention above (and almost every other contemporary analysis of the doctrine) assume that Indian moral psychology is fundamentally Humean in that it accepts the so-called 'desire-belief' account of motivation – an account that has only recently become the preferred view in the West. (Hume himself begins the famous passage in which he defends this view by characterizing the opposing view – according to which reason can motivate action without the help of desire – as a philosophical dogma of his day.[24])

THE APPLICATION OF *LAKṢAṆĀ*

So the question is: How do we reconcile these demands and dangers? Not surprisingly, I want to argue that the Indian exegetical principle of *lakṣaṇā* should be used but that it should be used very carefully. To begin with, it's worth drawing a distinction between what might be called the 'unrestrained' application of the principle of *lakṣaṇā* – the kind exhibited by the Nyāya argument against a literal reading of the claim that *mokṣa* is *sukha* – and what might be called the 'restrained' application.

The unrestrained application of the principle seeks to make a text consistent at any cost. Fundamental to this strategy is the assumption that the text is both perfectly consistent and entirely true. The strategy does not allow the option of simply ascribing an inconsistency or falsehood to the text under analysis. Neither Śaṅkara nor Rāmānuja dismisses a claim of the *Upaniṣads*, *Brahmasūtra*, or *Bhagavadgītā* as simply false. They apply the principle of *lakṣaṇā* without restraint.

The restrained application, in contrast, does not accept the assumption that the text is perfectly consistent and entirely true. It admits both that the author or authors that composed the text might have overlooked inconsistencies, and that the tradition that accepts the text as authoritative might have overlooked inconsistencies as well. It admits that the author or authors that composed the text might have asserted things that were untrue, and that the tradition that accepts the text as authoritative might have overlooked these falsehoods.

We see the distinction between these two applications of the principle in the Indian traditions themselves. When an author comments on a text that he takes to be authoritative, he applies *lakṣaṇā* in an unrestrained way because he assumes that the author of the text is infallible, and hence that every word of the text is true, and every claim of the text consistent with every other. Indeed, under the assumption that the author of the text is infallible, this kind of strategy is justified.

In other cases, however, commentators are willing to attribute mistakes to those texts on which they comment simply because they do not take the authors of the texts to be infallible. In these cases, they apply the principle of *lakṣaṇā*, but not in an unrestrained way. They utilize the restrained application of the principle.[25]

This is most obvious in cases in which an author considers an opponent's position. If the author utilizes the unrestrained application of *lakṣaṇā* in these circumstances, there would be no disagreements left to resolve. The Vedāntin, for example, would simply state the Nyāya view in a way that reflects innovative interpretation on the part of the Vedāntin. Instead, however, the Vedāntin notes the differences between the Vedāntin and Nyāya view and argues for the falsity of the latter.

This brings us back to the matter of how contemporary scholars should apply the principle of *lakṣaṇā*. The first point I want to make is that, since the unrestrained application of the principle is appropriate only under the assumption that the original author was or is infallible, contemporary scholars will rarely apply the principle in this way just because contemporary scholars tend not to operate under this assumption. So only the restrained application of the principle of *lakṣaṇā* need be addressed here.

In order to utilize the restrained application of *lakṣaṇā*, at least two criteria must be met. (These criteria are not meant to be exhaustive.)

(1) The premises of the argument that demonstrates the contradiction or absurdity that follows from the literal reading of the claim must be plausibly attributed to the text, author, or tradition of which the text is a part.

(2) The inference from the premises to the conclusion of the argument that demonstrates the contradiction or absurdity that follows from the literal reading of the claim must be plausibly attributed to the text, author, or tradition.

In order to justify reverting to a non-literal reading of a claim, an interpreter must argue that the literal reading of the claim entails a contradiction or absurdity. The first criterion states that the claims that constitute the premises of the argument that demonstrates the contradiction or absurdity must be plausibly attributed to the text, author, or tradition of which the text is a part.[26]

Consider an example. Radhakrishnan, whom I mentioned above, argues for a non-literal interpretation of Kṛṣṇa's advice to act without desire in the following way:

> **Premise One:** Kṛṣṇa advises Arjuna to act without desire.
> **Premise Two:** Desire is a necessary condition of action.
> **Premise Three/Conclusion One:** Hence taken literally, Kṛṣṇa's advice is a contradiction – he advises Arjuna to both act and not act, or to both act without desire and act with desire.
> **Premise Four:** If Kṛṣṇa's advice, taken literally, entails a contradiction, then the advice should be taken non-literally.
> **Conclusion Two:** Hence Kṛṣṇa advises Arjuna to act without certain desires. Other desires are permissible.

The argument is convincing, however, only if premise two is plausibly attributed to the *Gītā*. If premise two is true but cannot be plausibly attributed to the text, then, all other things being equal, the most plausible interpretation of Kṛṣṇa's advice is the literal – and inconsistent – one. Kṛṣṇa advises Arjuna to act without desire even if he is mistaken in some way in doing so. Hence Radhakrishnan's argument is not convincing as it stands. Some further argument is needed for the claim that premise two is plausibly attributed to the *Gītā*.

Some of the authors who offer a similar argument argue that, since a number of other seminal Indian texts and traditions accept the claim that desire is a necessary condition of action, the *Gītā* does as well.[27] Radhakrishnan and others,[28] however, seem to want to say that, since this claim is obviously true, the *Gītā* must accept it. So there are at least two different strategies for justifying the attribution of a claim to a text. The first is to find the claim in the text or tradition of which it is a part.[29] The second is to say that the claim is self-evident and hence that the original author must have accepted it, even if there is insufficient textual evidence to support the claim that the original author accepted it.

I want to leave the first strategy aside and focus on the second, since relatively little has been said about the second. Obviously, the fact that a claim is now widely accepted does not entail that it was obviously true or self-evident to the author of an ancient text.[30] It seems forbidding, however, to try to codify all of the additional conditions that would have to be met in order for an interpreter to be justified in attributing a claim to a text on this basis. Instead, I want to point out a single additional condition, the violation of which is the basis for many mistakes in Indian exegesis: the claim that is attributed to a text on the basis that it is self-evident must at least be true.[31]

Consider another example. Ian Whicher argues that verse 1.2 of the *Yogasūtra* (*yogaścittavṛttinirodhaḥ*) should not be taken literally to read: "Yoga – *yogaḥ* – is the cessation – *nirodhaḥ* – of the modifications (that is, states and activities) – *vṛtti* – of the mind – *citta*." Instead, it should be taken non-literally to mean: "Yoga is the cessation of [the misidentification with] the modifications (*vṛtti*) of the mind."[32]

One of the arguments that Whicher offers for this conclusion goes as follows:

> **Premise One:** Assume *nirodha* (cessation) is the ontological elimination of mental modifications. (This is what *Yogasūtra* 1.2 says, if taken literally.)
> **Premise Two:** If *nirodha* is the ontological elimination of mental modifications, then it is the willful suppression of mental modifications.
> **Premise Three:** If *nirodha* is the willful suppression of mental modifications, then *nirodha* is a *rajasic* and *tamasic* state (a state characterized by aggression, laziness, and delusion).
> **Premise Four/Conclusion One:** Hence if *Yogasūtra* 1.2 is taken literally, *nirodha* is a *rajasic* and *tamasic* state, which is absurd.
> **Premise Five:** If *Yogasūtra* 1.2, taken literally, entails an absurdity, then *Yogasūtra* 1.2 should be taken non-literally.

> **Conclusion Two:** Hence the advice in *Yogasūtra* 1.2 to eliminate the modifications of the mind is just the advice to eliminate the identification with the modifications of the mind.[33]

Whicher seems to want to say that premises two and three are self-evident. He doesn't cite the *Yogasūtra* or any of its commentaries in their support. Whicher assumes, in premise two, that in order to eliminate a mental state or activity, one must suppress it straightaway. This would seem to be false, however, in light of the following example.

In a related context, Paul Williams points out that the Buddhist *Prajñāpāramitā Sūtras* repeatedly describe the bodhisattva as without discursive thought. Williams points out that to take this to mean that the text advises "simply cutting discursive thought, making the mind a blank" straightaway, however, amounts to the fallacy of "confusing the result with the cause." Instead, a practitioner should first extend her analysis of reality as a means of deepening her understanding of *śūnyatā* (emptiness). As an eventual but not immediate result, discursive thought ceases.[34]

Likewise in the context of yoga, the practitioner should eliminate the *kleśas* (defilements) by means of morality, dispassion, and concentration (rather than simply trying to suppress the mind directly). As an eventual but not immediate result, mental activity ceases – that is, there is an ontological elimination of the mental modifications. If this is right, then premise two of Whicher's argument is false. If the premise is false, then it cannot be plausibly attributed to the text (author and so on) on the grounds that it is self-evident.[35]

Thus, in summary, the first criterion states that the claims that constitute the premises of the argument that demonstrates that a contradiction or absurdity results from a literal reading of a textual claim must be plausibly attributed to the text. In order for a claim to be plausibly attributed to a text, at least one of two conditions must be satisfied. Either (a) there must be sufficient evidence from the text or tradition, or (b) the claim must be self-evident. If an interpreter attributes a claim to a text on the basis that it is self-evident, then minimally the claim must be true. Sufficient textual evidence is a sufficient condition for attributing a claim to a text. The truth of a claim, however, is merely a necessary condition. Indeed, it is a rather meagre condition. Nonetheless, failure to meet this condition accounts for many mistakes in the interpretation of Indian philosophical texts.

The second criterion for the application of the principle of *lakṣaṇā* states that any inference within the argument that an interpreter offers to justify reverting to a non-literal reading of a claim must be plausibly attributed to the text, author, or tradition.[36] Suppose an interpreter offers an argument for a non-literal reading of a claim, and each premise of the argument is plausibly attributed to the text. It still might not be the case that the argument as a whole is plausibly attributed to the text. In addition to whatever evidence makes the attribution of the claims plausible, further evidence is typically needed for the plausibility of attributing to the text the combination of claims in the form of an argument. Many of Socrates' dialogues demonstrate that his interlocutor accepts inconsistent claims without realizing it, and of course each of us has been and is guilty of the same kind of oversight. We should leave open the possibility that a text or author is capable of this kind of oversight as well. So, rather than simply assume that the author draws every justified inference, a case should be made for each inference that is attributed.

There are at least two different strategies for justifying the attribution of an inference to a text, and the two strategies parallel those for justifying the attribution of a claim to a text. (For the sake of simplicity, in what follows, I assume that the first criterion is met.) The first is to find sufficient evidence for the inference within the text or tradition of which it is a part. This might mean establishing that the very argument that is being attributed to the text is explicit within the text or tradition itself. Otherwise, it might mean establishing that a sufficiently similar line of argument is advanced, perhaps repeatedly, in the text or tradition.

The second strategy is to say that the inference is self-evident, and hence that the original author must have accepted it, even if there is insufficient textual evidence to support the claim that the original author accepted it. If the inference is attributed to the text on these grounds, then it must meet the very meagre condition of being justified, just as the attribution of a claim to a text on the grounds that it is self-evident must meet the minimum (and only necessary) condition of being true.[37]

So in summary, the second criterion states that the inferences within the argument that demonstrates that a contradiction or absurdity results from a literal reading of a textual claim must be plausibly attributed to the text. In order for an inference to be plausibly attributed to a text, at least one of two conditions must be satisfied. Either (a) there must be sufficient evidence from the text or tradition, or (b) the inference must be self-evident. If an interpreter attributes an inference to a text on the basis that it is self-evident, then minimally the inference must be justified. Sufficient evidence from the text or tradition is a *sufficient* condition for attributing an inference to a text. That an inference is justified, however, is merely a *necessary* condition.

LAKṢAṆĀ AND CONTEMPORARY INTERPRETERS OF INDIAN PHILOSOPHY

The two criteria that I have defended here might be combined to read:

> The argument that demonstrates the contradiction or absurdity that follows from the literal reading of the claim must be plausibly attributed to the text, author, or tradition of which the text is a part.

If the argument is plausibly attributed to a text, then presumably each premise of the argument is plausibly attributed to the text and any inference between premise(s) and conclusion(s) is plausibly attributed to the text. Still, it is helpful to keep the two criteria distinct, since each amounts to a distinct task that comes with its own obstacles. In closing, I want to say something about the skills that are required to deal with these obstacles.

First, an interpreter should know the text and traditions that he or she interprets as well as possible and attempt to align the text under analysis with its cultural, philosophical, and historical milieu. Facility with the original language in which the text was composed is an important component in this range of skills. This skill will generally be of most use in establishing the plausibility of a claim or inference on the basis of evidence from the text or tradition of which it is a part. This point can be reduced to the advice to simply employ a certain kind of hermeneutic and historical rigour that many scholars already employ.

Hermeneutic and historical rigour is not enough, however. Thorough knowledge of the traditions under interpretation does not ensure that the interpreter will correctly identify possible contradictions and accurately discriminate between more and less plausible interpretations. In order to do this, the interpreter must also employ a certain kind of philosophical rigour – a careful analysis of concepts and their implications, the broad consideration of alternatives, and an ability to evaluate his or her own arguments honestly – much like that employed by classical Indian authors.

This is not to say that the careful historian and philosopher never imposes his or her own convictions, intuitions, conceptual schemes, and so on, onto a text. My point is that some of the grossest instances of this can be avoided by means of the strategies I have outlined. Without these strategies, there are literally no limitations on what an interpreter might claim a text implies.

There are both altruistic and egoistic reasons to produce research of this sort. To the extent that we do, we contribute toward building a community of scholars with a common set of standards. With a common set of standards, we produce work that is useful and interesting to a larger audience. We also work towards avoiding obvious mistakes and the relatively effortless refutations of those who have mastered skills that we have not. In short, we improve our work by making it more convincing.

CONCLUSION

Contemporary interpreters of Indian philosophy employ something like the classical Indian exegetical principle of *lakṣaṇā*. While this principle is indispensable to current scholarship, contemporary scholars will benefit from appreciating the rigour with which it was applied in the classical Indian commentarial traditions themselves, and by following their examples.

Notes

1 The translation is authored by Wendy Doniger and Brian K. Smith, but this portion of the introduction is written by Doniger and reflects her interpretation of the text, which differs from Smith's. See footnote 3, p. xvi.

2 Wendy Doniger and Brian K. Smith, *The Laws of Manu* (London: Penguin, 1991), xliv–xlv.

3 Edward Said, *Orientalism* (New York: Random House, 1994), 36.

4 Doniger and Smith, *Laws of Manu*, xlvii.

5 Arindam Chakrabarti, "Meat and Morality in the *Mahābhārata*," *Studies in Humanities and Social Sciences* 3 (1996): 261.

6 Rajendra Prasad, *Varṇadharma, Niṣkāmakarma and Practical Morality* (New Delhi: DK Printworld, 1999), 59–60.

7 Sarvepalli Radhakrishnan, "The Ethics of *Bhagavadgita* and Kant," *International Journal of Ethics* 21 (1911): 475.

8 See Christopher G. Framarin, *Desire and Motivation in Indian Philosophy* (London: Routledge, 2009), 6–8.

9 There is disagreement over whether a word or a sentence is the fundamental unit of meaning.

10 Consider examples of each claim. Maṇḍanamiśra begins his *Brahmasiddhi* by attributing the following argument to his opponents: "Indeed, others [that is, my opponents] think that since, when there is a grasping of [the *Upaniṣads'*] primary meaning, there is a contradiction … with perception, and so on, [therefore] they are [to be taken] in [their] secondary meaning" (Framarin, *Desire and Motivation in Indian Philosophy*, 156). Vācaspatimiśra, in his commentary to the *Nyāyasūtra*, says, "only if the primary (*mukhya*) [meaning] is inconsistent is the secondary (*gauṇa*) [meaning] reverted to" (Framarin, ibid., 151).

11 Vātsyāyana offers these examples in his commentary to *Nyāyasūtra*, 2.2.59.

12 K. Kunjunni Raja points out that the English sentence "The village is on the Ganges" might be understood to mean that the village is on the bank of the Ganges without reverting to its secondary meaning, since part of the primary meaning of the word 'on' in English is something like "in the vicinity of" (K. Kunjunni Raja, *Indian Theories of Meaning* [Madras: Adyar Library and Research Centre, 1969], 232).

13 Shastri Gajanana Shambhu Sadhale, ed., *Bhagavad-gītā with Eleven Commentaries* (Delhi: Parimal Publications, 2000), 83.

14 Ibid.

15 Ibid.

16 Ibid. See also Christopher G. Framarin, "The Problem with Pretending: Rāmānuja's Arguments against *Jīvanmukti*," *Journal of Indian Philosophy* 37 (2009): 399–414.

17 Sadhale, *Bhagavad-gītā*, 331.

18 Ibid.

19 This is a standard claim accepted by both the Naiyāyikas and Vedāntins. The thought is that if something comes into being, then it is partite, and if it is partite, then it inevitably reduces to its parts.

20 Framarin, *Desire and Motivation in Indian Philosophy*, 144–45.

21 As these examples make clear, the use of *lakṣaṇā* is widespread by the time of the oldest extant commentaries throughout a variety of traditions.

22 Tinu Ruparell raised this kind of objection against the strategy in a discussion at the Comparative Philosophy and Religion Workshop in Calgary, AB, October 2006.

23 Doniger and Smith, *Laws of Manu*, xlvii.

24 David Hume, *A Treatise of Human Nature*, ed. P. H. Nidditch (Oxford: Clarendon Press, 1978), 413.

25 Vācaspatimiśra and Udayana, for example, simply deny Vātsyāyana's claim (at *Nyāyasūtra*, 1.1.10) that the self is imperceptible, rather than attempt to interpret him in a way that is consistent with this claim (which would anyway be an impossible task).

26 This point is implicit in what Kisor Kumar Chakrabarti calls 'GAIE' – "the principle of general acceptability of inductive examples," which requires that the counter-example offered to an opponent is one that the opponent already accepts. Kisor K. Chakrabarti, *Classical Indian Philosophy of Mind: The Nyāya Dualist Tradition* (Albany, NY: SUNY Press, 1999), 8.

27 See, for example, Roy W. Perrett, *Hindu Ethics: A Philosophical Study* (Honolulu: University of Hawaii Press, 1998), 23, and Tara Chatterjea, *Knowledge and Freedom in Indian Philosophy* (Lanham, MD: Lexington Books, 2002), 125.

28 See, for example, Jagat Pal, *Karma, Dharma, and Moksha: Conceptual Essays on Indian Ethics* (Delhi: Abhijeet Publications, 2004), 53.

29 It might be that in order to determine whether a text or tradition asserts the premise, an additional argument, the conclusion of which is the premise under analysis, must be considered. This additional argument, in turn, must also meet the criteria that I outline here.

30 In what follows, I assume that a claim that is self-evident might still require some reasoning along the following lines. If someone has drawn on the wall with a crayon in the past fifteen minutes, and only a parent and her child are in the house, it might be self-evident to the parent that the child drew on the wall.

31 If a claim is plausibly attributed to a text on the basis of additional textual evidence, however, then the claim need not be true.

32 Ian Whicher, *The Integrity of the Yoga Darśana: A Reconsideration of Classical Yoga* (Albany, NY: SUNY Press, 1998), 152.

33 Whicher says, "Such willfulness leading to suppression, and so forth, is simply a form of misguided effort based on *rajasic* and *tamasic vṛttis* and predispositions in the form of aggressive or deluded ideas or intentions.... The disempowerment of *avidyā*

(ignorance) over the mind is not to be confused with the *guṇa* [quality] of *tamas*!" (ibid., 163).

34 Paul Williams, *Mahāyāna Buddhism: The Doctrinal Foundations* (London: Routledge, 2008), 49.

35 Whicher offers at least two additional arguments for his interpretation of *Yogasūtra*, 1.2. The more convincing of the two points out that if all mental modifications of an individual cease, then the individual cannot act in the world. If a liberated person cannot act in the world, then no living liberated teacher can exist. This, Whicher claims, is absurd, since the tradition admits liberated teachers. In an earlier draft of this paper, I argued that this argument is unconvincing, since it attributes the later doctrine of *jīvanmukti* (the possibility of a living liberated person) to the original text. Since then I've become less convinced of my objection. Even if the original text does not mention the doctrine of *jīvanmukti* per se, the problem that Whicher points out does seem rather obvious. Whether Whicher is justified in drawing the conclusion that *Yogasūtra*, 1.2 ought to be translated as he suggests, however, is a further question.

36 I use the word 'inference' to refer to any inferential move from premises to a conclusion. The conclusion might be an intermediate conclusion or a final conclusion. If a premise contains a conditional – such as, 'If *P*, then *Q*' – then the first criterion, rather than the second, requires that it be plausibly attributed to the text.

37 If the inference is plausibly attributed to a text on the basis of additional textual evidence, then the inference need not be justified.

Women's Rights as Human Rights: Explorations in Intercultural Philosophy and Religion[1]

MORNY JOY
University of Calgary

The subject of women's rights as human rights has been a topic of much discussion in a number of disciplines recently. It seems to me that many of the issues raised in connection with women's rights have a particular resonance with religious matters. Unfortunately, however, these matters have not been treated in a sustained manner within the discipline of Religious Studies.[2] This is because religion is often viewed as one of the principal obstacles to women's rights. It is basically from this problematic perspective that women's rights have been approached in Religious Studies, with an emphasis on fundamentalist forms of religion.[3] One of the reasons for this is that a number of countries have refused to be full signatories at the United Nations to declarations where women's rights are concerned. They have claimed reservations because of tradition and/or culture – which are basically shorthand terms for religion.[4] While there have been various eloquent indictments of this situation by feminist philosophers, political and legal theorists, and activists of many stripes,[5] there have been few voices from feminists in Religious Studies, especially from a comparative outlook.[6] In this essay then, I would like to undertake some preliminary observations as to specific areas of interest that hold promise for a comparative study of women's rights and religion. In the present climate of fundamentalist claims, this would seem to be a matter of some urgency. Until there is a form of co-operative dialogue between women scholars of various religious backgrounds, who also support women's rights, it appears that the present unproductive exclusive divide between the secular and religious domains, as mirroring exactly the liberal separation of the public and the private worlds, will remain entrenched. This is not to say that I oppose the separation of church and state as a general principle, but I think that, in particular circumstances, religion can no longer claim to be a private haven, shielded from the law when the law has been violated. The finer legal details of this needed modification are beyond the scope of this paper,[7] but what I plan to describe in this essay are some of the problematic areas concerning the interaction of religion and the rights of women where I believe that women scholars in religion could contribute both pertinent and valuable insights.

WOMEN'S RIGHTS AND RELIGION

In 1997 Martha Nussbaum published an article entitled: "Religion and Women's Human Rights."[8] In it she made a statement to the effect that no systems of religious law should be allowed to interfere with the basic rights of citizens. Her particular concern was the situation of women throughout the world where religions have not always respected women's rights, in accordance with the equal dignity and the inviolability of their persons, as promulgated by the United Nations in Universal Declaration of Human Rights (1949) and the Convention on the Elimination of all Forms of Discrimination Against Women or CEDAW (1979). For Nussbaum, this manifests itself in the need to control women, specifically in matters involving sexuality, marriage and divorce, reproduction and guardianship or custody of children. Since this publication, much discussion has occurred on the merits of Nussbaum's liberal political position, and of certain inherent tendencies that have been labelled by postcolonial thinkers or conservative religious figures as "western" or "Northern" impositions on women in cultures where secular values, such as equal rights are inapplicable.

In the same year, another article in a similar vein appeared, "Is Multiculturalism Bad for Women?"[9] Here political scientist Susan Moller Okin worried that cultures "that endorse and facilitate the control of men over women in various ways – even informally – limit their capacity to live with human dignity equal to that of men and boys, and to live as freely chosen lives as possible."[10] Moller Okin was especially concerned about the way in which this played itself out when people from these cultures migrate to countries such as the United States. Okin's short essay provoked an extremely animated discussion. A number of responses were published in a volume with the same name as her essay, edited by Joshua Cohen, Michael Howard, and Martha Nussbaum.[11]

There were telling observations among these responses. One response from Nussbaum herself called on Okin to account for a seeming dismissive attitude towards religion as not having anything constructive to contribute to human beings and society.[12] Another reply from Homi Bhabha alleged that Okin depicted a stark dualism posited between religion and secularism that tended to reinforce existing stereotypes regarding the religious practices and orientations of minority migrant communities.[13] She was also criticized by Bhabha for her determinate view of culture as static[14] because it did not take into account the dynamic, if sometimes controversial, encounters that can often bring about positive change in attitudes and behaviour for both parties. Finally, she was also charged with ignoring the fact that women in minority cultures are not necessarily passive recipients and many resist existing conditions by protesting against imposed standards that do not acknowledge their integrity.[15]

In her response, Nussbaum also placed particular emphasis on the notion of freedom of religious expression, specifically as it is expressed in the American Constitution. Nussbaum acknowledged the complex and difficult nature of the competing claims of the right to equality of treatment with the right to freedom of religious practice, involving the constant testing of the limits of toleration in a politically liberal state.[16] She also admits that she is in favour of the position that such a state – specifically the United States – "would give religion specific deference, on the grounds that minority religions have been especially vulnerable in all societies and are consequently in need of special protection."[17] Yet how congruent is this observation with her earlier remark that religious law should never impede the rights of citizens? For it would seem to me that deference to certain religious practices, which claim the authority of law and tradition, particularly in regard to women, could be extremely problematic. Are these practices then to be given deference or to be contested?

It is this contested area where I believe that there are no easy or immediate answers, especially in countries such as Canada, where multiculturalism has been official policy, in contrast to the United States where the metaphor of "melting pot" is preferred. These crucial decisions need to be painstakingly worked out through the courts, and through Parliament – at both federal and provincial levels – and in public debate. As an illustration of the way that the introduction of religion to these debates can complicate the question of women's rights in specific societies, I will present the basic outlines of two recent case studies in Canada. These are: 1. The situation of the Aboriginal women of Canada, particularly those on reservations governed by the Indian Act.[18] The rights of these women to housing, food, or shelter can still be lost if they marry a non-Aboriginal man – they become legally non-Indian. 2. The recommendation made in early 2005 in the province of Ontario in favour of permitting Islamic tribunals to use *Sharī'a* law to settle family disputes.

THE SITUATION OF ABORIGINAL WOMEN IN CANADA

The narratives of the Aboriginal women of Canada testify to injustices enacted, not only because of prejudices resulting from perceived differences of pigmentation or genetic inheritance, but specifically because of gender difference. This is evident in the ongoing failure to recognize Aboriginal women's rights to community or band membership and to respect their position as trusted guardians of the tradition. It is also manifested in the disproportionate rates of Aboriginal women subjected to judicial procedures and subsequent incarceration. But most especially and tragically it is all too obvious in acts of violence and murder that are inflicted upon them. These are forms of discrimination that contemporary justice has failed to rectify, and their continuation indicates a pattern of enduring injustice. As if to emphasize the seriousness of this situation, in 2004, Amnesty International issued a report entitled: "'Stolen Sisters': A Human Rights

Response to Discrimination and Violence against Indigenous Women in Canada."[19] The then president of the Native Women's Association of Canada[20] (hereafter NWAC), Beverly Jacobs, a Mohawk member of the Six Nations of the Grand Rivers, wrote one of the reports presented to Amnesty. In documenting the untold instances of violence against the Indigenous women of Canada, Amnesty states: "The social and economic marginalization of Indigenous women, along with a history of government policies that have torn apart Indigenous families and communities, have pushed a disproportionate number of Indigenous women into dangerous situations that include extreme poverty, homelessness and prostitution." The report also states: "Despite assurances to the contrary, police in Canada have often failed to provide Indigenous women with an adequate standard of protection."[21]

Previous to the settlement of European immigrants, the status was very different for Aboriginal women. They were not regarded as inferior to men. Though Bea Medicine, an Indian Lakota anthropologist,[22] warns against any compensatory notion of an inclusive or universalized indigenous women's spirituality, given the many tribal differences and regional distinctions,[23] she does acknowledge that "in most pre-contact societies, Native women shared equally with men in social, economic and ritual roles."[24] Women were full participants in certain religious ceremonies where, though their roles differed from those of the men, they were equally regarded as ritual specialists. This, unfortunately, is not the representation of women that is found in early colonial studies. These works mirror the colonialist attitudes, which cast Aboriginal peoples in stereotypical dualist comparisons where they represented evil.

Today Aboriginal women are taking up their cause for recognition. Yet Emma LaRocque, a Métis scholar, is only too well aware that the attitudes of the Aboriginal peoples themselves have become influenced by the same colonialist imaginary, specifically in its contemporary views of women. She states: "Sadly, there are insidious notions within our own communities that we as Native women should be 'unobtrusive, soft-spoken and quiet,' and that we should not assume elected leadership, which is taken to mean 'acting like men.' That 'traditional Indian woman' is still often expected to act and dress like an ornamental Pocahontas/'Indian Princess.'"[25]

Other contemporary Aboriginal women, such as Teressa Nahanee, a lawyer and member of the Squamish Nation, affirm that the status and rights of women now need to be protected under the *Canadian Charter of Rights and Freedoms*[26] rather the Indian Act. Nahanee cites with approval the words of Mary Eberts, counsel for a successful appeal launched by NWAC in 1992 for protection of women's rights under the *Canadian Charter of Rights and Freedoms*: "Aboriginal women are at a watershed: taking action under the Charter provides them with perhaps their only opportunity to secure a future in which they will have available at least some tools with which to fight the massive, persisting systemic discrimination, on grounds of gender and race, which they face at every turn."[27]

Yet this strategy has not been welcomed in some communities. Joyce Green, a Métis scholar, has described the negative attitude that has arisen towards Aboriginal women who adopt this position: "Women advocating the explicit protection of women's equality rights were attacked for undermining the greater cause of Aboriginal rights."[28] Nahanee herself understands the situation as particularly fraught, but she refuses to let the situation be framed in terms of rights versus the community, which she views as counterproductive.[29] "As long as the dominant forces within the Canadian and Aboriginal patriarchy continue to use the prison of collective rights to denigrate the Aboriginal women's struggle for sexual equality rights as a dichotomy of individual/collective, women will be unable to capture popular support inside and outside the community."[30] Both Nahanee and Green consider the individual rights/community issue as a false dichotomy. Nahanee asserts: "Each and every individual comprises the collective; there is no collective without them."[31] She believes that an individual inextricably interconnected with their community in extremely complicated ways that are not always in accord with the dominant view.

Canadian Native women's struggle to regain their rights can also be viewed from the perspective of religion, where religion is cast by them in a positive light. For the Aboriginal women to regain the rights that are being denied them, their former religious status is of utmost priority. Its restoration represents both the personal and communal integrity that many of them believe they are now being denied. It is a rather unique set of circumstances where human rights and religious rights are not at variance but, in fact, coincide. The dynamics of this appeal and the differing responses of the Aboriginal peoples themselves remain part of an ongoing internal debate that is part of the claim of the Aboriginal peoples to a form of self-government. Such a debate is also continuing at federal and provincial government levels, where certain treaties are still being renegotiated as the different peoples that comprise Canada's First Nations seek just restitution and just solutions to long-standing neglect of their rights.

THE CASE OF SHARI'A IN ONTARIO, CANADA

On 17 January 2005, former Ontario Attorney General Marion Boyd, who had been appointed by the provincial government to evaluate the situation, caused something of a stir in the Canadian community by recommending that Islamic tribunals be allowed to use *Sharīʿa* law to settle family disputes in that province. Was this an example of multiculturalism, within in a liberal democracy, going too far in its deference? For many women in Canada, including moderate Muslims, this seemed to be the situation. The decision, however, was not without precedent. Since Ontario's *Arbitration Act* was passed in 1991, Orthodox Jews, among others, have used such tribunals to arbitrate family problems and marriage disputes. This arrangement was viewed as a way of alleviating heavy case-loads in the civil courts. Boyd's recommendation was not binding, however, and both it and the act itself were then submitted to review.

The main supporter of the proposal to introduce *Sharīʿa* tribunals into the province of Ontario was Syed Mumtaz Ali, a member of the Islamic Institute for Civil Justice, a retired lawyer, who was born in India. Mr. Ali has affirmed that he believed his proposal was in keeping with the multicultural policies of his friend, the late Pierre Elliott Trudeau – Prime Minister of Canada when the *Charter of Rights and Freedoms* was instituted in 1982. Islamic proponents of the tribunals stated that this was an acceptable method of arbitration, as no decision could be made in such courts that would violate the *Canadian Charter of Rights and Freedoms* (1982). There was the added proviso that, if a person was dissatisfied with a decision, he/she could appeal to the civil court system.

In opposition were a number of women's groups, including those of Muslim women, who did not appreciate *Sharīʿa* as conforming with the rights of women to equality under the *Canadian Charter*. Other principal concerns of Muslim women who disagreed with the implementation of

Sharī'a were about gender bias, and especially of the intimidation that could be exerted on recent immigrant women who may not be informed of their rights. There was concern that such women could also be pressured by family into such arbitration under threat of rejection. Another basic worry was that, though the arbitration itself was not compulsory, many women would be led to believe that they were bound by the ruling and would not be told that they could appeal to civil courts if they were unhappy with the judgment. A further major concern was that there would not be enough trained personnel to review the implementation on the tribunals, which was also one of Boyd's recommendations.

After more consultations, however, in a decision, dated 11 December 2005, Dalton McGuinty, the premier of Ontario, rescinded the act that had allowed family court proceedings to be judged by any religiously affiliated tribunal. This was then an instance of a case where freedom of expression trumped freedom of religion. What is more intriguing than the decision itself, however, are the reflections of certain feminist thinkers on the issue. A Canadian professor of law, Natasha Bakht, commented on the situation. She was worried that the move to traditional legal arbitration reflects an attitude on the part of the government to wash its hands of dealing adequately with the status of women in religions – particularly in a time when fundamentalism is increasing. The state seems to be reluctant to take responsibility for matters that are considered private, especially decisions on matters of religion. Bakht fears that such non-regulation by government amounts to maintenance of the status quo, i.e., "support of pre-existing power relations and distributions of goods within the 'private' sphere."[32] She arrives at this conclusion because, in Canadian law, the burden of proof for a breach of the *Charter of Rights and Freedoms* is on the person who is making a charge of such a breach. Such an onus places women in a difficult and demanding position.

Bakht also makes an intervention, however, on behalf of Muslim women who may want to accept arbitration by *Sharī'a*. She states that one cannot automatically presume that such women are either ignorant or oppressed in making such a choice. To do so would be to "infantilize" Muslim women in discriminatory ways. She further declares: "In fact, making an overly generalized argument regarding women's capacities or experiences homogenizes women and potentially eliminates important differences based on intersecting grounds of oppression."[33] In support of her stance, she quotes Fareeda Shaheed of the network Women Living Under Muslim Law (WLUML), who were opposed to the implementation of *Sharīʿa* law: "WLUML recognizes that living in different circumstances and situations women will have different strategies and priorities. We believe that each woman knowing her own situation is best placed to decide what is the right strategy and choice for her."[34]

Another feminist scholar, Sherene Razack, who is a Professor of Sociology and Equity Studies in Education at the Ontario Institute for Studies in Education of the University of Toronto, and whose principal areas of scholarship concern race and gender issues in the law, warns against a strategy that she believes was all too prominent in the debate. Though she concedes that something positive may have resulted from this exercise, in that the "plans of a small conservative religious faction may have been upset," she believes that there has certainly been a narrowing of focus and attitudes that she understands as damaging for all concerned. This is because the harmful dualisms have been reinforced. These dualisms are: "Women's rights versus multiculturalism; West versus Muslims; enlightened Western feminists versus imperilled Islamic women."[35] From her perspective, such divisions have rather pernicious consequences, especially as they concern feminism. "I argue that in their concern to curtail the conservative and patriarchal forces within the Muslim community, Canadian feminists (both Muslim and non-Muslim) utilized frameworks that installed a secular/religious divide that functions as a colour line, marking the difference between the white, modern, enlightened West, and people of colour, and in particular, Muslims."[36] In a post 9/11 climate, such a facile distinction serves to both "keep in line Muslim communities at the same time that it defuses more radical feminist and anti-racist critique of conservative religious forces."[37]

Both of these reactions by Bakht and Razack express the disquiet that much current debate on rights and religion, particularly in relation to women, is presented in ways that simply reinforce a situation where a secular society is positioned in opposition to religion. On the one hand, this leaves no space available for public dialogue between concerned moderates of different religions. At the same time, however, this debate, with its seeming extremist depiction of all Muslims, forecloses any productive debate of the problems posed by all forms of fundamentalism for women.[38] In this way, it only serves to reinforce the division between public and private, which has been responsible for the fact that religious practices that are harmful to women have largely remained impervious to prosecution. A number of radical feminists, as well as contemporary atheist commentators, e.g., Richard Dawkins, seem to be of the opinion that no one in their right mind would have anything to do with religion, and they recoil at any attempt at accommodation within a secular society. This, I believe, excludes any constructive attempt at a public discussion that could be informed by a comparative study of the topic that takes into account the various positions of different religions and does not only focus on fundamentalism. It is in this connection that I believe scholars in Religious Studies do have something to offer by way of mediation in the face of this fundamentalist reading of all religion.

THE FUNDAMENTALIST CHALLENGE

Before embarking on an investigation of certain problems posed by fundamentalisms and their dictates,[39] I would quickly like to survey one approach that has had some success in breaking down the binaries involved in the opposition of the secular and religion. This approach can be expressed, though not in a glib way, by the feminist catchphrase: "The personal is the political." In an early article in 1983, Carole Pateman neatly summarized the issues involved as feminism strove to avoid either a denial of all things private in favour of integration with the public sphere, or any false idealization of the private. She observes: "Feminism looks toward a differentiated social order within which the various dimensions are distinct but not separate or opposed, and which rests on a social conception of individuality, which includes both women and men as biologically differentiated but not unequal creatures."[40] She is nonetheless realistic in admitting that, at that time, "A full analysis of the various expressions of the dichotomy between the public and private has yet to be provided."[41] Some progress has since been made, especially in attempting to move beyond Pateman's emphasis on individuality.

One of the areas where the separation of public and private has been addressed with a degree of success is that of violence against women. While she bemoans the fact that insufficient progress is being made, and that non-prosecution is still prevalent in many parts of the world in cases of violence against women, Hilary Charlesworth describes the strategy that needs to be adopted on this matter. Recognizing that "the traditional construction of civil and political rights ... obscures the most consistent harms done to women,"[42] i.e., that they mostly occur in the private sphere, Charlesworth advocates the adoption of another stance: "[I]f violence against women is understood not just as aberrant 'private' behaviour, but as part of the structure of the universal subordination of women, it can never be considered a purely 'private' issue: the distinction between 'public' and 'private' action in the context of violence against women is not a useful or meaningful one."[43] This issue has been addressed by the UN in 1994 in its Declaration of the Elimination of Violence against Women (DEVW). In the same year, it appointed a special *rapporteur* on violence against women. Then, in 1995, the Platform for Action from the Beijing Fourth World Conference on Women declared: "Violence against women throughout the life cycle derives essentially from cultural patterns, in particular the harmful effects of certain traditional or customary practices and all acts of extremism linked to race, sex, language or religion that perpetuate the lower status accorded to women in the family, the workplace, the community and Society."[44]

As Sally Engle Merry notes, both the Vatican and certain Islamic countries were opposed to the final statements in the conference Platform.[45] Unfortunately, as Engle Merry also reports, "Many states have opposed this conception of human rights on cultural or religious grounds and have refused to ratify women's rights treaties such as DEVW, or have done so only with reservations."[46] Courtney Howland views these actions as actually in contravention of the UN.[47] Such activity by religious groups is extremely worrisome. It would seem that they are making a concerted effort to counteract all the gains that women had been making in connection with rights, particularly at the UN, during past half-century.

There have recently been a number of books and articles that chart this emergence of women into the public realm at the UN during the past century.[48] Radhika Coomaraswamy, who was the first *rapporteur* to be appointed by the United Nations specifically on the issue of Violence Against Women in 1994, spoke in 1996 on this development in relation to human rights: "A revolution has taken place in the last decade. Women's rights have been catapulted onto the human rights agenda with a speed and determination that has rarely been matched in international law. There are two aspects to this process: first, the attempt to make mainstream human rights responsive to women's concerns; and second, the conceptualization of certain gender-specific violations as human rights violations."[49]

At the same time, however, Amrita Basu adds a sobering qualification: "Parallel to the evolution of transnational women's movements, and equally important, has been the phenomenal growth of transnational networks of the religious right. We saw this in the 1994 Cairo conference on population and development, and again in the Beijing [women's] conference of 1995. In both these contexts one found a thoroughly transnational alliance of groups on the religious right, not only official organizations but also members of non-state organizations, including religious bodies like the Catholic Church."[50]

Judith Butler describes her own reaction to one of their offensives. She was alarmed when she learned of the manoeuvrings of the Vatican in the lead-up to the Beijing conference on the status of women in 1995: "The Vatican not only denounced the term 'gender' as a code for homosexuality, but insisted that the platform language [of the conference] return to the notion of sex, in an apparent effort to secure a link between femininity and maternity as a naturally and divinely ordained necessity."[51] Joan Wallach Scott, an American critical theorist, describes another such interference that occurred in the United States around the same time, when a sub-committee of the U.S. House of Representatives reviewed submissions that cautioned morality and family values were under attack from so-called "gender feminists."[52] As Scott describes it, it appeared that the opponents of "gender" insisted that "gender feminists" regarded manhood and womanhood, motherhood and fatherhood, heterosexuality, marriage and family as "culturally created, and originated by men to oppress women."[53] No doubt they had been informed of Butler's variations on the theme of gender, which she had explored in her book *Gender Trouble*.[54] The authorities were troubled that women were beginning to take decision-making into their own hands, specifically concerning basic reproductive issues, and saw "gender" as a sufficiently dubious term with which to attack this development.[55]

Since this initial intervention by the Vatican on the subject of "gender feminism," it has attempted to influence members of the Catholic communities from a number of countries (especially in Central and South America[56]), as well as organize coalitions with Islamic countries, to support its own position.[57] Part of its tactic is to argue that human rights for women, especially in the context of gender, is a "western," i.e., colonialist, imposition. This alignment by the Vatican with the colonized and underprivileged of this world, as well as with non-exploitative interests, is patently disingenuous. It is simply another example of the manner in which it has orchestrated, often with the help of ruling regional elites, the appropriation and deployment of idealized "feminine" norms. These traditional formulas are designed to keep women in their proper maternal place, as the unsullied guardians of a nation's morality.

From this perspective, women's increasing demands for self-determination are decried as nothing less than selfish self-fulfillment. As mentioned previously, the struggles against expanding women's rights since the Beijing conference in various UN committees, ostensibly on the grounds of protecting religious traditions, are evidence of this reactionary agenda. In this way, as is blatantly obvious in the contemporary United States, but also in other religions and countries of the world, the battle lines are being drawn by fundamentalists and neo-conservatives. By means of these activities, they are perpetuating traditional dichotomies. Some scholars are wondering if it is even worth continuing the struggle for women's rights at the UN, so effectively organized has the opposition become.[58]

Judith Butler's own response to this outcome is intriguing. While she is reluctant to approve of the notion of human rights in the abstract, as it involves the implementation of a universal category without due consideration of particular circumstances, she has become perturbed by the advances that fundamentalism and neo-conservative interests have made. As a result, she is willing to concede that: "Although many feminists have come to the conclusion that the universal is always a cover for a certain epistemological imperialism, insensitive to cultural texture and difference, the rhetorical power of claiming universality for say, rights of sexual autonomy and related rights of sexual orientation within the international human right domain appears indisputable."[59] This concession demonstrates that there is a willingness, even amongst those who are opposed to universals as they often tend towards prescription, to allow strategic use of a universal statement as a tactic of resistance.

It is by analyzing these developments from within the purview of Religious Studies, with the help of insights garnered from feminist scholars in other fields, such as philosophy and anthropology, that women scholars in religion could provide assistance to further discussions of this fraught topic. This is because they could help to break down the false, and even extreme dichotomy posed by the clash of values that both fundamentalists and militant secularists seem to want to maintain between religion and rights.

THE QUESTION OF CULTURAL ESSENTIALISM

One of the grounds that certain nations have claimed as a basis for their reservations against declarations at the UN is that of "culture," which is often associated with another term, "tradition." Both of these terms are regarded as alternative words for religion. A number of women scholars have been extremely vocal in their criticisms of the reified notion of culture that is appealed to in these situations. Firstly, the anthropologist Sally Engle Merry cautions that: "There is a critical need for conceptual clarification of culture in human rights practice. Insofar as human rights rely on an essentialized model of culture, it does not take advantage of the potential of local cultural practices for change.... A more dynamic understanding of culture foregrounds the importance of translators to the human rights process and the possibilities for change in local cultural practices."[60]

In Engle Merry's view, instead of being regarded as a stable or static concept, and as a non-negotiable item, culture needs to be appreciated in a more dynamic way. She describes the manner in which culture is understood in contemporary anthropology as "a far more fluid and changing set of values."[61] As a result, culture is now conceived of: "as unbounded, contested, and connected to relations of power, as the product of historical influences rather than evolutionary change."[62] In addition, for Engle Merry, cultural practices always need to be appreciated within their specific contexts and with an awareness that the meaning of culture and its effects will change with any alteration in a context.[63]

Another scholar who is similarly suspicious of essentialized definitions of culture, be they Eastern or Western, is Uma Narayan. In her book, *Dislocating Cultures*, she issues a warning: "We need to be wary about all ideals of 'cultural authenticity' that portray 'authenticity' as constituted by lack of criticism and lack of change. We need to insist that there are many ways to inhabit nations and cultures critically and creatively."[64] From this perspective, Narayan takes issue both with Western colonial impositions of "feminine" ideals, particularly in India, where she was born and also with India's own attempts to invoke essentialist categories, especially as they have done with Hindu fundamentalism (or Hindutva).[65] While Narayan adroitly exposes the idealized projections of a "national and cultural identity" and their false association with Hinduism, she is particularly articulate about their exploitation of exalted depictions of women as central components of "cultural identity." She describes how, in consequence, women who stray from such models are labelled as "stooges of western imperialism" or worse. Narayan expands on this: "The social status and roles of women are often represented as of central import to the task of 'resisting westernization' and 'preserving national culture' [thus] reducing Third World feminist contestations of local norms and practices pertaining to women as 'betrayal of nations and culture.'"[66] Narayan also remarks on the rather selective process involved here. This involves apologetic attempts to allow for certain "borrowings" that are characterized as "modernist," e.g., those of an electronic nature and other contemporary conveniences, in contrast to those designated "Western" ones. In all such categorizations, human rights are inevitably Western. The reality behind all such rhetorical flourishes is that it is the women who bare the brunt of the responsibility for keeping faithful to religiously prescribed cultural roles.

What is especially striking is the false nostalgia involved in these claims, with their obvious religious associations. These have been criticized by other Indian women scholars, notably by Uma Chakravarti in "Whatever Happened to the Vedic *Dasi*,"[67] and by Kumkum Roy, in her ironically titled essay: "Where Women Are Worshipped, There the Gods Rejoice."[68] These essays have influenced and support Narayan's argument against any form of cultural essentialism. Such a manipulation of history, in order to promote a glorious past from which contemporary society has sadly fallen and which needs to be re-established, is a hallmark of many fundamentalist religious movements. It is both sad and extremely telling that, in many of these religions, the cause of a nation's fall from grace is blamed on women's waywardness, especially their purported sexual deviance. As a result, women thus need to be rescued from their fallen ways and returned to supervision and subservience. Gender, insofar as it enters into these calculations, features as a divinely ordained decree. Both men and women are directed, under pain of sin or a bad rebirth, to follow the gendered scripts that provide the rigid backbone of a stable, god-fearing society.

Narayan will have none of this. In drawing her own conclusions about these directives, she states that, just as there can be no one essential description of the female gender, so there is no authentic cultural identity. In expanding this position, Narayan finally rejects not only "the idea that there is anything that can solidly and uncontroversially be defined as 'Indian culture,' but also the idea of an 'African culture' or [for that matter] 'Western culture'"[69] Yet Narayan is not completely dismissive of religion, allowing that: "Many religious traditions are in fact more capacious than fundamentalist adherents allow. Insisting on humane and inclusive interpretations of religious traditions might, in many contexts, be crucial components in countering the deployment of religious discourses to problematic nationalist ends."[70] Narayan's critiques of both "gender" and "culture" and their faulty appropriation by religion can help to counteract the effects of their being invoked in idealized and inflexible formulas that prevent constructive exchange on any level.

Another contemporary educator and activist for women's rights is Mahnaz Afhkami, who was formerly a minister of state in pre-revolutionary Iran. She is the founding president of the Women's Learning Partnership and has written extensively on women, religion, and rights. Her sentiments on the inroads made by fundamentalism and its distortions are similar to those of Narayan. "The Islamist discourse seeks to establish a particular rendition of Muslim religion as the true image of Muslim societies as they 'actually' exist. This presumed image is then presented as the actual 'culture' of the Muslim people. All 'rights' then, including Muslim women's, naturally flow from this culture."[71]

In a later essay, again concurring with Narayan, she observes: "In Muslim societies, women are particularly targeted because there is no better proof of return to a golden past than pushing them back into their 'natural' place. Thus women's position becomes the yardstick, the measure for the success of the fundamentalist agenda."[72] She is also cognizant of the machinations of the Islamists who have worked in concert with the Vatican, and others opposed to women's rights, to impede the growth of rights by implying that it is solely a Western construct. "By suggesting that the West has invented the idea of universality of rights in order to impose its way of life on others, the Islamists attempt to disparage the validity of the argument for rights in the eyes of their peoples, including women."[73]

Afhkami is particularly committed to breaking down many of the binaries that continue to restrict women's access to religious and political freedom. In addition to the public/private and secular/religious divisions, she would like to encourage a change so that the notion of human rights does not focus solely on the individual but understands the individual as always situated within a particular community: "We must move beyond the theory of women's human rights as a theory of equality before the law, of women's individual space, or a 'room of one's own,' to the theory of the architecture of the future society where the universality of rights and relativity of means merge to operationalize an optimally successful coexistence of community and individuality."[74]

It is worth noting that Afkhami's program does contain certain provisos deemed necessary for its success, and one of these is directed squarely at the enforced directives inflicted on women: "We must insist that no one, man or woman, may claim a right to a monopoly of interpretation of God to human beings or a right to force others to accept a particular ruling about any religion. The upshot of this position is that women ought not to be forced to choose between freedom and God. The same applies on the part of tradition."[75]

CONCLUSION

In these various analyses and testimonies by women from very different areas of interest, regions of the world, and religious backgrounds, there is a strong affirmation of the need to support human rights as women's rights. There is also a clear insight into the fact that religious and cultural claims can insist on false divisions that interfere with women's access to such rights. Fundamentalist religion is one of the worst culprits. As a result, one of the counter-strategies is that many women scholars and activists support forms of mediatory intervention in an attempt to moderate the stark binary oppositions that all too often characterize the conflict between religion and rights. Universal claims by both sides need to be put into a perspective that allows for types of global and local, community and individual interactions where very careful attention is paid to the specific context. None of these recommendations will be uncomplicated to implement – and they do not necessarily all sit easily together – but they are suggestive of a start that holds promise.

As fellow participants in undertaking such an approach, I believe that women scholars in religion could provide both relevant information and appropriate methodological assistance. From both philosophical and hermeneutical standpoints they are familiar with both textual interpretation and historical particularity, and they can call attention to spurious claims. Their training also supplies them with the relevant tools to detect readings that are either distinctly literalist in their translations or highly selective in determining their applications. My hope is that this paper will stimulate interest for women scholars in religion to begin to undertake collaborative study and discussion of a comparative nature on this most important topic.

Notes

1 Some parts of this essay previously appeared in: "Gender and Religion: A Volatile Mixture," *Temenos* 42, no. 1 (2006): 7–30, and in "Women's Rights in the Context of Religion," *Svensk religionshistoriskarsskrift* [Swedish Yearbook of the History of Religions] (April 2008): 181–200. Reprinted with permission.

2 One person who was particularly active in this area was the late Lucinda Peach. See: "Human Rights Law, Religion, and Gender," *The Global Spiral*; http://www.metanexus.net/magazine/ArticleDetail/tabid/68/id/6004/Default.aspx and "Human Rights Law, Religion and Gendered Moral Order," in *Varieties of Ethical Reflection*, ed. Michael Barnhart (Lanham, MD: Lexington, 2002), 203–30.

3 See the work of John Stratton Hawley (ed.), *Fundamentalism and Gender* (Oxford: Oxford University Press, 1993).

4 See Ann Elizabeth Mayer, "Religious Reservations to the Convention on the Elimination of all Forms of Discriminations against Women: What Do They Really Mean?," in Courtney W. Howland, *Religious Fundamentalisms and the Human Rights of Women* (New York: St. Martin's Press,1999), 105–16.

5 See the collection of essays in Courtney W. Howland, *Religious Fundamentalisms and the Human Rights of Women* (New York: St. Martin's Press, 1999), and also in Jurate Motiejunaite (ed.), *Women's Rights: The Public/Private Dichotomy* (New York: Idebate Press, 2005).

6 See Amanda Whiting, and Carolyn Evans (eds.), *Mixed Blessings: Laws, Religions and Women's Rights in the Asia-Pacific Region* (The Hague: Martinus Nijhoff, 2006), and also an essay by Lucinda Peach, "Buddhism and Human Rights in the Thai Sex Trade," in Courtney W. Howland, *Religious Fundamentalisms and the Human Rights of Women* (New York: St. Martin's Press, 1999), 215–26.

7 See Lori G. Beaman, *Defining Harm: Religious Freedom and the Limits of the Law* (Vancouver: UBC Press, 2008) and also Lucinda Peach, Legislating Morality; Pluralism and Religious Identity in Lawmaking (Oxford: Oxford University Press, 2002).

8 Martha Nussbaum, "Religion and Women's Human Rights," in Paul Weithman (ed.), *Religion and Contemporary Liberalism* (Notre Dame, IN: University of Notre Dame Press, 1997), 93–137.

9 Susan Moller Okin, "Is Multiculturalism Bad for Women?," *Boston Review*, October–November, 1997. Also published in: *Is Multiculturalism Bad for Women?* Joshua Cohen, M. Howard, and M.C. Nussbaum (eds.) (Princeton: Princeton University Press, 1999), 7–26.

10 Okin, "Is Multiculturalism Bad for Women?," 3.

11 Joshua Cohen, M. Howard, and M. Nussbaum (eds.), *Is Multiculturalism Bad for Women?* (Princeton, NJ: Princeton University Press, 1999).

12 Nussbaum, "A Plea for Difficulty," in *Is Multiculturalism Bad for Women?* Cohen et al. (eds.), 106–7.

13 Homi Bhabha, "Liberalism's Sacred Cow," in *Is Multiculturalism Bad for Women?* Cohenet al. (eds.), 79.

14 Ibid., 82.

15 Ibid., 81.

16 Nussbaum, "A Plea for Difficulty," 113.

17 Ibid., 111.

18 The *Indian Act* came into effect in1876. Aboriginal peoples of Canada who signed treaties with the Canadian government were termed "status" or "registered Indians". They thereby gained certain rights, but status could be lost by a woman marrying a man who was not a "status Indian." While this was amended in 1985 under Bill C-31, many bands still make the situation very difficult for such women.

19 See the report by Amnesty International: "'Stolen Sisters': A Human Rights Response to Discrimination and Violence against Indigenous Women in Canada" at: http:www.amnesty.ca/stolensisters/am200034/pdf.

20 See the "Sisters in Spirit" webpage at http://www.sistersinspirit.ca. This page was set up by the Native Women's Association of Canada (NWAC). They launched the national Sisters in Spirit Campaign in March 2004 to raise public awareness of the alarmingly high rates of violence against Aboriginal women in Canada. NWAC believes there is an urgent state of affairs with regard to the safety of Aboriginal women in Canada.

21 Amnesty International, "Stolen Sisters," 2.

22 The word "Indian" is used in the *Constitution Act* of Canada. The Aboriginal people of Canada, Indians, Inuit, and Métis, are named in both the *Constitution Act* of 1867 and of 1982.Though today the term, "Indian," has fallen somewhat into disfavour, it is used still in legal discussions where the status of Indians under the *Act* is being discussed. The term, "First Nations" is the preferred term used by bands today who have status in terms of the *Indian Act*. Each of these terms has varying levels of acceptance among the indigenous peoples of Canada. In this paper, various terms, such as "indigenous," "native," "Aboriginal" are also used, usually in connection with a specific writer's preference. Bea Medicine uses the term, "Indian" to refer to herself.

23 Beatrice Medicine and Patricia Albers, *The Hidden Half: Studies of Plains Indian Women* (Washington: University of America Press, 1983), 191.

24 Medicine and Albers, *Hidden Half*, 154.

25 Emma LaRocque, "The Colonization of a Native Woman Scholar," in Christine Miller and Patricia Chuchryk (eds.), *Women of First Nations: Power, Wisdom and Strength* (Winnipeg: University of Manitoba Press, 1996), 14.

26 The *Canadian Charter of Rights and Freedoms* came into force on April 17, 1982. Section 15 of the *Charter* (equality rights) came into effect three years after the rest of the *Charter*, on April 17, 1985, to give governments time to bring their laws into line with section 15. The *Charter* is founded on the rule of law and entrenches in the constitution of Canada the rights and freedoms Canadians believe are necessary in a free and democratic society. It recognizes primary fundamental freedoms (e.g., freedom of expression and of association), democratic rights (e.g., the right to vote), mobility rights (e.g., the right to live anywhere in Canada), legal rights (e.g., the right to life, liberty and security of the person), and equality rights and recognizes the multicultural heritage of Canadians. It also protects official language and minority language education rights. In addition, the provisions of section 25 guarantee the rights of the Aboriginal peoples of Canada. http://www.pch.gc.ca/progs/pdp-hrp/canada/freedom_e.cfm.

27 Teressa Nahanee, "Dancing with a Gorilla: Aboriginal Women, Justice and the Charter," in *Aboriginal Peoples and the Justice System* (Ottawa: Royal Commission on Aboriginal Peoples, Minister of Supply and Services, 1993), 367.

28 Joyce Green, "Constitutionalising the Patriarchy: Aboriginal Women and Aboriginal Government." *Constitutional Forum* 4, no. 4 (1993): 114.

29 It needs to be noted that there is a disagreement among Indigenous women themselves on this. Some would prefer to take their in-house complaints to Native sentencing circles. See Jennifer Koshan, "Sounds of Silence: The Public/Private Dichotomy, Violence and Aboriginal Women," in Jurate Motiejunaite (ed.), *Women's Rights: The Public/Private Dichotomy* (New York: Idebate Press, 2005), 211–34.

30 Nahanee, "Dancing with a Gorilla," 370.

31 Ibid.

32 Natasha Bakht, "Family Arbitration Using Sharī'a Law: Examining Ontario's Arbitration Act and its Impact on Women," *Muslim World Journal of Human Rights* 1, no. 1 (2004): 23.

33 Ibid., 22.

34 Ibid.

35 Sherene Razack, "The Sharia Law Debate in Ontario," *Feminist Legal Studies* 15 (2007): 29.

36 Ibid., 6.

37 Ibid.

38 A comprehensive study of the forms of fundamentalism and their implications for women in the major religions can be found in Courtney Howland, "Women and Religious Fundamentalism," in *Women and International Human Rights Law*, Kelly D. Askin and Dorean M. Koenig (eds.) (New York: Transnational Publishers, 1999), 533–621.

39 With reference to the use of the term 'fundamentalisms,' I basically follow the work of Martin Marty and Scott Appleby in *Fundamentalisms Observed* (Chicago: University of Chicago Press, 1991), though I find a paucity of study on women in their various works. I do not wish to restrict my understanding, however, to that designated by a particular species of nineteenth-century American Protestantism. Ideally, there are different terms applicable to specific religions to account for this phenomenon, such as Islamist and Hindutva, that would need to be developed in a larger study. For the purposes of this paper, one of the main intentions of which is to demonstrate the collaboration of these movements to restrict women's further access to rights, I will simply use the term 'fundamentalisms.'

40 Carole Pateman, "Feminist Critiques of the Public/Private Dichotomy," in S. Benn and G. F. Gaus (eds.), *Public and Private in Public Life* (London: Croom Helm, 1983), 300.

41 Ibid.

42 Hilary Charlesworth, "Human Rights as Men's Rights," in Julie Peters and Andrea Wolper (eds.), *Women's Rights Human Rights: International Feminist Perspectives* (New York: Routledge, 1995), 107.

43 Ibid.

44 UN Report on the Fourth World Congress on Women, Annex II, Platform for Action, Chapter 4, Section D, par. 119; http://www.un.org/esa/gopher-data/conf/fwcw/off/a--20.en.

45 Sally Engle Merry, "Women, Violence, Human Rights," in Marjorie Agosín, ed., *Women, Gender, and Human Rights* (New Brunswick, NJ: Rutgers University Press, 2001), 91.

46 Ibid.

47 Courtney Howland states with regard to these reservations: "These assertions of a religious fundamentalist position … in response to accusations of a treaty violation and reservations to treaties should not be viewed merely in the context of the particular

treaty in question.... A state's act of making a reservation is a public international act equivalent to the issuance of *opinio juris*.... The Charter specifically eschews religious law as the source for human rights, and, thus, any particular religious law may not determine the standards for the 'without distinction' language.... Thus, these declarative statements and reservations represent the state taking a public position which is contrary to the Charter. Public statements contrary to the Charter demonstrate bad faith and violate the state's two-fold duty to cooperate and not to undermine. Thus, these states, by making these assertions are in violation of their legal obligations under articles 55 and 56." Howland, "Women and Religious Fundamentalism," 618.

48 See, especially, Leila J. Rupp, *Worlds of Women: The Making of an International Women's Movement* (Princeton: Princeton University Press, 1998), and Jain Devaki, *Women, Development, and the UN: A Sixty-Year Quest for Equality and Justice* (Bloomington: Indiana University Press, 2005).

49 Radhika Coomaraswamy, "Reinventing Women's International Law: Women's Rights as Human Rights in the International Community," Edward A. Smith Lecture, 1996; http://www.law.harvard.edu/programs/HRP/Publications/radhika.html.

50 Amrita Basu, "Women's Movements and the Challenge of Transnationalism"; http://www.womencrossing.org/basu.html.

51 Judith Butler, "The End of Sexual Difference?" in Elisabeth Bronfen and Misha Kavka (eds.), *Feminist Consequences: Theory for the New Century* (New York: Columbia University Press, 2001), 423. The conference platform did not eliminate the word "gender."

52 Joan Wallach Scott, *Gender and the Politics of History* (New York: Columbia University Press, 1999 [1988]), ix.

53 Ibid., ix.

54 Judith Butler, *Gender Trouble: Feminism and the Subversion of Identity* (New York: Routledge, 1990).

55 The word, "gender" has had a checkered history over the past two decades. See Morny Joy, "Gender and Religion: A Volatile Mixture," *Temenos* 42, no. 1 (2006): 7–30.

56 Laura Guzmán Stein, "The Politics of Implementing Women's Rights in Catholic countries of Latin America," in Jane H. Bayes and Nayereh Tohidi (eds.), *Globalization, Gender, and Religion: The Politics of Women's Rights in Catholic and Muslim Contexts* (New York: Palgrave, 2001), 127–55.

57 "In Beijing, the coalition of Catholic countries that joined the Vatican included Guatemala, Honduras, Ecuador, Peru, Bolivia, and the Philippines. These were joined by the Muslim countries of Iran, Sudan, Libya, Egypt, and Kuwait.... During the 1995–2000 period, other Catholic Muslim cooperative efforts occurred.... In 2000 at the Beijing Plus Five Conference in New York, the conservative religious alliance continued its opposition to the initiatives involving sexuality, abortion, and for some, even the issue of women's rights as human rights (arguing instead for

human dignity)" (Bayes and Tohidi, *Globalization, Gender, and Religion*, 3–4).

58 Posadskaya-Vanderbeck, Anastasia, "International and Post-socialist Women's Rights Advocacy: Points of Convergence and Tension," in Joanna Kerr, E. Sprenger, A. Symington (eds.), *The Future of Women's Rights: Global Visions and Strategies* (London: Zed Books, 2004), 196.

59 Judith Butler, "The End of Sexual Difference?", in Elizabeth Bronfen and Mischa Kavka (eds.), *Feminist Consequences: Theory for a New Century* (New York: Columbia University Press, 2001), 243.

60 Engle Merry, "Women, Violence, Human Rights," 11.

61 Ibid., 14.

62 Ibid., 15.

63 Ibid.

64 Uma Narayan, *Dislocating Cultures: Identities, Traditions, and Third World Feminism* (New York: Routledge, 1997): 33.

65 Ibid.

66 Uma Narayan, "Essence of Culture and a Sense of History: A Feminist Critique of Cultural Essentialism," *Hypatia* 13, no. 2 (1998): 90.

67 Uma Chakravarti, "Whatever Happened to the Vedic *Dasi*? Orientalism, Nationalism and a Script from the Past," in Kumkum Sangari and Sudesh Vaid (eds.), *Recasting Women: Essays in Colonial History* (New Delhi: Kali for Women, 1989).

68 Kumkum Roy, "'Where Women Are Worshipped, There the Gods Rejoice': The Mirage of the Ancestress of the Hindu Woman," in Tanika Sarkar and Urvashi Butalia (eds.), *Women and Right-Wing Movements: Indian Experiences* (London: Zed Books, 1995), 10–28.

69 Narayan, "Essence of Culture," 102.

70 Narayan, *Dislocating Cultures*, 35.

71 Mahnaz Afkhami, "Gender Apartheid, Cultural Relativism, and Women's Human Rights in Muslim Societies," in Agosín, *Women, Gender, and Human Rights*, 236.

72 Mahnaz Afkhami, "Rights of Passage: Women Shaping the Twenty-First Century," in Joanna Kerr, Ellen Sprenger, and Alison Symington (eds.), *The Future of Women's Rights* (London: Zed, 2004), 60.

73 Ibid., 66.

74 Ibid., 66.

75 Ibid., 65.

NOTES ON CONTRIBUTORS

DR. TAMARA ALBERTINI is an associate professor of Philosophy at the University of Hawai'i at Manoa, specializing in Renaissance and Islamic thought. She has a Lic.phil. from the University of Basel (Switzerland) and a Dr.phil. from the Ludwig-Maximilians-Universität in Munich (Germany). Within Islamic philosophy, her publications include: *The Oxford Handbook of Islamic Philosophy* (in preparation); "Dreams, Visions, and Nightmares from the Prophet Muhammad to the Fundamentalist Mindset," in *Dreams and Visions*, ed. by Nancy van Deusen (2010), "Crisis and Certainty of Knowledge in al-Ghazzali and Descartes," *Philosophy East and West* 55, no. 1 (2005): 1–14; "The Seductiveness of Certainty: Fundamentalists' Destruction of Islam's Intellectual Legacy," *Philosophy East and West* 53, no. 4 (2003): 455–70; and "Islamic Philosophy: An Overview," in *The Companion to World Philosophies,* ed. by Eliot Deutsch and Ron Bontekoe (Blackwell, 1997).

ARINDAM CHAKRABARTI is Professor in the Department of Philosophy, University of Hawai'i, Manoa, where he was formerly the Director of the Center for South Asian Studies. After his doctoral work at Oxford on philosophy of language, he taught analytic philosophy and Indian philosophy at Calcutta, London, Seattle, and Delhi. In addition to his book *Denying Existence* (Kluwer Academic, Synthese Library series, 1997), he has co-edited *Knowing from Words* (1994) with Professor Bimal K. Matilal, and *Universals, Concepts and Qualities* (2006) with Professor Sir Peter Strawson. His publications include numerous papers in comparative and analytic philosophy, two collections of essays in Bengali, and one book in Sanskrit on modern Western epistemology. Currently he is working on a book on moral psychology of the emotions.

FRANCIS X. CLOONEY, S.J., is Parkman Professor of Divinity and Comparative Theology at Harvard University. His primary areas of scholarship are theological commentarial writings in the Sanskrit and Tamil traditions of Hindu India and the developing field of comparative theology, a discipline distinguished by attentiveness to the dynamics of theological learning deepened and complexified through the study of traditions other than one's own. Professor Clooney is the author of numerous articles and books, including *Hindu God, Christian God* (Oxford University Press, 2001), *Beyond Compare: St. Francis de Sales and Sri Vedānta Deśika on Loving Surrender to God* (Georgetown University Press, 2008), and *The Truth, the Way, the Life: Christian Commentary on the Three Holy Mantras of the Srivaisnava Hindus* (Peeters Publishers [Leuven], 2008).

CHRISTOPHER G. FRAMARIN is an assistant professor in the Philosophy and Religious Studies departments at the University of Calgary. He is author of *Desire and Motivation in Indian Philosophy* (Routledge, 2009). He is currently working on a book on the value of animals in the Hindu tradition.

KATRIN FROESE is an associate professor of Religious Studies and Philosophy at the University of Calgary. Her current research compares continental European and Chinese philosophical traditions. She is the author of *Nietzsche, Heidegger and Daoist Thought: Crossing Paths In-Between* (SUNY, 2006) and *Rousseau and Nietzsche: Toward an Aesthetic Morality* (Lexington Books, 2001).

MORNY JOY is University Research Professor in the Department of Religious Studies at the University of Calgary, Canada. In May 2011 she received an Honorary Doctorate from the University of Helsinki. Morny works and has published in the area of philosophy and religion, postcolonialism, and intercultural studies in South and South-East Asia, as well as in the all-important area of women and religion. She has recently co-edited two posthumous volumes of the work of Grace Jantzen and has published a volume on *Continental Philosophy and Philosophy of Religion* (Springer 2011).

CHEN-KUO LIN is University Professor of Buddhist Philosophy in the Department of Philosophy and Graduate Institute of Religious Studies at National Chengchi University, Taiwan. In 1999–2000, he was invited to hold the European Chair of Chinese Studies at the International Institute of Asian Studies, The Netherlands, and taught at the Institute of Sinology, Leiden University. His research project focuses on the issues of language and knowledge in the Mādhyamika and Yogācāra schools. He is also interested in bridging dialogues between Buddhist philosophy, Continental philosophy (phenomenology, hermeneutics, and deconstruction), the Kyoto School, and modern Confucianism. His intellectual journey can be surveyed in two books: *Emptiness and Modernity: From the Kyoto School, Modern Neo-Confucianism to Multivocal Buddhist Hermeneutics* (Taipei: New Century Publication, 1999) and *A Passage of Dialectics* (Taipei: New Century Publication, 2002).

DAN LUSTHAUS (PhD, Temple University) has published extensively on Indian and Chinese philosophy and religion. Publications include *Buddhist Phenomenology: A Philosophical Investigation of Yogācāra Buddhism and the Ch'eng wei-shih lun* (Routledge Curzon, 2002), *A Comprehensive Commentary on the Heart Sūtra (Prajñāpāramitā-hṛdaya-sūtra) by K'uei-chi* (translated in collaboration with Heng-Ching Shih) Berkeley: Numata, 2001), and numerous articles on Buddhist, Hindu, and Daoist thought. He has taught at UCLA, University of Illinois Champaign-Urbana, and Boston University, and has been a research associate at Harvard University since 2005.

MICHAEL McGHEE is Senior Fellow in the Department of Philosophy at the University of Liverpool. With the publication of his book, *Transformations of Mind: Philosophy as Spiritual Practice* (Cambridge University Press, 2000), he charted new waters for the practice of comparative philosophy of religion. A pioneer in the engagement of analytic philosophy with Buddhist (primarily *mahāyāna*) thought, McGhee develops a sophisticated hermeneutics of suspicion from the Buddhist perspective, interrogating Ango-American philosophical presuppositions of neutrality and rationality. He is also the author of various articles on themes in aesthetics, ethics, and the philosophy of religion.

MICHAEL OPPENHEIM is a professor in the Department of Religion at Concordia University in Montreal. His latest book, *Jewish Philosophy and Psychoanalysis: Narrating the Interhuman* (Lexington, 2006), compares the work of Jewish philosophers of encounter (Rosenzweig, Buber, and Levinas) with post-Freudian psychoanalysts (Klein, Erikson, Fairbairn, Winnicott, and Irigaray). He has published books and articles in the areas of modern Jewish philosophy, Judaism in the modern period, philosophy of religion, and psychology of religion.

TINU RUPARELL is an associate professor in the Department of Religious Studies at the University of Calgary. Trained in both analytic and Continental philosophy, he is particularly concerned to put these modes of thought into comparative conversation with Hinduism. He has published and presented widely in intercultural philosophy, focussing on the areas of interreligious dialogue and comparative hermeneutics. He is the author of the forthcoming *Dialogue and Hybridity* (Albany: SUNY Press, 2012) and has coedited *Encountering Religion* (Oxford: Blackwells, 2001) and *Christian Thought in the 21st Century* (Eugene, Oregon: Wipf and Stock, 2011).

VINCENT SHEN is the holder of Lee Chair in Chinese Thought and Culture, Department of East Asian Studies and Department of Philosophy, University of Toronto. His research interests lie in the area of Chinese Philosophy, Comparative Philosophy, Phenomenology and Philosophical Problems of Technology, Culture and Religion. His recent publications include *Philosophy of Paul Ricoeur* (Taipei: Sanmin, 2000), *Contrast, Strangification and Dialogue* (Taipei: Wunan, 2002), *Technology and Culture* (Taiwan: Open University Press, 2003), *Ideas of University and Spirit of Strangification* (Taipei: Wunan, 2004), *An Anthology of Shen Tsing-song* (Jinan: Shandong Education Press, 2005) and *Confucian Ethics in Retrospect and Prospect* (edited with Kwong-loi Shun, Washington, DC: Council for Research in Value and Philosophy, 2007).

AHMAD F. YOUSIF is currently a professor at the International Institute of Islamic Thought and Civilization, in Kuala Lumpur, Malaysia. He has previously taught at the University of Winnipeg, the University of Ottawa, the International Islamic University Malaysia, and the University of Brunei Darussalam. Yousif teaches postgraduate courses on religious and Islamic studies. He is the author of three books, and numerous articles published in scholarly journals. As a professor of Islamic Studies, Yousif is widely credited for having pioneered research concerning Muslims in Canada, Islam in Southeast Asia, and Comparative Religion.

INDEX

A

Abdallah b. Mahmud al-Ka'bi, 87
abhidhā, 242
Abhidharma, 61, 209, 211
Abhidharmaśabhāsya, 207
Abhidharmasamuccaya, 158
Abhinavagupta, 75
Aboriginal women, 260–63
Abraham, 104–6
  and Isaac, 104
absent-mindedness, 61
Academy for Jewish Philosophy, 129
ācārya, 187
actionless action, 112
afterlife, 127, 159
Agniveśa, 139
agnostic humanity, 37
agon, xv, 32, 35
aḥkām, 227, 228
ākāśa, 60
al-Baghdadi, xviii
al-Biruni, xviii, 78, 86–88
al-e Ahmad (Iranian writer), 30
al-Faruqi, Ismail Raji, xviii, 77
al-Ghazālī, 231, 236
al-Ḥakīm, 227
al-Kalbi, xviii
al-Qadi 'Abd al-Jabbar, 78
al-Shahrastani, xviii
aḻvār, 191
Amnesty International, 260–61
angst, 45
aniyata-visayaka, 65
antaḥkaraṇa, 60
anthropology, xi, 45, 270
  anthropological method, 89
  and religious studies, 269
anumāna, 160, 161
Anuśāsana Parva, 188
apprehension, 207
appropriation, viii, 6, 14, 15, 20, 269
Appuḷḷār, 177, 178, 190–91
āpta, 159
āptopadeśa, 159
Aquinas, Thomas, xii, 43, 57, 140, 142, 180, 225, 234, 235
  Summa Theologica, 234
Aranya Kanda, 190
Arbitration Act (Ontario), 263
Archimedes, 235
Aristotelian rationalism, 225
Aristotle, xvii, 7, 67, 143, 149, 150, 179, 180, 193, 198, 199, 225, 232, 235
  being as being, 8
  and Chinese philosophy, 141
  De Anima, 57, 58, 66
  episteme, 7
  and happiness, 180
  and Ibn Rushd, 232, 234
  Ibn Rushd's commentary on, 73, 230
  inner sense-organ, 66
  and Islamic scripture, 231
  and Jewish philosphers, 145
  leisure and recreation, 7, 8
  and logic, 152, 232
  ontology, 8
  sensus communis, xvii, 58, 66, 68
  on *Sleep*, 67
  theory and praxis, 7
  theory of the eternity of the world, 232
Asaṅga, 156–58
asattva, 159
āstika, 61
astronomy, 148
ātman, 58, 67, 159, 160

Ātreya, 139
Aufhebung, 4, 153
Augustine, 180, 181, 198, 234
aum, 190, 191
avatāra, 191
Averroës (Ibn Rushd), xvii, 73, 74, 142, 148, 221–36
Averroism, 233
Averroistic heresy, 225
Avicenna (Ibn Sīnā), 142, 148, 149, 152, 236
avidyā, 216
awakened experience, xxii, 204, 205
awakening
  phenomenology of, xxi–xxii, 203–4, 210, 217–18
awakening (*bodhi*), xxii, 38, 157, 211, 214, 217

B

bādha, 242, 243
bahuvrīhi, 190
Barnes, Michael, 48
Barthes, Roland, 44
Beethoven, Ludwig van, 68
Begründung, 17, 18
Beijing Fourth World Conference on Women, 267–69
being, 8, 12, 109–11, 189
  and knowing, 26, 27, 37, 193
  and nothingness, 110
Being vs. Nonbeing, 153
being-with, 213, 216
Berkeley, George, 10
Bhagavad Gītā, 70, 72, 142, 241–46, 248
bhakti, 242
Bhartṛhari, 57
Bhattacharya, Krishna Chandra, 30, 32, 38
Bible, 81, 86
  Hebrew, 124
biblical exegesis
  Christian tradition of, 234
bodhi, xxii, 38, 157, 211, 214, 217
Book of Changes, 4, 8
Brahmasūtra, 246
Bṛhadāraṇyaka Upaniṣad, xvii, 58, 62
bricolage, 49, 50
bricoleurs
  philosophers as, 49, 54
Buber, Martin, 124, 125, 142
Buddhism, 2, 16, 121, 144, 145, 146, 156, 158, 203
  artistic forms, 38
  Buddhist and Brahmanical schools, 38
  Buddhist philosophers, 139, 207
  in China, 16
  and conditioned co-arising, 144
  and ethics, politics, and economics, 16
  and Hinduism, 158
  Huayan, 144
  and Husserl, 205
  medical theories and practices, 157
  and medicine, 156
  meditational psychology, 61
  ontology, 147
  Pali, 144
  phenomenology, 204
  philosophical texts, 38
  philosophical traditions, 37
  practice of, xv, 38
  Pure Land, 144
  schools, 38
  Tantra, 144
  texts, 34, 156, 209
  Yogācāra, 156, 204, 208, 209–10, 211
Butler, Judith, 268, 269

C

caitasika, 61
Canada, 260, 261, 263
Caraka, 139
Caraka-saṃhitā, xx, 139, 141, 156
Carama Śloka, 190, 191
Catholic communities, 268
Catholicism, xxi, 147, 180, 182
CEDAW (Convention on the Elimination of Discrimination Against Women), 258
Charmides (Plato), 27
Charter of Rights and Freedoms (Canada), 262–64
cheng, 13, 16
China, 2, 9, 12, 16, 121, 155
Chinese philosophers, 10
Chinese philosophy, 10, 16
Chinese philosophy and religion, xiv, 22
Christian God, 99
Christian Gospel, 86
Christian love, 100

Christian mysticism, 175
Christian philosophers, 225
Christian philosophy, 143
Christian philosophy and theology, 225
Christian religion, 226
Christian theology, 234
Christian tradition, 121
Christian world view, 222
Christian writers, 87
Christianity, ix, 78, 79, 99, 100, 145, 146
apologetic strategy, 181
and Islam, 77, 78
kenosis, 53
morality, xviii
and Platonism, 37
Christians, 79, 80, 81, 86, 143, 146
medieval, 225
citta, 61, 70, 73, 249
civilization
clash of civilizations, 30
future of, 21
Hindu, 86
Islamic, xvii, xxiii, 77
Western, 3
cognition
Buddhist theory of, 207
Cohen, Hermann, 142
Cohen, Joshua, 259
commentaries
halachic and aggadic, 124
communal life, 121, 123
communication, 14, 15, 18, 19, 49, 80
communicative action, 17, 19
comparative philosophy and religion, 3, 22
Comparative Religious Ideas Project (CRIP), 174–75, 186
comparative studies, xx, 1, 2
comparison
as mode of understanding, 45
concealment, 36, 207
conditioned co-arising (*pratītya-samutpāda*), 144
Confucian codes, 145
Confucian rituals, 112
Confucian tradition, 109
Confucian values, 108
Confucianism, xiii, xiv, 2, 11–14, 16, 19–20, 95, 113, 144
Confucius, 8, 11, 13, 108, 113, 114
consciousness, 60, 67, 70, 127, 157, 204–5, 206–10, 211, 213
states of, xv, 38
structure of, 204, 209, 210
Convention on the Elimination of Discrimination Against Women (CEDAW), 258
conversion, 89
Corbin, Henry, xv, 25, 33–34, 36–38
correspondence, 10, 11
covenant, 124
Crescas, 142, 144
CRIP (Comparative Religious Ideas Project), 174, 175, 186
critical theory, 22
Critique of Pure Reason (Kant), 63
culture, x, xi, 2, 43, 89, 120, 124, 225, 241, 270–73
African, 272
Arabian, 224
Chinese, 12, 14, 17
Indian, 272
Islamic, 222, 234
medieval, 225
Western, 272
and Western values, xi

D

dao, 6, 11, 12, 13, 107–13, 115
Daodejing, xviii, xix, 107, 108, 109, 110, 113, 142
Daoism, xiv, 2, 11, 12, 13, 14, 16, 20, 95, 107–13
and nature, 13
and self-identity, 115
strangification, 20
Daoist experience of *Dao* and *wu*, 16
Daoist morality, 96, 109, 145
Daoist philosophy, xviii, xix, 95, 96, 107
Daoist sage, 111, 113, 114, 116
Daoist theory of language, 147
Daoist thinkers, xix, 95, 108, 114, 115
and conventional morality, xix
Daoist thought, 112, 115
darśana, 187
dāsatva, 178
Dawkins, Richard, 266

De Anima (Aristotle), xvii, 57, 58, 66, 73
debt, 99
Declaration of the Elimination of Violence against Women (DEVW), 267
deep sleep, 68, 189
defilements, 216, 250
Deleuze, Gilles, 21, 44
dependent-arising, 210
Derrida, Jacques, 21, 44, 140
Descartes, René, 9, 140
desire and aversion, 244
desireless action, 241, 242
Dewey, John, 42
dharma, 61, 187, 212
Dharmakīrti, 57, 140
Dharmapāla, 210
dharma-śāstra, 145, 147, 148
dhārya, 187
dhātus, 160
dialogue, xvi, 6, 18, 19, 20, 22, 35
  inter-religious, viii
  as mutual strangification, xv
  Platonic, xv
Dignāga, 139, 141, 158, 209
din, 81, 82
Diocles of Carystus, 149, 150
Diotima, 26, 28
Dīrghāgama, 17
Divinity, 144, 193
Doctrine of the Means (*Zhong Yong*), 10, 13
Doors of Perception (Huxley), 147
duḥkha, 156, 245
Dvaita school of Vedānta, 69
Dvaya Mantra, 190, 191
dynamism of nature, 13

E

East-West divide, 142
East-West Philosophers' conference, 125
Eco, Umberto, 146
ecological movement, 22
ego, 101, 208
ego attachments, 102
egoism, xviii, 96, 98, 101, 102, 115
eightfold consciousness, 208
elenchus, xv, 35
empirical idealism, 213
empiricism
  classical, 10
emptiness, 12, 195, 214
  Buddhist teaching of, 16, 211–16, 250
enlightened experience, 210
enlightenment, 207, 211, 216
  and ignorance, 206
Epictetus, 198, 200
episteme, 6, 7
epistemology, 121, 146, 150, 162, 204, 206
  Buddhist, 207
  feminist, 120
  Indian, 139
  Islamic, 90
epoche (phenomenological), 90
Essence of the Three Mysteries (*Śrīmad Rahasyatrayasāra*), 173, 175–78
ethics, 178
  bedroom, 145
  centrality of, 124, 131
  Chinese, 16
  Christian, 78
  criticisms of, xviii
  critique of, 95
  egalitarian, 17
  as first philosophy, 128
  Indian, 245
  and philosophy, 128, 132
  and reason, xiii
  as the foundation for philosophy, 132
  virtue ethics, 246
  Western, xviii
Europe
  medieval, 226
evil, xix, 70, 98, 108, 114, 127, 261
Evil One, 98
exegesis
  Christian tradition of, 234
  Indian, 239, 249
existentialism, 21
experience
  enlightened, 205–6, 210, 214
  mundane, 205
  non-enlightened, 205–6
experience and knowledge, 205

F

face of the other, 53
faith, xviii, 38, 81, 82, 83, 96, 99, 105, 106, 129, 178
  in God, 102
  Islamic, 233
  in Kierkegaard, 103, 104, 115
  and morality, 102, 103
  and reason, 225
  vs. reason, 145
falsafa (philosophy), 227, 234
falsification, 11
family, 148, 155, 224, 264, 267, 268
family disputes, 260, 263
family problems, 263
family values, 268
farḍ, 228
Faruqi, 78, 80–81, 82, 86, 90
Faṣl al-Maqāl (*The Decisive Treatise*)(Ibn Rushd), 222, 227, 229–32
fatwā, 229
Fear and Trembling (Kierkegaard), 104, 106
feminism, 127, 129, 130, 265, 266, 268
  definition of, 127
  and Judaism, 123
feminist critique, 265
feminist philosophers, 120, 128, 130, 257
feminist standpoint epistemology, 120
feminist thinkers, 130, 132, 264
feminist thought, 128
feminists
  Canadian, 265
  gender feminists, 268
First Nations, 263
Foucault, Michel, 44
Fox News, 45
Frege, Gottlob, 140
fundamentalism, xxiv, 141, 264, 265, 266, 269, 272
fundamentalist challenge, 266
fuquha', 82, 84

G

Gadamer, Hans-Georg, 205
Geist, 153
gender, 20, 120, 124, 127–28, 130, 268–69, 271, 272
gender bias, 264
gender difference, 260
Gersonides, 142, 148
ghosts, 217
globalization, xiv, 1, 2, 21
God, 180, 199
  and Abraham, 104
  awareness of, 38
  Christian, 99
  creator, 231, 232
  death of, 27, 99, 143
  dedication to, 183
  dependence on, 178, 184
  devotion towards, 244
  existence of, 127
  faith in, 104, 115
  and freedom, 273
  and human pleasure, 193
  Judge Wilhelm's, 103
  and *kenosis*, 52
  in Kierkegaard, xviii, 95, 102, 107
  knowledge of, 232
  love of, 179, 180, 196–200
  and man, 179, 180, 193–95
  and *manas*, 75
  in Nietzsche, 99
  personal, 12
  as radically other, 104
  religions without, 144, 145
  and sensual fantasies, 104
  and sin, 180
  surrender to, 175, 176
  transcendent, 105
  unity of, 198, 199, 200
  unity with, 175
God-man, 51
good and evil, 96, 97, 100, 102
Gospel, 86
Gradinarov, Plamen, 204
grammar, 59, 148, 155
  and structure of reality, 156
Greek science, 149
Greeks, 85, 121, 155, 227, 234, 236
guan, 20
guanxin, 211
guilt, 99, 100, 106
guṇas, 187, 188
Guttmann, Julius
  Philosophies of Judaism, 129

H

Habermas, Jürgen, 17, 19, 20
Hadot, Pierre, xv, 25, 26, 28
ḥakam, 227
Halacha, 123, 124
halakhah, 145, 147, 148
hallucinations, 147
happiness, 180, 244
    and Aristotle, 180
ḥarām, 228
Hasidic tales, 146
heaven, 6, 11, 12, 13, 110
    and earth, 107, 109, 110, 112
hedonic states, 64
Hegel, G.W.F., xx, 4, 125, 140, 153, 154, 163
    as Christian thinker, 143
Hegelian dialectics, 4
Heidegger, Martin, 2, 9, 30, 36, 142, 205, 213
hermeneutics, xiii, 22, 148
    diatopical, xii
    of suspicion, xi
Hermes Trismegistus, 199
ḥikma, 226–27, 229, 234, 235
Hindu fundamentalism, 271
Hindu medical theories, 157
Hinduism, viii, ix, xxi, 80, 86, 121, 145, 175, 271
    and Buddhism, 158
    civilization, 86
    ontology, 147
    texts, 157, 158
    Vedic, xvii
Hindutva, 271
Hippocrates, 198
history, 45
    Hegel's view of, 153–54
    Jewish, 123
Holocaust, xvi, 123–24
Holy War (*jihad*), 146
Hourani, 222, 226
Huayan, 144
Huayan Buddhism, 144
ḥukm, 227, 229
human beings, 6, 12, 29, 74, 96, 97
human nature, 32, 183, 197
human resources, 72
human rights, x, xxiv, 257–64, 267–73
humanness, 6, 16
Hume, David, 10, 45, 125, 246
humility (Christian), 99
Husserl, Edmund, xxii, 153, 203–6, 211, 213, 215, 217
    and Buddhism, 205
Huxley, Aldous
    Doors of Perception, 146
Huxley, Thomas H., 163

I

Ibn Ḥazm, xviii, 86, 87, 88
Ibn Masarra, 230
Ibn Rushd (Averroës), xvii, 73, 74, 142, 148, 221–35
    and Aristotle, 232, 234
    The Decisive Treatise (*Faṣl al-Maqāl*), 222
Ibn Sīnā (Avicenna), 142, 148, 149, 152, 236
idolatry, 79, 199
ignorance, 7, 58, 79, 192, 207, 216, 244
    and enlightenment, 206
imagination, xvii, 57, 68–69, 74, 75
    and memory, 68
Indian Act (Canada), 262
Indian medicine, 139
Indian philosophers, 60, 161, 162, 240, 242–43
Indian psychology, 60
Indian thought, 46
Indian women, 271
indigenous women
    and violence, 261
indriya, 59, 61, 65
inference, 158–62, 240
infinity, 155, 216
inner sense, xvii
inner sense (*manas*), xvii, 57–68, 71–75
Insanity, 156, 157
insider-outsider question, 46
insight, xxii, 205–10, 215, 216
    and knowledge, 209
    non-discriminated, 207
    three forms of, 208, 216
    threefold, 208
    trans-in-mundane, 207
    trans-mundane, xxii, 205, 207
    Yogācārin notion of, 209
insight of all modes of phenomena, 215, 216

instrument (*karaṇa*), 60
intentional objects, 212
inter-religious dialogue, 15, 22, 50, 51
intoxication, 157
irony
  Platonic, 28
Islam, xvii, 77–91, 131, 145, 146, 222, 232, 233
  and Aristotle, 231
  and Christianity, 77
  and Judaism, 78
  Qur'ān, 79–81, 84, 86, 90, 230–31
  Qur'ānic law, 231
Islamic civilization, xvii, xxiii, 77
Islamic epistemology, 90
Islamic Institute for Civil Justice, 263
Islamic law (*shāri'a*), 145, 223, 225–26, 234, 260, 263–65
Islamic methodology, 91
Islamic Schools of Law, 222
Islamic thought, 221
Israel, 124

J

Jaimini, 177
Jainism, 144
Japan, 121
Jewish beliefs, 124
Jewish experiences, 123, 124
Jewish history, 123
Jewish identity, 123
Jewish law, 123, 148
Jewish life and thought, 123
Jewish philosophers, 123–25, 129–31, 141
  and Aristotle, 145
Jewish religion, 123
Jewish thought, 129
Jewish women, 130, 132
Jews, 79–80, 86, 126, 263
  persecution of, 148
ji, 111
jihad, 146
jīvas, 187
jña, 60
jñāna, 207
jñānendriya, 71
Johnson, Mark, 62
ju, 212
Judaism, 79, 123–24, 128–29, 145, 146
  and Islam, 78
Judeo-Christian tradition, 85, 96
Judge Wilhelm, 103
jurisprudence, 90, 148, 228, 231
  religious, 146
justification
  task of, 127

K

Kalām, 222, 226, 234
Kaṇāda, 72
Kant, Immanuel, xvii, 11, 57, 58, 62–64, 103, 125, 145–46, 148, 155, 205
karaṇa, 60
karma, 152, 156, 192
karmendriya, 71
kenosis, xvi, 51, 53
kenotic incarnation, 51
Kern, Iso, 204
Kierkegaard, Søren, xviii, 35, 95–96, 102–7, 114–16
  and Abraham, 104–5
  and conventional morality, xix
  on egoism, 115
  and faith, xviii, 103, 115
  God, 107
  and morality, 95–96, 102–4, 107
  and sacrifice, 106
  and self-identity, 115
kleśa, 38, 250
knowledge
  discriminated, 207
  innate, 19
  and insight, 205, 208–9
  mundane, xxii, 205, 210, 215
  non-concealed, 207
  non-discriminated, 206
  non-discriminative, 205
  trans-mundane, 205, 208
knowledge of knowledge and ignorance, 27, 28
Korea, 121
Kṛṣṇa, 241, 242, 244, 248
kunya, 224

L

lakṣaṇā, principle of, xxiii, xxiv, 239–40, 242–43, 245–47, 251–53
Lakṣmaṇa, 183, 190, 191
language games, 6, 14, 17
Laozi, 4, 20, 142
law, 227, 228, 229, 230, 232
  Christian, 226
  Indian, 245
  Islamic, 145, 223, 225, 226, 231, 234, 260, 263–66
  Jewish, 123, 148
  and philosophy, 225, 226, 227
  Qur'ānic, 231
  Sunni schools of, 231
  and wisdom, 234
leap of faith, 106, 107
legitimacy, 19, 20
Leibniz, Gottfried, 9, 43
Levinas, Emmanuel, xvi, xx, 53, 122, 125, 128, 132, 142
  and the Other, 53
liangzhi, 19
liberation, xxii, 61, 72, 73, 127–28, 207, 218, 244
  definition of, 72
life, 12
  meaning of, 12
  ways of, 89
life-form, 6
Life-world, 13, 14, 18, 215
līlā, 146, 154
Lindbeck, George, 47
linguistics, 3, 148
Locke, John, 10
logic, 227–28
  Aristotelian, 152, 232
  in Chinese philosophy, 9
  Indian, 161
  in Oriental thinking, 240
logical positivism, 10
love (Christian), 100
Lyotard, Jean-François, 14

M

madhhabs, 82
Mādhyamika, 210–11
mādhyati, 157
Magians, 80
Mahābhārata, 68–69, 188, 241
mahābhūtas, 160
mahān, 74
Mahāprajñāpāramitāśāstra, 208
Mahāyāna, 156
Maimonides, 142, 148, 152
Maitrayani Upaniṣad, 73
makrūh, 229
Mālikī methodology, 231
manas (inner sense), xvii, 57–75
mano-bhūmi, 156
manomayakosa, 72
mano-vijñāna, 61
mantra, 69, 190
Manusmṛti, 240–41
maqāl, 226
Marxism, 144
master-slave dialectic, 97
mathematics, 9, 155
McGuinty, Dalton, 264
medical texts, 139–40, 151, 156–57, 159
  Buddhist, 157
medicine, 139, 148–50, 155, 156–57, 161
  and Buddhism, 156
  forensic, 158
  Indian, 139, 157
  and philosophy, 149
Medicine, Bea, 261
meditation, xxii, 38, 181, 191, 205, 211, 214–15
  Buddhist, 206, 214
  method of, 213, 214–15, 217
memory and imagination, 68
Mencius, xiii, 43, 205
mental construction, 216
Mercury Trismegistus, 199
Merleau-Ponty, Maurice, 62
metaphors
  root, 155, 163
metaphysics
  Indian, 246
Middle Ages, 148–49, 221–22, 225, 234
middle way, 214, 215, 216
Midrashic tales, 146
millah, 81, 82
Mīmāṃsa, 144

Mīmāṃsā Sūtras, 177
mimesis, 48–53
mind, 12, 58, 74, 210–13, 216, 217, 249, 250
  and body, 72, 97
  contemplation of, 211
  deluded vs. enlightened, 211, 213
  Indian metaphysics of the, 59
  Indian philosophies of, 59
  metaphysic of the, 61
  pure, 213
  states of, 27, 31
  theories of, 58
  Vedic, Puranic, and Sāṃkhya-Vedāntic metaphysic of, 74
  and world, 211
  Zhiyi's conception of, 216
mind and world
  correspondence between, 212
Mishna, 124
Mishneh Torah, 148
missionaries (Christian), 81
Mnesitheus of Athens, 150
Mohanty, J. N., 204
Mohezhiguan (*Great Calming and Contemplation*), 215
mokṣa, 73, 131, 244–46
moral virtue, 111–13
moralism, 145
morality, 110, 115
  bourgeois, 103
  Christian, xviii, 100
  conventional, xix
  critique of, 95
  and Daoism, xix, 96, 108–9, 111–12, 114, 116
  and the face of the other, 53
  and faith, 102–3
  and family values, 268
  and immorality, xviii
  in Kierkegaard, 95, 107
  Nietzsche's critique of, 95, 96, 114
  slave, 98
  and society, 98
  standards, 98
  and yoga, 250
Muhammad, 79
Muhammad al-Jamil al-Rahman, 222
Muhammad b. Jarir at-Tabari, 78
mukhya, 242
Müller, Max, 83
multiculturalism, 3, 21, 22, 29, 259, 260, 263, 265
mundane knowledge
  vs. insight, 210
muqaranah, 83
muqaranat al-adyan, 83
Muslim philosophers, 222, 225
Muslim scholarship, 77–78, 84, 90
Muslim women, 263–66, 272
mystic ecstasy, 89
mystical wisdom, 207
mysticism (Christian), 175
myth, 88, 146

N

Nāgārjuna, 57, 153
Naiyāyikas, 244, 245
Name of the Rose (Eco), 146
namo, 190, 191
Nāṉmukaṉ Tiruvantāti, 191
Narayan, Uma, 270-71, 272
Nārāyaṇa, 175, 190, 191
nāstika, 159
Native Women's Association of Canada, 261
natural attitude, 206, 215
nature, 12, 13, 14, 18, 22, 150, 181, 188
  and Daoism, 13
  dynamism of, 13
  rhythm of, 14
Neo-Confucian metaphysics, 147
Neo-Confucianism, 22
neo-Marxism, 22
Neo-Platonism, 145
neuro-psychology, 71
New Testament, 85, 181
Ni Liangkang, 204
Nietzsche, Friedrich, xiii, xviii, 27, 95–102, 104, 107, 114–16, 143
  and conventional morality, xix
  and morality, 95–97, 100, 114
  and self-identity, 115
  Thus Spoke Zarathustra, 99, 100
nirodhaḥ, 249
nirvikalpa-jñāna, 205
niṣkāmakarma, 241, 246

niyamya, 187, 189
niyanta, 187
noesis-noema, 210
non-being, 109, 110, 153
nothingness, xix, 109–12, 114
and being, 110
Nussbaum, Martha, 258, 259
Nyāya, xvii, 58, 61, 62, 64, 66, 67, 69, 70, 158, 246, 247
Nyāya philosophers, 64
Nyāyasūtra, 139, 242, 245
Nyāya-Vaiśeṣika, 60

O

Old and New Testaments, 83
Omnipresent Self, 73
On Sleep (Aristotle), 67
ontology, 4, 7, 12, 146, 155, 206
Buddhist, 147
Hindu, 147
science of, 8
Orientalism, xi, 81, 88, 89, 240, 245
orientational pluralism (Rescher), 44
Other, xv, xvi, xx, 18, 20–21, 41, 44, 48–53, 77, 107, 111, 112, 115, 132, 153, 189, 205
absolute, 22
radical, xviii
otherness, xii, xvi, 52, 53

P

paganism, 79, 181, 200
pain, 245, 271
and pleasure, 64, 65, 72, 144
Pali Buddhism, 144
panentheism, 147
Panikkar, Raimundo, xii
pantheism, 147
paratantra, 210
parikalpita, 210
pariṇāma, 162
Parmenides, 2, 149
parrhesia, 26
participant observation, 89
path, 146, 155, 211, 214, 217
perception
and inference, 151, 158, 209
phenomenological attitude, 205, 206, 215
phenomenological method, 89
phenomenologists
Nyāya, 64
phenomenology, xxii, 21, 61, 204–5, 208, 212, 217
Buddhist, xxii, 204
Husserlian, xxii, 204
soteriological, xxii, 205
transcendental, 206
phenomenology of awakening
Buddhist, xxi, xxii, 203–4, 210, 217–18
phenomenology of consciousness, xxii, 204
phenomenology of insight, xxii, 204
phenomenology of mundane experience, xxii, 203
philology, 45
philosophers
Anglo-American, 142
Indian, xxiv
as strangers, 25, 26, 27
Philosophers' Conference (1939), 126
philosophical dialogue, x, 18, 34, 35, 217
philosophical texts, xxi, xxiii, 4, 38, 47, 61, 140, 142, 151, 162, 203, 250, 251
philosophical traditions, 16, 36, 48, 140, 142
Philosophies of Judaism (Guttmann), 129
philosophy
as a way of life, 25
agon of, 32
analytic, viii, xv, 31, 34, 38, 129
ancient, 25, 149, 163
Buddhist, 121, 204–6
Chinese, xiv, xxii, 1–24, 121, 131, 132, 141, 143, 155
Christian, 131, 143
comparative, 1, 25–39, 130–32, 140–43
Confucian, 121
contemporary, xv, xix, 21, 25, 128
of contrast, 4
Crescas' ethical philosophy, 144
Daoist, xviii, xix, 95, 96, 107
definition of, 122, 128, 229, 230
dialogue, 35
different styles of, 152
discipline of, 120, 121, 123
eastern vs. western, xiii

and education, 26
ethical, 107
and faith, 183
feminist, xix, xx, 126–30, 132
forms of, 42
future of, 21
Greek, 9, 121, 131, 221
Hindu, 86
history of, 96, 128
Ibn Rushd, 225
Indian, xxiii, xxiv, 121, 122, 139–44, 151, 155, 239–40, 252–53
inner sense, xvii
intercultural, 14, 15, 21, 41–45, 47–50, 52–54, 182
as intrinsically comparative, 31
in Islam, 222
Islamic, xix, xxii, xxiii, 126, 221, 230
Jewish, and Islamic traditions of, 121
Jewish, xix, xx, 119, 120, 123–24, 126, 128–32
Kantian, 34, 155
and law, 225–27
and logic, 227, 228
mainstream, 32, 43
and medicine, 149
medieval, xx, 163
method, 4, 44, 86, 89, 120–21, 123, 129, 143, 146, 152, 183, 204, 206, 211, 214–15
modern academic practice of, 43
modern, 131
moral, 198
national, 21
nature of, 119, 122
Neo-Confucian, 121
non-Western, 141
ontology, 7
philosophical dialogue, 34
politics of, 32
post-Christian, 121, 131
presuppositionless, 153
and reason, 143
and religion, viii, ix, xii, xiv, xviii, xx, xxiv, 1, 2, 3, 15, 148, 152, 226
and religious studies, 269
and science, 149
and scripture, 180
as self-critical, 122
Socratic conception of, 35
study of, 229
Taoist, 121
and theology, 233
theoria, 7
Tiantai, xxii, 217
traditions of, 121, 132
training in, 129
and truth, 128
twentieth-century, 21
types of, 144
as vocation, 26, 27
Western, 2, 6, 7, 8, 9, 10, 32, 121, 122–24, 126, 128–29, 131, 142–43, 155, 163, 204
and wisdom, 179
world, 21
and worldviews, 121
Yogācārin, 209
philosophy and religion
intercultural, 1, 2, 3, 5, 22
Western, 2
philosophy of religion, 83, 119, 120, 122, 125, 126–27, 130, 163, 185
comparative, 132
and feminist philosophy, 127
intercultural, 45
and Jewish philosophy, xix, 126
Western, 126
physics, 22, 148, 155
Plato, xv, xx, 2, 26–28, 57, 140, 141, 145, 149, 153, 163, 198, 199, 232
divided line, 153
Republic, 233
Platonic irony, 28
Platonism, 36
Christian, 37
two worlds doctrine of, 29
Platonists, 31, 37
Cambridge and Persian, 36
pleasure, 65, 193
and pain, 64, 65, 72, 144
pluralism, xiv
politics of recognition, 3
postmodernism, xv, 20, 22, 44, 45
prajñā, 205, 207, 209, 216
prajñā-parādha, 162

Prajñāpāramitā Sūtras, 250
Prajñāpāramitāśāstra, 215
prakṛti, 70
pramāṇa, xx, 139
pramāṇa theory, xx, 140
pramāṇas, 139, 156–63
pramāṇa-theory, 158
prānāyāma, 71
prapatti, 190
pratitantra, 178, 187
pratītya-samutpāda (conditioned co-arising), 144
pratyakṣa, 159
pratyakṣa-pūrva, 161
praxis, 7, 8, 13
prayer, 89
prejudice, 79
proper-being, 190
prophetic traditions, 90
Protestant Reformers, 86
psychology, 61, 71, 83
  Buddhist meditational, 61
  Indian, 61, 67, 72
  Western, 72
Pure Land Buddhism, 144

Q

qadhf, 231
qiyās, 84
qiyās al-ma'nā, 231
Quine, W.V.O., 57
Qur'ān, 79–81, 84, 86, 90, 230, 231
Qurtubi, 82

R

race and gender issues, 265
rāga and *dveṣa* (desire and aversion), 244
rahasya mantra, 190
rajas, 159
Ralbag, 148
Rāma, 183, 190
Rāmānuja, 43, 177, 192, 243–44, 246
Rāmāyaṇa, 190
Rambam, 148
Raphael, 235–36
rationalism, 9
rationality, 3, 5, 9, 11, 91, 230
Reality, 4, 13, 189
  nature of, 33
Reality Itself, 12, 13, 16, 18, 20
reason, 159
  analogical, 85
  in different philosophies, 143
  and ethics, xiii
  and faith, 225
  inductive, xx, 159, 161
  in Islam, 222
  jurisprudential, 146
  philosophical, 153
  semantic, 232
reasoning, 234
reasoning techniques, 234
recovery
  hermeneutic of, 50
reflection
  and self-critique, 15
religion
  anthropological approach to, 89
  Christian, 102
  comparative, 45, 77, 81–84, 88, 90–91
  feminist philosophy of, 127
  Hindu, 86
  historical approach to, 89
  history of, 81, 83, 87
  and philosophy, ix, x, xi, 152, 206, 226, 227
  psychological approach to, 89
  sociological approach to, 89
  and truth, 85
religious dialogue, 15, 16, 20, 82
religious faith, 123
religious pluralism, 123
religious studies, 43, 44, 45, 81, 84, 85, 90, 257, 269
  and anthropology, 269
  and feminism, 258
religious texts, xvii, 34, 38, 57–58, 62, 67, 73, 77–81, 84, 86–88, 90, 107–8, 111–13, 124, 142, 148, 156, 158–59, 173–75, 176, 182–86, 189, 209, 215, 222, 225, 230–31, 241, 244, 246, 248, 250
reluctant other, 50, 51, 52
ren, 6, 13, 19
Rescher, Nicholas, 44
ressentiment, 98, 146

rhetoric, 144, 148, 184
Ricoeur, Paul, 205
right and wrong, 109, 110, 112
rights of women, xxiv, 146, 257–58, 260, 262–63, 265, 267, 269, 272–73
Roman Catholicism, xxi, 147, 180, 182
Roman Empire, 226
Rorty, Richard, 49, 122, 142
Rosenzweig, Franz, 123, 125, 142
  Star of Redemption, 123

S

śābdabodha, 69
śabda-pramāṇa, 158, 159
sacrifice, 104, 105, 199
  in Kierkegaard, 106
sādhya, 190
Said, Edward, 240
Sākyamuni, 17
Sales, Francis de, xxi, 175–76, 179–83, 186
Samādhi, 73
sāṁkalpa, 69, 70
sāṁkalpa-sukta, 70
Sāṁkara, 62, 75
Sāṃkhya, xvii, 58, 60, 70, 71, 74, 144
Sāṃkhya Kārika, 70, 242
Sāṃkhya-Vedānta, 60
Sāṃkhya-Yoga, 70
sāṃvika ahamkāra, 60
samyagjñāna, 207
san-di (threefold truth), 214
san-guan (threefold meditation, 215
Śaṅkara, 243–44, 246
san-zhi (threefold insight), 215
śarīra, 177, 187
sarvākārajñatā, 216
sattva, 159
scholars
  feminist, 269
  Muslim, xviii, 78, 80, 84, 87, 90, 91
  women, 258, 270, 271, 273, 274
scholarship
  Muslim, 77, 78, 84, 90
School of Athens (Raphael), 235, 236
Schopenhauer, Arthur, 34
Schuld vs. *Schulden*, 99
science, 7, 15, 139, 148
  Chinese, 156
  European, 9
  modern, 9, 10
  and philosophy, 149
  and technology, 11, 13, 21, 22, 30
scientific method, 91, 153
secularism, 29, 32, 123, 126, 129, 259, 266
self, 111, 159
  and body, 71, 187
  construction of, 49
  emptying of (*kenosis*), xvi
  narcissistic obsession with, 99
  in Nyāya, 64, 67
  and other, 111, 112
  as other, 48
  as pure consciousness, 70
  split self, 101
  and the other, 115, 153
  true, 13
self-awareness, xi, 13, 71, 204, 209
self-consciousness, 208
self-contempt, xviii, 99
self-contentment, 15
self-critique, 16, 22
  and reflection, 15
self-denial, 51
self-deprecation, 99
self-enclosure, 18
self-government, 263
self-identity, 14, 22, 111, 115, 154
self-interest, 105, 115
self-knowledge, 71, 180
self-overcoming, 100, 115, 116
self-realization, 153
self-recognition, 154
self-reflection, 16, 18–20
self-transformation, xvi, 53
self-understanding, 22, 131
semantic reasoning, 231
semantics
  Navya Nyāya, 69
Seneca, 198
sense-organs, xvii, 58–61, 63–71, 75, 159
  common, xvii
  external, 61, 64
  inner, 61, 62, 66, 71
śeṣa, 187, 191
śeṣa-śeṣi, 177
śeṣatva (dependence), 178

śeṣi, 187
Sextus Empiricus, 151
Shahrastani, 78, 86, 87, 88
Shankara, 45
shāri'a, 145, 223, 225, 226, 234, 260, 263–65
    tribunals, 263
shen, 111
shixiang, 211
shu, 19, 20
siddha, 190
siddhānta, 187
sin, 179, 180, 197, 198, 200, 271
    original, 180
sincerity, 13, 16, 20
Sītā, 183, 190
Śiva, 146, 154
Six Nations, 261
śloka, 188
society, 42, 44, 89, 273
sociology, 45, 83
Socrates, 26, 198, 199
Socratic dialogues, 251
Song of Songs, 180, 183, 195
sophrosune, 27, 28
    translation of, 27
soul, 60, 103, 127, 193
Spain, 148
Spinoza, Baruch, xx, 9, 142, 143, 144, 163
Spirit, 4, 154
spiritual life, 72, 148, 178
Śrī, 175
Śrī Bharata, 190
Śrī Raṅgam, 189
Śrī Śatrughan, 190
Śrīmad Rahasyatrayasāra (*Essence of the Three Mysteries*), xxi, 173, 175, 176
Śrīraṅgarājastava, 189
Śrīvaiṣṇava, 178, 182
Śrīvaiṣṇava tradition, 175, 176
Star of Redemption (Rosenzweig), 123
stranger
    philospher as, xvi, 25
strangers, xiv, xvi, xix, 6, 26, 37, 48, 51, 197
    philosophers as, 25, 26, 27
strangification, xii, xiv–xvi, 1, 6, 10, 11, 14–20
    linguistic, 15, 16, 17, 18
    mutual, xiv, xv, 6, 15, 22
    ontological, 6, 16, 18, 20
    pragmatic, 15, 16, 18
structuralism, 4, 5, 22
sukha, 244–46
Summa Theologica (Aquinas), 234
Sunnah, 86
Sunni Schools of Law, 231
śūnyatā, 250
Suttapitaka, 206
svabhāva, 190
Symposium (Plato), 26, 28
synaesthesia, 66
syncretism, 52

T

Talmud, 124
tamas, 159
Tantra, 144
Tantra Buddhism, 144
taṣdīq, 232, 233
tathātā, 207
tatpuruṣa, 190
Taylor, Charles, 3, 121
testimony, 69, 158, 159, 193, 197, 198
texts
    Buddhist, 17, 34
    medical, 139, 140, 151, 156, 157, 159
    philosophical, xxi, xxiii, 4, 38, 47, 61, 140, 142, 151, 162, 203, 250, 251
    religious, xvii, 34, 38, 57–58, 62, 67, 73, 77–81, 84, 86–88, 90, 107–8, 111–13, 124, 142, 148, 156, 158–59, 173–76, 182–86, 189, 209, 215, 222, 225, 230–31, 241, 244, 246, 248, 250
theology, 175, 182, 185, 222
    Christian, 86, 180
    feminist, 130
    Islamic, 230
    mainstream, 43
    and philosophy, 233
theoria, 6, 7, 9
theory and praxis, 5
Theotimus, 195, 197, 198, 199, 200
thinking (conceptual), 208
threefold contemplation, 216
threefold insight, 214, 215, 216
    Zhiyi's theory of, 215
threefold meditation, 215

threefold truth, 214, 215, 216, 217
theory of, 217
Thus Spoke Zarathustra (Nietzsche), 99, 100
tian, 6
Tiantai Philosophy, 203, 204
Tiantai School of Buddhism, xxii, 203
Tillich, Paul, 144
Tirosh-Samuelson, 128, 129, 130
Tiru Mantra, 177, 178, 190, 191
Tiruvaṭi, 191
Torah, 86, 148
Tractatus (Wittgenstein), 46
traditions
non-Western, xxii
philosophical, xiv, xvi, xxi, 2, 3, 5, 6, 14, 15, 21, 22, 37, 143, 183, 222, 242
Traité de l'Amour de Dieu, xxi, 173, 175
transcendental idealism, 213
translatability, 5
translation, 16, 17, 20, 48, 49, 50, 53
Treatise on the Love of God, xxi, 175
Trinity, 180
Trismegistus, 198
trisvabhāva, 210
tṛṣṇā, 144
Trudeau Pierre Elliott, 263
truth, xii, xxii, 7, 10, 18, 20, 205, 211, 213, 214, 215, 233, 244
abstract vs. concrete, 216
disclosure of, 204
Mādhyamikan theory of, 214
as proposition vs. truth as evidence, 217
and religion, 85
scriptural, 233
truth and falsehood, 80
truth values, 233
two truths, 214
Buddhist theory of, 206

U

Udayana, 57
Ultimate Reality, 11, 12, 13, 16, 18, 20
ummah, 81, 82
understanding, 5, 207, 209
and comparison, 45
and interpretation, 12
mutual, xviii, 2, 3, 18–20, 79
United Nations, xxiv, 257, 258, 267
Universal Declaration of Human Rights, 258
unmādyati, 157
upacāra, 242
upalabdhi, 207
Upaniṣads, 57, 67, 70, 142, 189, 244, 246
utilitarianism, 245
uttrāsa-bhayata (mental trauma), 157

V

Vaiśeṣika, 61, 67, 158
Vaiśeṣika Sutra, 72
values (Christian), 99
van der Eijk, Philip, 149
Vāsudeva, 188
Vatican, 267–69, 272
vedanā, 144
Vedānta, xvii, 58, 61, 69, 70, 74, 177, 187, 245, 247
Vedānta Deśika, xxi, 175–78, 181–83, 186
Vedāntin, 245, 247
Vedārtha Saṃgraha, 177
Veṅkaṭanātha, 175
Verfremdung (strangification), 15
verification, 11
vijñāna, 205, 207, 209
Vijñaptimātratāsiddhi, 208
vikalpa, 208, 209, 210, 216
Vimāna-sthāna, 159
vinaya, 145
violence, 260
against women, 266–67
and indigenous women, 261
virāt, 74
Virgin Mary, 147
virtue, xiii, 7, 97, 106, 109, 113, 114
cultivation of, 113
moral, 112
virtue, cultivation of, 108
viṣaya, 207
viṣayaṃprativijñapti, 207
visual-consciousness, 207
vṛtti, 242, 249
Vyoma Śiva, 63

W

waitui
 mutual, xiv, xv, 1, 6, 15, 18, 19, 22
waitui (strangification), xii, xiv, 1, 6, 10, 11, 14–20
wājib, 228
Wallner, Fritz, 15
wanwu
 Daoist concept of, 21
Western traditions, 145
westernization, 29, 36, 271
Whitehead, Alfred North, 140
wisdom, xv, xvi, 8, 25–27, 226–27, 234
 and law, 234
 love of, 26
 and philosophy, 179
wisdom of contrast, 4, 5
Wittgenstein, Ludwig, xx, 6, 27, 45, 46, 57, 163
Wittgensteinians, 45, 46
women, 126, 127, 128, 257–73
 Aboriginal, 260, 261, 262
 in Canada, 260
 equality rights, 262
 and fundamentalism, 265, 266
 Indian, 271
 Indigenous, 260, 261, 262
 in Islam, 146
 Jewish, 130, 132
 Muslim, 263, 264, 272
 and patriarchy, 31
 status of, 268
Women Living Under Muslim Law, 265
women scholars in religion, 269
Women's Learning Partnership, 272
women's movement, xxiv, 268
women's rights, xxiv, 146, 257–58, 260, 262–63, 265, 267, 269, 272–73
wonder, 7
world
 mundane, 215
world religions, xviii, 78, 85, 90, 91
worldview, 32, 82
worldviews, 124
wu, 109
wulun, 21
wuwei, 112

X

xenophobia (philosophical), 142
xin, 6
Xuanzang, 208, 210

Y

Yajurveda, 69, 70
Yellow Emperor, 109
Yin, 8
Yoga, 72, 209, 249, 250
Yoga-bhasya, 70
Yogācāra, 156, 204, 210, 211
 Chinese sects, 211
 consciousness, 204
 literature, 207
 literature of, 208
 philosophy, 209
 theory of the eightfold consciousness and fourfold insight, 208
 theory of the three natures, 210
Yogācārabhūmi, 156, 207
yogaścittavṛttinirodhaḥ, 249
Yogasūtra, 242, 249, 250
yukta, xx, 159–62
Yukti-dīpikā, 70

Z

Zaehner, Richard, 147
Zahirite methodology, 86
Zarathustra, 100–2, 115
Zen, 146
Zhiyi, xxi, xxii, 203–5, 210–18
 Great Calming and Contemplation (*Mohezhiguan*), 215
 philosophy, 210
 theory of mind/consciousness, 211
Zhiyi's philosophy, 204, 205, 207, 208, 214
Zhong Yong (*Doctrine of the Means*), 10
zhongsheng
 Chinese Buddhist concept of, 21
Zhuangzi, xviii, xix, 108, 110–15, 142, 146, 205
Zoroastrianism, 100

www.ingramcontent.com/pod-product-compliance
Lightning Source LLC
Chambersburg PA
CBHW052012290426
44112CB00014B/2218